The
SCOTTISH
GOVERNMENT
YEARBOOK
1988

edited by
DAVID McCRONE & ALICE BROWN

First published 1988

Published by

Unit for the Study of Government in Scotland
Department of Politics
University of Edinburgh
31 Buccleuch Place

ISBN O 9509 626 6 X

Printed by
Drummond Street Reprographics Unit
University of Edinburgh

2

The Scottish Health Education Group

The Group applies a vigorous health education policy across Scotland. Objective is to improve the lifestyle of the population in relation to health.

Programme includes:
alcohol, smoking, immunisation,
dental health, mental health,
the elderly etc.

Aims to help each person to make the best possible choice for optimum health and well being...

"Be All You Can Be."

**Media and Pubility Officer,
John W. Dennison,
Woodburn House, Canaan Lane,
Edinburgh EH10 4SG.**

Office: 031-447 8044   **Home: 031 339 6372.**

IBM in Scotland-more than three decades of growth.

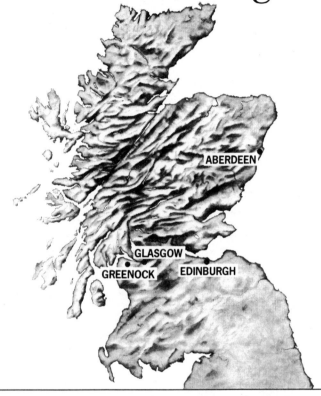

IBM has been an integral part of the Scottish economy since 1951 – the year IBM United Kingdom was formed. That year, IBM UK established its first manufacturing plant at Greenock on the banks of the Clyde, where 100 people built typewriters and accounting machines.

Today, 2,700 people work there producing advanced information technology products including Display Systems and the IBM Personal Computer. Over 85 per cent of IBM Greenock's production is exported to countries in Europe, the Middle East and Africa.

Through branch offices in Edinburgh, Glasgow and Aberdeen, IBM UK serves more than 4,000 Scottish customers; from banking and insurance to North Sea oil and gas; from manufacturing to retailing and distribution; from education to local and central government administration.

IBM's operations in Scotland, those of our customers and of the 2,000 British suppliers to the Greenock plant, contribute significantly to the prosperity and welfare of Scotland and to the economy as a whole.

IBM

IBM UNITED KINGDOM LIMITED, BUCHAN HOUSE, 21 ST. ANDREW SQUARE, EDINBURGH EH2 1AY.

TABLE OF CONTENTS

The Yearbook is edited on behalf of the Unit for the Study of Government in Scotland at The University of Edinburgh. Additional copies of the Yearbook, backcopies of the eleven previous volumes and further information about The Unit's activities can be obtained from Mrs. Helen Ramm at 31 Buccleuch Place, Edinburgh EH8 9JT, Scotland.

A COMMENTARY

The Editor

The governance of Scotland is a mess. This is not to say that Scotland is inefficiently administered, for since the days of Tom Johnston we have had an enviable system of services coordinated through the Scottish Office, and as long as the local authorities did its bidding with a minimum of grumbling, it worked pretty well. This somewhat corporatistic system which had evolved from Johnston and Churchill through Secretaries of State, Labour and Tory, to meet the challenge of modernising an economy bequeathed by Victorian prosperity has broken down at last. Or at least, it has lost its legitimacy. The irony is that the attack has come from the Right not the Left, and with it the whole basis of the United Kingdom has begun to rock. Consider the facts. It seemed fanciful to imagine before the 11th June that the Tories would receive such a hammering at the election in Scotland. 'Doomsday' seemed to belong to leader-writers who always like to rummle up the readers over breakfast. And yet while the Tory vote did not fall too far, it slid in the wrong places, leaving ministers ashen-faced the morning after, and wondering how to make a living. It dawned on them and the rest of Scotland that an important threshold had been crossed, and Malcolm Rifkind saw it more clearly than most as he sought to gather the bits of wreckage together. For a few days, he was shell-shocked, and only found solace in the bosom of the Tories' English victory. Like the advocate he is, he recited the fact that the 'unionist' parties in Scotland had done well, but found uncomfortable the fact that proportional representation would have provided more lobby material in Westminster.

If things have gone quiet over the recess, it is because all parties are coming to realise that the ball-game has changed. None can take comfort from what has happened. The Tories have been pushed further into the Thatcherite bosom, and many of their own supporters, brave souls, realise that their party is wrong – at least over its anti-devolution stance. For the rest, Labour is feart; the Alliance is lost; and the SNP indulges in loud whistling in the dark.

Looking back over the last thirty years of Scottish politics, we can see more clearly the direction. It takes a major effort of memory to remember that once upon a time (it is almost a fairy story) the Conservatives took 50% of the popular vote. And only 22 years ago. Much has been made of the North-South divide, and much of it is misleading. Scotland's story is not simply to explained by geography, but by economics, and culture. It was the very success of the Scottish Establishment – the Lithgows, the Frasers –

which helped to alter the climate of opinion so that we Scots thought in a Scottish dimension. As the old Unionist and Imperial families were replaced by a managerial elite, so the Conservatives lost an empire and failed to find a new Scottish role. The SNP were the beneficiaries of the new Scottish focus in the late sixties, and while much, perhaps too much, has been made of their distinctive contribution to Scottish politics, underneath it all the gap between the Tory success in England and the lack of it in Scotland simply grew. Labour likes to think that it has wooed the electorate to its way of thinking, and certainly it has unprecedented success, at least in terms of seats. But it would do well to remember that the 1987 result was, in terms of the popular vote, its 5th worst out of 13 elections since the war. Labour's advance in Scotland is far more uneven than the Tories' decline. At the four elections after the war, it did worse in Scotland than elsewhere, and between 1964 and 1974, this happened again. Its success relative to England only manifests itself since 1979, and there is a suspicion that it doesn't really know why this has happened. It is put down to a better organisation, or, somewhat negatively, to the lack of a 'loony left' on the London model. There are few things Scots enjoy more than lecturing recalcitrant brethren, and there has been plenty opportunity for this to happen now that the Scots represent one quarter of the Parliamentary Labour Party. Its unease with its mandate has led it into some curious moves. For the government (or at least the St Andrews House bit of it), it is all a bit of a joke, but they jest at their peril perhaps. Labour's impotence is ultimately structural – the result of virtually all power being vested in the government's hands, power which will not be given up easily. At least Mrs Thatcher realises that devolution of any sort means a loss of power in Whitehall. The arch-centralist of post-war politics is not about to allow a mere 10% of the population to take power away when she has been busily gathering it in from local authorities and any remaining sources of potential opposition.

And ironically, and dangerously for them, Thatcherism has provided the motifs for a new opposition north of the border. It shows quite remarkable ineptitude or blindness for Allan Stewart (who believes in these things anyway) and Michael Ancram (who probably doesn't but regales the Bearsden Ladies' Tea Club with them) to call for more 'standing on our own feet', 'resolution and independence'. The Nats can hardly believe their ears. If Scotland has become a side-show in British politics, it is one in which we are busily playing our own shadow game on the walls of the tent.

If we are gloomy about the state of governance in Scotland, it is not because we do not have good adminstrators, but because the problems of Scotland are not being, and probably cannot be, tackled under our ramshackle system of government, a system which suited both sides of the border in the first half of this century, but which has become more and more redundant. The fact that our political parties cannot agree to cooperate on even the most trivial of issues is a reflection that the electoral system is outmoded. The problems of Scotland, whether it is our prison service, the system of local democracy, the funding of local services, as our contributors make plain, show no signs of solution. Stewart and Ancram are probably right; we have little resolution or independence; we cannot stand on our own feet; we have a 'dependence' mentality. But they will not like at all the political and economic means which will make us more resolute, more independent, more upright. These are interesting times.

In this issue of the Yearbook, we review the General Election and its aftermath, the new crises of our society – our prisons which fester, our local democracy which needs freedom, and our old problems of sectarianism. This year we are examining in detail the politics of the environment – our planning system, pollution, and nuclear power –, and our Scottish economy – the impact of the North-South divide, local government initiatives, and industrial change. The editors are indebted to all our contributors who submit copy without reward (except in heaven) and more or less to time and length. Since its inception in 1977, we have relied on the concern of many people with Scotland's problems both to write for us and to read what we have written. These have not been rewarding times in which to study our system of government, although they have been interesting ones. Throughout the period we have been able to rely on our regular writers – to Chris Allen, Hamish Henderson, Allan Macartney and Richard Parry, and we owe them a considerable debt. My co-editor, Alice Brown, has helped to share the editorial task, and has brought fresh insights and enthusiasms to the Yearbook. Helen Ramm does all but write the Yearbook (and we are not sure that she doesn't from time to time), and without her it simply would not appear. A special thanks should go to our new printers who have made the transition so well that we have hardly noticed the change. Sheila Edgar is largely the reason why. Without our advertisers, we could not hope to produce such a moderately priced volume, and we have used their valuable support to increase considerably our readership. A special mention must go to Ferranti who have continued to support us even though there are so many claims made on them. To all who write for us, read our contributions, and help us in so many ways, our thanks.

David McCrone

THE YEAR AT WESTMINSTER

ALL CHANGE?

Martin Dowle

The 1987 General Election produced a seismic change in the complexion of party strengths at Westminster, virtually producing the much-dreaded Doomsday Scenario under which the Conservatives won a landslide victory in seats in England, while Labour took the lion's share in Scotland.

The initial assumption as the dust settled on the morning of June 12 was that the combination of an Opposition of 62 MPs (comprising 50 Labour, 7 Liberal, 3 SNP and 2 SDP members) and only 10 Conservative MPs would make the position of the Government in the Commons impossible.

In theory, this appeared to be the case. The first problem for Malcolm Rifkind, the Scottish Secretary, was to find a ministerial team, having lost Michael Ancram and John Mackay, his two under-secretaries, and Peter Fraser, the Solicitor-General for Scotland, among the casualties in the election.

His initial problems of manning the front bench, let alone the backbenches, were compounded by the refusal of Alick Buchanan-Smith, who narrowly held on against a strong Liberal challenge in Kincardine and Deeside, and of Allan Stewart, dropped from the Scottish Office team in the reshuffle in September 1986, to rally to the call from the party hierarchy to serve in the Rifkind team in its hour of need.

Their differing reasons illustrated the magnitude of Rifkind's problem. Buchanan-Smith declined to serve by arguing that the election results in Scotland demonstrated deeper roots to the problems for the Conservatives than the conduct of policy inside the Scottish Office alone.

"This is the moment when the losses in the election results mean that we should be looking for sensitivity on a wider front, and I believe that I can better serve the Conservative Party in Scotland with the freedom to speak," he said after he had resisted strong pressure in the weekend following the election from the Tory Party hierarchy to come to the aid of the cause[1].

While Buchanan-Smith, whose differences with Margaret Thatcher stretched back to his resignation as Shadow Scottish Secretary in 1976 when she refused to back devolution, opposed the approach of the Government from the liberal wing of the Tory Party, Stewart was doing so from the Right.

His argument was that the Conservatives had polled so poorly because they had failed to implement Thatcherism in Scotland, and he therefore felt that since Rifkind intended to continue with an interventionist course at the Scottish Office, he could best assist his party's cause from the backbenches[2].

He was backed in this view by the most populist Right-winger on the Scottish Tory backbenches, William Walker, the MP for North Tayside. He received a warm reception from the Prime Minister at a meeting in early July when he pressed upon her the view that the Conservatives could not match Labour in pledging subsidies to buy votes.

Walker argued instead that the Conservatives should do what they were best at – returning the assets held by the state to the people, as they had done in other Government departments through the philosophy of 'popular capitalism'.

To illustrate his case, he argued that the pandering of the Government to those seeking subsidies simply encouraged people to vote for Opposition parties as the best guarantee for gaining more of them – as, he claimed, in the Highlands,which in 1987 returned one Labour and five Alliance MPs, leaving it with no Conservative representation for the first time in its history[3].

The refusal of Buchanan-Smith and Stewart to serve was a significant blow for Rifkind, leaving much of the party's remaining talent on its backbenches. As a consequence, Ian Lang was promoted to the post of Minister of State to oversee industry and local government, while Michael Forsyth, the Right-wing ideologue who narrowly survived at Stirling was brought in as Under-Secretary for health and education, and Lord James Douglas-Hamilton, dropped as a whip in 1981, was brought back to be in charge of the environment and prisons.

The problem of losing the Solicitor-General in the Commons was solved by keeping Fraser at his post, and dropping the special 10 minute Law Officers' question time. Instead they were amalgamated with general Scottish questions to be answered by Rifkind himself, taking their place in the ballot for the four-weekly one-hour Scottish Office question time. Perhaps the knowledge that Labour too might have to have a Solicitor-General outwith the Commons in the event of coming to Government muted Opposition criticism of this move.

Rifkind's other problem lay in the manning of committees. Reduced from 21 to 10 MPs, the Government had fallen below the threshold of around 13 MPs which had previously been considered essential for keeping Scottish business going in the Commons. His difficulties were alleviated by the expedient of appointing David Maclean, the Inverness-born MP for the Cumberland constituency of Penrith and the Border as the Scottish whip. This instantly raised the number of "Scottish" MPs to 11, though in practice it still remained at 10 since George Younger, as Defence Secretary, was clearly not available to participate in day-by-day Scottish politics at Westminster.

The Scottish Grand Committee, composed of all 72 Scottish MPs posed little problem since the Conservatives in Government had had no majority since the principle of 15 English added members had been abolished shortly after the Tories returned to power in 1979. As all votes in the committee are instantly referred to the floor of the House, the Government's position was little worse than in the 1983 to 1987 Parliament.

The Scottish Standing Committees, which consider Scottish legislation on a line-by-line basis, present a greater problem for the Tories. These must have 16 members, thus requiring 9 Tories for a Government majority. The Tories can scrape that majority by placing all their Scottish members (plus Maclean) except for Rifkind and Younger on the committee.

The difficulty for Ministers (and thus the Opposition's opportunity) lies in the prospect of a multiplicity of Government legislation which could tie down Ministers simultaneously in more than one committee. When the Conservatives had the luxury of 21 MPs, this posed no problem. Now it is a potential nightmare.

Rifkind sought to avert this problem with the tendering out of local authority services by placing the Scottish and English legislation into the same Bill. This caused apoplexy on the Labour benches, where the 50 MPs (some of whom had been selected to serve on the Local Goverement Bill standing committee) pointed out that there was no Scottish Office Minister serving to deal with the clauses and amendments relating to Scotland.

Following lengthy negotiations before the Commons rose for the summer recess in July 1987, Rifkind agreed that Douglas-Hamilton should sit on the Local Government Bill, but only when questions of Scottish interest were being discussed. Labour MPs were determined that from October onwards, Douglas-Hamilton would be sprinting up and down the committee corridor as befitted an Oxford boxing blue serving simultaneously on the Local Government Bill and the legislation to reform housing and education in Scotland.

Labour's main hope at the start of the new Parliament lay in attempting to exhaust the Government by using its superior strength of numbers in the select committees – a problem which the Government could only deal with through agility in the arrangement of business or by the unpopular route of adding English members to deal with Scottish legislation, a course which it knew well enough would play into the hands of the small but lively contingent of 3 SNP MPs returned in the election[4].

The other problem for the Government lay in the manning of the Scottish Select Committee which in the previous two Parliaments consisted of 13 members. Its proportion of Government to Opposition membership has historically been chosen according to the UK strengths of the various parties at Westminster, resulting in 8 Tories, 4 Labour and 1 Alliance sitting on the committee in the 1983 to 1987 Parliament. The Scottish imbalance thereby created had been alleviated by allocating the chairmanship to Labour[5].

Even if, with the fall in the Government's overall majority from 143 to 101 at the election, the Conservatives were to claim just seven seats, they would still be unable to man the committee with only 5 backbenchers. Two schools of thought emerged inside the Tory Party over the committee – the first, headed by John Wakeham, the Leader of the Commons, that the Scottish Conservatives should soldier on with a smaller committee, and the second headed by Stewart and Walker arguing that the select committee was too time-consuming, and in any event only provided a platform for Opposition parties to criticise Government policies in Scotland.

The first of the two camps was thrown a lifeline early in the internal Government debate by the previous Labour chairman, David Lambie, who agreed that 13 was too large a number for the committee, and that a smaller size would enable it to work more effectively. His view immediately undermined Labour's strategy of trying to tie up as many Tories as possible in committees, and in the process give sufficient work to the otherwise undeer-employed contingent of 50 Labour MPs.

After the initial euphoria of achieving its target of 50 MPs subsided, Labour began to realise that its numerical superiority might prove to be as much of a problem as a strength.

True, it had won the golden prize of establishing itself as a truly national party of Scotland. Donald Dewar considered the gaining of the Western Isles, South Aberdeen (his old seat) and Dundee East, along with strong showings in Dumfriesshire and Inverness, Nairn and Lochaber as the perfect answer to the old canard that Labour was simply the party of the old industrial heartland of the west of Scotland[6].

But Labour soon found itself torn over the mandate question. If its MPs suggested that the Conservatives had no mandate to govern Scotland, it would run into the old and uncomfortable fact that the past three Labour Governments had been elected only on majorities secured in Scotland and Wales, and not in England. Similarly, the preferential level of public expenditure of 124p for every pound spent in England left the mandate question an even more difficult one to argue.

Evidence that Labour MPs wanted to approach the Scottish question with caution came in the election for the executive of the Scottish group of Labour MPs. Sam Galbraith, the newly-elected MP for Bearsden and Strathkelvin, comfortably defeated Dennis Canavan, a strong advocate of disruptive parliamentary tactics, for the chairmanship of the devolution sub-committee of the group[7].

The group meeting held before the first Scottish question time of the new Parliament also firmly rejected Canavan's proposals for disrupting Commons proceedings as a protest at the refusal of the Conservatives to modify their policies in recognition of their defeat at the hands of the Scottish electorate.

But the hopes of the 50 Labour MPs that with their new lively intake of 19 members they would be able to trounce a weakened Scottish Office team on the floor of the Commons ended in total disarray.

Instead of going on the defensive, the Tory Right organised a group of English backbenchers to participate in Scottish questions, thus squeezing out many of the Labour MPs who had wished to speak. Labour members were outraged as Conservatives such as the exiled Right-wing Scot, Eric Forth and other right-wingers such as Gerald Howarth and Neil Hamilton asked why insufficient progress was being made on the privatisation of hospital services and pointed to the higher level of public expenditure in Scotland north of the Border.

All MPs are entitled to participate in the debates relating to any specific part of the United Kingdom (indeed, during the Unionist Boycott of Westminster following the signing of the British-Irish Agreement, Northern Ireland question time was dominated by non-Ulster MPs). But Scottish MPs have jealously guarded the tradition that such interventions should be kept to a minimum and not impede Scottish MPs from asking questions.

The temperature rose as it became clear that Labour MPs would be unable to ask questions, while English Conservatives could regularly speak on account of the scarcity of their Scottish colleagues. The baiting proved too much for Canavan, who in contravention of the group decision only two nights before, excitedly and repeatedly called out "I spy strangers" until the Speaker was forced to call a division.

The ensuing quarter of an hour turned out to be a disaster for Labour. As Canavan and his allies pressed forward with the vote against the express wishes of Dewar, a verbal slanging match between Willie McKelvey, the Labour MP for Kilmarnock, and the Shadow Scottish Secretary took place only feet in front of the Mace, in full view of astonished Conservatives and members of the Press Gallery. When the vote came, it showed that 15 members of the Scottish Labour group had supported Canavan, along with one Liberal.

For the Alliance, the internal difficulties of the merger question prevented it from capitalising on the strength of its new intake of MPs which in Menzies Campbell and Ray Michie contained a strong commitment to Home Rule. The SNP intake, however, swiftly established its position, despite the loss of its parliamentary leader, Gordon Wilson. Margaret Ewing, as the former MP for Dumbarton East, assumed the parliamentary leadership, while the new MP for Banff and Buchan, Alex Salmond, soon established a reputation as a left-wing MP determined to point out the weakness of Labour's position in claiming to defend the Scottish people from the ravages of Thatcherism.

The Poll Tax – The Calm Before The Storm.

The tragedy for the Opposition on the Scottish legislation introducing the community charge was that it was safely on the Statute Book before the one group of MPs who could have successfully challenged it – namely, English backbench Tory sceptics – woke up to its implications.

This led to the bizarre situation after the General Election where concessions for England and Wales on poll tax looked highly likely because of the Government's insecurity on the issue, while those in Scotland had been of a minor nature before the election since the Government had been determined to maintain the integrity of the principle for the Conservative manifesto.

Mrs Thatcher's determination to proceed with the introduction of the legislation formed the central part of a somewhat weak legislative programme in the Queen's Speech in November 1986.

Consequently, the Scottish Conservative whip, Gerry Malone, knew he had few rivals in the queue for completion of all parliamentary stages in time for a likely Dissolution of Parliament in May 1987 in time for a June election. Possibly only the Criminal Justice Bill, parts of which ultimately had to be sacrificed for the early election, ranked in importance in the mind of the Prime Minister.

But equally the Government had little time to play with, notwithstanding the fact that the Abolition of Domestic Rates (Scotland)

Etc Bill (ADRES as it came to be known in an awful St Andrew's House acronym). It was consequently rushed to an early Second Reading on December 9, and placed in committee before the Commons rose for the Christmas recess.

Mr Rifkind sought to justify what was clearly a very contentious plan (as the Conservatives found to their cost in the subsequent election) by argying that 85 per cent of single pensioners would benefit, with 30 per cent of those standing to gain more than £1 a week. Other single households would also fare well, with 80 per cent gaining, with 50 per cent of those gaining more than £1 a week.

Such statistics, used by Mr Rifkind at the time of the Queen's Speech and in the Second Reading debate, were viewed by Opposition parties as selective, since 3.85 million adults would now be required to pay at least an element of the charge, some 700,000 people more than the combined number of ratepayers and their spouses.

The atmosphere between the two parties at the start of the legislation's passage was not of the best, as illustrated by the confusing row which broke out between Government and Labour whips in early December over the apparently short notice given to the Alliance and SNP parties over the calling of a Scottish Grand Committee debate in Edinburgh on agriculture and fisheries[9].

An assortment of 25 Liberal, SDP, SNP and Labour MPs used an unusual Commons device to block the meeting, with an angry James Wallace, the Liberal MP for Orkney and Shetland, complaining: "The Government treats the Scottish Grand Committee with contempt. The short notice for this meeting indicates its casual attitude to Scottish affairs."

Some MPs accused the Scottish Labour whip, Allen Adams, of failing to inform other Opposition parties of the debate, a task which Labour said belonged to the Government. The Government whip, Gerry Malone, said he was astonished by the blocking of the Grand Committee meeting, saying that the Opposition parties would have known about the debate three weeks before if they had read the newspapers.

In the debates on the Bill before Christmas, Opposition parties concentrated on portraying the measure as unworkable, and ridiculing the claim of Malcolm Rifkind that it would be fair and simple to operate.

Labour, the Alliance and the SNP alike predicted chaos for the new scheme, earmarked to start in May 1989, and questioned how the complexity of the rebates could work, how students would be reimbursed, or how the Government would succeed in enforcing the payments.

The Opposition onslaught was somewhat hampered then (and for much of the debate in 1987) over the Government's failure to explain how the rebate system (widely assumed to result in those on benefits securing an 80 per cent return for their poll tax payments) would fit into the social security reforms, the shape of which was not to become clear until its implementation in May 1988.

Tempers rose again when the Opposition learned that Gerry Malone had determined to "double bank" the sessions of the standing committee virtually from the start, in an effort to clear the Commons stages of the Bill by Easter. From his viewpoint this was sensible, since it was clear that the problem for the Government would lie more in the Lords than in the Commons.

During the 1986/7 session, their Lordships registered their 100th defeat of the Government, and memories were still fresh of the defeat inflicted upon the government in the summer of 1986 over the proposal by Mrs Thatcher to insist on recipients of supplementary benefit paying 20 per cent of their rates bills, a measure only secured by the Government demanding its inclusion after a further vote in favour in the Commons.

Labour, for its part, retaliated against this unusually early attempt to force along the Bill by producing a filibuster in its first week. This unfortunately resulted in a late-night appearance by Dennis Canavan, who was not a member of the committee, turning up to protest that the measure had no support in Scotland. The meeting was adjourned twice as the chairman tried to persuade Canavan to withdraw. The resulting chaos, viewed by an audience of English MPs including John Biffen, the Leader of the Commons, and John Wakeham, the Government Chief Whip, agog at the pre-Christmas spectacle, backfired badly for Labour in publicity terms and let the Government off the hook over Dewar's allegations that Parliament was being "railroaded" over an important piece of legislation.

When the committee resumed in the New Year, Labour changed its tactics and concentrated on finding arguments against the Bill[10]. Its arguments centred on the unfairness of the measure (favouring the rich); problems of collection (producing snoopers and invading privacy); and led to disenfranchisement of those seeking to escape payment of the tax (notwithstanding the two parallel registers for voting and for collecting the charge).

But its campaign made little impact on the Scottish public. Ken Fagan, the president of the Convention of Scottish Local Authorities (COSLA), drew a parallel with the bus deregulation legislation, pointing out that the public outcry did not materialise until it was clear that their buses were not going to turn up – by which time it would be too late.

But Labour's low-key campaign and failure to raise the issue in the public consciousness mainly arose from the decision of Donald Dewar not to serve on the committee. As a consequence of its failure to deploy its big guns on such a crucial matter, the battle was never really joined between the two sides. Ministers, led by the Government's expert on the issue, Michael Ancram, were also constantly able to turn the tables back on Labour by pointing out that it had no alternative beyond the continuation of the present rating system, though possibly with an improved rebate scheme.

The committee stage involved one fascinating clash between Ancram and the SDP's representative, Robert Maclennan, before he shot to fame after the election as the party's third leader. Maclennan compared the proposed role for the registration officers of drawing up a list of those eligible to pay the poll tax, which he maintained would involve them investigating peoples' private lives, with what happened in police states.

Ancram said that he heard Maclennan make both literary speeches and incomprehensible speeches, but none like his present one which had "gone over the top". He dismissed it as both inaccurate and sensational, and demanded that Maclennan withdraw his comments about the apparatus of police states, which he promptly refused to do.

After 100 hours of debate, with only half of the 34 clauses debated, the Bill was guillotined in early February. Despite ritual Opposition indignation, few observers lamented its passing. Nicholas Fairbairn, who counted himself privileged not to have sat on the committee, suggested as an epitaph: "Delivered from death by boredom with a guillotine."[11]

Two weeks after the guillotine had been imposed, Malcolm Rifkind surprised MPs by abandoning the proposed three-year transition to the new system and opted instead for the "clean-break" in May 1989, a move which he said would be easier for both the public and local authorities. His arguments about avoiding the need for two bills – one an element of rates, the other an element of poll tax – landing on the doormat cut little ice with the Cabinet in July 1987 which opted for a five-year transitional phase in England, against the advice of Nicholas Ridley, the Environment Secretary.

After the Third Reading in the Commons, the Bill underwent a stormy passage in the Lords where it came under strong attack from the Lord Ross of Marnock, the former Scottish Secretary, and a line-by-line scrutiny from Alliance and sceptical Tory peers, who appeared shocked by the regressive nature of the tax. Under the pressure of time, the Government ultimately conceded exemption for the severely mentally handicapped and increases for student grants and supplementary benefit to take account of the extra which those affected would have to pay for the poll tax. Afterwards,

Ministers maintained that the mentally handicapped concession had been on offer to Labour in the Commons, but that its spokesmen had failed to notice the olive branch put out by the Government side.

As it became clear at the start of May that the Government needed to clear the decks for the June 11 General Election, the poll tax became a matter of renewed controversy in the Commons. Neil Kinnock proclaimed that the measure would be fought all the way.

In order to secure the remaining stages of the Bill – mostly Commons agreement to the concessions in the Lords – the Government forced a second guillotine on the Bill, limiting discussion in the dying days of the Parliament to 90 minutes on each amendment. The move was denounced by Neil Kinnock, the Labour leader, who argued that the measure was too important for debate to be restricted in such a way, particularly since it would become a major issue in the impending election.

His arguments cut no ice with John Biffen, the Leader of the Commons, who insisted that there was no good reason why the timetable limits on the Bill should not be implemented.

On May 13, in a final acrimonious debate in the Commons, the Bill completed its parliamentary stages, with further attempts by Labour to secure more concessions for the disabled being defeated by a Government majority of 112. The bitterness between parties which the measure provoked came to the surface once more when John Home-Robertson, a Labour front-bench spokesman, told Michael Ancram to "go to hell".[12] Opposition anger was intensified by the fact the guillotine left only two hours for the Commons to cover 132 amendments.

Perhaps the tiredness of those involved was best illustrated when Michael Ancram, who for two years had been trying to persuade everyone to refer to the "community charge", followed the example of Mrs Thatcher by talking about the "poll tax". To the merriment of the assembled MPs, he repeated the gaffe later in the debate. But the Government nevertheless secured the measure in time for Mrs Thatcher to tell a delighted Scottish Conservative conference in her Friday night rally speech that the Queen had given the measure its Royal Assent.

Conclusion: Doomsday Arrives

Though the Conservatives at an extraordinarily buoyant conference proclaimed the Act as the flagship for their election effort, its enactment proved to be little more than rearranging the deck chairs on the Titanic.

But as the dust settled on the General Election result, the political position of the Tories turned out to be far from disastrous. Though in disarray through the refusal of Alick Buchanan-Smith and Allan Stewart, to serve Malcolm Rifkind was soon able to portray at least a superficial picture of business as usual.

When Margaret Thatcher undertook her annual visit to Scotland in September 1987, she had already abandoned her earlier intention that she should simply listen to the Scots in an effort to understand why her party failed to secure more than 24 per cent at the polls. Instead, she characteristically launched into a denunciation of devolution, and again proclaimed a greater dose of Thatcherism as the path to success for Scotland.

Despite the post-election promise by Malcolm Rifkind that the Scottish Conservative Party would undergo a major re-think of the relevance of its policies (with no possibilities, including devolution, ruled out), it was soon clear that little in the Government's mind had changed.

Truly it could be said that Mrs Thatcher had come to much the same conclusion as her illustrious predecessor, Benjamin Disraeli, who as Chancellor under Lord Derby declared: "The Scotch shall have no favours from me until they return more Tory members to the House of Commons".

Martin Dowle was Chief Political Correspondent of *The Scotsman* from 1985 to 1987 and is now Parliamentary Correspondent of the BBC.

References

1. *The Scotsman*, 16/6/87.

2. Personal conversation with author.

3. *Glasgow Herald*, 10/7/87.

4. See Ewen Macaskill "A Dilemma Designed by Committee", *The Scotsman*, 18/7/87.

5. The job was taken by David Lambie, MP for Cunninghame North.

6. See Donald Dewar, "Scotland, The Way Forward", in "Labour's Next Moves Forward", Fabian Tract 521.

7. *Glasgow Herald*, 21/7/87.

8. *Hansard*, 22/7/87.

9. *The Scotsman*, 5/12/86.

10. *The Scotsman*, 11/2/87.

11. *Hansard*, 9/2/87.

12. *The Scotsman*, 14/5/87.

THE 1987 GENERAL ELECTION IN SCOTLAND

John Bochel & David Denver

Introduction

In our report on the 1983 General Election in Scotland we noted that the results deviated sharply from those in England and Wales[1]. Amongst other features peculiar to this part of Britain two obvious and significant differences were noted. The first was that the two major parties (Labour and Conservative) together obtained a much smaller share of the votes in Scotland than they did in England and Wales. The second difference was the growing Labour domination in Scotland in contrast to Conservative progress in the rest of the country.

Between 1970 and 1979 the combined Labour and Conservative share of the votes here had fallen from 82.5 percent to 73.0 percent (having gone as low as 61.0 percent in October 1974). Over the same period their share in England and Wales fell from 91 percent to 83.7 percent over the decade (with the lowest being 77.6 percent in February 1974). So, although the decline in the two-party share of the vote was a British-wide phenomenon, the fall was much steeper in Scotland. There is no great mystery about the reason for the growing differential. Unlike most of the rest of the country Scotland had a four-party system and increasing electoral support for the SNP accounts for the bulk of the difference. Of perhaps greater significance and certainly more intriguing in retrospect, is the growth in Labour support in Scotland compared with its dismal failure elsewhere. The decade began with Labour having a lead of 6.5 percentage points over the Conservatives in Scotland and, with some variation, it ended with Labour 10.2 points ahead. In England and Wales, on the other hand, Labour had a deficit of −3.1 points in 1970 and this rose to −8.9 in 1979.

The results of the 1987 election show that Scotland continues to diverge in both of these respects. The two major parties together continue to have a lower level of support here than in England and Wales (Table 1), although the gap has narrowed a little. The slight revival in the fortunes of the SNP was, in this context, more than compensated for by the decline in Alliance support. The most striking and certainly the most newsworthy aspect of the 1987 General Election in Scotland, however, was the advance by Labour and the further decline of the Conservatives. The former's lead over the latter rose from 6.7 points in the election of 1983 to 18.4 points in 1987; this compares with a Labour deficit of almost 15 points in England and Wales. In respect of the gap between the Conservatives and Labour, then, the divergence between Scotland and the rest of the country has increased. In 1983, the difference between the Conservative lead in England and Wales and the Labour 'lead' in Scotland was a massive 24 points. In 1987 it was a staggering 33 points. Without survey evidence it is impossible to be sure about the sources of Labour's increased share of the vote but it seems likely that most of it came from former Alliance voters, although some seepage from the Conservatives cannot be ruled out.

Table 1:   Scotland's Electoral Divergence 1983-1987

	SCOTLAND			ENGLAND & WALES		
	1983 %	1987 %	1983-87 %	1983 %	1987 %	1983-87 %
Con	28.4	24.0	−4.4	45.1	45.3	+0.2
Lab	35.1	42.4	+7.3	27.6	30.4	+2.8
All	24.5	19.2	−5.3	26.2	23.5	−2.7
SNP	11.7	14.0	+2.3	−	−	−
Lab lead	+6.7	+18.4	+11.7	−17.5	−14.9	−2.6
Con + Lab	63.5	66.4	+2.9	72.7	75.7	+3.0

Indicators of trends in party support in Scotland between 1983 and 1987, if carefully read, suggested that Labour would make significant advances in Scotland in 1987. There were no parliamentary by-elections here between 1983 and 1987 but it seems unlikely, given the recent votability in by-elections, that these would have provided a very reliable guide to voting trends in Scotland. Opinion polls, certainly over a lengthy period, provide a better view, but even their results must be treated with caution in the periods between elections. The MORI polls which are published regularly in the *Scotsman* and the results of which are presented in Table 2, cannot be said to be inaccurate because we have no way of checking the figures against 'reality', but they do seem to exaggerate the level of Labour support, underestimate that of the Conservatives and, allowing for sampling error, get the Alliance and SNP shares more or less right over the period. But even though there may be some dispute about the precise figures, the trends as compared with the 1983 election were correct, that is Conservative decline, Labour advance, Alliance loss and SNP progress.

Experience suggests that, in Scotland at least, local government elections are very important indicators of trends; not local by-elections, but the biennial District and Regional elections. The 1986 Regional election results (Table 3) one year before the General Election certainly confirmed the trends suggested by opinion polls and, in addition, as can be seen later, made it possible to make reasonable projections as to the electoral status of individual constituencies. National shares of votes in local elections are a

Table 2: Party Support in Mori Scotsman Polls 1984-1987

		Con %	Lab %	Alliance %	SNP %	Other %
1984	March	28.0	49.0	13.0	10.0	*
	May	27.0	47.0	13.0	12.0	1.0
	September	26.0	46.0	14.0	14.0	1.0
	November	28.0	46.0	12.0	13.0	1.0
1985	May	22.0	47.0	18.0	13.0	*
	September	21.0	42.0	24.0	13.0	*
	November	24.0	42.0	23.0	11.0	*
1986	March	22.0	41.0	24.0	13.0	*
	May	21.0	45.0	19.0	14.0	*
	November	26.0	45.0	16.0	13.0	*
1987	March	19.0	47.0	21.0	12.0	1.0

* Less than 0.5%.

crude measure because they do not take account of the differing numbers of candidates put forward by the parties. In 1986, for example, the Conservatives had 70 fewer candidates than the SNP, Labour had 13 fewer and the Alliance 85 fewer. The second column in Table 3 attempts to eliminate the biases caused by these differences by showing the results in the 165 regional divisions in which the Labour, Conservative, Alliance and SNP parties all promoted candidates. The trends revealed are much the same. The figures coincide almost exactly with those of a MORI poll published in the *Scotsman* at the time of the regional elections. Perhaps more surprisingly the party shares of the votes relate quite closely to those obtained at the subsequent General Election.

Table 3: Party Shares of votes in 1986 Regional Election

	Scotland %	Four-Party Contests %
Con	16.9	20.8
Lab	43.9	45.8
All	15.1	18.5
SNP	18.2	14.9

Studying local elections is always worthwhile because they can give a picture of the state of party morale and organisation. The failure of the Conservatives to contest a large number of regional seats was perhaps a reflection of low morale and/or weak organisation at local level and this in turn had implications for the General Election. The 1987 results should, therefore, have come as no great surprise to those who had kept an eye on inter-election indicators of electoral trends.

The Scottish Results 1987

Although Scotland produced the most spectacular results of any 'region' in Britain in relation to Conservative losses and Labour gains, it is salutory to note that the level of Labour support is greatest in the North region of England and that Labour received a larger share of the vote in Wales than in Scotland. The North region also boasts a higher proportion of Labour seats than does Scotland. Nevertheless the attention paid to the 1987 results in Scotland is justified because it was here that the greatest Conservative losses were suffered in share of votes (−4.4 points) and in seats (−11) and where Labour made its greatest gains with a 7.3 increase in its share of the votes, more than double that in England as a whole. Scotland also accounted for over half of the Conservative loss of seats in Britain, and for nearly half of net Labour gains. The Alliance too, suffered their biggest loss of support in Scotland and Wales (−5.3).

Table 4: Party Share of Votes by Standard Region

	Con %	Lab %	All %	SNP/PC %	Other %
North	32.3	46.4	21.0	–	0.3
Yorkshire & Humberside	37.4	40.6	21.7	–	0.3
East Midlands	48.6	30.0	21.0	–	0.4
East Anglia	52.1	21.7	25.7	–	0.5
Greater London	46.5	31.5	21.3	–	0.7
Rest of South East	55.6	16.8	27.2	–	0.5
South West	50.6	15.9	33.0	–	0.5
West Midlands	45.5	33.3	20.8	–	0.4
North West	38.0	41.2	20.6	–	0.2
Wales	29.5	45.1	17.9	7.3	0.2
Scotland	24.0	42.4	19.2	14.0	0.3

The Conservatives had their worst results this century in terms of share of the vote in Scotland but Labour is still some way short of *its* best result achieved in 1964 with 48.7 percent of the votes, and it has not yet achieved the 50 per cent which the Conservatives had in 1955, admittedly in an era of weak 'third' parties. The Conservatives held on to only 10 of the 72 seats in Scotland, their worst performance since 1910 when, in the face of a Liberal triumph, they got nine.

Despite its failure to break through to 50 per cent of the vote, the geographical distribution of its support and the operation of the electoral system ensured that Labour did much better in its tally of seats. It gained

27

eight seats from the Conservatives, one from the Alliance and two from the SNP to reach 50 for the first time, a figure only bettered this century by the Liberal's 58 in 1910.

Although the Alliance suffered a five point decline in its share of the vote compared with 1983, it emerged with a net gain of one seat resulting from two gains from the Conservatives and the loss of one to Labour, giving a total of nine seats. The SNP's modest improvement in its share of the vote brought it a net gain of one seat, from two to three, having lost two to Labour and gained three from the Conservatives.

Regional Variations in Scotland

As usual, as shown in Table 5, there were considerable regional variations within Scotland. Labour's great strength in the central belt was confirmed and reinforced. It had an absolute majority of the votes in Strathclyde, almost 50 percent in Central region and around 45 percent in Fife. Labour's poorest region remains the Borders and it continues to be weak in the relatively urbanised regions of Grampian and Tayside. The greatest increases in Labour's share of the vote are to be found in its heartland of Strathclyde, Fife and Central, but it made progress in all regions. From a nationwide perspective commentators have noted that Labour's advance was most marked in its 'heartland' areas like Scotland and the North of England. But even within Scotland there was a tendency for Labour to do best where it was already strong.

Table 5:   Party Shares of Votes in Regions

	Con %	Lab %	Alliance %	SNP %	Other %
Borders	33.6 (−0.9)	10.0 (+2.5)	49.6 (−4.6)	6.8 (+3.0)	−
Central	22.9 (−2.8)	48.9 (+7.7)	12.6 (−7.5)	15.8 (+2.8)	0.2
Dumfries & Galloway	41.2 (−3.4)	19.3 (+3.0)	16.4 (−2.2)	22.5 (+2.0)	0.7
Fife	23.4 (−5.2)	44.5 (+9.0)	21.7 (−5.1)	10.4 (+2.2)	−
Grampian	32.6 (−5.2)	22.5 (+3.6)	25.2 (−1.5)	19.7 (+3.1)	0.1
Lothian	27.3 (−3.0)	41.6 (+6.0)	20.5 (−5.8)	10.2 (+2.8)	0.4
Strathclyde	19.3 (−4.9)	53.3 (+9.2)	15.7 (−6.8)	11.5 (+2.6)	0.2
Tayside	30.6 (−3.1)	26.7 (+5.9)	11.0 (−4.9)	31.6 (+2.2)	0.1
Highlands & Islands	19.5 (−7.3)	23.1 (+7.3)	41.6 (−2.9)	12.7 (−2.9)	3.1

Table 6: Distribution of Seats in Regions

	Con	Lab	Alliance	SNP
Borders	–	–	2	–
Central	1	3	–	–
Dumfries & Galloway	2	–	–	–
Fife	–	4	1	–
Grampian	1	2	1	2
Lothian	2	8	–	–
Strathclyde	2	30	1	–
Tayside	2	2	–	1
Highlands & Islands	–	1	4	–
TOTAL	10	50	9	3

The Conservative share declined in every region. Their best region was Dumfries and Galloway where they gained 41 percent of the vote, but with only two seats it can contribute little to their parliamentary strength.

The Alliance share also declined in every region; they lost the majority which they had in the Borders, although they are still close to 50 percent, but again this is a small region with only two seats and can make only a modest contribution to the tally of seats. Apart from the Borders, the best Alliance territory is Grampian where its share fell least and where it still holds around a quarter of the vote.

The SNP, like Labour, increased its share in every region and it is strongest in Tayside with getting on for a third of the vote, but only one seat.

Grampian is the only truly competitive four-party region and the only one in which all the parties have a member of Parliament.

Constituency Results

The 1987 General Election was fought on the same constituency boundaries as existed in 1983, so a direct comparison of performances in individual constituencies is possible.

One important item for comparison between the two elections is the parties' share of the vote in each constituency. Although there are large variations in the *size* of changes in shares from one seat to another (which could be treated as swing if four-party politics did not make this a poor measure), there is a striking consistency in the *direction* of change. The Conservative share of the vote fell in all but one of the seventy-two constituencies, (the exception being Tweeddale, Ettrick and Lauderdale with an increase of 0.7 percent); Labour's share rose in all but one, (Banff and Buchan −0.3 percent); the Alliance share declined in sixty-four, and the SNP improved its vote in sixty seats (excluding Orkney and Shetland which it did not contest in 1987, and Fife North East where it remained the same).

A second comparable feature is the outcome in marginal seats. In all elections the movement in these is crucial to the overall result. Labour's failure to gain many Conservative marginals and to retain some of its own in England and Wales doomed it to defeat nationally.

If we define as marginal those seats in which the incumbent party had a majority of 10 per cent or less, then on the 1983 results the Conservatives in Scotland had twelve marginals to defend, Labout had three and the Alliance three; neither of the seats held by the SNP were marginal. Six of these Conservative seats were, on the statistics, vulnerable to the Alliance, three to Labour and three to the SNP; in the Labour marginals the Conservatives challenged in two and the Alliance in another; two of the Alliance seats were vulnerable to the Conservatives and one to Labour.

The 1983 Conservative majorities in their marginals ranged from 1.1 in Edinburgh West to 9.9 percentage points in Edinburgh Pentlands. As it happens these were the only two of the twelve that succeeded in holding and in which the decline in their share of the vote was less than 1 percentage point. Despite the marginality of these two seats the odds were on the Conservatives to hold them. A projection to constituencies of the 1986 Regional election results showed the incumbents ahead in both by roughly the margin achieved in the General Election. On the other hand, all of the Conservative losses, including the non-marginal Argyll and Bute were projected on the same basis[2].

Similar projections for the three Labour marginals suggested that none of them was in danger and, of course, they were not only retained but with significantly increased majorities. The one Alliance seat (Glasgow Hillhead) which was vulnerable to Labour showed a clear Labour lead in the Regional results and they duly gained it, but the two in which the Conservatives were challengers produced very much greater shares of the votes for the Alliance incumbents. Although the SNP had no statistically marginal seats it lost the two that it held (whilst gaining three others). But by other than statistical criteria both SNP-held seats were marginals. The Western Isles had been for many years a Labour seat, but a local Labour party row, a general upsurge of support for the SNP and an obviously attractive local candidate enabled Donald Stewart to capture the constituency for the SNP in 1970. His retirement in 1987 left this unique constituency up for grabs again, and Labour reclaimed its inheritance to the surprise of few. The defeat of the SNP leader and incumbent MP Gordon Wilson by Labour in Dundee was, however, a surprise to many. Wilson won this seat in February 1974 and retained it against the odds in three succeeding elections. Projections from local elections showed this in recent times to be 'really' a Labour seat, but they had been unable to recover it. It is ironic that they should have done so at an election in which SNP fortunes were on an upturn. An exceptional Labour organisation combined with a sensible choice of candidate seem to be the most likely explanation for this gain.

TABLE 7:   Parties 'Best' Results

Conservatives   Mean Fall in Share of Votes = 4.3

Ten 'Best Con. Results		Ten 'Worst' Con. Results	
Tweeddale, Ettrick & Lauderdale	+ 0.7	Dunfermline	− 14.4
Dumbarton	− 0.1	Ross, Cromarty & Skye	− 14.0
Greenock	− 0.2	Gordon	− 10.1
Perth & Kinross	− 0.7	East Kilbride	− 9.5
Edinburgh Pentlands	− 0.9	Glasgow Hillhead	− 9.2
Edinburgh West	− 0.9	Glasgow Cathcart	− 8.1
Banff & Buchan	− 1.0	Glasgow Govan	− 7.8
Western Isles	− 1.5	Monklands East	− 7.1
Stirling	− 2.2	Kincardine & Deeside	− 7.1
Falkirk East	− 2.3	Eastwood	− 7.1

Labour   Mean Increase in Share of Votes = 7.4

Ten 'Best Lab Results		Ten 'Worst' Lab. Results	
Greenock & Port Glasgow	+ 17.1	Banff & Buchan	− 0.3
Paisley South	+ 14.8	Caithness & Sutherland	+ 0.6
Dunfermline East	+ 13.2	Kincardine & Deeside	+ 0.8
Western Isles	+ 12.6	Fife North East	+ 0.9
Strathkelvin & Bearsden	+ 12.5	Galloway & Upper Nithsdale	+ 1.5
Ayr	+ 12.4	Roxburgh & Berwickshire	+ 1.5
Clydebank	+ 12.0	Edinburgh West	+ 2.1
East Kilbride	+ 11.9	Linlithgow	+ 2.3
Glasgow Garscadden	+ 11.5	Angus East	+ 2.8
Glagow Central	+ 11.5	Argyll & Bute	+ 2.8

Alliance   Mean Fall in Share of Votes = 5.2

Ten 'Best' Alliance Results		Ten 'Worst' Alliance Results	
Western Isles	+ 14.9	Greenock & Port Glasgow	− 18.4
Ross, Cromarty & Skye	+ 10.9	Ayr	− 10.8
Argyll & Bute	+ 9.8	Glasgow Maryhill	− 10.4
Kincardine & Deeside	+ 6.9	Clydebank & Milngavie	− 9.9
Gordon	+ 5.6	Dunfermline East	− 9.6
Fife North East	+ 4.6	Dumbarton	− 9.6
Caithness & Sutherland	+ 1.6	Inverness, Nairn & Lochaber	− 9.2
Galloway & Upper Nithsdale	+ 1.5	Stirling	− 9.0
Eastwood	− 0.4	Paisley South	− 9.0
Glagow Hillhead	− 1.1	Kilmarnock & Loudoun	− 9.0

SNP Mean Increase in share of Votes = 2.4

Ten 'Best' SNP Results		Ten 'Worst' SNP Results	
Kilmarnock & Loudoun	+ 9.2	Western Isles	− 26.0
Tayside North	+ 8.6	Glasgow Provan	− 7.7
Moray	+ 8.0	Dundee East	− 3.6
Clackmannan	+ 7.9	Strathkelvin & Bearsden	− 2.1
Banff & Buchan	+ 6.8	Ross, Cromarty & Skye	− 2.0
Linlithgow	+ 6.5	Dundee West	− 1.8
Angus East	+ 6.4	Kincardine & Deeside	− 1.2
Motherwell South	+ 5.5	Caithness & Sutherland	− 0.7
Inverness, Nairn & Lochaber	+ 5.0	Glasgow Pollock	− 0.3
Paisley North	+ 4.9	Glasgow Central	− 0.3

In purely statistical terms the 'best' Conservative result was against David Steel in Tweeddale, Ettrick and Lauderdale, where their share increased by 0.7 percentage points and their worst was in Dunfermline East where it fell by more than 14 points. Better than average results in Edinburgh Pentlands, Edinburgh West and Stirling probably saved them these seats, but the rest of their 'good' results were in a sense, wasted. None of their 10 worst results put any of their seats at risk. Labour's 'best' result was in Greenock and Port Glasgow and their worst was in Banff and Buchan (0.3 points). Above average results were needed to win the Western Isles and Strathkelvin and Bearsden, and these were forthcoming. Otherwise most of Labour's 10 'best' results were in safe Labour seats with the exception of Ayr where they came very close to achieving a coup of considerable proportions. For the Alliance, the 'best' result was in the Western Isles where their share increased by 14.9 percentage points, the largest increase by any party anywhere except for Labour's 17.1 in Greenock and Port Glasgow. Above average performances enabled them to gain Argyll and Bute and Fife North-East, but elsewhere their best performances were either in seats that they held or in those that were safe for other parties. Apart from Fife North-East, none of the marginals in which they lay second appear amongst their 10 best performances. The 'worst' Alliance performance was in Greenock and Port Glasgow (−18.4 points) and they had poorer than average results in two of their own seats, Inverness, Nairn and Lochaber (−9.2) and Tweeddale, Ettrick and Lauderdale (−8.6). Otherwise the biggest Alliance losses tended to be in safe Labour seats. The 10 'best' SNP results were very productive in terms of seats, above average performances gaining them Moray, Banff and Buchan and Angus East. The 'worst' result was in the Western Isles (−26.0) suggesting that Donald Stewart had a huge personal vote there.

The question of tactical voting got more publicity in 1987 than ever before and more precise guidance was offered to electors about how to deploy otherwise 'wasted' votes than at any previous election. But the tactical voting campaign, which was a frankly anti-Conservative ploy was not, it would appear, very successful. The complex movements of votes which produce the result in an individual constituency cannot be identified from aggregate statistics, but it seems clear that there was, in 1987, far less tactical voting than many had hoped for. There is some evidence of a modest amount of such voting in Banff and Buchan, the second most marginal Conservative seat, which was lost to the SNP. The Conservatives had a majority of 2.3 percent here in 1983 and their share of the vote fell by only 1.0 point in 1987. But this was the only seat in which Labour's share actually declined and, although the fall in the Alliance share was just above average, the bulk of defectors seem to have gone to the SNP. In Renfrew West and Inverclyde, Strathkelvin and Bearsden and Edinburgh South, Labour came from third place in 1983 to gain the seats, hardly evidence of tactical voting, unless voters there had a greater sophistication than that with which they are usually credited. In the other seats that Labour gained from the Conservatives, Aberdeen South, Cunninghame North and Edinburgh South, the SNP share of the vote increased and the decline in the Alliance share equalled the Scottish average in the first and was only slightly above average in the other two.

Apart from Banff and Buchan, the other SNP gains from the Conservatives were also made with no apparent surge in tactical voting. In both Moray and Angus East the Labour share, which had collapsed on previous occasions when the SNP won, actually increased and, whilst the Alliance share fell by slightly more than the average in Moray, it decreased by slightly less than average in Angus East. Nor did the Alliance victories in Argyll and Bute and Fife North-East seem to be the result of tactical voting. In both of these seats the Labour share increased; the SNP vote did fall by a significant margin in Argyll and Bute, but it held steady in North East Fife.

Turnout

Overall, turnout in Scotland was 75.0 percent compared with 72.7

33

percent in 1983 which was the lowest of the post-war period. It is difficult to know what factors affect turnout. It seems to vary little if at all with the weather, number of candidates, age of the register, demographic structure of the constituency or peoples' perceptions of the likely result. Nor does the amount of publicity given to campaigns in the mass media seem to have much positive effect on turnout. On the whole, turnout has, with a few ups and downs, been declining over the years, although not dramatically.

In only five seats did turnout go down in 1987 compared with the 1983 election and that by a very modest amount. In individual constituencies the highest increase was five percentage points in Aberdeen North which raised it from a lowly 65 in 1983. The greatest drop in turnout was in Monklands West, down by 3.4 points to just about the Scottish average. The highest turnout in 1987 was in Strathkelvin and Bearsden (82.1 percent) which was also in top place in 1983, and the lowest in Glasgow Central (65.6 percent) which occupied the same position in the previous election. Marginality seems not to have had a consistent positive effect on either total turnout or increase over 1983. Only five of the Conservative marginals had turnouts of more than two percentage points above the average, four were below and three were around average. If marginality alone is not an important influence on turnout, competitiveness may be. In four of the five Conservative marginals in which turnout was more than two points above average, the Alliance came a close second in 1983 with Labour not very far behind making contests genuinely three way. In all the other Conservative marginals (except Edinburgh South) only one party was a clear challenger.

Conclusion

There is little doubt that the most striking aspect of the 1987 General Election results in Scotland is the extent to which the Scots have continued to turn away from the Conservatives. The Conservative decline between 1983 and 1987 can be readily attributed to the discontent in Scotland, within the Conservative party as well as more generally, over the government's handling of Scottish issues. In matters such as rating revaluation, and the subsequent proposal for a community charge to replace domestic rates, the closure of the Gartcosh steel plant, welfare payments during severe weather and, more generally, unemployment and industrial decline, the government appeared insensitive to Scottish opinion. What is striking about the Conservative decline in Scotland, however, is the fact that it has been in progress almost continuously since 1955. If the process is not arrested the Conservatives are in danger of being obliterated in Scotland.

While Conservative decline is easy to describe it is less easy to explain. Long-term social changes – in housing patterns for example – might be presumed to *favour* the Conservatives, but they clearly have not. British-wide developments, in particular, the loosening of traditional party ties, have clearly contributed to electoral change in Scotland with the SNP and the Alliance benefitting at the expense of the major parties. (It should be remembered that Labour's 42.4 percent of the vote in 1987 was *lower* than they received in any election between 1945 and 1970.) Nonetheless the problem remains that in Scotland it is the Conservatives who have suffered most whereas in most of the rest of the country it is the Labour party which has seen its support slump. Has there, then, been something specific to Scotland or to Scottishness that explains this? This, however, is a question that merits more serious consideration than can be offered here.

John Bochel, University of Dundee
David Denver, University of Lancaster

References

1. J M Bochel and D T Denver, 'The 1983 General Election of Scotland' in D McCrone (ed.) *The Scottish Government Yearbook 1984*, Edinburgh, Unit for the Study of Government in Scotland, 1984.

2. J M Bochel, *An Analysis of Party Support in Scottish Parliamentary Constituencies Based on the 1986 Regional Election Results*, Dundee, Election Studies, 1987.

"MAIR NOR A ROUCH WIND BLAWIN..."

Alan Lawson

The 1987 Result

Although the 1987 election result in Scotland did not immediately cause a revolution of any kind, there are certainly grounds for regarding it as a political milestone in the process – a process which has been gaining speed over the past 25-30 years – whereby Scotland re-establishes a separate identity, politically and in other fields, and effectively de-colonises itself from the British ascendancy. On June 11th 1987, "the winds of change" (H MacMillan) turned into "a rouch wind blawin" (H Henderson).

The election results are analysed in detail elsewhere in this journal, but some figures have to be cited at the onset here by way of introduction. Labour's 50 MPs was the highest number for any party (ie, excluding Coalitions) since the Liberals' 58 in 1910. The Tories' 10 seats represented their worst result since 1910, and is the smallest number of MPs which a government party has ever had in Scotland. (The only remotely similar situation was their 13 seats in the Conservative Government of 1922-23.) And it is in this respect that the National Question has moved centre-stage, since the Tories now have the task of running the political system in Scotland with a team which is so short on numbers (not to mention talent). And it is certainly the Tories weakness and the challenging of their 'mandate to govern Scotland' that is creating the potential for change, rather than the increased strength of Labour (important though that is).

The fact that the Tories now have such a problem stems from the concessions which have been made to national sentiment and political pressure over the past hundred years, from the appointment of the first Scottish Secretary in 1885, through the setting up of the Scottish Office in the 1930s (and the subsequent expansion of its functions), to the advent of the Scottish Select Committee at the start of this decade (as part of the setting up of the many UK Select Committees), and the growing prominence (although not power) of the Scottish Grand Committee. It is these past developments which now make the Tories' position so embarrassing, and which make Scotland so different from those areas in the North of England where the Tories did poorly against Labour.

Yet historically, the Tories regularly did much worse in Scotland than in England from 1900 until the Second World War. It was only in the period

1945-55 that they were able to do as well (or even a little better) here than in the south. Ever since 1959 they have polled worse in Scotland than their counterparts in England, and the Labour Party have been the majority party in Scotland now for almost 30 years. In the 13 post-war elections, the Scottish Labour lead (in seats) over the Tories has been: 10, 6, 0, –2, 7, 19, 26, 21, 19, 25, 22, 20, 40. That sequence shows how strong the trend has been and how marked the latest result is.

The significance of the 1987 result is strengthened by the degree of tactical voting which apparently took place. In the marginal seats held by the Tories, votes seemed to swing to the immediate challenger, regardless of party, in order to displace the incumbent MP. Hence, Labour were able to win seats in middle-class areas, whilst the Liberals – despite suffering quite a downturn in their support – were able to win seats like North-East Fife and Argyll. In the seats which the SNP gained, there was hardly any increase in the Labour vote... in marked contrast to elsewhere. (A further point of interest was the marked rise in turnout in most seats, indicating perhaps a renewed sense of purpose on the part of the electorate: only 14 of the 72 seats showed a lower turnout that in 1983 – of which 10 were the Tory wins and the other 4 Alliance wins.) During the campaign there was some encouragement given to the electorate to vote tactically against the Tories. An organisation called TV'87 (Tactical Voting 87) tried to attract prominent supporters and gain publicity, whilst the *Glasgow Herald* called on its readers to "make a statement about the way that Scotland is governed".

The extent to which people increasingly voted anti-Tory (a) because they wanted some form of Scottish self-government, as against (b) because they didn't like Tory policies, is not easy to ascertain, but the two may be becoming so closely fused (as argued later) that it may represent less and less of a distinction as time goes on. If there is truth in (a), then the electorate have shown a considerable degree of sophistication over the past 15 years in their ways of supporting self-government... by voting SNP in the early/mid-70s, then by voting 'yes' in the 1979 referendum, and now by voting tactically anti-Tory.

Are The Trends Irreversible?

The ways in which the parties in Scotland will approach the somewhat bizarre situation they now face has (at time of writing) only partly been revealed, but their approaches will be conditioned by the extent to which the political trends – at Scottish and UK level – appear to be inevitable and irreversible. The recent voting figures don't look good for the Tories in this respect: in 1979, they reassured themselves when they won back the seats lost to the SNP in '74; but in 1987, in the face of Rifkind forecasts of re-taking the seats narrowly lost to the Alliance in '83, those Alliance MPs were all returned with greatly increased majorities (and despite the

Alliance's Scottish vote falling from 25% to 19%). So it seems to be getting harder and harder for the Tories to take back lost ground.

A further factor which makes the Tory position more difficult to reverse is that they are now 'below the PR line' – ie, they get far fewer seats than their vote would allow them under a PR voting system. (They can hardly complain, of course, since party policy is opposed to PR.) But whilst they have been winning *slightly* fewer seats than their deserts over the past 30 years, the latest result gave them only 10 when their share of the vote (24%) should have entitled them to 17. In turn, this 'disadvantage' leaves them so short of talent to run the Scottish political system that the performance of those selected for office is quite likely to further discredit the party and damage its future electoral chances. (On the plus side, the behaviour of Lord James Douglas-Hamilton keeps the political satirists of the land well stocked with stories.)

But in seeking to discover whether current trends are likely to continue, it is necessary to look beyond the immediate election figures, for, given the socio-economic make-up of the Scottish population and given statistics like average income per head, our voting patterns should be more in line with the English Midlands. This large, and growing, discrepancy requires a wider treatment, involving sociological and cultural factors.

Some of the structural reasons for the Tories' decline in Scotland over the past 30 years were outlined in an article by Stephen Maxwell in *Radical Scotland* No.15 (June/July 1985). He suggested that Scottish Toryism no longer seemed to make any contribution at intellectual level (apart from the freelance ideologues of the Smith and Hume Institutes in London) as compared with the 19th and early 20th centuries. Further, the great industrial Tory families of the inter-war period had disappeared and not been replaced, due to the many take-overs from the south and the subsequent branch-economy nature of industry in Scotland. In terms of image, the appointment of landed gentry and such-like Public school figures as Secretaries of State (eg, Noble, Campbell, Younger) gave the party a "grouse-moor" feel to it. In more direct voting terms, the consistently higher Scottish rate of unemployment (since the '60s) has tended to turn people away from the Conservatives, whilst even the old working-class Orange vote which the Tories used to get has apparently largely deserted them.

The only one of these factors which seems capable of being reversed is the "grouse-moor" image, but recruitment by the Party is so low that any 'new image' is likely to be of the young radical right – something liable to cause even greater disenchantment amongst the Scottish electorate. Indeed, it has been the 1970s rise of the New Right in the south which has perhaps caused the greatest reaction by the Scottish electorate against the Tory Party. The new zeal for economic liberalism has been perceived as bad news for Scotland, with an increase in damaging take-overs in the private sector and a decline in support (ideological and financial) for Regional Aid in the public sector. Currently, the driving ahead of the Chunnel project may symbolise for many Scots the new centralist and 'south-east corner' mentality of the Tory Government.

And there are other aspects of the New Right's thinking which strike faulty chords in Scotland. As sociologist Isobel Lindsay states in *Radical Scotland* No.29 (Oct/Nov 1987), "the current harsh social Darwinism is not an ideology which fits well with the experiences of 20th century Scots. We have been too conscious of the fact that many of the problems and ills that have beset us and our parents were not of our own making. Even in the last ten years, the best things to have happened in Scotland – environmental, cultural, recreational – have been primarily primed by public money; the worst things that have happened – high unemployment and cuts in services – have been caused by lack of public funding or by the ruthlessness of private institutions."

Further problems have arisen for the Tories on the policy side. The closure of Gartcosh (which caused a revolt within their own ranks) was seen by many as symbolic of a lack of concern for and interest in industry generally and Scottish heavy industry in particular. The ham-fisted handling of the cold climate allowance issue during the winter of '86/87 was the kind of thing that remains in people's minds for a long time, adding 'geographism' to the list of 'isms' associated with the Tory party. The use of Scotland as a testing-ground for legislative experimentation (extended police powers, poll tax) represents a quite remarkable insensitivity to Scottish feelings. Again, there is no sign that any of this will change.

And then we come to the question of self-government, which is increasingly damaging for the Tories. It's not just that the Tory party is setting its face ever more firmly against self-government at a time when political and economic developments have tended to increase the demand and the enthusiasm for it; it's the way that the Tories have gone about it. When Lord Douglas-Home was trotted out to tell everyone in 1979 to "vote NO and we'll provide a better form of devolution", it was only a short-term strategy; the ploy is now seen so clearly to have been downright dishonest that the Tories are now perceived as the Party which is 'economical with the truth' even on the matters of greatest importance. It is unlikely that people will forget that manoeuvre.

On the positive side, the last 20 years – and the post-79 period in particular – have seen many aspects of a national revival, especially on the cultural side. Given the increasingly mono-cultural nature of English society, all such developments represent a potential strengthening of the desire for self-government and the determination to pursue it. Advances have taken place in publishing in particular, with an apparently ever-increasing stream of books on all things Scottish, especially history. Meanwhile, attempts to introduce more Scottish material into the schools' curriculum seem to be making headway. The opening of the Burrell and the Scottish National Gallery of Modern Art have boosted national prestige, as have the host of small specialist and local museums. The rise and rise of Scottish pop groups now complements the high standard of the many successful professional folk-groups. On the sports field national teams and individuals usually acquit themselves with dignity, if not always with success, but it is the former which is the more valid litmus-test of a reviving self-confidence. On the spectating side, the contrasting behaviour of Scottish and English travelling football supporters perhaps has as much to tell us about the relative healths of the two societies as any other measure. This, and the fact that Scottish football clubs now buy *English* players, should not be underestimated as an influence on the state of the national self-confidence.

On the international front, a further division between Scotland and Thatcher's England was seen at the time of the Commonwealth Games in 1986, when a number of persons prominent in Scottish society were prepared to align themselves with a call for sanctions against South Africa, thereby creating an alternative Scottish viewpoint on an international issue of the day. At a lower level, our efforts to assist the third world are increasingly being made on a direct basis (eg, through organisations like SCIAF and Scottish Aid for Nicaragua) rather than just through southern 'national' headquarters.

The intensity of these increasing differences between the two societies has of course been heightened by the apparent permanence of the Tory government and of Mrs Thatcher as Prime Minister. One of the consequences of this has been the way in which Mrs Thatcher has come to represent English nationalism. As Isobel Lindsay puts it: "The enthusiasm which many working-class as well as middle-class English feel for Margaret Thatcher is related to their perception of their national identity; she represents an assertive, maudlinly sentimental English nationalism – fulfilling a yearning for renewed imperial glory. The role of the British bomb has had much more to do with the desire for prestige and status than to do with defence needs. This dominant strand of English nationalism strikes few chords in Scottish hearts. Scottish national sentiment has developed in different directions. We are David rather than Goliath; we are the underdogs, with considerable sympathy for other underdogs; we are less xenophobic (if for no other reason than that so many of our friends and relatives live abroad); we have no delusions of potential 'great power' status. Therefore, Thatcher's strand of English nationalism which has been accepted so warmly in the South, has produced attitudes ranging from the ambivalent to the antagonistic here."

These powerful underlying trends within Britain are very important for any attempt to determine where we are now and what is likely to happen in the next few years. They are more important than a simple study of the policies of the different parties or the precise results of particular elections. And the significance of them is that they all seem to point in the direction of a further decline in support for the Tory party in Scotland (or, at the very least, no real recovery.) If the Tories continue to be the government of the United Kingdom – which seems pretty likely for the foreseeable future – then their weakness in Scotland does create a political instability, if not a crisis.

The Parties' Initial Responses

The possibility of any change in the attitude of the Tory party seems small. At UK level they can apparently do no wrong, and the policies of the radical right continue to be fed into the party machine and continue to be acted upon. In Scotland, although there has been a fair amount of internal discontent – much of it showing an understanding of the points which have been made above – and although the question of devolution was raised in several quarters post-election, the *official* line is against any policy change, and the line against self-government in particular has hardened, with Lord Goold leading the way, Allan Stewart finding an apparent new lease of life in this crusade, and with various ex-MPs almost having to join the NUJ, so frequent are their appearances in the columns of the Scottish quality press 'explaining' the election result and pointing the way ahead. (Michael Ancram actually appeared with major articles in both the *Glasgow Herald* and *The Scotsman* on the same day on one occasion!) The Party at grass roots level seems to have too little clout to cause any serious challenge at this stage, and given that they were unable to find 72 Scottish candidates to fight the election in June (having to import various 'radical righters' and 'Sloane Rangers' from London for some of the Glasgow constituencies, who became known as 'The White Knights'), their relative weakness within the Party machine is fairly understandable. Meantime, further moves by the establishment included a flying visit to Glasgow by the Adam Smith Institute's representatives, ringing calls for "more Thatcherism" from the White Knights, and a conference publication from Eastwood constituency. It is doubtful, however, whether these manoeuvres did more than highlight the Tories' Scottish weakness.

The position of Malcolm Rifkind is particularly interesting, since it is clear that (a) he remains committed in principle to some form of self-government for Scotland, and (b) he is unlikely to believe that more Thatcherism will reverse his Party's decline in Scotland. Indeed, in an interview with the *Press and Journal* (September), he described the introduction of further right-wing policies in Scotland as "a high-risk strategy", thereby apparently distancing himself from any future falling masonry (and/or falling support). His close acquaintance Brian Meek, Tory leader on Lothian Regional Council, stated in an interview (September) that he believed that "devolution was inevitable and that our Party should be the one to do it". Meek also viewed the hard line with some scepticism, and reckoned that the May 1988 District Elections would be a crucial test for the Party's recovery or otherwise, and that if it were otherwise then the devolutionists might become more prominent again.

For the Labour Party in Scotland, the result induced a kind of political schizophrenia, with their best-ever Scottish result coinciding with a further desperate defeat in the south. The immediate response of the frustrated 'Gang of 50' in the House of Commons is described elsewhere in this volume, and there is no doubt that the result caused a difference of view within the Party as to what should or could be done about challenging the Tories' mandate in Scotland. The Party establishment – epitomised by Donald Dewar – wanted to do nothing out of the ordinary, whilst a number of the MPs and an indeterminate section of the Party membership were looking for serious political action. Three major intellectual challenges faced the Party: first, confronting the very real possibility that Labour would not win the *next* General Election; any who took this view would clearly distance themselves from Donald Dewar's "long haul" approach (ie, a 5-year approach.) Second, was the possibility that if a Scottish Assembly were to be won from an unenthusiastic Tory Government, then there might be a price to be paid in terms of (a) a reduction in the number of Scottish MPs at Westminster, and (b) the possible withdrawal of Scottish MPs during debates on 'devolved business' for England & Wales; such concessions would clearly make the job of the UK Labour Party in winning and exercising power that bit more difficult. And thirdly, there was the prospect that any serious action on the National Question might well have to involve co- operation with other pro-Assembly forces, including political parties. (Initial forays into cross-party activity by Labour in the shape of a Festival For Scottish Democracy (in September) were tentative, with the SNP and the Alliance deciding not to participate due to being only half-heartedly or compromisingly invited.) All three of these points would represent *major* departures from traditional Labour thinking. At the same time, Labour had by now won just about everything there was to win in Scotland apart from the Scottish Cup; from such a position it was clearly difficult to go up, and fairly easy to go down.

The prominence of the National Question in all such deliberations within the People's Party was further heightened by the problems of opposing the unpopular poll tax, due to be introduced in Scotland first (starting in April 1989, with the Registration process beginning in April 1988). For some Party members, the STOPIT campaign should be founded on the 'No Tory Mandate in Scotland' issue, whilst for others the campaign was attractive as an alternative to or even a diversion from the constitutional issue.

The only fixed item on the agenda (as far as the National Question was concerned) was the presentation of an Assembly Bill to Parliament on 30th November. There were several problems connected with that move (such as tactics, publicity, and campaigning), but since the Bill was going to be defeated by the massed ranks of the Tory faithful, the *real* question was what – if anything – was going to be planned as a response to that Tory rejection. There would be two distinct options at that stage: (1) to attempt (with other forces) to set up some kind of forum of MPs, Councillors, and other elected and non-elected representatives of Scottish life, thereby challenging the British right to rule in Scotland, and discussing important Scottish matters and the form of any future Scottish government, or (2) minor forms of protest could be undertaken which would represent no such challenge, and which would therefore be a recognition that nothing could be done to advance the Assembly cause this side of the next election (and a Labour victory in that election). It is certainly possible that a pressure group of some kind will appear in the Labour Party to further the cause of option 1, an option which is being pursued by the cross-Party Campaign for a Scottish Assembly, using a Steering Committee as a springboard. Whatever the outcome, it is the most traumatic situation the Party in Scotland has ever found itself in, and therefore any simple resolution of the problems (and the divisions) is unlikely. As Tom Nairn (the author of *The Break-up of Britain*) put it in a short analysis in the July issue of *Marxism Today*: "Caledonian Labourism has always been ultra-conscientious in its obeisance to all the icons of Windsordom. The irony is that Scotland's quest for a more modern and distinct identity has ended in the clammy embrace of the party historically most hypnotised by Britishness. The question is whether the Scottish Labour Party can eventually change its own nature and become both national enough and, more importantly, democratic enough to assume the responsibility which history seems to have thrust upon them."

The SNP, did not enjoy the best of results in the election (2 losses, 3 gains), and the loss of chairman Gordon Wilson's seat was a great disappointment to the Party. (His resolve to stay on as chairman due to the persuasions of Mrs Winnie Ewing looked a dubious life-support system for him in a Party which has been cultivating a modern and left-of-centre image for several years now.) However, the Party – whilst less successful than it would like – has been doing nothing wrong for almost 5 years, an achievement not to be underestimated in a Party where commitment is so strong and disappointments have been so many. Given its improved presentation in the media and given the growing trends towards national self-confidence, the Party must be dismayed that considerably increased support has not been forthcoming. Yet they are well positioned: with the Tories in disarray, Labour seeming to be at a peak and faced with a major political conundrum, and with the Alliance falling away due to merger wrangles, it seems that the SNP must go up soon. Hopes for the District Elections in May 1988 are high, and if Labour's opposition to the 'Tory mandate' falls flat, then major gains for the SNP seem likely. Local by-election results already point in that direction.

The Alliance also came out of the election with mixed feelings: a good showing in Scotland with 1 loss and 2 gains, giving 9 seats, but failing to 'break the mould' in the UK. It seems unlikely that the Alliance parties will (separately or together) set the heather on fire in Scotland over the next few years. The merger negotiations will likely take up an inordinate amount of activists' time and energy; the Liberals – a small party on the ground – sends too much of its available talent to Westminster (starting with the leader); the Young Libs seem to be an ex-force; and the SDP is a very small party in Scotland. The prospects for the Alliance in Scotland would seem to rest almost entirely on their TV image and the success (or otherwise) of the merger process.

It is perhaps an indication of the significance of the National Question now in Scottish politics that all four/five of the parties seem to be in a weak position in one way or another, and that seems to suggest an unreality about the situation which seems unlikely to continue indefinitely.

Summary

The election of '87 created what might be called 'an unstable equilibrium', and there are basically three possible outcomes. First, that situation could be challenged by the opposition forces in Scotland, although that would not be easy and it would certainly involve tactics not formerly seen. Secondly, the Tories could alter policy on the National Question and introduce a scheme which was of considerable benefit to the Tory Party at UK level (ie, an Assembly scheme with reduced representation for Scotland – and hence Labour – at Westminster); however, this scenario looks pretty unlikely as long as (a) Mrs Thatcher remains Tory leader (since she has always hated the whole idea of devolution for Scotland), and/or (b) the Tories seem likely to win the next election fairly comfortably anyway. The third possibility is that very little happens, with the Tory 10-man team struggling along and 'brass-necking' their weak position and general unpopularity.

However, if the question remains unresolved by the next General Election, then for the many reasons outlined earlier in this article, it is highly likely that the Tories will lose a further block of Scottish seats (4 of their seats have majorities of 2,000 or less) leaving them in a *rely* impossible position next time. Whichever of these scenarios comes to pass, the view that "Devolution is inevitable" (Brian Meek) does now seem to be the case, and it is also likely that any shift of political power to Scotland would now go far beyond the devolutionary ideas of the '70s and would be closer to some kind of 'quasi-federalism'.

And although the 1987 election may not of itself have brought a major shake-up of the constitutional arrangements within the United Kingdom, it will probably be seen in retrospect as a very significant milestone on that road, a point from which there is unlikely to be any turning back.

Alan Lawson is editor of *Radical Scotland* magazine.

THE COMMUNITY CHARGE AND LOCAL GOVERNMENT FINANCE IN SCOTLAND

Archie Fairley

Introduction

The Abolition of Domestic Rates (Etc) Scotland Act received Royal Assent on May 15th 1987. Any lingering doubts about its eventual implementation appear to have been dispelled by the Conservative victory in the UK General Election on June 11th although there is press speculation that the Scottish implementation date of April 1989 may be delayed to coincide with the introduction of similar legislation for England and Wales, which was announced in the Queen's Speech on June 25th 1987. Any such delay would be viewed as a response to the apparent unpopularity of the community charge or poll tax and to the scale of Conservative defeat in Scotland on June 11th.

The Act is based on the Green Paper "Paying for Local Government" in which the reform proposals – the abolition of domestic rates, the introduction of the community charge, and the centralisation of non-domestic rates – are described as "the most radical re-structuring of local government finance this century"[1] – a verdict with which few would disagree.

This chapter will locate the reform proposals in their historical context by examining broad trends in the development of local government finance, with particular reference to the conflicts and tension between central and local government which have developed since the mid-1970's and to the impact of revaluation in 1985. The proposals will be examined to see how far they are consistent with Conservative fiscal and local government policies as they have developed since 1979. Attention will be paid to the nature and effectiveness of the opposition campaign inside and outside Parliament and the impact of the proposals on the future of Scottish local government will be discussed.

Historical Background – The Road to the Poll Tax

Local government in 19th century Scotland lacked uniformity and effectiveness until a series of Acts of Parliament in the late 1880s and 1890s, culminating in the 1900 Town Council (Scotland) Act which established a framework giving elected local authorities the powers to tackle major issues such as sanitary and housing reform. The development of municipal services, with Glasgow in the forefront, proceeded throughout the 19th century, but it is from the 1890s that a recognisable and uniform local government system can be traced. Throughout the 19th and 20th centuries, local government has been financed by central government grants and rates – a local property tax. Rates have come under periodic attack and criticism but have survived, probably because of the attributes most clearly stated in the Report of the Layfield Committee which was set up in 1974 to review the whole system of local government finance in England, Scotland and Wales.

"(i)   a tax on property is particularly suitable as a local tax. There is no difficulty in attributing the yield to even the smallest units of local government, since this yield depends on the physical location of immovable property;

(ii)   the form of tax is relatively simple and understandable, however much less easy it may be to comprehend the underlying details;

(iii)   over many years there has been considerable stability in the operation of rating, with relatively small changes from year to year;

(iv)   property is visible and easily identifiable; it cannot be shifted geographically in response to change in rates of tax;

(v)   the yield of the tax is readily predictable and certain;

(vi)   evasion is extremely difficult;

(vii)   the cost of maintaining rating is not high in proportion to the yield;

(viii)   rates are a perceptible tax; the demand, expressed as a lump sum at yearly or half-yearly intervals, brings the tax prominently to the notice of ratepayers;

(ix)   because rates are perceptible, and because deliberate decisions have to be taken to raise rate poundages to meet increased costs, the tax promotes accountability;

(x)   there are no problems of confidentiality of the taxpayers' personal income or circumstances (save now, when rebates are claimed)."[2]

As a result of central government policy and rising expectations, local government current expenditure in Scotland grew steadily in the 1960s and into the 1970s at an average annual rate of around 4% more than the rate of inflation.[3] Expenditure doubled in real terms between 1964 and 1975. This growth in expenditure was encouraged by central government and matched by growth in rate support grant (RSG) which peaked at 75% of local government spending in 1975/76.

1975 proved to be a turning point with the announcement by Tony Crosland, then Secretary of State for the Environment, that "the party's over" signalling the end of local government expansion financed largely by central government grants. 1975 was also the year of local government reorganisation in Scotland. As a result of significant inflation in the economy and the reorganisation, rate bills in Scotland rose by 28% provoking complaints from ratepayers and contributing to the terms of reference for the Layfield Committee.

In considering the nature of the crisis, Layfield concluded that short-term problems – "the virtual cessation in the rise of real national income...the rapid increase in inflation and...the reorganisation of local government"[4] – had highlighted longer-term fundamental problems concerning the financial and political relationship between central and local government.

Having criticised the ambiguity which, in his Committee's view characterised this relationship, Layfield went on to produce proposals which themselves contained significant elements of ambiguity and contradiction and were, at the end of the day, unacceptable to both central and local government.

The Committee took the view that "the only way to sustain a vital local democracy is to enlarge the share of local taxation in total local revenue and thereby make councillors more directly accountable to local electorates for their expenditure and taxation decisions".[5] To realise this objective, they proposed the introduction of a local income tax (LIT) to supplement the rating system. The rating system would be retained and extended to agricultural land and buildings. LIT would be an additional source of revenue for "top tier" authorities – in the case of Scotland, the regional councils. Both regions and districts would continue to levy rates. This formula would allow central government grant to be reduced to around 40% of local government expenditure thus enhancing local democracy and local accountability.

However, and in apparent contradiction to the emphasis on local democracy and accountability, Layfield also asserted central government's right to control levels of local government expenditure in the interests of macroeconomic policy.

Layfield's proposals found little favour with either central or local government but they set the scene for the debates of the 1980s and provided ammunition both for the supporters of the rating system and the advocates of LIT.

Aggregate Exchequer Grant as a percentage of local government spending in Scotland fell from 75% in 1975/76 to 68.5% in 1978/79. Expenditure reductions and rates increases became the order of the day but the effect of the pay restrictions embodied in the Social Contract kept the level of expenditure (and rates increases) down because of the labour intensive nature of local authority services.

Prior to 1979, RSG reductions had been a pragmatic response to external economic pressures. Following the election of the Conservative government in 1979, the curtailment of local authority spending was elevated to a policy objective in its own right. This policy objective has been pursued through reductions in central government grant on the one hand (expressed as a percentage of Scottish local government expenditure, RSG was cut from 68.5% in 1980/81 to 56.1% in 1986/87) and the enactment of legislation which gave the Secretary of State for Scotland widespread powers to restrict local government spending.

This radical and ideological approach swiftly turned local government into one of the main political battlefields of the Thatcher years. The emergence from the mid 1970s, of a new breed of Labour councillor, committed to a radical examination and extension of local government services, fuelled the conflict. The other major opponents of the government's economic and social policies, most notably the trade unions, experienced a series of crushing defeats in the 1980s. This trend reinforced the view of many on the political left that local government was the main agency for opposing central government policies and defending living standards while for those on the right, Labour local government came to be viewed as a major obstacle to the implementation of Conservative economic and social policies.

The 1979 Conservative manifesto contained a commitment to re-open the debate on the rating system. The result was the 1981 Green Paper "Alternatives to Domestic Rates" which canvassed alternatives to the rating system, including a poll tax. This was followed by a White Paper, produced in 1983, which came to the following conclusion:

"The Government were fully prepared to propose to Parliament the abolition of domestic rates if consultation had revealed broad-based support for an alternative system of local taxation which satisfied the criteria. However, it was clear from the response to the Green Paper and from the evidence given to the Environment Committee that no consensus can be found for an alternative tax to replace domestic rates. The Government recognises that rates are far from being an ideal or popular tax. But they do have advantages. They are highly perceptible to ratepayers and they promote accountability. They are well understood, cheap to collect and very difficult to evade. They act as an incentive to the most efficient use of property. No property tax can be directly related to the ability to pay; the rate rebates, now incorporated in housing benefit, together with Supplementary Benefit, have been designed to reduce hardship. The Government have concluded and announced to Parliament that rates would remain for the foreseeable future the main source of local revenue for local government."[6]

Average rates increases in Scotland of 30% in 1980/81 and 34% in 1981/82 fuelled the anger expressed by ratepayers' groups and sections of the business community, but rates reform did not emerge as a serious issue in the 1983 election campaign and the poll tax did not even merit a mention.

Following the 1983 election, the government pressed ahead with its legislative, financial and ideological attack on local government, but there appeared to be a consensus that there was no realistic alternative to the rating system. That consensus was shattered by the 1985 rating revaluation in Scotland.

Revaluation – Instant Crisis

Revaluations of property for rating purposes have been carried out in Scotland in 1971, 1978 and 1985.

The 1975 Local Government (Scotland) Act prescribes quinquennial revaluations, but the Secretary of State used his powers to delay the full revaluation of the 1978 Valuation Roll from 1983 to 1985. Revaluation redistributes the rating burden between sectors of ratepayers and between individual households. Significantly, there has been no revaluation in England and Wales since 1973.

The 1985 revaluation entailed a significant shift of the rating burden from industrial to domestic ratepayers and what the Green Paper "Paying for Local Government" described as "arbitrary and unpredictable impositions"[7] on many Scottish households. In spite of government measures to mitigate the effect of revaluation, including a special rebate scheme, over 100,000 households had an increase of more than 33% in their rate bills between 1984/85 and 1985/86. There were also significant fluctuations in the commercial and industrial sector.

Not surprisingly, revaluation provoked an outraged response from a range of domestic and non-domestic ratepayers, many of whom were traditional Conservative supporters. If revaluation after 7 years had this effect in Scotland, it didn't take a great deal of imagination to work out what the consequences would be in England and Wales where there had been no revaluation for 12 years. The hunt for alternatives to the rates now began in earnest with the publication of the Green Paper "Paying for Local Government" at the end of January 1986. Any lingering doubts amongst Conservatives about the unpopularity of revaluation were dispelled at the Regional Council elections in May 1986, when the Conservatives lost control of Tayside and Grampian Regions and suffered serious reverses elsewhere, notably in Lothian. Conservative councillors attributed much of their unpopularity to rating revaluation and saw the community charge and the abolition of rates as their electoral saviour.

The Main Themes of the Act

The 1987 Act has four main features:

(i)   the abolition of domestic rates;

(ii) the introduction of a system of community charges;

(iii) the transfer of control over the level of non-domestic rates from local authorities to the Secretary of State for Scotland;

(iv) the replacement of rate support grant by revenue support grant.

These reforms are to be implemented in April 1989. When similar legislation has been enacted for England and Wales, it is proposed to introduce a Uniform Business Rate (UBR) for Scotland, England and Wales.

The Case for Reform

The case for the proposed reforms has two main planks. On the one hand, there are the principled arguments and criticisms of the existing rating systems contained in the Green Paper. On the other hand, there is the hidden agenda – the desire to control the high profile "big spending" authorities, to undermine support for local government in Scotland dominated as it is by the Labour Party and to secure or shore up traditional Conservative support which, it was believed, had been lost by revaluation in particular and the government's alleged failure to protect "the ratepayers" from rate increases substantially above the rate of inflation in general.

These two strands often overlap and interact. Their co-existence goes a long way to explaining the theoretical poverty and inconsistencies of the Green Paper, which have been widely noted by most academic commentators. Its 133 pages have all the appearance of a document for which the conclusions were written first and the analysis to justify the conclusions produced as an afterthought. The contrast with, say, the style and methodology of the Layfield Report produced 10 years earlier is striking and speaks volumes about the changing style of government over the decade – there is now a failure to seriously examine alternative arguments or evidence which does not sit neatly with the predetermined conclusions. The comments of Martlew and Bailey that the Green Paper's examination of the evidence is "narrow and partial in focus"[8] or of Midwinter and Mair that its proposals "mark the triumph of ideology over analysis"[9] are not untypical.

Before examining the Green Paper's arguments and conclusions, a further criticism of its content and methodology must be made. The Green Paper's origins lie, to an extent, in developments in Scotland, particularly revaluation. Its conclusions for Scotland are similar to those for England and Wales, but there are significant diferences and they are to be implemented earlier and in a different way from the reforms in England and Wales. However, there is no integrated, sustained or convincing presentation of the Scottish evidence.

The Green Paper's numerous charts and tables break down as follows:

Related to	No of Charts/tables
England only	30
Great Britain	21
Wales only	9
United Kingdom	7
Scotland only	7
England and Wales	2

Of the seven Scottish tables, six contain background information on the characteristics of households and tax units, the population of communal establishments and comparative yields of national and local taxes. The seventh details the sources of funding of Scottish local government in 1985/86. There is no serious attempt to evidence the consequences of the proposals for domestic and non-domestic ratepayers, and local authorities in Scotland. For a Scottish reader, promised specific Scottish legislation, reading the Green Paper is a frustrating experience. Irrespective of any other political arguments, it is difficult to imagine such a flawed Green Paper being produced had it been subject to examination by the committees of a Scottish Assembly.

The case for the replacement of domestic rates by the community charge, the centralisation of non-domestic rates and the ultimate introduction of a national Uniform Business Rate (UBR) is based on economic and political arguments.

Economically, it is argued that central government has a responsibility for controlling public expenditure, that public expenditure squeezes the private sector and should therefore be reduced, that local government expenditure is a significant component of public expenditure, that local government expenditure is out of control and that central government, because of inherent defects in the rating system, is unable to bring local government expenditure under control. The economic theories which underlie these propositions are beyond the scope of this article. However, it is difficult to reconcile the assertion that local government expenditure is out of control with the evidence that local authority expenditure in the UK has fallen from 28% of public expenditure in 1979/80 to 25% in 1985/86. At the time the Green paper was published, planned expenditure by Scottish local authorities was only 3.2% above Government guidelines, which hardly seems likely to rock the macroeconomic boat. The power of central government to control local authority expenditure was formidable before 1979, but since then successive Acts of Parliament first applying to Scotland and then, in a different form, to England and Wales, have given the Secretary of State unprecedented powers to control the general level of spending, and the spending and rating decisions of individual local authorities.

It is at this point that we move from the economic to the political arguments, for the Green Paper concedes that the government has been successful in restraining local authority expenditure, but complains that central/local relationships have worsened and that local authorities have not been willing partners. The argument, implicit in the Green Paper, but made explicit in the House of Commons, then proceeds to assert that local electorates continue to elect recalcitrant local authorities and goes on to ask why this should be so.

Here we come to the key political argument of the Green Paper – accountability. Local authorities are not accountable to their domestic and non-domestic ratepayers who, together with central government, finance their spending policies. They are accountable to an electorate, the majority of whom do not pay rates. As a result, claims the Green Paper, "Many electors are indifferent to how much their local council spends or are encouraged to vote for ever higher expenditure on services."[10] The results are unfair to domestic ratepayers and damaging to the competitive position of non-domestic ratepayers both within the UK and in an international context. Let us examine the evidence.

Out of the Scottish electorate of 3.9 million, 1.9 million adults are householders liable to pay rates. Of that 1.9 million, 1.1 million pay full rates, 400,000 pay no rates at all and a further 400,000 receive a partial rebate. However, the simple assertion that only 1.1 million out of 3.9 million adults pay full rates fails to reflect the fact that 1.3 million of the 2 million non-householders are spouses of ratepayers and most organise their finances jointly. In the real world you don't have to be the householder in order to pay a share of the rates.

Furthermore, amongst the volumes of research on voting patterns, there is no evidence to support the proposition that electors vote for high spending policies because they will not have to finance them. Indeed, there is some evidence to the contrary, in that those least likely to pay rates and therefore with most to gain from high spending policies (young adults) are also less likely to vote than older people and less likely to vote in local rather than national elections.

The alleged unfairness experienced by domestic ratepayers has in the past been argued on the basis that rates are not related to ability to pay (ie: that rates are a regressive form of taxation). This is certainly true, although rates, it can be argued, are a tax on property, which while not necessarily relative to ability to pay do at least reflect a choice about household expenditure.

However, clearly it would be ridiculous to criticise domestic rates on the ability-to-pay argument when the proposed alternative is a poll tax which bears absolutely no relationship to ability to pay. In fact, the argument has now shifted. It is now argued that the balance of local authority services has historically swung from property services (water, gas, electricity and protective services) to personal services (education, social services, libraries). It is therefore consistent to argue that the tax base should shift from a property tax to a personal (or poll) tax. The use of the term "community charge" to describe what is undoubtedly a head tax or poll tax is partly a cosmetic exercise but also reflects government philosophy. "Moving from rates to a flat-rate community charge would mark a major change in the direction of local government finance back to the option of *charging* for local authority services."[11]

No convincing case has been made to establish that non-domestic rates affect the competitive position of firms either within the UK or in an international context. The Green Paper concedes that "Hard evidence of the effects of rates on business is scarce" and that "How far business rate increases do affect the location and viability of businesses in particular areas must therefore still to a large degree be a matter of conjecture."[12]

Nevertheless, on the basis of this shaky evidence, the 1987 Act removes non-domestic rates from the control of Scottish local authorities with effect from April 1989. The maximum non-domestic rate for each authority will be determined by the Secretary of State in accordance with movements in the Retail Price Index (RPI). When revaluation practices in Scotland, England and Wales have been standardised, the government proposes to introduce a Uniform Business Rate (UBR) throughout Great Britain. The proceeds would be distributed to authorities on a per capita basis although safety nets would be required initially in view of the dramatic gains and losses which individual authorities would otherwise incur.

The final argument advanced for reform is that the 1985 revaluation in Scotland has caused "widespread loss of public confidence in the present Scottish rating system and a vociferous demand for reform."[12] No evidence is produced to indicate how widespread the loss of confidence or the demand for reform is.

The Green Paper is, by consensus, poorly researched and argued. Its conclusions represent a complete reversal of the conclusions of the Layfield Committee and of the government's own 1983 White Paper, which found that the rating system was effective and that there were no reasonable alternatives to it. It is difficult to avoid the conclusion that the Green Paper's proposals are based on short-term electoral expediency and a longer-term aim of further eroding the revenue-raising powers of local authorities.

The Act and Conservative Policy

If electoral expedience was, at least in part, behind the Act's proposals, the 1987 election results in Scotland must have disappointed its architects.

However, it is important to note that the 1987 Act complements and promotes the government philosophy which has been current since 1979. This applies particularly in relation to fiscal policy, local government policy and policy towards Scotland.

The government's preference has been to make the taxation system as a whole more regressive. The replacement of domestic rates with a system of community charges furthers this objective. The poll tax is more regressive than the rating system which, while not directly rated to ability to pay, at least bears some relationship to income and wealth since households living in the most expensive and desirable housing pay the highest rates. Everyone, irrespective of housing, income and wealth pays the same poll tax.

A string of Acts of Parliament since 1979 have brought unprecedented central government control of local authority rating and spending decisions in Scotland, England and Wales. The 1987 Act will further tilt the central/local relationship towards central control. By taking control of non-domestic rates, central government will have control of 80% of Scottish local authority income (compared with 56% at present) thus increasing the already powerful leverage which it can apply. Furthermore, the Act empowers the Secretary of State to reduce the level of community charge of any authority whose expenditure is judged to be "excessive and unreasonable" by Parliament.

Scotland has been used as a test-bed for government legislation throughout the first two Thatcher governments, most notably in the field of rate-capping. The poll tax continues that trend. The rationale has been most eloquently, and offensively, explained by Sir George Young, MP for Ealing Acton and former Under-Secretary at the Department of the Environment:

> "While my own rates – at one point in the debate – would have gone down from over £2,000 to around £400, many voters in marginal seats would inevitably have to pay more.....So, I, for one, am glad that the Scots are taking the shine of the new ball before the English go in to bat."[13]

Opposition Campaign

The poll tax has found few supporters in Scotland. All the political parties, except the Conservatives declared their opposition as did 63 out of 65 Scottish local authorities, the STUC, and a range of community and voluntary organisations.

Most public criticism of the Green Paper and the 1987 Act has focused on the "winners and losers" and the redistributive and regressive nature of the poll tax. There has also been some discussion of the practical difficulties associated with levying and collecting the tax. In addition, attention has been focused on the effects on the central/local relationship, the democratic implications, civil liberties and the Scottish dimension.

The community charge is a poll tax (or head tax) because, with a few specified exemptions, it is a flat rate tax levied on all adults over the age of 18. Terminology was the first battleground. The fact that the tax is popularly referred to as a poll tax (the derogatory term favoured by its opponents) rather than a community charge (as its supporters would prefer) is an indication of how the battle has gone.

Research has confirmed the commonsense proposition that the "winners" are most likely to be single adult households and households living in property with a high rateable value and that the "losers" are most likely to be households with three or more adults and households living in property with a low rateable value.

Only prisoners, long-term hospital patients, the severely mentally handicapped and people living in residential and nursing homes will be exempt. The severely physically disabled will be eligible for 100% rebates. Everyone else will be required to contribute at least 20% of their poll tax. Shortly before the 1987 election, the government announced that income support claimants will have their benefits uprated to allow them to pay their rates or poll tax.

In general terms, the redistributive consequences within local authority areas are obvious and intended, and are in line with the government's fiscal policy. Shifts in the burden of paying for Regional Council services will also cause a significant transfer of tax burdens between local authority areas. The areas to benefit will be those with relatively high domestic rateable values. For example, within Strathclyde Region, areas like Eastwood and Bearsden and Milngavie will gain at the expense of areas like Glasgow, Cumnock and Doon Valley and Clydebank. There will be further transfers between local authority areas when the Uniform Business Rate and the "pooling" system are eventually introduced.

The Act has come under fire from professional associations largely on the grounds of practicality and the cost implications. The decision to bring in the poll tax in one "big bang" in 1989, rather than phase it in over 3 years, will ease the administrative problems, but it will certainly not remove them.

The costs of implementing the Act and the likely collection levels are matters of fierce dispute and will not be finally resolved until after the event, but a number of serious practical difficulties do exist and will have to be tackled.

Research commissioned by COSLA and the Scottish Consumer Council has identified the scale of some of the problems:

Amongst a representative sample of 18-24 year old Scots, there was found to be a high degree of mobility – 34% had 3 or more addresses since the age of 18 – and a reluctance to register to vote – 32% said they were not registered. These factors clearly pose problems for the compilation of the community charges register.

People on maximum rebates could be due to pay £50 – £60 a year. Experience of companies collecting from this type of consumer and expressed preferences indicate that the most effective forms of collection (such as a weekly visit) are likely to be the most expensive to staff and administer. Collection with rents may reduce the scale of the problem, but will undermine the stated objectives of perceptibility and accountability.

Widespread default is likely. A significant number of 18-24 year olds indicated that they had no goods worth poinding (the legal term for impounding) and sheriff officers were concerned about the legal complications of poindings against non-householders. The most effective means of recovering arrears – a speedy and personal visit to the client – was also likely to be the most costly.

For the first time in British history, there is now a direct financial incentive for citizens to keep their names off the Electoral Register. While the Community Charges Register will be kept separate from the Electoral Register, cross-checks between the two will be made and many young people in particular will be tempted to avoid liability for taxation by giving up their right to vote.

Compilation of the Community Charges Register will require canvassers to ask intrusive personal questions in order to compile the Register and to provide local authorities with the information necessary to levy the tax.

Registration, levying and collection will all be more expensive than current systems because of the requirement to keep the Community Charges Register up to date on a day to day basis and because many more demands and payments will require to be processed.

The administration costs and loss of revenue are the subject of some controversy but finance officers have estimated that collection levels could be as low as 80% due to the practical dificulties in registration, collection and enforcement. This compares with a collection level of around 99% for domestic rates. Any shortfall will be reflected in the level of community charge. An 80% collection rate would mean a 25% "surcharge" for those actually paying the tax. Government figures on "winners and losers" have to date been based on the untenable assumption that there will be a 100% collection rate.

If the poll tax is in accordance with the government's general fiscal policies, it is certainly true that the centralisation of control over non-domestic rates is a logical extension of the government's centralising policies.

The government will take control of non-domestic rates, leaving local authorities with control over less than 20% of their income. The result is that very minor reductions in revenue support grant, even a failure to allow for a realistic rate of inflation, will have a multiplier effect on the level of community charge. This is because the entire shortfall has to be made up by what was previously the domestic ratepaying sector, without any contribution from business ratepayers. The example below shows that,

	Year 1	Year 2
Council Expenditure	100	105
Government Grant	60	57
Business Rate Income	28	29.4
Balance from Community Charge	12	18.6

with inflation running at 5%, a standstill Council budget in real terms, and a 5% cut in government grant, the net result is a 55% increase in the personal community charge.

A decision to increase council spending has a similar multiplier effect on community charge levels.

Central government will have even more power to influence local spending policies, but the act still reserves the government's right to reduce community charge levels if an authority's spending is judged "excessive and unreasonable" by Parliament.

An opinion poll commissioned by the Scottish Local Government Information Unit in November 1986 found that 80% of Scots were opposed to the introduction of the poll tax in Scotland ahead of England and Wales.

Of course, this is not the first time that Scotland has been used as a test-bed for local government legislation. Ratecapping, in particular, was tried out in the early 1980s in Scotland. The justification advanced by the government on this occasion relates to the 1985 revaluation and the effect this had on the credibility of the existing rating system.

The opposition campaign did not achieve the always improbable objective of keeping the Bill off the statute book but it can be judged to have been successful to the extent that public opinion swung against the poll tax and it certainly had a number of interesting features.

COSLA (the Convention of Scottish Local Authorities) took the unprecedented step of establishing a "Bill team" to follow the Bill through Parliament and to brief politicians, press and others on the details of the legislation. COSLA's member authorities provided experts on local authority law, finance, electoral registration, rating, welfare rights, housing benefits and public relations, who met on a regular basis to provide information on and analysis of the Bill. COSLA's activities reflected both the significance of the Bill for the future of Scottish local government and the changing role of COSLA itself. As co-operation and consensus between local and central government have broken down, COSLA's traditional role as a mediator and sounding board has become less important, and it has increasingly become a forceful advocate and publicist of local government interests.

The Scottish media have, for the most part, been hostile to the terms of the Act, particularly the poll tax. This brought complaints from defeated Conservative candidates in the 1987 election that the community charge had had a bad press and that the Scottish press was, unlike Fleet Street, anti-Conservative.

The Committee debates in the House of Commons were generally judged to have been of poor quality. The government side was content to use its majority to vote the Bill through without entering into serious debate while the opposition failed to exploit the political capital presented by the Bill or its technical weaknesses. Most political commentators judged that Lord Ross's contributions in the House of Lords were far more pointed and effective than anything heard in the Commons.

Perhaps the most effective opposition was carried out by the officers and members of the Scottish local authorities themselves.

Senior local government officers, normally reluctant to comment on matters of political controversy, attacked the reforms on technical grounds, while local government politicians lost no time in exposing the regressive aspect of the tax.

The Future for Local Government Finance

Local government has been bedevilled by committees of inquiry and reorganisations which have been concerned with structure or finance but have ignored the links between the two. In reality, decisions about structure have implications for the mechanisms used for finance and vice versa.

Because of the practical difficulties and the "gearing" mechanism referred to earlier, it is difficult to see how the 1987 Act provides a long term basis for financing the present structure of Scottish local government.

In view of the present government's centralist tendencies, the next step could be 100% central fu ding with local authorities left to administer a centrally determined block grant. If this scenario seems far-fetched, remember that the effect of the 1987 Act will be to reduce local authority control over income in Scotland from 44% to less than 20%.

Alternatively, the provisions of the 1987 Act might be more practical if local government was stripped of major functions. In view of the current proposals for privatisation of key services and the downgrading of local authorities as providers of education and housing, this scenario, too, may not be wholly unrealistic.

The opponents of the 1987 Act favour either a reformed rating system or local income tax. While they disagree over an alternative to the rates, they are united in their support for a Scottish Assembly which would presumably, if they were successful, have the final say.

The 1987 Act does not provide the basis for effective, democratic local government. It is not just the inequity of the poll tax which is the problem. The massive tilt towards the centre in the central/local financial relationship has a similar effect on the central/local political relationship.

In any future reforms, local government structure and finance should be looked at together, not in isolation, with the objective of defining a method of financing local government appropriate to a pluralist political system in which local government has the power to formulate, finance and implement policy within appropriate areas, subject only to the approval of its own electorate.

Archie Fairley, Director, Scottish Local Government Information Unit.

References

1. *Paying for Local Government*, HMSO, 1986, Cmnd 9714, p (viii).

2. *Local Government Finance : Report of the Committee of Inquiry*, (Layfield), HMSO, 1976, Cmnd 6453, p 145.

3. Cmnd 9714, *op. cit.*, p 61.

4. Cmnd 6453, *op. cit.*, p 46.

5. *Ibid.*, p 301.

6. *Rates : Proposal for Rates Limitation and Reform of the Rating System*, HMSO, 1983, Cmnd 9008, p 14.

7. Cmnd 9714, *op. cit.*, p 61.

8. C Martlew and S J Bailey, *Local Taxation and Accountability : An Assessment of the 1986 Green Paper – "Paying for Local Government" – and its Effect in Scotland*, Public Finance Foundation Discussion Paper No. 10, p 32.

9. A Midwinter and C Mair, *Rates Reform : Issues, Arguments and Evidence*, Mainstream, 1987, p 117.

10. Cmnd 9714, *op. cit.*, p 38.

11. *Ibid*, p 25.

12. *Ibid*, p 13.

13. Sir George Young M.P. in *Public Service and Local Government*, January 1987.

"GOING LOCAL TO SURVIVE"

Bill Taylor

Decentralisation, or "going local" as it is sometimes known is being seen in many quarters as the answer to the seemingly faceless bureaucracy and inefficiency that so often characterises local government. This article examines the rapid rise of the going-local initiatives which have become increasingly popular in many parts of England, and looks at the implications for Scottish local government. We do this by looking at the inability of local government to deliver a sufficiently high standard of service, with adequate accountability to local people, and importantly the steps which have been taken by some authorities to correct this. We also touch – albeit very briefly – on the potential of decentralisation as a vehicle for social and political change. Finally, we examine a case study; Edinburgh District Council's detailed strategy for going local.

What's wrong with local government? Most politicians of all parties would agree that there is a problem. They would accept that local authorities tend to be too remote and inflexible, a bureaucracy which provides services to the public which are often less than satisfactory. Politicians whilst agreeing that a problem exists, do of course, fundamentally disagree when it comes to problem-solving. Broadly speaking their responses can be categorised as follows:

Cut it?

This school of thought believes that the "frontiers of the state" – including the local state – should be rolled back. Privatisation of many local authority services would provide the freedom for ratepayers to spend their money as they like. The rationale implied here thus stresses not only ideological commitment, but also an economic one, in that inefficient local authority services should be supplanted by the private sector operating within a free market according to the natural laws of profit. (This view, is of course, generally accepted as current Government policy).

Improve it?

This school is personifed by some "traditional" Labour Councils. They accept the need to improve services, but argue that this can best be achieved within the traditional town hall framework. All that is required is increased resources and some careful political management. This school sees nothing wrong with centralised services so long as they are properly run.

Decentralise it?

Recently, many people have come to realise that the problems of bureaucracy and inefficiency in local government cannot be overcome either by embarking on an ideological crusade on behalf of local government against cuts and privatisation, nor however, do they believe that more resources are all that is needed. Proponents of decentralisation argue that radical restructuring of local government is required.

"What is needed.....is an entirely new approach to local government. An approach that puts the public first. The world has to be turned upside down. They have set about a radical new vision for local government, it's called Going Local".[1]

Decentralisation of local authority services along with a measure of devolvement of power to local people, is becoming increasingly fashionable. It appears to be building up a tidal wave of popularity which at times looks like sweeping all before it.

However, before charting its progress, it is important to define what we mean by decentralisation. The challenge to traditional Labour machine politics has been well documented throughout the 1980's. The seeds of such a challenge, however, dates back to the 1960's with the proliferation of radical movements – feminism, black consciousness, student radicalism, and peace movements. Their critique on perceived Labour paternalism has had a significant influence on the ideas of the 'new urban left' of the 1980's.

"Their criticisms of state services, their demands for greater personal and popular control over key political and social decisions, and the emphasis in their own organisations on finding non-hierarchical and participative ways of working have provided a major stimulus to new ways of thinking. It is no accident that many of the officers and councillors who have worked towards new forms of service delivery and new ways of working have been, and in many cases remain, involved in these political movements".[2]

Labour's traditional approach since 1945 has been very much a centralist one, where nationally led initiatives and national legislation have been the lynch-pins of Labour Party policy making. The new left have challenged this centralist faith, by proposing a new concept of policy – local socialism. Undoubtedly the starting point for the Labour Councils who have attempted to 'go local' is a critique of existing structures and practices. The Labour Coordinating Committee captured the mood of this critique when they suggested that "all too often Labour Councils have been indistinguishable from Tory ones remote bureaucracies run by an elite incapable of responding to democratic demands".[3] Local Government – including those authorities under Labour control – are thus being seen as paternalistic and bureaucratic in the way they make decisions and deliver services.

Towards a New Type of Local Government

In the field of local government, new left Labour authorities have been in the fore-front of recent initiatives which have never been far from the headlines – "overspending", ethnic/womens/gay groups, municipal enterprise. One of the principle vehicles for local socialism has been the decentralisation of local authority services and the devolution of power to local groups.

Beuret and Stoker[4] suggest that broadly speaking, decentralisation strategies initiated by Labour Councils involve five main objectives:

To develop a more personal service through the creation of Neighbourhood Offices.

To create a corporate approach to problem-solving; that is, to deal with people's problems in one office and as they occur and not to refer them elsewhere, or 'fob them off' to other 'specialist' departments.

To encourage community development, through involvement and participation.

To increase accountability to local people – the devolution of decision-making.

To increase the efficiency of the Council and thus create a more effective service for public consumption.

(It should be noted that all of the above objectives have not been achieved by *any* of the Councils who have embarked on decentralisation).

On top of the problems caused by the bureaucratic nature of local government, the last 10 years have meant a period of severe financial constraint coupled with more direct central government control through legislation.

The historical bureaucracy, coupled with the recent severe cash crisis, helped create a climate where local government's reputation is not altogether a good one. The criticisms of Councils and their services include: unresponsiveness; unnecessary bureaucracy; inefficiency; slowness; remoteness; inaccessibility; too much red tape; hostility and rudeness.

Whilst not all of these criticisms are valid for every local authority in the country, it must be recognised that they are not without foundation.

If local government is to meet these challenges successfully, radical changes are required. In order to make radical changes, it is however, necessary firstly to identify the problem areas. We should also note that local government is not quite as bad as it is often painted, and indeed has made many achievements and has much to be proud of.

Much of this, however, is achieved, despite, rather than because of, certain key features in local government.

What then are the problem areas for local government? Firstly, it is a bureaucracy with rigid departmental structures. By bureaucracy we mean large, centralised organisations, which deliver a wide variety of services to a very large number of consumers. As a rule, Council departments identify and manage their particular responsibilities and operations in a fairly distinct manner. These distinctions are inevitable and serve many useful purposes. What frequently renders them problematic is the chronic inability to work across these boundaries when required.

For the customer, these boundaries are often meaningless. When an individual has a problem which requires assistance, the nature of that problem does not always fall into the neat departmental categories which have been devised. As a consequence, Council's do not find it easy to provide an interdepartmental or corporate response. Indeed, there are even specialisms within departments, with in some cases little or no interaction between them.

This means that when members of the public have a problem they must tackle the following obstacles:

Decide which agency deals with their problem – not always obvious.

Decide which department deals with their problem – again not always not obvious.

If phoning, they must know the right section/person to ask for and if they do not, they could find themselves making a frustrating and expensive series of phone calls.

If calling in person, they firstly must find out where the relevant department is situated, then work out how to get there, and then make the journey.

If their problem involves several departments then the above procedure may have to be repeated with wearying frequency. To illustrate the point, consider the problem council tenants may face trying to get something done about the unacceptable state of some waste ground near their estate. Whom should they contact? The Housing Department? Parks and Recreation? Planning? Environmental Health? In other words the route to a solution, through the departmental jungle, is not always obvious and elderly or infirm people, for example, will find these problems particularly acute.

Nor do these structures lend themselves to a flexible, sensitive and rapid response to clients' needs. Rather, Councils tend to be rigid in what is offered and cumbersome in the way that the service is delivered. Another unwelcome characteristic of local government is that there tends to be a certain obscurity about it and about the work that is undertaken. Ask anyone in the street what local government is or what the Council does and often people will be unable to give a meaningful answer. The truth of the matter is that they deliver a great many services to a large number of people but somehow manage to remain anonymous in so doing.

Given the above, it is hardly surprising that local government is frequently accused of being impersonal. Very often, by the nature of the services provided, people are required to seek help at those moments in their lives when what they least need is to be faced by an impersonal, bureaucratic structure which sometimes defies penetration.

Why then do Councils appear impersonal?

Most Council offices are centrally based with city wide catchment areas and so must operate on a large scale.

Premises are, in the main, large and daunting.

Given the large number of staff engaged in public contact work, continuity of contact with the same member of staff throughout cannot be guaranteed.

All these features of its operation can combine to give the distinct impression of an endless roundabout.

Going Local ..... Putting the Problems Right

Some commentators would not disagree with the above diagnosis. They would however, argue that traditional organisation and management techniques are all that is required. Put simply, a rationalisation programme for local authorities which examines the structures, procedures and management practices would suffice. If successful, these changes would undoubtedly improve efficiency and managerial accountability. They would do nothing, however, to bring the local authority physically closer to the people nor involve them in the decision-making process.

In theory it could be argued that it is possible to marry local decision making with a centralised structure. In practice, such a merger is unlikely to work, since it fails to provide local people with a convincing framework for participation. Decentralisation, on the other hand, if successfully implemented and properly managed, can resolve bureaucracy-related difficulties whilst involving the community in decisions affecting their local services. It does this by bringing local authorities physically closer to the people they serve, by improving service delivery and by increasing accountability.

Proponents of decentralisation[5] argue that the objectives for improved service delivery via decentralisation should include:

Improving the accessibility of Council services. This can be achieved by physically locating local offices – service delivery points – in the very heart of local communities.

Breaking down the barriers *between* departments. Corporate delivery of services will eliminate the tendency for the public to be shunted around from one department to another.

Breaking down the barriers *within* departments. The development of generic forms of working (ie. staff building up skills to cover a wide range of work) would make it much easier for staff to deal with consumers' problems without having to pass them on to another section of the department.

A major objective is that staff in local offices have the power to deal directly with consumers' needs without constantly having to refer back to headquarters. This will be achieved by the devolution of decision making. In addition, this means a flatter, less hierarchical management structure and clear lines of accountability. The benefits will be less red tape and less delay.

Promoting the equal opportunities of local government and anti-discrimination policies both as an employer and a service provider.

Adding a local element to decision making. Decentralisation aims to push as much of the decision making process as possible down to a local level through the use of forums and committees made up of local representatives and District Council elected members.

We mentioned earlier that decentralisation does not aim to abolish the structure of local government but to transform it into a system which will both improve the accessibility of services and increase the speed of service delivery once need has been identified. To achieve this, three principles of traditional practice have to be modified:

centralised decision-making;

narrow operating lines;

the centralist model.

Centralised Decision Making

Decentralisation aims to modify the traditional practices of central decision-making. Amendment of the traditional Committee structures allows an element of local control to be introduced to local authority Committee systems. In addition, decentralisation should encourage the maximum possible delegation of decision-making and responsibility to local office staff.

Narrow Operating Lines

Decentralisation aims to reverse the tradition in local government of rigid job specialisms which are not always necessary. Setting up a system of generic working will greatly enhance this process, as does the physical location and concentration of staff from different departments within each local office. This offers greater flexibility and better communications between specialisms, which in turn, can only improve the ability to respond to the needs of local people.

The Centralist Model

Decentralisation seeks to change a system which traditionally provides council services throughout a city with little regard to tailoring services to suit the needs of local people either as individuals or as a group with specific needs. Under decentralisation it is recognised that the style and method of service delivery between local authorities and local communities may well differ, the intention being to match services much more flexibly to local needs. Decentralisation can greatly assist in this by having small teams based locally, dealing with the needs of a specific community.

Decentralisation – The Political Dimension

At this juncture, it is perhaps opportune to focus, albeit very briefly, on decentralisation as a potential for creating a vehicle for social and political change. Whilst there is little evidence to support this thesis, it is worthwhile mentioning it for two reasons. Firstly, it is a theory which has been at the centre of much academic discussion within the field of urban sociology. Secondly, Scottish politics is currently in a vacuum, with a huge anti-Conservative majority, yet with little possibility in the foreseeable future of a Scottish Assembly or the solving of Scotland's social and economic malaise. With this in mind, there may be those who would seek to apply the decentralist local authority model to broader political objectives.

Colin Fudge argues that three aspects of political activity have potential at the neighbourhood level. These are:

officially sponsored local decision making;

local party political intervention;

urban social movements.

The benefits which can be derived from local authority sponsored devolved decision-making initiatives are that local people can have a greater measure of control over the services which are delivered in their area. This can cover frequency, style and quality of service delivery. Critics would, however, charge this model as being purely tokenistic, (as the song says, "a spoonful of sugar helps the medicine go down"). We will examine this model in more detail shortly, when we review Edinburgh District Council's plans for decentralisation.

Local party intervention at the neighbourhood level has been best exemplified in the country by the Liberal Party's community, or grassroots initiatives. This strategy is ideal for the politics of opposition in that it can highlight area-specific problems, and galvanise local opinion against the local authority. This strategy can therefore be used to gain electoral support and broaden the popular base of the party. Cynics would say that this strategy smacks of opportunism, and that in any case the Liberals' performance in those areas of the country where they are in control, is no more sensitive to community needs than anyone else.

The third, and most theoretically developed thesis, is that of urban social movements. At the centre of any discussion in this field is Manuel Castells analysis of spatial forms[6]; by which he means neighbourhood structures within towns and cities, these being the product of given modes of production mediated by specific historical conditions in any given society. Within capitalist societies, he argues that urban units provide the capability for the productioin of labour power, this being utilised in turn by capitalist enterprises.

The production and reproduction of labour power is achieved through the provision of collective consumption – housing, education etc. The key question which Castell's poses is this – does this state intervention in this process have any effect on the nature of capitalism? The logic of profit maximization and capital accumulation remain unchanged, as does, therefore, the basic contradiction between consumption and production. However, state intervention does – and this is for Castells crucial – tend to help focus people's attention on the issues of consumption and it is no longer a series of amorphous and disparate services. State intervention leads to the emergence of (in the words of Habermas) a 'visible agent', more specifically a visible political agent.

Castells however, is careful to argue against the inevitability of the politicization of consumption issues leading necessarily to the raising of class consciousness, for, very often, mechanisms can be used by the state to encourage participation and integration. The key point here is that urban contradictions need a political focus ".....everything depends on the articulation of the contradictions and practices or, to put it another way, on the dialetic between the state apparatus and the urban social movement."[7] The unmasking of this contradiction can with the appropriate political leadership lead to the politicization of consumption issues which in turn can lead to the raising of class consciousness.

Many criticisms can be made of Castells' theories, including his flawed assertion that there is somehow a coherent social base within urban social movements, and that this movement can somehow be transformed into a political force. Evidence from this country and elsewhere suggests the social base for urban movements is characterised by divisions based on class, ethnicity old established residents versus newcomers, owner occupiers versus tenants, etc. These are real divisions reflecting different material interests, and these cannot be easily overcome.

However, Castells responds by positing that while urban dwellers may be divided on some issues, they will be united around some other, for example, education, health, public transport (even these seemingly 'unifying' examples however, seem somewhat problematic). For Castells the catalyst that will transform struggles around these 'unifying elements' into class struggle, is the introduction of political organisation.

One thinks here of the Leninist concept of a "gigantic leap in imagination" between economic and political consciousness, and the party's role in this process. However, unlike Lenin, Castells appears to give no indication as to how practical this is to be achieved. Further, what evidence do we have to suggest that socialist politics have a monopoly on urban social movements? It would appear that they can attract party political intervention from a variety of ideological perspectives. Whilst the Communist party has been in the forefront of 'local urban struggles' in Italy, it is, as we mentioned earlier, the Liberal Party in Britain which has immersed itself in neighbourhood or community politics. There is no reason to view urban political activity as necessarily socialist orientated.

It is worth noting, that the proponents of 'going local' as a vehicle for political change in this country have all but disappeared. The radicals at Walsall and Hackney Councils have lost the leadership positions within their Councils. Instead the initiative for going local has been taken up by 'soft left' Labour and to a lesser extent by Liberal Councils. The rationale here is not decentralisation for the sake of the class struggle, but rather it is driven by much more pragmatic aims. Put simply, more efficient managerial techniques which are tailored to fit local demand, along with an element of community participation.

EDINBURGH – A CASE STUDY

So far, we have examined the theory and practice of decentralisation at an abstract level. We now proceed to discuss briefly the progress made in Scotland, and in particular, we focus on Edinburgh's ambitious plans for going local.

Decentralisation within local authorities has over the years taken a number of forms, the most obvious of which is the area-based social work teams operated by many Regional Councils.

Other Scottish develoments have included Stirling District Council's[8] scheme of local offices in selected areas, and Glasgow's Area Management schemes[9]. The Glasgow scheme is particularly interesting in that for the first time in Scotland, Senior Officers, (in the shape of Programme Area Teams) along with decision making Area Management Committees comprising of local people, MP's and Councillors have come together jointly to tackle local problems. Despite the impressive start to decentralisation made by Glasgow, it nevertheless is limited in many ways. The districts covered by the area teams are huge – often as large as many towns in Scotland – the service offered is not comprehensive for it is limited to Council tenants only; and the services offered to tenants are themselves restricted.

Let us now proceed to examine the comprehensive and ambitious plans outlined by Edinburgh District Council.[10] This scheme, if it is successful, will be Scotland's first fully decentralised local authority offering a full range of services locally, along with community decision making. As such, it may serve as a model for others.

The system outlined for Edinburgh was the product of a great deal of effort by both politicians and staff. A Project Team of six Senior Officials were seconded to work full-time on the scheme for a four month period. In addition senior councillors met frequently to supervise the project on an on-going basis. It is also worth noting that the Trade Unions, staff and public were kept fully informed of progress as it was made.

The Edinburgh scheme attempts to analyse the strengths and

weaknesses of the various operational models of decentralisation. In particular, it was influenced by the schemes at Birmingham and Walsall Councils.[11] It needs to be stressed, however, that Edinburgh's scheme has been specifically geared to meet that city's needs.

The principles of decentralisation have been tested in a number of environments and in a number of different ways. Before describing the experience of decentralisation within a local authority context, it should be noted that many of the components which make up decentralisation are already being used extensively within many sectors of business, commerce and industry. For example, building societies now operate through an expanding network of local offices, whilst the idea of generic working, team building and pride in product is used extensively in a number of successful companies.

None of the above examples advocates that small is beautiful as such. Rather the intention is to create smallness *within* large organisations. This provides a basis for a principal objective of decentralisation in a local government context, that is the need to marry economies of scale with sensitivity to local needs, through the establishment of smaller units for service delivery and decision making.

The Edinburgh model argues that the best way forward is for them to develop their own approach to decentralisation, one which is unique and specifically matches consumers' needs and organisational resources. By examining experience elsewhere it soon becomes apparent that valuable lessons can be learned. However, there is no blueprint for decentralisation, no one package that can be taken off the shelf, dusted down and used.

Edinburgh's Decentralisation Strategy, is different from that of any other authority. Other authorities who have moved towards decentralisation have decided to begin by either opening up a single office in an area of deprivation (eg. Carlisle District Council) or by limiting their city wide offices to a single service (eg. Walsall Metropolitan Borough Council). Edinburgh's strategy rejects the experimental pilot area project in favour of city wide scheme. It rejects the decentralisation of the Housing Department in isolation, in favour of a system which deals with all Council departments. It proposes a scheme where staff working in local offices will deal with a wide range of enquiries and tasks. It suggests a management structure which will promote interdepartmental working and maximise staff involvement, and it advocates local people being directly involved in decision taking.

Edinburgh's strategy for decentralisation is unique. It has been designed specifically for the city and its people.

Edinburgh's Local Service Delivery

The Edinburgh Scheme proposes 30 local offices which would be established throughout the city.

The local office is the Council's link with the community. It is the vehicle through which it will provide information and advice, deliver local services, receive applications and encourage community involvement in council affairs. As the Council's open-door to the community, it is the key to the Decentralisation Strategy.

Broadly speaking, the local offices will do what the present centrally based departments do in serving the community. The difference is, by being locally baed, less bureaucratic, and with devolved responsibility, it will do it better, more quickly and more responsibly.

It will provide information and advice, deliver services and receive applications for: Housing; Cleansing; Planning; Recreation; Economic Development and Estates; Technical Services and Environmental Health.

In fact it will provide any Council services required by the public. In addition, the local office will be the focus for tenant and resident participation in Council affairs through the establishment of local forums. Continued liaison between the Council and the Community will be encouraged through the provision of staff and facilities in the local office.

Although each local office will have an area for which it is responsible, the advanced telecommunications and information systems will allow the public to use any local office.

Local offices require to be in or close to the areas where Council services are in greatest demand. They need to create a friendly environment and be of a size that overcomes the impression of an uncaring bureaucracy. Balanced against this is the need to minimise overall costs, and to have sufficient workload for each unit to be run economically.

The strategy argues that the city requires around *thirty local offices*, to serve local communities. This number allows for service delivery points throughout the city and at the same time allows for managerial effectiveness. The distribution of the offices and their size reflects the anticipated demands placed upon the services to be decentralised. Accordingly, the greatest concentrations of large offices are in the local authority housing areas and of medium sized offices in the older, tenemental areas of the inner city. Those sectors of the community which are more mobile and rely less on Council services, will be served by a wider distribution of smaller offices.

The Local Office and Its Staff

Edinburgh's staffing proposals and the location and design of the offices, will make a significant impact on improved service delivery.

The external appearance of local offices will vary considerably and will largely depend upon the nature of the properties used. Shops, schools and purpose built premises are all possibilities. The common theme will be the clear display of the Council's logo and the name by which each office is known.

Internally, the office will be open plan design where possible. Where privacy is required, interview rooms will be available. Consumers will be encouraged to approach any of the Community Services Assistants, and an indication of each member of staff's role eg. housing, community services, together with their names will be clearly displayed at their work areas. Offices will have comfortable waiting areas.

Main provisions will be:

A Cashier Point – a secure room through which all transactions will be handled.

A Meeting Room – with separate access arrangements for local forum and other meetings.

A Play Area – for callers with young children.

Multi-Lingual Notice Boards and Information Display – for Council and local interest material.

Toilet Facilities – including provision for specialist needs, eg. disabled people and baby care.

Opening hours will be the subject of consultation with the Trades Unions and the local people. They will be geared to meet the needs of the consumer and include at least one late night opening per week. Staff training needs will also be catered for, eg. by later opening or early closing on certain days.

Most Local Office Assistants will have at their work stations a computer terminal giving direct access to the council's on-line information and service files. Tenants calling to report recognised repairs will have their requirements fed immediately into the "repairs file" and be given a receipt. Similarly, applicants for a house will be shown where they are on the waiting list for different types of houses in different areas and be given a printed statement to this effect.

The layout, facilities and working environment of the local office are designed to create an atmosphere of mutual confidence and trust.

The number of staff in each local office will vary with the workload generated by the area.

On entering the local office, initial contact will be with a COMMUNITY SERVICES ASSISTANT. His or her duties will include the following: Providing general advice on all Council services; delivering directly a limited number of basic services eg. logging a repair request; referring requests for more specialised services to the Housing Assistants or other departmental officer in the local office; referring or initiating request to departments and ensuring that such requests are satisfactorily progressed. These staff are fundamental to the success of the local office in that they are the first contact between the Council and the consumer.

Although the Community Services Assistant will endeavour to deal with as many enquiries as possible without referral, there will be a need for staff from other departments to be based in the local office on a full-time or part-time basis. Housing is a major area of service delivery and each office will have a team of LOCAL HOUSING ASSISTANTS whose role is to deliver a comprehensive housing service. Rather than dealing with only one housing specialism as at present, Housing Assistants will cover a much wider range.

Where a department is particularly active in a local area, then those staff immediately concerned would be based in the local office eg. Planning Officers during the preparation and consultation period of a local plan.

One of the fundamental objectives of the strategy is to involve the public in the decision-making process, initially through local forums, which will precede the opening of the local office. It will be the task of the COMMUNITY DEVELOPMENT ASSISTANT to service the local forum, support local groups and assist in developing interest and involvement from within the community.

Cash transactions, including rent and rates collection will be supervised by the CASHIER. The ADMINISTRATIVE OFFICER supported by CLERICAL ASSISTANTS will deal with financial, personnel, typing/word processing and other staff support services within the office.

The internal management of the office will be the responsibility of the LOCAL OFFICE MANAGER and one or two ASSISTANT

LOCAL OFFICE MANAGERS. In the larger office, one Assistant Manager will be responsible for housing matters and the other for community services ie. non-housing matters.

This new approach to the delivery of local government services can only be achieved by adopting a generic form of working whereby staff become local government officers with the emphasis on local needs rather than specialist activities. Generic working can provide a more varied workload and a greater degree of responsibility and job satisfaction. This will require not only a re-appraisal of working methods and attitudes but also an effective management structure; a review of the remaining centralised departments; and a major programme of staff training. Staff will be encouraged to respond directly to the needs of the people within their area, to present the effective, caring and friendly face of local government.

Decision Making

An innovative and exciting aspect of Edinburgh's decentralisation proposals will be the active participation and involvement of the local community in decisions that affect them and their area. This move towards greater local accountability is at two levels – the Local Forum and the Area Committee.

Local Forum

The Local Forum will consist of the ward Councillor(s) who represent the area, together with representatives of a wide range of local groups. Open to the public, they will meet regularly in the area served by their local office. There will be one Local Forum for each local office catchment area. They will be properly constituted advisory committees of the Council. The Chair of the Committee will be a ward Councillor elected annually by the Forum.

The Local Forum will have an evolving role. Inititally its purpose will be to give views on the plans for the local office. It will be consulted on the matters of location, design, opening arrangements, access, etc, prior to the opening of the office.

Once the office is operational, the Local Forum will have a crucial role in advising on local service delivery and, hopefully, developing a close working relationship with the staff of their office.

The functions of the Local Forum will continue to operate after the introduction of Area Committees, which are to be established when all the local forums and offices are established. Each Forum will elect one representative with full voting rights to sit on the Area Committee. A number of non-voting representatives can also be appointed to attend this meeting. The Local Forum will provide an essential local element to the working of the Area Committee. They will have a continuing role in advising Councillors on local issues and ensuring through the Area Committees that the District Council's programmes and policies take into account the needs of particular localities.

The Local Forum will be serviced by staff from the local office. The Forums will ensure an effective use of resources at a local level by using the knowledge and expertise of ward Councillors, local office staff and local people.

The Area Committee

The role of the Area Committees will be to consider and determine all matters relevant to the area. This will mean that they will replace some of the Council's Sub-Committees.

The general context within which the decision making powers should be defined is outlined below:

To prepare and amend programmes for the expenditure of such budget for local projects as may be allocated to the Area Committee.

To identify local needs, and to assist in the development of central policies and programmes.

To make recommendations on the quality and level of service being delivered at the local level to the relevant committee.

To act as a sounding board for establishing local opinion on such matters as referred by the Council.

To make decisions on matters delegated to it. This will include items which are area-specific and are within centrally determined policy guidelines.

To make representations concerning the extent of Area Committee powers.

To promote Local Forums, residents' associations, tenants associations, etc.

To consult with Statutory Undertakers, community councils, police, fire, etc and other agencies, eg. bus companies, on the provision of services.

Area Committees will report directly to a Policy and Resources Sub-Committee as well as having access to main committees. This reflects politically the matrix management of the administrative structure. The Policy and Resources Sub-Committee should include the Leader of the Council and the Chairs of the main committees to ensure corporate decision-taking.

As experience is gained with the new working arrangements, Area Committees' delegated powers will be monitored and reviewed.

At the outset each Area Committee should be allocated an annual budget of £50,000. This will enable it to decide on a number of small projects in its area which it considers important. These projects could range from support for local organisations such as tenants' groups to local environmental improvements projects, a community minibus or local newsletter.

For more expensive projects there will be a central budget which will supplement Area Committee budgets. Allocations from such a fund will be determined by Policy and Resources Committee in response to bids from Area Committees. It will be possible for an Area Commitee to seek an increase in its allocations on a special needs basis.

Financial responsibility for Area Committees is essential if they are to function effectively and use limited resources to the best possible advantage for their area. In addition, it will highlight at a local level the difficulties the Council faces concerning the allocation of money to projects when resources fall far short of total need.

With regard to representation, in a Scottish context, it is important to be aware of the legislation concerned with the setting up of such Committees. The relevant statute is the Local Government (Scotland) Act 1973, which allows amongst other things for only a ratio of community representative to three councillors on any co-opted committee. This obviously limits the voting input of local people.

Consequently it is not a simple exercise to decide upon the representation of Councillors and non-elected members on each Area Committee. However, it is suggested that the following principles have been adopted –

Each Local Forum selects a community representative to serve on its Area Committee. This representative will have full voting rights. The Forum will also appoint a number of representatives who will attend Area Committee meetings but *not* have voting rights.

Each District Ward Council will serve on the appropriate Area

Committee and have full voting rights.

Because the number of Local Forums and number of wards in each Area Committee vary, it will be necessary for four Area Committees to co-opt additional Councillors to ensure the correct proportion of elected members/community representatives.

Regional Councillors and Local MPs will be invited to sit on Area Committees. They will not have voting rights.

Area Committees will reflect the political make up of the area. This may not be the same as the District Council.

Edinburgh's Problems

Independent academic and local government observers have praised Edinburgh's proposed plans, both in terms of the boldness of the concept and as a well drafted and comprehensive strategy document. It is however clear that as with so many other authorities that have dabbled with decentralisation, that its introduction in Edinburgh will be far from plainsailing.

There would appear to be a number of hurdles to be cleared before Edinburgh could begin to decentralise its services and decision making. Agreements with the trade unions are a possible sticking point, although it has to be said that given the current relatively cordial relationships, the likelihood of trade union support is much stronger than in other authorities. Entrenched departmentalism is another possible pitfall; although the appointment of a Chief Officer based within the Chief Executive's Department with the appropriate management support, should act as a strong counterbalance to any moves away from the corporate approach. Lack of community support for the concept poses yet another potential problem; here however the initial meetings with the various community groups in the City to discuss decentralisation have met with a largely favourable response.

The above potential difficulties can be overcome, Edinburgh's real quandary revolves around two connected problematic areas; namely the political commitment of the Labour Administration and the financial crisis facing the Council.

Despite manifesto commitments, the Labour Administration initially appeared to see decentralisation as something of a luxury, rather than as a vehicle to promote their policy of 'Improving Services ....'. It has only been in the latter half of the lifetime of this Administration that plans for going local have been seriously developed. Even then it is fair to say that decentralisation has not had unanimous support. It is also worth noting the views of the opposition groups on the Council: the Alliance group have given a full commitment to the policy, whilst the Conservatives have sought to make decentralisation unworkable by denying it the initial capital and revenue investment required.

Decentralisation on the scale contemplated by Edinburgh requires it to be a top political priority. This brings us to the final hurdle – finance. In August 1987 the Secretary of State for Scotland had a Parliamentary Order passed which forced the Council to reduce its budget for the third consecutive year. This has forced the Council to examine areas for restricted or 'negative' growth. Within 1987/88, this had meant budgetary reductions in a number of areas including decentralisation. Statements by the Labour group have indicated that going local is still very much on the agenda, but in a restricted form and at a slower pace.

In short, decentralisation in Edinburgh faces the problems beset by dynamic ambitious local authorities throughout the country – how to expand and enhance services in an era of severe financial restrictions. All in all, Edinburgh District Council's decentralisation scheme makes an ideal case study – its success or otherwise will prove a useful pointer to other local authorities.

Going Local .... the next move

This paper has tried to outline the theory and practice of decentralisation. We have seen that its rationale is twofold – the promotion of good quality delivery of local services, along with increasing the opportunity for local people to become involved in making decisions which affects their community.

Given the centralist nature of Government policy since 1979, with its constant stripping of powers, the reduction in local authority spending, the proposed 'Scottish Homes' legislation, and the planned privatisation of council services, going local may provide the potential for the effective defence of local government. The 'big brother knows best' attitude, along with poor standards of service delivery, can be combated by effective management of resources at a local level along with the promotion of local democracy. Going local may therefore be less of an option, and more of a strategy for survival.

Bill Taylor is head of the Councillors' Research Unit at the City of Edinburgh District Council. He has been involved in drawing together plans for Decentralisation both in Edinburgh and at Walsall Council.

This article is written in a personal capacity.

References

1. The Decentralisation Research and Information Centre, Polytechnic of Central London, "Going Local Factpack", Polytechnic of Central London, 1985.

2. M Boddy and T Fudge *Local Socialism*, School of Advanced Urban Studies, Bristol University, 1984.

3. Labour Co-ordinating Committee: "Can Local Government Survive?" London, 1983, p.14.

4. M Beuret and G Stoker, Paper to the 1984 PSA Annual Conference, *The Attack on Labour's Centralist Faith*.

5. Boddy and Fudge, *ibid*.

6. See for example Castell's work in *The Urban Question*, Heineman, London 1977 and *The City and the Grass Roots*, Heineman, London, 1984.

7. Castells, (1977), p 463.

8. Stirling Council's decentralisation plans are outlined in the Summer 1987 issue of *Going Local* Polytechnic of Central London Newsletter.

9. Glasgow District Council's decentralisation plans are outlined in the Spring issue of *Going Local*.

10. This article draws extensively on Edinburgh's *Decentralisation Strategy Document*, Edinburgh District Council, November 1986, as well as a number of personal interviews.

11. Details of the Walsall and Birmingham schemes were obtained from journal articles and personal interviews.

THE SCOTTISH DIFFERENCE:

POLICY AND PRACTICE IN COMMUNITY CARE

David J Hunter & Gerald Wistow

Introduction

The development of community care has been an objective for health and social work services in Scotland for more than a quarter of a century as, indeed, has been the case in England and Wales. In a recent study, we have shown that the Scottish commitment to community care has been more muted than elsewhere in Britain.[1] Nonetheless, it has been official policy since the Mental Health (Scotland) Act of 1960, if no earlier, to develop an extended range of services 'in the community' which would operate alongside a proportionately reduced level of hospital facilities. This approach has been reflected in Scottish Office planning for the priority groups of elderly, mentally ill, mentally handicapped and physically handicapped people.

A central policy goal for the priority care groups has been to develop a more flexible spectrum of care as a replacement for services historically focussed on long stay hospitals. Underpinning this approach has been the belief that it would enable the variety of individual needs to be met by a variety of responses. This and a number of the other essential elements of community care have been well expressed by the DHSS in England in the following terms: 'community care is a matter of marshalling resources, sharing responsibilities and combining skills to achieve good quality modern services to meet the actual needs of real people in ways those people find acceptable and in places which encourage rather than prevent normal living'[2] The range of resources to be combined is indeed extensive. Government functions with a potential role in the provision of community care include health, social work, social security, housing, education, transport, employment and physical planning. Voluntary organisations, the private sector and the informal caring networks of family and neighbourhood have increasingly been seen also to have important contributions to make.

It follows from these considerations that a number of conditions must be fulfilled if community care is to be implemented effectively. First, it depends upon the achievement of high levels of inter-service and inter-sector co-ordination in the delivery of care and, thus, in planning the availability of appropriate service mixes. Moreover, such inter-service planning is necessary at the level of both Scottish Office departments and local field agencies. Second, it requires community services to accept larger – and hospitals smaller – roles in the total pattern of care than has historically been the case. Third, it implies that this new balance of agency responsibilities must be adequately funded: the flow of resources into community services (and specially social work departments) needs to be commensurate with their planned increase in responsibilities.

Given the breadth of its functions, the Scottish Office would appear well placed corporately to initiate and carry through a coherent programme of community care. Yet, in practice, the instruments necessary for implementing a community care strategy have been developed more slowly in Scotland than in England, or in Wales. This situation, in turn, reflects a relatively weak commitment to community care objectives in Scotland compared with elsewhere. In what follows, therefore, we critically assess the nature of Scottish community care policies and attempt to explain why Scotland has been relatively strongly wedded to hospital (and other institutional) options for the care of priority client groups.

Administrative Responsibilities for Community Care

The Scottish Office comprises five departments, three of which share an involvement in community care – the Scottish Home and Health Department (SHHD), the Scottish Education Department (SED) which has the Social Work Services Group (SWSG) attached, and the Scottish Development Department (SDD) which is, *inter alia*, responsible for housing.[3]

While appearances may suggest that by bringing together a range of functions under a single Minister, the Scottish Office is able to take a more corporate view of policy and administration and to achieve a greater degree of coordination than is possible in England, the Scottish Office is far from monolithic in its operation. Functions are divided between its departments, often in a curious way. This is no more evident than in community care where health and social work services are split between SHHD and SED respectively. Such divisions are especially apparent in a context where, as Gibson puts it, 'the old intense departmental loyalties have not yet been fully replaced by a strong Scottish Office loyalty'.[4]

Since 1979 there has been a Minister for Health and Social Work embracing the functions of the SHHD and the SWSG.[5] Generally the move is seen as beneficial although integration has been slow. A number of examples are cited as evidence of a closer working relationship, including the 1985 circular on community care, joint planning and support finance[6] and the interdepartmental working group which revised health priorities (see below).[7] Not surprisingly, in view of their differing traditions and distinct organisational separation a lot of which is in contrast to practice elsewhere in Britain, there is not complete harmonisation between the SHHD and the SWSG. Indeed, a Rayner scrutiny suggested that the possibility of locating the SWSG within the SHHD should be studied with a view to eliminating overlap in the work of the two departments.[9] There exists no obvious reason, other than trying to achieve a balance in the size of departments, why the SWSG is located within the SED. Working across the administrative boundaries separating the SHHD and the SWSG has proved difficult as Wiseman found in a study of collaboration within the Scottish Office.[9]

Of course, the issue of interdepartmental working is much more than a structural matter. Individuals, their personalities and operating styles, are of crucial importance in any intervention. Departmental tradition and culture can also either aid or impede interpersonal contact and contribute to frontier problems. Wiseman's point about an absence of direct political input at the formative stages of policy development while not peculiar to the Scottish Office is particularly acute there. The centre of the political stage is in Westminster and not in Edinburgh. Such factors are not unimportant in the evolution of community care policy and provision in Scotland.

Resource Profile

The level of spending on the health service in Scotland is strikingly high compared with England and Wales. In 1985, as table 1 indicates, per capita expenditure was 28 and 19 per cent greater than that in England and Wales, respectively. These additional resources enable services to be made available which are considerably more extensive than their English and Welsh counterparts. For example, in 1985 the number of available beds in all specialities was 59 per cent higher than that in England and 39 per cent above the Welsh figure (table 2). In the same year, the number of medical and dental staff in hospital and community health services (and overwhelmingly in the former) was 44 and 39 per cent greater than the equivalent figures for England and Wales, respectively (table 2). These data indicate that Scotland's additional resources are disproportionately allocated to hospital services. In addition, an earlier study has shown that in 1980 there were 43 per cent more hospital nurses and hospital medical staff per 100,000 population in Scotland than in England.[10]

Personal social services expenditure is also greater in Scotland than south of the border: 20 and 37 per cent above that in England and Wales, respectively (table 1). Moreover, just as a higher proportion of health spending goes into the hospital service, so a higher proportion of personal social services spending was allocated to residential care in Scotland than in England and Wales: 21.9 per cent compared with 17.4 and 15.8 per cent respectively.[11] Part of the differential in overall spending levels is accounted for by the inclusion of the probation service within the Scottish personal social services whereas it remains a separate service in England and Wales. Nonetheless, Scotland remains the best resourced part of Britain for both health and personal social services functions with a bias towards institutional (hospital and residential) rather than community (ie domiciliary) care.

Developing Community Care Policies

The lead in the development of community care policies has come nationally and, in the main, from the Scottish Health Service Planning Council (SHSPC) which advises the Secretary of State on health policy. The Council's relationship with the SHHD has been an uneasy one as its first Secretary has documented.[12] Four reports produced by the Council's multidisciplinary programme planning groups between 1979 and 1985 dealt specifically with the care of the priority groups and with community care issues.[13] [14] [15] [16] The SHSPC reports did not represent firm government statements in the manner of White Papers, each report being obliged to carry a disclaimer to this effect, although many of their main recommendations subsequently found their way into the national priorities document, *Scottish Health Authorities Priorities for the Eighties (SHAPE)*, published in 1980.

SHAPE represented the first serious attempt in Scotland to determine future priorities for health care. Unlike the programme planning group reports, upon which much of the priorities document was based, *SHAPE* was a solo SHHD production rather than, as might have been expected, a joint report with the SWSG. Criticism of this exclusion appears to have been a factor in the decision to establish an *interdepartmental* working group in 1985 to review *SHAPE*. Its Report, *Scottish Health Authorities Review of Priorities for the Eighties and Nineties (SHARPEN)*, is presently being considered by the Planning Council. No decision has yet been taken on when the final report will be published. In its current form, *SHARPEN* does not represent government policy and it is likely that the final approved version will be substantially different. All subsequent references to *SHARPEN* are to the consultative version.

The major thrust of *SHAPE* and *SHARPEN* is away from the acute hospital services and towards increased provision for community care and long-term services for elderly people and people with mental disorders. As a general and overriding concern in respect of its priorities across all the care groups, *SHAPE* made it quite clear that:

> ...collaboration in planning and in the sharing of resources between health boards and local authority services is crucial to the success or failure of attempts to achieve the proposed objectives. Failing close collaboration *at every level*, results will continue to fall short of what

is attainable...[17]

SHARPEN's four priorities – services for old people with dementia; care in the community with particular reference to elderly, mentally handicapped and mentally ill people; prevention and health promotion; services for the younger physically disabled – involve services and client groups all of which fall within the category A priority of *SHAPE*. Where *SHARPEN* departs from *SHAPE* is in recommending that the priority for service development for older people, and for people with a mental handicap or a mental illness, lies in care in the community and not in institutional provision. Considerable emphasis is placed on the need for joint approaches by health boards and local authorities, and within the Scottish Office.

We review below the extent to which collaboration at local level has been developed since *SHAPE*. First, however, we comment on the policies specifically developed for each of the three main priority groups – elderly people (including those who are mentally infirm), mentally ill people and mentally handicapped people – in order to demonstrate the distinctive nature of community care policy and thinking in Scotland.

Elderly People

Historically, as we have noted, Scotland has enjoyed a high level of NHS beds. For example, the level of geriatric bed provision in Scotland in 1980 approached twice the level in England and Wales (13.3 per 1,000 population aged 65 and over as against 7.8). Hospital beds therefore dominate the service system. According to *SHAPE*, the overall objective of policy was 'to prevent inappropriate admissions to long-stay hospital accommodation by means of increased emphasis on care and support of the elderly in the community'.[18] *SHAPE* endorsed the recommendation of the programme planning group on services for elderly people that the target level for provision of geriatric beds should be related to the 75 and over age group, and that the proposed basic minimum ratio should be 40 beds per 1,000 population aged 75 and over.[19]

It was pointed out that geriatric hospital provision could not be considered in isolation from community provision. On the basis of the latest figures then available (1976), residential places in local authorities and voluntary homes were being provided at the rate of 19.9 places per 1,000 persons over 65 compared with the target of 25 places. The provision of sheltered housing and amenity housing places fell well short of the programme planning group's targets of 50 places and 100 places respectively per 1,000 persons over 65.

In terms of day hospital places, again *SHAPE* accepted the programme planning group's target of two geriatric day hospital places per

1,000 population aged 65 and over.

SHAPE emphasised the importance of health boards and local authorities cooperating closely in drawing up plans for residential provision for elderly people which would achieve a balance between hospital and community care. *SHARPEN* centres on the need for community care on the grounds that the targets for hospital provision have largely been met.

In regard to elderly people with mental disorders, *SHAPE*, again drawing on the relevant programme planning group report, recommended hospital provision for old people with dementia of 10 beds per 1,000 population aged 65 and over, half of which would be in units called continuing care units which would vary in size from 40 to 60 beds at one extreme to 20 beds at the other.[20] The authors of *SHAPE* thought it would be some time before the target would be attained and suggested that the best hope for progress at reasonable cost lay in adapting existing units. The target may be contrasted with that in England of three beds per 1,000 over 65 although it is expected in England that the majority of elderly people with mental disorder who require inpatient care are likely to be dealt with in general psychiatric beds where the guideline is 0.3 to 0.5 per 1,000 total population.

In regard to psychogeriatric day hospital places, *SHAPE* recommended a target ratio of 2.5 places per 1,000 population over age 65. It noted that very few health boards provided special day facilities for elderly people with mental disorders.

SHARPEN, broadly endorsing *SHAPE*, recommends an increase in the number of hospital beds – the current rate of 6 beds per 1,000 population aged 65 and over falls far short of the *SHAPE* target of 10 beds – and support services.

Mentally Ill People

SHAPE appeared before the completion of the programme planning group's report on mental health services for adults in Scotland.[21] The report recommended a far greater emphasis on community care and adopted the DHSS's guideline in England for day places.

In regard to the provision of inpatient care, *SHAPE* reported that an increased demand for hospital psychiatric services was likely to be offset by a higher turnover rate and a decrease in the number of occupied beds. *SHAPE* endorsed the programme planning group's main objective which was to work towards a community based service for mental illness. However, the group's report was not unequivocal on this point. It stated: 'despite the shift of emphasis towards community care, the psychiatric hospital will continue to play a major role, albeit a changing one, in the future'.[22] Each year some 25,000 people are admitted to Scottish psychiatric hospitals of whom two thirds have already been inpatients on or more occasions.[23] Although the number of beds in psychiatric hospitals fell from 20,200 in 1965 to 16,900 in 1980, Scotland still had in that year almost twice as many people in psychiatric hospitals for the size of population as England.[24] SHARPEN, following SHAPE, emphasises the need for an expansion in community-based services and for a reduction in the levels of institutionalised care.

A policy of maintaining a long stay institutional sector has been defended on the grounds that it is better that individuals be looked after in hospital than be neglected altogether, particularly when there will always be a need for some hospital beds. While there is some force in this argument, inherent contradictions in policy abound but are not conceded. For example, a decision by Grampian Health Board with Treasury and SHHD approval to spend £16 million on the major redevelopment of a 700 bed psychiatric hospital (the Royal Cornhill) has caused many to ask what has happened to community care and joint planning. In endorsing the decision the Health Minister at the time (John MacKay) denied that it would have an adverse effect on community care. But the revenue implications of running a new hospital and starting up new community care developments will be major and are likely to defeat the Minister's optimism, especially when the twin aims of policy prove to be incompatible. As a psychiatrist put it, 'if you build you will fill'.

Mentally Handicapped People

Plans to shift the balance of care for mentally handicapped people were drawn up by the Scottish Office in 1972[25] and were further developed in the 'Peters Report' of 1979.[26] The latter document formed the basis for the SHAPE report's mental handicap planning targets. Hospital services continue to be the dominant form of provision and all the more so compared with the remainder of Britain. The number of residents aged 16 and over in mental handicap hospitals at the end of 1984 was some 42 and 62 per cent greater than the equivalent figures for England and Wales, respectively. Also, local authorities provided proportionately fewer residential places but more day care than in England or Wales.

In general terms, the relatively higher rate of hospitalization is consistent with official policy goals. The Peters Report set planning targets of 1.2 per 1,000 population for hospital places but only 0.6 per 1,000 for residential places in the community. (By contrast the English and Welsh target for hospital places was only 0.65 per 1,000, including 0.10 for day patients.[27]) The report did suggest that the balance between hospital and community places might subsequently be adjusted in favour of the latter but emphasized that 'many mentally handicapped people may be more lonely and more restricted in an uncaring community than in an arguably artificial but at least richer social life enjoyed in hospital'.[28] However, a recent balance of care study conducted by the Scottish Health Service's Information Services Division contains indications that, in certain respects, the quality of life for hospital residents was significantly lower than that for residents of other staffed accommodation.[29]

The same study also throws into question how far hospital provision is necessary for so large a proportion of the client group as Scottish Office policy has historically assumed. Indeed, it suggested that 'perhaps 90 per cent or more of those resident at the time of the study in mental handicap hospitals or hospital units would be capable of living outside hospital in the kind of facilities which already existed somewhere in Scotland'.[30]

Over the past year there have been some indications of a shift in thinking taking place within the Scottish Office. A recent official statement has made it clear that 'the Government accept that more mentally handicapped persons than previously envisaged could live in the community, subject to the provision of facilities and services for them, and that the time has come to move beyond the Peters targets'.[31] The Secretary to the Scottish Health Service Planning Council has been more specific, suggesting that it may be time to reverse the ratio of places set out in the Peters Report and provide 1.2 places per 1,000 in the community and 0.6 places per 1,000 in hospital.[32] SHARPEN backs this approach and envisages that long-stay accommodation should be provided by both the health service and social work departments in small-scale units in the community. A growing role for district council housing provision and housing association schemes is also advocated.

Even if such a policy shift were adopted, it would still leave Scotland some distance from what has become official policy in Wales and what is rapidly becoming conventional wisdom in parts of England, namely, that all mentally handicapped people, irrespective of their degree of handicap, should have access to accommodation in ordinary housing with support services appropriate to their needs.

Implementing Community Care: Joint Planning and Support Finance

The Scottish Office has developed two mechanisms for promoting inter-agency cooperation: joint liaison committees (JLCs) and support finance. Significantly, each of them was not only introduced somewhat later than their English and Welsh equivalents but they also operate on a more discretionary basis than elsewhere in Britain.

Joint Planning

Joint liaison committees were introduced following the recommendations of the Mitchell Committee of 1977. Their prescribed role was to 'establish the principles of cooperation' and to 'advise on the planning and operation of services of common concern'.[33] They were to consist of members and senior officers, meeting preferably not less than three times a year but without executive powers as 'this would amount to an unacceptable erosion of responsibility' from their constituent authorities.[34] The recommendation was adopted on an experimental basis in a circular published in 1980 and a review was promised in the light of experience.[35] Thus joint liaison committees were not established until four years after their English and Welsh counterparts and without the latter's statutory basis, though health boards and local authorities were placed under a general statutory obligation to cooperate with each other in the 1972 National Health Service (Scotland) Act.

The promised review of experience was completed five years later when new guidance replaced the original circular.[36] The new circular reflected the widely held view that collaboration, in general, and the joint liaison committees, in particular, had 'not been uniformly successful'.[37] This should be interpreted as civil service understatement for very low levels of activity indeed in some localities. A survey of the arrangements for collaboration in Scotland found that joint liaison commitees met, on average, 2.4 times during 1984 and in some health board areas such meetings represented the full extent of inter-authority contacts. Only six health boards reported the existence of senior officer support groups to the joint liaison committees and only seven joint planning subgroups were reported for the whole of Scotland.[38] By contrast, a similar survey in England found that, while joint consultative committees met no more frequently than in Scotland, their support machinery was much more substantially developed: all but one locality had a senior officer support group and the average number of joint planning subgroups was almost three per locality.[39] Against this background, the 1985 circular reaffirmed the importance of effective inter-authority cooperation and asked authorities to prepare, through their joint liaison committees, joint ten year plans for the provision of services to the main priority client groups. The first round of plans were to be drawn up by the end of March 1986 and kept under continuing review thereafter.

However, the circular explicitly eschewed enforcing this timetable by insisting on the submission of plans to the Scottish Office: 'they need not be formally submitted to the Secretary of State, and will not require his approval, although it would be helpful if copies were sent to him'.[40] Perhaps not surprisingly in these circumstances, only three joint plans (from Orkney, Shetland and Lothian) reached the Scottish Office by the March deadline. Though further health boards subsequently submitted plans, by no means all have yet done so.

The delay in submitting such plans suggests that local joint planning arrangements remain under-developed. Ample evidence exists to support this conclusion. Information collected by Scottish Action on Dementia, for example, points clearly in that direction[41] as do survey data showing that the April 1985 circular made little impact in some areas and none at all in others.[42] Official sources have drawn similar conclusions. Thus, the Secretary to the Scottish Health Service Planning Council has publicly stated that 'we have not developed community care, we have not developed joint planning with local authority and voluntary bodies and as a result we have not made adequate provision for the care of the (priority groups)'.[43]

The failure of the joint liaison committee to provide an effective focus for joint planning has led to pressure for joint planning to be placed on the same statutory basis in Scotland as in England and Wales. Primarily originating from external lobbies (such as the Care in the Community Scottish Working Group, an alliance of 22 voluntary groups), this pressure resulted in the insertion of a clause to the 1986 National Health Service (Amendment) Act which provides the Scottish Secretary with reserve powers to establish the joint planning machinery on a statutory basis if the present voluntary arrangements fail. It remains unclear in what circumstances the Secretary of State would deem it necessary to trigger the operation of his reserve powers. Although in January 1987 Lord Glenarthur, the former Health Minister, told an Edinburgh conference on joint planning that a circular was being drafted on the new reserve powers, nothing had appeared by the summer of 1987. Such a lack of urgency on the Scottish Office's part is, as we have indicated, consistent with its approach to joint planning since the early seventies.

Support Finance

Alongside the recommendation in 1980 that joint liaison committees be established, the Scottish Office also introduced support finance as a financial incentive to greater health board and local authority collaboration.[44] Just as the joint liaison committees were six years behind their English and Welsh counterparts, so the support finance initiative was launched four years after the equivalent joint finance arrangements in England and Wales.[45] In essence, support finance was a mechanism under which limited health service finance could be made available to support elements of the cost of statutory and voluntary organisation projects sponsored by social work departments and of benefit to the NHS. More specifically, under the terms of the 1980 circular, funds were top-sliced from the NHS Vote and retained by SHHD as an earmarked central fund for which health boards were invited to bid. Generally, the programme provided no more than 60% of the capital and/or revenue costs of particular projects. The local authority had to meet the balance which, in the case of revenue projects, increased to the full long-term cost as the support finance contribution tapered out, normally over a period of five years.

The amounts available under the programme, although lower than under the English joint finance scheme, increased from £1m in 1980/81 to £4.6m in 1984/85 with take up of funds growing from 40 to 90 per cent over the same period. However, take up was geographically uneven as the two largest local authorities (Strathclyde, from the outset, and Lothian, subsequently) refused to participate in the scheme on the grounds that the scheme effectively pre-empted growth and distorted local government priorities in future years. This essentially political stance worked to the advantage of some of the smaller authorities, notably Highland, who were able to obtain larger sums than would have been the case had the funds been allocated to all health boards on a population related basis, as in England. Indeed, in contrast to the SHHD's preference for a 'hands off' relationship with health authorities, the centralised bidding process meant that there was far tighter central control over the management and distribution of support finance than existed in England where the allocation of resources to particular projects was determined by individual health authorities.

Within the Scottish Office concern grew that the central bidding system was becoming administratively burdensome as the programme expanded. In additionm local authority and voluntary organisations were critical of the lower level of support finance in Scotland compared with England. Such considerations influenced a review of support finance which resulted in a number of amendments to the original arrangements. Thus some concessions were made in the terms of support finance grants: the English arrangements of seven year revenue support including three at 100 per cent were followed and housing and education projects were brought within the scheme, in line with the position in England and Wales. Health boards were also empowered (as their counterparts in England and Wales had been in 1983[46] [47]) to make lump sum or continuing payments to help meet the cost of moving patients into more appropriate forms of community care. Responsibility for the day-to-day administration of the programme was also completely devolved to health boards from 1985/86. The centrally reserved fund was discontinued and in its place each board was given a non-mandatory indication of the sum it was expected to devote to support finance projects from within its normal revenue allocation. This indicative allocation is based on population size, weighted to account for those in long-term care. Unlike the position in England, boards are free to exceed this indicative allocation or to direct it to NHS spending.

The indicative allocation system raises doubts about how far the sums nationally allocated to support finance will actually be used to support local authority and voluntary organisation projects. Evidence is only just beginning to emerge and a final judgment would be premature. Nonetheless, Scottish Office data show that only £3.2m of the £6.1m indicative allocation for 1985/86 was set aside for projects.[48] Other sources suggest that only 40 per cent of the Greater Glasgow Health Board's indicative allocation of £1.8m was made available to Strathclyde Regional

Council and only 18 per cent actually spent on projects.[49]

While the 1985 changes failed to satisfy fully bodies outside the health service, the new system also created anxieties for health boards. In particular, those boards which did well out of the previous bidding system feared receiving smaller amounts in their indicative totals. There is also concern that, by spreading the resources more thinly, the new arrangements will constrain the type and scale of development for which support finance can be made available. More fundamentally, however, support finance needs to be seen for what it is: a pump priming mechanism too limited in scale to support anything but a marginal shift in the balance of health and local authority responsibilities. More widespread progress depends upon increased mainstream resources for social work departments. However, local authority interests continue to argue that current funding levels are inadequate for this purpose.[50]

An Assessment

Throughout *SHAPE*, and the programme planning group reports on which it is largely based, there is a commitment to the retention of a role for hospitals, to the development of community care alternatives, and to interagency collaboration. Crucially, and in striking contrast to policy in England, the commitment to community care is not to be at the expense of hospital development. Preventing inappropriate admission to, rather than encouraging discharge from, hospital is the thrust of national policy in regard to the three key priority groups we have considered. Such a policy stance involves at best a juggling act between maintaining the hospital sector for existing patients while at the same time developing community provision in order to avoid admission to hospital. At worst, the existing hospital services continue to absorb the bulk of available resources for development at the expense of the necessary expansion in community services. While *SHARPEN* moves further away from a commitment to hospital based provision it remains to be seen what impact this shift will have on policy at national and local levels.

To date, there is virtually no evidence of health boards shifting substantial resources into community services regardless of the care group involved.[51] On the contrary, and as we noted earlier, in regard to mental health services for example, some boards are intent upon investing in new or improved hospital facilities on the grounds that many of their buildings are unsuitable for psychiatric care. Ministerial statements in recent years have revealed a continuing commitment to a mix of hospital and community provision. But whereas hospital services already exist and in some cases are ripe for upgrading or replacement with numerous staff groups advancing the cause, the development of community care services is uneven, faltering and lacking in direction either nationally or locally. In June 1986, addressing the centenary conference of the Psychiatric Nursing

Association Scotland, former Health Minister, John MacKay, reaffirmed the Scottish Office's commitment to such a policy. He attached great importance to the replacement of old hospital buildings with new or upgraded facilities. This had to be done in tandem with building up community care services. 'I'm not one of those people who thinks it's an either or, I think it has to be both'.

SHARPEN apparently contains a softening of this approach in favour of a less ambiguous commitment to community services but it is unclear how far it will be carried through. Past history suggests that a degree of scepticism is in order. As a former Chief Medical Officer at the SHHD, Sir John Brotherston, has commented recently, 'it has proved easier to state objectives than to achieve them'.[52] Sir John argued that while limited progress had been made in building up geriatric services, little had been achieved in the way of improved services for people with mental disorders. In virtually no sector, however, had the build up of community care services in conjunction with local authorities and voluntary bodies been a top priority despite *SHAPE* and the monitoring of its implementation which appears to have had no impact on events. *SHARPEN* confirms these findings following an analysis of returns made by health boards.

Sir John believes that resource constraints, a 'vigorous defence mounted on behalf of the prestigious acute hospital service', and determined and well organised public opposition to hospital closures have in combination been responsible for the inertia afflicting comunity care policies. He predicts gloomily that:

> unless more funds are made available to the Health Boards or the public come to accept that resources should be transferred from acute hospital services to finance the expansion of community and long-stay services, it seems clear that progress towards the goals set by *Priorities for the Eighties* will continue to be unacceptably slow.[53]

If resource constraints offer a partial explanation for the state of affairs Sir John and others have catalogued, we do not believe them to be wholly responsible. After all, as we pointed out earlier, Scotland already enjoys the highest level of *per capita* funding in Britain. In theory, therefore, it ought to be easier and less painless to engineer the desired shift in service mix. Paradoxically, the healthier resource position may have blunted the desire to secure a shift from hospital based to community based care given the other obstacles to change. In our view, however, there are more fundamental and deep-seated problems and obstacles which account for why community care policies in Scotland remain substantially different from their counterparts elsewhere in Britain.

In Scotland the notion of community care does not sit easily alongside the traditional concepts of care which largely determine health policy and which are widely held by sections of the medical profession and other professions. At all levels, political, administrative and professional, a more hospital-oriented perspective has been the dominant influence and there has been no sustained attempt to challenge it. In part this may be because the relatively high numbers of beds and other health resources has minimised cost-push and demand-pull pressures for the development of alternatives to hospital provision, especially for elderly people. Yet the continued reliance on relatively large-scale hospital provision for mental illness and mental handicap suggests the influence of additional factors located in the wider professional and social culture.

There has always been great caution in Scotland among doctors about letting go of beds and embracing community alternatives. This reflects a traditionally stronger emphasis on institutional, if not custodial, forms of provision: institutions for mentaly handicapped people and other groups all house more inmates than their English counterparts. Martin points out that the 'heavy dependence on hospital care went hand-in-hand with a low level of activity in the local health and welfare services'.[54] One could be cynical and argue that the maintenance of long-stay beds has made it easy for local authority social work departments to fail to acknowledge any responsibilities on their part, a luxury denied England and Wales where the pressure to close hospital beds and whole hospitals has been greater. Such an imbalance has probably also made it harder to make the shift towards community care *within* the NHS.

To some extent the Scottish Office may be criticised for failing to give a lead and develop stronger policy instruments. At the same time, its inclination to decentralise responsibility for implementation to field authorities can be criticised as either self defeating or, in an age of sustained resource scarcity, politically convenient. Nonetheless, it remains the case that pressure from the field to extend community care has been relatively weak and to that extent the centre might have little to gain by stepping too far ahead of opinion at local level. However, even a minimalist administration could require plans to be submitted and monitor their implementation. At the same time, it is becoming clear that joint planning requires more than a minimal financial underpinning. In England and Wales the case for more substantial funding of the shift to community care over and above the joint finance programme is being accepted through increased growth for social services departments in the former and the All Wales Strategy in the latter. In a context where the allocation of even the indicative support finance allocation to community care is now in question, it is evident that the financial no less than the planning mechanisms for achieving this goal continue to be poorly developed.

In the light of the Audit Commission's trenchant critique of community care policies in England and Wales [55] and the government's response which was to invite its health adviser, Sir Roy Griffiths by the end of 1987 to complete a wide-ranging review of community care policies, [56] it is conceivable that Scotland will not for much longer escape the need for change. Pressure for it is steadily mounting.

David J. Hunter, King's Fund Institute, London.

Gerald Wistow, Centre for Research in Social Policy, Department of Social Sciences, Loughborough University of Technology, Loughborough.

References

1. D J Hunter and G Wistow, *Community Care in Britain: Variations on a Theme*, King Edward's Hospital Fund for London, London, 1987.

2. Department of Health and Social Security, *Government Response to the Second Report from the Social Services Committee*, 1984-1985 Session, CMND 9674, HMSO, London, para. 3, p.1.

3. For a discussion of the structure of the Scottish Office, see M Macdonald and A Redpath, 'The Scottish Office 1954-79', in N Drucker and H M Drucker (eds.), *The Scottish Government Yearbook 1980*, Paul Harris, Edinburgh, 1979, pp.101-134.

4. J S Gibson, *The Thistle and the Crown: a History of the Scottish Office*, HMSO, Edinburgh, 1985, p.181.

5. Between 1985 and 1986 home affairs was included in the ministerial brief; following the September 1986 ministerial reshuffle, the Highlands and Islands and tourism were substituted; following the general election in June 1987 the brief changed again with education replacing the Highlands and Islands and tourism.

6. Scottish Office, *Community Care: Joint Planning and Support Finance*, NHS 1985 (GEN18), SW5/1985, SDD15/1985, SED1127/1985, Scottish Office, Edinburgh, 1985.

7. Scottish Health Service Planning Council, *Scottish Health Authorities Review of Priorities for the Eighties and Nineties*, Edinburgh, 1987.

8. W. Moyes, *Scrutiny of the Central Advisory Service (Social Work Services)*. Report to the Minister for Home Affairs Health and Social Work, Scottish Office, Edinburgh, 1985.

9. C Wiseman, 'Policy Making in the Scottish Health Services at National Level', in N Drucker and H M Drucker (eds.), *The Scottish Government Yearbook 1980, op.cit.*, pp.135-160.

10. P Cole, A McGuire and P Stuart, *More Money – Better Health Care?*, Health Economics Research Unit, University of Aberdeen, 1985, p.11.

11. Hunter and Wistow, *op.cit.*, p.65.

12. T D Hunter, 'Close Encounters of a Bureaucratic Kind', *The Political Quarterly*, 58, 2, 1987, pp.180-190.

13. SHHD and SED, *Services for the Elderly with Mental Disability in Scotland*, HMSO, Edinburgh, 1979.

14. SHHD and SED, *A Better Life. Report on Services for the Mentally Handicapped in Scotland*, HMSO, Edinburgh, 1979.

15. SHHD and SED, *Changing Patterns of Care. Report on Services for the Elderly in Scotland*, HMSO, Edinburgh, 1980.

16. SHHD and SED, *Mental Health in Focus. Report on the Mental Health Services for Adults in Scotland*, HMSO, Edinburgh, 1985.

17. SHHD, *Scottish Health Authorities Priorities for the Eighties*, HMSO, Edinburgh, 1980, paragraph VII.1, p.74.

18. *Ibid.*, paragraph II.56, p.29.

19. SHHD and SED, *Changing Patterns of Care, op.cit.*

20. SHHD and SED, *Services for the Elderly with Mental Disability in Scotland, op.cit.*

21. SHHD and SED, *Mental Health in Focus, op.cit.*

22. *Ibid.*, paragraph 87, p.119.

23. D Hunter, 'Planning for Mental Health: More Rhetoric Than Commitment', in N Drucker (ed.), *Creating Community Mental Health Services in Scotland, Volume 1: The Issues*, Scottish Association for Mental Health, Edinburgh, 1987, p.106.

24. *Ibid.*

25. SHHD and SED, *Services for the Mentally Handicapped*, SHHD,

Edinburgh, 1972.

26. SHHD and SED, *A Better Life, op. cit.*

27. DHSS and Welsh Office, *Better Services for the Mentally Handicapped*, CMND 4683, HMSO, London, p.42.

28. SHHD and SED, *A Better Life, op.cit.*, para.7.24, p.74.

29. N Baker and J Urquhart, *The Balance of Care for Adults with a Mental Handicap in Scotland*, Information Services Division, Scottish Health Service, ISD Publications, Edinburgh, 1987, para 7.4, p.108.

30. *Ibid*, para. 6.1.1, p.96.

31. *Services for the Mentally Handicapped in Scotland – Government Statement*, Scottish Office, Edinburgh, 16th January 1987, para 2.

32. W Farquhar, *The Shape of Things to Come: What Remains to be Done?*, Paper to the Centenary Conference of the Psychiatric Nurses' Association, Scotland, Stirling, 27-28th June, 1986 (mimeo) p.6.

33. SHHD, *Working Party on Relationships between Health Boards and Local Authorities* Report, SHHD, Edinburgh, 1977, para.4.2, p.4.

34. *Ibid.*, para. 4.5, p.6.

35. SHHD, *Joint Planning and Support Financing Arrangements*, NHS Circular No.1980 (GEN)5, SHHD, Edinburgh, 1980.

36. Scottish Office, *Community Care: Joint Planning and Support Finance, op.cit.*

37. *Ibid.*, para.4.

38. University of Aberdeen/Loughborough University, *Survey of Arrangements for Health and Local Authority Collaboration in Scotland; Analysis of Responses*, Department of Community Medicine, University of Aberdeen, 1986, (mimeo).

39. G Wistow and S Fuller, *Collaboration Since Restructuring: the 1984 Survey of Joint Planning and Joint Finance*, Centre for Research in Social Policy and National Association of Health Authorities, Loughborough and Birmingham, 1986.

40. Scottish Office, *Community Care: Joint Planning and Support Finance, op.cit.*, para. 6, p.2.

41. Scottish Action on Dementia, *An Analysis of Responses to the SAD Policy Document 'Dementia in Scotland: Priorities for Care Strategies for Change'*, Edinburgh, 1986, para.2.5, p.13.

42. Care in the Community Scottish Working Group, *Community Care Survey*, Edinburgh, 1986 (mimeo).

43. Farquhar, *op.cit.*, p.1.

44. SHHD, *Joint Planning and Support Financing Arrangements*, *op.cit.*

45. For an account of the detailed differences between the arrangements adopted in each country, see Hunter and Wistow, *op.cit.*, chapter 7.

46. DHSS, *Health Service Development: Care in the Community and Joint Finance*, Circular HC(83)6/LAC(83)5, DHSS, London, 1983.

47. Welsh Office, *Health and Social Services Development; 'Care in the Community'*, Welsh Office Circular 15/83, Cardiff, 1983.

48. J Gulstad, *The Right to be Ordinary*, Centre for Housing Research, University of Glasgow, 1987, p.15.

49. S Black, 'Pruning the Thistle', *Social Services Insight*, 1st May 1987, p.7.

50. S Black, 'Getting Nowhere Fast', *Social Services Insight*, 24th April 1987, p.18.

51. See, *inter alia*, N Baker and J Urquhart, *op.cit.; J Gulstad op.cit.*; N Drucker, 'Lost in the Haar: A Critique of Mental Health in Focus', in D McCrone (ed.), *The Scottish Government Yearbook 1986*, Unit for the Study of Government in Scotland, Edinburgh, 1986, pp.70-92; N Drucker (ed.), *Creating Community Mental Health Services in Scotland*, 2 volumes, Scottish Association for Mental Health, Edinburgh, 1987; Unit for the Study of the Elderly, *Patterns and Pathways in the Care of Elderly People in Scotland*, Final Report to the Chief Scientist Office, Department of Community Medicine, University of Aberdeen, Aberdeen, 1987.

52. Sir J Brotherston, 'The NHS in Scotland 1948-84' in G McLachlan (ed.), *Improving the Common Weal : Aspects of Scottish Health Services 1900-1984*, Edinburgh University Press, Edinburgh, 1987, p.147.

53. Brotherston, *op.cit.*, p.148.

54. F M Martin, *Between the Acts. Community Mental Health Services 1959-1983*, The Nuffield Provincial Hospitals Trust, London, 1984, p.67.

55. The Audit Commission for Local Authorities in England and Wales, *Making a Reality of Community Care*, HMSO, London, 1986.

56. DHSS, *Sir Roy Griffiths to Review Community Care*, Press Release B6/410, 16 December 1986.

Table 1: Expenditure on Health and Personal Social Services Great Britain 1985

	Spending on Health Services		Proportion allocated to*			Spending on Personal Social Services	
	Total	Per Capita	Hospital Services	Community Health Services	Family Practitioner Services	Total	Per Capita
	(£000)	(£)	%	%	%	(£000)	(£)
England	12,986.5	275	54.0	6.0	21.4	2,353.1	50
Wales	838.8	298	53.4	6.1	22.1	123.1	44
Scotland	1,812.4	353	57.9	5.6	17.6	306.1	60

* Central administration, other services and capital expenditure percentages of total have been omitted.

Sources:

1) NHS data: Central Statistical Office, 'Regional Trends 22', 1987, HMSO.

2) PSS data: 'Personal Social Services Actuals 1984/5', CIPFA 1986 (for England and Wales); 'Rating Review: Actual Income and Expenditure 1984/5,Service Volume', CIPFA Scottish Branch, 1986 (for Scotland).

Table 2: NHS Staffing and Bed Levels
Great Britain 1985

	Available Beds*	Occupied Beds*	Medical and Dental Staff**	Nursing and Midwifery Staff**	General Practitioners**
England	6.9	5.6	82.4	835.7	54.8
Wales	7.9	6.2	85.4	938.9	53.3
Scotland	11.0	9.0	118.8	1,207.0	68.1

*   Per 1,000 population
** Per 100,000 population

Source: Central Statistical Office, 'Regional Trends 22', HMSO, 1987.

THE POLITICS AND IDEOLOGY OF THE PRISON CRISIS

Richard Kinsey

After this article was written, a second wave of riots and hostage-taking occurred in Scottish prisons. This has mot in the author's view materially affected his arguments.

1. The Politics of Prison Secrecy

> We are struck, first, by the loss of publicity which the transfer of the administration from local to central government has involved. Since 1878 the prison has become a "silent world", shrouded so far as the public is concerned, in almost complete darkness. This is due, in the first place, to the policy, to which every well-ordered administration is prone, of "No Admittance except on business". (Sydney and Beatrice Webb, 1922, pp.235- 6)

Prisons may not deter too much crime but they certainly frighten off politicians. No Scottish Office Minister likes to say why in Scotland we send twice as many people to prison as they do down south. Are we more evil than the English or is the Scottish system unfair? The astute answer is of course another question: well what is *your* answer to the problem of law and order? The opposition retreats in embarassed disarray. Better to call it a draw and in future to keep quiet. It seems the prisons must either force themselves onto the political agenda – literally, as we have seen so often this year – or be sacrificed in an expedient conspiracy of silence.

The politics of prison secrecy is by no means new. As long ago as 1922, Sydney and Beatrice Webb identified the system of central government control of the prisons introduced in 1878 and the consequent lack of public accountability as the two conditions, which allowed outsiders to be excluded and insiders to exercise their hidden powers beyond the public gaze. "Along with the practice of exclusion of the outsider," they wrote, "there goes an official policy of deliberate reticence, in order not to give any opportunity for troublesome questions to be raised in Parliament, and so as not to afford material for critical articles in the public press"[1]. The researches of John Howard and Henry Mayhew in the eighteenth and nineteenth centuries, they complained, would no longer be tolerated in the twentieth century "by the Home Office of today, on the ground that they would constitute an unnecessary interference with the official administration".

Times may have changed since the Webbs complained that inquiries into "alleged scandals" were held in secret and reports *never* published – although some cynics still share their worry that the "deliberate policy has been to ensure that the only source of authoritative information about what is going on in our prisons should be the series of annual reports by the Commissioners themselves, which naturally only tell the public so much of the facts as the Commissioners think to be, in the public interest, expedient"[2]. Access for independent research is still notoriously difficult to obtain and when it is obtained conditions are regularly imposed on publication. And there still appears some truth in the observation that "no person engaged in the administration is allowed to publish any book or article on the subject of his work without the permission and imprimatur of the Commissioners, which, as a rule, they appear reluctant to give"[3] – readers may recall newspaper reports of the difficult career of Mr Ken Murray's attempts to speak out on his experience as a prison officer in the Barlinnie Special Unit (*The Scotsman* 14.1.87).

But, even so, the absolute control over public information, policy making and resources inside the prisons, which typified the Scottish prisons' administration fifty years ago, is now under pressure – albeit largely from the inside. Since 1914, when the clandestine and illegal National Union of Police and Prison Officers was formed, an increasingly effective trade unionism has emerged, so that today the Scottish Prison Officers' Association (SPOA) is probably the most influential voice in prison affairs – both inside and outside the Scottish Office. Recently professional associations and representative organisations – such as the Scottish Prison Governors' Committee and the Prison Governors' Branch of the Society of Civil and Public Servants – have given increasingly public voice to grievances previously aired only in private. Less systematic but still effective has been the impact of the medical profession, social workers, psychologists and psychiatrists, whose professional allegiances outside the prison system have presented at least a limited challenge to the administrative priorities and bureaucratic orthodoxy described by the Webbs. The closure of the Detention Centre at Glenochil must, at least in part, be put down to the highly critical Chiswich Report (Scottish Office 1985).

Such developments are important but it remains the case that the politics of imprisonment in Scotland is still the preserve of a very few. Thus, for example – and really for much the same reasons that the Webbs gave – none of the political parties has a clear and identifiable analysis of why, in particular, Scottish prisons should have such an appalling record of riots, hostage-taking and disorder. Likewise, not one of the political parties – and this is true of the UK at large – has a clear and identifiable view of the purposes, effectiveness and future of imprisonment.

Fulfilling the Webbs' predictions, "prison reform" has thus become a classic example of the single-issue campaign, perceived by all concerned – by the participants as much as the MPs, journalists and the public – as a minority interest, outside mainstream politics. As a result, whenever a major incident occurs inside a prison, those who appear in the television debates or contribute articles such as this – whether as former prisoners, "campaigners", as prison staff or as Scottish Office civil servants – are almost without exception drawn from a very narrow community of activists, academics and other "prisons' professionals", who have little if any connection with the political system proper and as such are accountable to no one but themselves.

The word "community" is carefully chosen. Certainly each member of this community has a different corner to fight and allotted public role – the civil servant must shield the minister from political embarrassment, the civil libertarian reformer must represent the underdog, the academic should maintain distance and impartiality and so on. However, behind the sharp images and divisions that appear on our television screens, the reality is more truly represented as a sequence of dependencies and power relations, which still protect to great effect our prison secrets.

For example, state-subsidised voluntary organisations like SACRO (The Scottish Association for the Care and Resettlement of Offenders) are financially dependent on the Scottish Home and Health Department for funding, as are academic departments for research grants and access to information. Financial dependence of course need not spell political subservience but doubts – real or imagined – are always there. For example, academics are frequently involved with organisations such as the Scottish Council for Civil Liberties and SACRO, which have been critical of the Prison Department, which is a section of the Home and Health Department, which in turn funds the academics' research or even worse the research of their colleagues.

Add to this the fact that professional advancement in both the prison service and the SHHD is increasingly dependent on university qualifications – especially at the post-graduate level and frequently taught and examined by those same academics – and we have in effect what has become, whatever the appearances to the contrary, an extremely tight network of individuals with clear personal, institutional, professional and financial ties and obligations and in which questions of privilege and confidentiality, of conflicts of interest and professional advancement lurk awkwardly beneath ideals of the free exchange of knowledge, ideas and information.

Indeed, frequently I find myself trapped within precisely this same network of conflicting interests and values, in which obligations of confidentiality appear to be the price of acquiring the kinds of background information essential to advancing understanding. This article is a case in point. Many of the propositions and empirical claims I make must, it seems be stated in general and unattributable terms. Permission to cite completed research has not been granted; thus the reader must take on trust what in other and better circumstances might have been backed by chapter and verse.

2. The Cycle of Crisis

> The Scottish Prison Service carries out an onerous and often thankless task on behalf of the community and I believe there ought to be a proper recognition of their work in such difficult circumstances. (Mr Malcolm Rifkind, 6.5.87).

We have a double crisis in Scottish prisons. One is a crisis of ideals, the other is a crisis of control. The one has undoubtedly bred upon the other so that, without exaggeration, we now face the prospects of real and continuing trouble inside the prisons with apparently little genuine belief in the possibility of finding a solution. A culture of pessimism thus reinforces the politics of impossibilism.

There seems every reason to be pessimistic about the future of imprisonment. Both academic research and practical experience seem to lead to the same conclusion: prison does not work, or at least if it does, at enormous cost and with little certainty. It may be that some people will be deterred by the threat of imprisonment but we cannot say which ones. It may be that some will be rehabilitated but again we cannot say who they are. It may be that it is better to lock away and "incapacitate" those who are likely in the future to commit violent crimes but we have no way of predicting who will commit such offences[4].

As research has thrown doubt upon deterrence, rehabilitation and incapacitation so it has become fashionable to fall back on the simpler and perhaps more appealing idea of "just desserts" and the proposition that people should be sent to prison simply as punishment for past offences rather than with a view to their future conduct and well-being. But then other uncertainties creep in. Why and when is prison "deserved" – rather than a fine, corporal punishment or a community service order, for example? And if prison is appropriate, what should it be like? Should the regime be punitive and hard or is the simple denial of liberty sufficient in itself? And finally, does the just desserts idea make sense when it seems people are more likely to commit further offences if they are sent to prison than if they are not?

In truth, the evidence on prisons is contradictory and bewildering. Advocates of one position or another can always find something in their support and if not they can always say that the evidence against them is true only of the present situation and does not necessarily hold good for all time. In practice, however, the political impact has been definitive. In the face of such uncertainty and confusion, ideals have been abandoned[5]. In place of the rehabilitative ethic of prison rule 5 – "the purposes of training and treatment of convicted prisoners shall be to establish in them the will to lead a good and useful life on discharge and fit them to do so" – we now have an established "administrative penology", which prioritises what many practitioners and researchers believe always to have been the first but covert principle of prison administration, namely the control and processing of "bodies" within the prisons and thus the smooth running of the bureaucratic system.

From the point of view of those working within Scottish prisons there are two, working definitions of control, depending upon one's position within the administrative hierarchy. First, there is the view of the career civil servants in the central prisons administration (the Prison Department), whose primary role is to fine-tune the administrative structure rather than confront or solve the concrete problems of prison life and, according to some sources, above all to service the political master, the Secretary of State, and to ensure that he is not politically embarrassed. In the course of routine events, this would include avoiding undue public criticism of the system by those working within it – such as psychiatrists or the medical profession – and crucially by prison officers and SPOA. Indeed, it has been suggested that the power and influence of the SPOA within the prisons system rests upon a tradition within the Scottish Office of minimal confrontation and maximum accommodation to the wishes of the SPOA precisely in order to avoid the embarrassment of ministers.

From the point of view of those charged with the day-to-day running of a prison, however, control has a very different meaning. Where large numbers of prisoners associate, whether in the workshops or the wings, they necessarily outnumber staff and the immediate objective of control is, therefore, the smooth movement and processing of bodies through the institution with the aim of avoiding trouble and confrontation. It is generally recognised by prison staff that, for such purposes, the use of coercion as anything more than a remedy of the last resort is counter-productive. Indeed, a considerable body of research outside Scotland has shown that routine accommodations and negotiation of the formal rules between staff and prisoners – in dress or tobacco rations, for example – are common[6]. In Scottish prisons, however, while it is admitted that such practices have a place, it has been suggested that discipline is maintained, not through coercive sanctions, but through regimentation, organised movement, counting and assembly, which is intended to impose a psychology of order and deferrence to authority. In reality, therefore, for a period dating back decades rather than the last few years, the immediate demands of running the system – whether from the perspective of the civil servant or prison staff – have taken priority over what is now seen as the "rhetoric of rehabilitation".

More recently, however, control has broken down in both dimensions. There are two obvious and immediate reasons for this. First, in some prisons the infra-structure is literally collapsing – sanitation, accommodation and amenities in Victorian prison buildings – especially in the local prisons such as Saughton and Barlinnie – are now totally inadequate to cope with the number of bodies to be processed. (As I write, the Scottish Office has just announced a £6 million improvement scheme in Barlinnie). Secondly, in Scotland we have a rate of imprisonment about twice as high as England and Wales and which according to the most recent Council of Europe figures, is now the highest in Europe. However, it should be remembered that nearly three quarters of those who are sent to prison in Scotland are there either on very short sentences – as fine defaulters or for drunkenness offences – or on pre-trial remand. Not only does this mean that the local short-stay prisons are severely over-crowded, it also results in enormous pressure on the routine of these prisons and the work of prison officers, especially in terms of administrative duties involved in the constant turn-over of receptions and releases. In short, from the point of view of both prisoners and the staff, the fine social balance between formal control and informal accommodation and thus the possibility of a working consensus – however begrudging – has been all but collapsed, along with the buildings themselves. There is literally no room for manoeuvre.

As internal pressures on those working (and held) inside individual institutions have intensified as a result of social conditions and penal and sentencing policies, over which they have no control, so divisions between the central administration and staff "at the sharp end" have crystallised and become visible even from the outside. There are many examples. In December 1985 the Prison Governors' Committee felt it necessary to write to the *Scotsman* complaining that the closed prisons were "so overcrowded that they are straining accommodation and staff resources to the limit" and that they were working under conditions that were "really not acceptable in modern society". More recently and perhaps more unusual, the Scottish Prison Officers' Association thought fit to join with the Scottish Council for Civil Liberties in writing to the Prime Minister, urging that a Royal Commission on Scottish Prisons be set up. Among their reasons, they stated "we are not satisfied that the (Prison) Department, with its present policies and obligations, will find a resolution of the crisis that we can accept in a civilised society".

Such divisions and internal criticisms must not be put down simplisticaly to a failure of leadership or to the personal politics of those working within the Prison Department, however. It is a *structural* problem rooted firmly in the *centralised* administrative control of prisons, which is beyond scrutiny and effective accountability. In the crudest terms, among the "community of prison professionals", it is quite apparent that those who work full time in the prisons feel their own status and professional judgement is under-rated and frequently ignored by civil servants, whose long-term career patterns demand mobility between departments and who consequently have little understanding of the immediate problems of control and even less knowledge of the theory and practice of crime and punishment.

It is, in other words, a classic instance of bureaucratic goal displacement: decisions on the use of resources, the allocation of prisoners, staffing levels, conditions of work and "overall policy" are thus seen to be taken on criteria of bureaucratic efficiency. When as recently, both violent disorder and industrial action by staff have taken place, the response at the centre can be little else than crisis management and damage limitation. Inevitably, when such decisions are made behind the shield of "confidentiality" – and indeed the Official Secrets Act – interests of immediate political and administrative expedience take precedence.

3. The Failure of Ideals

It is said that Malraux saw as a key problem of our time whether it is "possible to pursue an active but pessimist philosophy that is not, in fact, a form of fascism". This seems to encapsulate the problem for the prison service. The abandonment of the rehabilitative ethic has led to a widespread abandonment of hope. The somewhat chilling phrase "secure and humane containment" seems to command growing support as policy. The rehabilitative ethic, and perhaps still more, the liberal-reformism which preceded it, was an ethic of coercive caring; but at least there was caring. Will there be real care in the era of humane containment? (Professor Tony Bottoms, *The Coming Penal Crisis*, 1980).

The most significant response on the part of the Scottish Office to the steadily intensifying crisis of control in the eighties has been to increase the use of the coercive sanction to deal with "difficult and disruptive" prisoners. The cages and punishment blocks at Inverness and Peterhead are the most obvious examples. As was noted earlier, it is widely believed within the system that, simply in terms of "managing bodies", such initiatives are counterproductive, as they disrupt the formal and informal systems of control by regimentation and negotiation. However, it is also very important to recognise that the number of "difficult" prisoners is in fact very small. The recent unpublished report of the Scottish Office Working Party on Alternative Regimes estimated on the basis of returns from prison governors that "there might be a total of around 250 such prisoners out of a population of approximately 3,000 convicted adult male prisoners". However, the figure of 250 covers not only aggressive and what are termed subversive and uncooperative prisoners, it also includes "inmates who challenge customary constraints by excessive use of normal channels of complaints"; "inmates who for personal reasons or because of the nature of their offence cannot be in normal association", and those "who for other reasons are at odds with the prison authorities".

In view of the breadth of these categories – not to mention the rather peculiar criteria employed – it is perhaps worth emphasising that the vast majority of prisoners – 92% on these figures – are *not* difficult or disruptive. It is, therefore, singularly disturbing but – in terms of the failure of policy and the failure of ideals, to which I have referred no longer surprising that the same working party should conclude that for the prison population *at large* "the concept of planned progression through the system was undermined by the lack of any coherent and consistent regimes, which might encourage prisoners to respond positively and behave well".

The failure of Scottish Office ministers and the Prison Department to confront the issues of penal policy directly has undoubtedly reinforced the double crises of control, which the prisons now face. The sense of frustration at Scottish Office inactivity, which at the time of the 1986 riots led to the deliberate leak to the press of the Working Party's report, is further intensified by the confusion of aims and the culture of pessimism, which appear to have taken root at all levels in the system. In recent months, this pessimism has surfaced in public in a debate over the future of rehabilitation, which at one point became so vitriolic that the Director of Prisons felt it necessary to threaten a journalist with legal action for misrepresenting his views (*The Scotsman*, 11.12.86).

Briefly stated, it is now maintained by many who work within the prisons that, as a matter of principle and law, the primary role of prison should be punish rather than rehabilitate; that, therefore, the role of prison staff lies properly within the criminal justice rather than the welfare system and that their function is to provide for the "secure and humane containment" of prisoners; that, especially given pressure on resources and the nature of imprisonment itself, the immediate and legitimate objective of staff must be the maintenance of order and control within the institutions. What was previously a tacit but tolerated working practice has thus been elevated to a statement of principle and policy.

At this point, however, opinion appears to split. On the one hand, there are the hard-liners who argue that effective containment and control demands restriction of association, the extension of formal sanctions and the further introduction of secure "segregation" or "control" units within the prisons. On the other side are the liberals, who maintain that "realistically" the best approach of the Prison Department and government would be to ensure that resources presently provided under the guise of rehabilitation are deployed simply to prevent deterioration of an individual as a result of the experience of imprisonment. Individuals should be provided with opportunities for "self-improvement", their rights should be respected and regimes should be liberal and geared to consent rather than coercion. Critically, advocates of this position recognise that, if humane containment is to work, there must be a sharp reduction in the number of people sent to prison. Even so, they tell us, the best we can aim for is that people go out of prison no worse than they came into it.

In comparison to the current orthodoxy of the Prison Department, the liberal argument is undoubtedly attractive, principled and progressive. In America, in particular, it has a long and respectable philosophical pedigree and has been very powerful in countering the more bizarre and brutal arguments of the political Right. It is also, in my view, very dangerous.

The liberal critique of the rehabilitative ideal and of the so-called "treatment model" is well established in the literature. The principle of rehabilitation is said to be theoretically faulty and ultimately discriminatory because it assumes deficiencies either in the individual or in his or her upbringing rather than in social inequality, the class structure and so on. Secondly, it is said to deny both the rights and rationality of the individual in favour of a modern paternalist philanthropy based on a determinist conception of human nature and on a false belief in the scientific basis of medical, psychiatric and psychological practices. The logical outcome of this, it is said, is the indeterminate sentence, under which prisoners should be held until they are "cured". In practical terms the danger, indeed the demonstrable outcome, is that techniques of behaviour modification or drugs therapy, for example, are employed under the guise of rehabilitation of the individual when the real aim is to secure the docility of the prison population at large – that it is used as an illegitimate means of maintaining control. Finally, besides all this and more, there is the wealth of research evidence which, alongside recidivism rates upwards of 80%, shows beyond doubt that rehabilitation has in fact failed.

The trouble is that little of substance is offered in its place. For example, the so-called "justice model", espoused by most liberal critics of rehabilitation, promises the elimination of arbitrary discretion and the professional sorcery of the psychiatrist, the psychologist and the social workers. "Administrative justice" behind closed doors of the parole board, for example, would be abolished in favour of strict determinate sentencing in open court on supposedly self-evident principles of "justice" and "dessert". The rights and responsibilities of the individual prisoner would be respected and protected – after all, the prisoner has a right to be punished rather than to be put through the hoops of the treatment model like a rat in the psychologist's maze.

The irony is that, despite their origins in well-meant liberal reform, such criticisms and the alternatives such as they are, as Professor Bottoms predicted in 1980, are only too "easily capable of appropriation by the

Right, who have no difficulty with concepts of dessert and equal sentencing, but would insist on *long* fixed sentences rather than the short fixed sentences proposed by justice model adherents"[7]. Today, the reality is that when you throw out rehabilitation, you simply abandon people to their rights.

There are answers to the criticisms which are made of the rehabilitative ideal. First, to argue that rehabilitation is simply incompatible with the coercive structure of the penal system and should therefore be the function of a separate and distinct welfare system is to misunderstand the nature of welfare provision, which itself rests in significant part upon use of sanctions – the threat to take a child into care, for example. As such, there is no logical reason to argue that rehabilitation and the welfare of the prisoner cannot and should not be the primary aim of imprisonment. Rather, it is an argument made by those whose frame of reference is dictated by the immediate demands of prison management.

Secondly, the identification of rehabilitation with the medical model of treatment and cure is, without doubt, an accurate description of rehabilitation as it has been practised in prison – although notable exceptions to this would include the Barlinnie Special Unit. But to consign the ideal of rehabilitation to the dustbin of penal history would be like jettisoning education because of the teaching methods of Mr. Gradgrind or Jeremy Bentham.

Thirdly, and most difficult to argue succinctly, it is both politically and sociologically too easy to reject rehabilitation in prison as an instance of unwarranted paternalism or, alternatively, of the unwanted ministrations of "the nanny state". Certainly, we must ask whether and under what conditions rehabilitation can best be achieved in prison; we should most certainly determine how and for what purposes it should and should not be undertaken in prison. But to say that rehabilitation does not and must not occur in prison is as daft as saying that socialisation does not and must not in schools, in families, in the civil service or, for that matter, in the Prison Department. In a broad sense rehabilitation in prison occurs, whether we like it or not. It occurs through the process of regimentation; it occurs through the informal negotiations and staff tolerance of rule-breaking by which the prisoner learns to play the system; most dramatically, it occurs in the production of recidivists. If, then, we are going to have prisons, we are going to have some form of rehabilitation, whatever thee political, philosophical of sociological position of the critic. It remains a political question as to what ends rehabilitation serves and whether we choose to make those ends explicit.

4. Somebody Else's Problem

"An SEP is something we can't see or don't see or our brain doesn't let us see because we think that it is somebody else's problem. That's what SEP means. Somebody else's problem. The brain just edits it out, it's like a blind spot. If you look at it directly, you won't see it unless you know precisely what it is. Your only hope is to catch it by surprise, out of the corner of your eye." (Ford Prefect in Douglas Adams, *Life, the Universe and Everything*.)

Derek McClintock, Professor of Criminology at Edinburgh University, has repeatedly and forcibly made the point that "prisons, except in a narrow administrative and technical sense, cannot be fruitfully considered in isolation from the substantive criminal law, the criminal justice process, sentencing principles and practice, and the nature and purpose of various non-custodial measures". Furthermore, he adds, as the prison service is "part of the State bureaucracy... penal affairs are therefore part of the political process and cannot be divorced from the theory of the State". To complicate matters further, he tells us that "the methods and practices of the prison service cannot be understood in isolation from the theories and explanations made as to criminal or deviant behaviour"[8].

He is of course absolutely right. Any serious attempt to unravel the problems of Scottish prisons in the eighties would take us through the infinitely complicated chain which, depending upon one's view of the world, either links together a rational administration of justice or hangs like a deadweight about its neck of reform. By way of illustrating the problems it is worth considering the following example given by Elliott Currie[9].

Suppose, Currie asks us, that state x imprisons a lot of robbers and has a low robberty rate, while state y puts proportionately fewer robbers behind bars and has a higher rate. Does this mean that the lower risk of imprisonment in state y is responsible for its higher robbery rate? Perhaps, he admits; but it could also mean that the high robbery rate in state y makes it hard to apprehend and convict robbers in the first place, and also makes it less feasible to send them, once convicted, to already overcrowded and volatile prisons. In which case, the crime rate isn't simply a response to criminal justice policies; to an important extent, the crime rate itself influences the effectiveness of the penal system.

Clearly, even in a simple example such as this, the interaction of penal policy, sentencing, policing and crime rates is far more intricate than appears on first sight. Yet, in a matter of hours after the riots last winter we had had all the answers – over-crowding, over-sentencing, insufficient resources, the failure of penal policy; inadequate social work funding, unemployment, educational deprivation, etc., etc. All of which appears to accord both with common-sense and empirical research. The trouble is that neither common-sense nor research are particularly helpful when we are confronted by a chain of decision-making and responsibility in which, it seems the buck is passed back through an ever widening circle.

What, for example, can the prison authorities or the Scottish Office do when the judiciary continues to incarcerate fine-defaulters (about 50% of all prison receptions in Scotland) and to remand those awaiting trial (20%) in preference to bail? But what can the judiciary do when crime is rising and social work departments are unable to fund alternatives to custody? What can the police or social workers do in the face of rising crime and cuts in public spending? But what can local or central government do when foreign multinationals disinvest and wreck the local economy? Ultimately, it is always somebody else's problem.

There is a reverse side to this. If the police arrest a young man and charge him with robbery, they know that it is the procurator fiscal's job to ensure that the prosecution is in the public interest. The fiscal knows that it is for the judge to determine whether or not a custodial sentence will be imposed. But the judge has the recommendation of the social work department and the social enquiry report to rely on and, if he then decides to imprison the offender, it is for the Prison Department to decide which prison to send him to and under what regime he should be held. Even then it is for the medical officer at the particular institution to determine whether he is fit in mind and body to undertake the rigours of, for example, the short, sharp, shock. At each point in the system, therefore, there are safety nets, but each net would appear to be torn. The hole in the net again is someone else's problem.

The institutional passing of the buck, which thus typifies the administration of criminal justice and the prisons in this country is perhaps less obvious than the problems of prison conditions, oversentencing and the funding of alternatives – and much more difficult to document. Nonetheless, it has further reinforced the crisis of confidence and imagination which now pervades both the prisons' bureaucracy and the political and intellectual world of prison reform.

Put very simply, as crime rises prison administrators are caught in yet another double bind. One moment they are accused of failing in their task – neither the deterrent nor the rehabilitative functions of prison are working. At the same time, more people are sent to already over-crowded prisons, so the less there is the possibility of rehabilitation and the greater the likelihood of more trouble. Understandably, those working within the system have become increasingly demoralised and defensive.

The problem is, of course, that where we have an advanced bureaucratic division of labour but inadequate accountability, crises – whether political, social or economic – can always be represented as somebody else's problem. This is even more likely when, as in the prison system, we are confused and uncertain about what it is that bureaucracy is meant to be doing. Is the object of imprisonment to deter and prevent future crime? Is it to punish past offences? Is it to rehabilitate offenders or simply to hold them meantime so that, for a while at least, they cannot commit any more wrongs?

These problems are even further compounded when the public sees the prisons burning and prison officers held hostage. We naturally want to lay the blame at somebody's door – but whose? Few people would wish to make scapegoats of individual prison administrators, members of staff or even government ministers. Quite properly, but too readily where there is no effective system of accountability and review, in such circumstances, we accept the collective responsibility of officialdom – for unless decision-makers can be held to account, it seems from the prisoners' point of view that we have one law for the prisoner and another for the imprisoner. From this real problems flow.

Take, for example, the recent changes in the system of parole, introduced by the Secretary of State for Scotland in December 1984. Under his powers, Mr Rifkind announced that prisoners serving five years or more for violent crime or drugs offences would only qualify for parole where the circumstances were exceptional. Likewise in relation to life prisoners, he decided that only in exceptional circumstances would he consider release in less than twenty years where the sentence was for the murder of police or prison officers, murder by terrorists, sexual or sadistic murders of children or murder by firearm in the commission of crime.

This is an horrific catalogue of offences, for which longer sentences may or may not have the desired deterrent effect. What is at issue here, however, is the immediate effect this change of policy had on the prisons. From the point of view of both those already serving sentences and expecting to get parole and from the perspective of staff attempting to keep control of increasingly tense situation, suddenly the goal posts had been shifted. Thus, HM Chief Inspector of Prisons wrote earlier this year that, during investigation of the troubles at Saughton and Peterhead:

> It became apparent to us that very many governors, staff and inmates had been shocked by and dismayed by this public announcement in December 1984. The prisoners felt unjustly treated in that the effect of the announcement was retrospective, that what they believed were realistic expectations had been thwarted and what light there had been at the end of the tunnel had been extinguished. They also felt that it was futile to apply, at least in the earlier stages of sentence, and that any faith they had had in the system had been destroyed. Staff on the whole felt that this change in policy could have been better managed, that prisoners in the system at the time of announcement had been dealt an unfair blow and that an attractive incentive, which often resulted in cooperation, had been removed in the early stages of a prisoner's sentence when the prisoner may be experiencing

difficult settling down.[10]

What doubtless had seemed to the Secretary of State a sensible measure designed to tackle violent crime in society thus appears to have had the effect of producing violent crime in the prisons. So much so that the Prisons' Inspectorate concluded that "the parole system must be reviewed in an attempt to restore confidence in it because, regardless of counter arguments, inmates and staff perceive the new policy as repressive and iniquitous".[11]

Despite the extraordinarily strong terms of this recommendation, it would seem that no public review of parole is planned and no doubt, at some point in the future, television studios will ring once again to the tones of "I told you so". But can anyone seriously say that Malcolm Rifkind is personally to blame for the particular actions of demoralised staff and prisoners in Scottish Prisons?

The sense of frustration of those within the community of prisons professionals is only itensified, however, when we read statements such as the following comment in a press release issued by Mr Rifkind in response to the Report on Peterhead Prison:

> Prison regimes by their very nature will never be ideal for those who have grievously offended against society. It is my view that we have had, in recent times, too great a concentration of attention upon the criminal element. The lawbreaker does not have the sympathy of the population at large. Their support lies with the forces of law and order, and while the Scottish prison system is passing through a particularly trying period our support for them is not in doubt and never will be. (Scottish Office, 6.5.87)

Mr Rifkind is undoubtedly correct to point out that in Scotland we have spent too little time investigating criminal victimisation and the responses and attitudes of victims towards offences and offenders. For this reason it is much to be regretted that the Scottish Office decided not to participate in the second British Crime Survey undertaken in England and Wales in 1983/4. Thus, the only hard information we have on patterns of criminal victimisation in Scotland therefore dates back to the Scottish Office survey of 5,000 members of the public, which was completed in 1981.

This provided some extremely valuable information which, as it would seem to confound common-sense, demands careful analysis. For example, the Scottish Office researchers commented that "the reputation of Glasgow as a city with high rates of violent crime is not substantiated by the initial findings from the survey. For most types of assault – serious, common and sexual – the rates in Glasgow are equal to or less than the Scottish average".[12] More important in the present context was, to some no doubt, the quite extraordinary finding that:

> Although for most crimes, victims expressed a preference for
> involving the courts, there were few indications that victims expected
> harsh sentences for their offencers... Only 13% thought a prison or
> other custodial sentence was the most appropriate for the
> offender.[13]

5. What Is To Be Done?

> The mood and temper of the public with regard to the treatment of
> crime and criminals is one of the most unfailing tests of any country.
> A calm dispassionate recognition of the rights of the accused; a
> constant heart-searching by all charged with the duty of punishment;
> a desire and eagerness to rehabilitate in the world of industry those
> who have paid their due in the hard coinage of punishment; tireless
> efforts towards the discovery of curative and regenerative processes;
> unfailing faith that there is a treasure in the heart of every man; these
> are the symbols which in the treatment of crime and the criminal,
> mark and measure the stored up strength of a nation and are sign and
> proof of the living virtue in it. (Winston S Churchill).

It is now nearly seventy years since Churchill gave voice to such
sentiments. In the meantime such attitudes have, it seems, fallen out of
favour and the Scottish prisons have become bogged down in an
administrative and political morass, which in fact has little if anything to do
with the electorate and which will take the equivalent of a Royal
Commission to sort out. It is hard to share the present Secretary of State's
view that such a body will take "too long to report to be of use". Clearly, we
need the evidence and research that a Royal Commission would be
empowered to collect, while the inherent advantage of such a strategy lies
in depoliticising what would otherwise become an overtly party political
wrangle over the failures or otherwise of government policy.

A Royal Commission might begin by asking such questions as why it is
in Scotland the judiciary send so many more people to prison for
comparatively trivial offences than, for example, in England and Wales.
But very soon it would find itself on the track of somebody else's problem.
Ultimately, it would have to confront the basic problem of accountability
posed so long ago by the Webbs and, more specifically, the relationship
between and the purposes of the modern institutions of the criminal justice,
welfare and penal systems.

For many people, the idea of political accountability in the area of
welfare, policing or prisons is anathema. The social worker or psychiatrist,
for example, is immediately concerned with issues of confidentiality, trust
and professional ethics. The civil libertarian can share with the politician

the fear of a political police force and totalitarian visions of prison camps and closed "psychiatric" wards. With apologies for going over well-trodden ground, therefore, it is as well to restate the essential reasons for accountability in the criminal justice system.[14]

First, in relation to criminal justice, political accountability – whether of the police, the prisons, or even the judiciary – in no sense should be equated with political control. Professional autonomy, negotiation and judgement in the particular case – as we have seen in relation to prison staff but equally for the judge, the social worker or the police officer – is not only inevitable but desirable in the interests of substantive justice. However, the exercise of discretion must always occur within the prescribed limits of the law, which in no circumstances should be subject to retrospective change. In that sense, direct political control by administrative fiat – such as Mr Rifkind's change in the parole system – is not only undesirable and counterproductive; it is totally incompatible with the rule of law and the principles of democratic accountability.

Secondly, political accountability refers to the formulation of future policy rather than legal responsibility for past actions. It is, or rather should be, for the legislature to determine the legal limits of discretion and for the courts to decide whether or not an official has acted within those powers. But it is surely for elected representatives in their executive capacity – whether at local or national level – to provide clear guidelines and policy directives on how and to what ends those powers are to be exercised in the particular case. For example, it is a question of law whether an individual prisoner has been mistreated by a particular prison officer; it is a matter of policy whether punishment blocks – such as the cages in Inverness – should be built in the first place and how disciplinary regimes should operate.

Third, and following from this, the purpose of political accountability is to hold up to public review and scrutiny the collective responsibility of those who make policy rather than to establish individual responsibility for the implementation of decisions taken. Especially as in many instances we will not know until after the event what the effect and unintended consequences of policy initiatives will be, the review and monitoring of the impact of policy is essential. At present, certainly in the penal and criminal justice systems, it appears that too often key decisions in one area are taken by unelected and unaccountable civil servants in ignorance of relevant information and without regard to the possible impact in another.

What is needed, therefore, is a separate and independent policy making body, in which the different policy requirements, priorities and interests of the various criminal justice, welfare and penal institutions would be represented. Such a body must be flexible in its policy making and fully representative of and sensitive to the competing interests both of those working within and of those served by the different institutions. For of two things we can be sure. First, interests and priorities change over time, sometimes very rapidly. Secondly, in circumstances where resources are scarce and objectives essentially contestable, we can expect dissensus rather consensus as between and within the different agencies involved, and the "consumers" of their services.

In relation to the prisons, one possible option would be to establish a Scottish Sentencing Commission, similar, for example, to those established recently in the states of Minnesota, Washington and Pennsylvania. Professor Andrew von Hirsch, for example, argues in his recent book *Past or Future Crimes*, that experience in the United States suggests that legislatures, judiciary and parole boards had proved singularly ineffective at elaborating effective sentencing principles:

> Legislatures when writing specific norms for sentencing have tended to become embroiled in law-and-order politics. The judiciary, when willing to draft sentencing standards at all, has been wont to rely on past sentencing practice and to avoid controversial issues of policy. Parole boards have occasionally drafted coherent standards for parole release decisions but cannot regulate judge's decisions about whether or not to imprison. [15]

There would seem more than a passing resemblance to the problems we face in Scotland. In von Hirsch's model, the Sentencing Commission is composed of a "small number of members, nominated by the jurisdiction's chief executive, and backed by a full-time professional staff". Such a commission would prescribe guidelines for sentences, which judges would ordinarily be required to observe, from which any departures would be subject to appellate review. These guidelines, von Hirsch argues "would be prescriptive, not merely reflective of past sentencing practice." But the commission's main function "would be to make considered, explicit policy decisions about what the basis of sentencing ought to be".

This is, as we have seen, an enormous task. In the present Scottish context, in order to determine what the objectives of sentencing ought to be, a Sentencing Commission would necessarily have to review, on a continuing basis, the provision and use of resources – in social work, prosecution and police as much as in the prisons themselves. Thus, alongside guidelines on both custodial and non-custodial sentencing, at the very least the Commission would be expected to lay down guidelines as to the nature and purpose of different regimes and, for example, the role of rehabilitation in prison.

In principle, the setting up of a Scottish Sentencing Commission along such lines would be an enormous step forward – and not one without precedent in jurisdictions of similar size, law and culture. There are many questions of detail and of principle that would have to be clarified. For example, it is not exactly clear why, according to von Hirsch, a non-elective Commission – presumably in Scotland appointed by the Secretary of State - should be under less "pressure to adopt posturing stances of toughness"[16] than one at least in part appointed by or composed of elected members of, for example, local authorities.

This is of particular importance, of course, when the problem here is so much a question of local versus central government control of the prisons. Certainly, if prisons like the police were made the financial responsibility of local authorities one might expect a greater involvement of local representatives in policy formulation and review. This would seem sensible when, for example, one considers the nature of many of the recommendations of the recent inquiry on Peterhead, which covered such matters as the provision of physical education staff and support services, the maintenance of prison buildings, catering services, transport arrangements for visitors etc., all of which could usefully be undertaken at local level through local authority departments. It would also be likely that the effectiveness and credibility of the Prisons Inspectorate would be enhanced. For, as the Webbs pointed out:

> When the power of and the responsbility for government is in one authority, and the inspectors are officers of another authority, a greater degree of impartiality, more fearless criticism, and a wider freedom of suggestion can be secured than is ever possible in practice when all the officers concerned – local administrators, inspectors and the office staff of the authority – are members of one and the same service, and, to a large extent, parts of a single official hierarchy.[17]

To conclude, I have not attempted in this article to cover the many particular questions of justice and injustice, of practice and principle which inform the current prisons debate. For those who wish to leaven the bread and water of official reports and committees of inquiry, I would recommend the recent reports of SACRO and SCCL[18]. Rather, I have tried to think politically and therefore, I hope, optimistically about the problems and to point out the underlying and perhaps less obvious features of the crisis we face.

These are the matters which, I believe, should properly be considered by a Royal Commission or, more realistically, its equivalent. I say "equivalent" because I am sufficiently pessimistic to believe that we will have a Scottish Assembly long before the present government allows a Royal Commission on Scottish Prisons. An Assembly, however, need not be pessimistic about the future of crime and punishment in Scotland. It is one more job that needs desperately to be done – but it is one which can be done.

Richard M J Kinsey, Centre for Criminology and the Social and

Philosophical Study of Law, University of Edinburgh.

References

1. Sydney and Beatrice Webb, English Prisons under Local Government, Longmans, Green & Co., 1922, p.236.

2. *op.cit.*, pp237-8.

3. *ibid*, pp.236-7.

4. For two excellent, recent reviews of the theoretical issues and empirical research in this area see Elliott Currie, *Confronting Crime; An American Challenge*, New York, 1985, especially chapters 2 and 3, and Andrew von Hirsch, *Past or Future Crimes: Deservedness and Dangerousness in the Sentencing of Criminals*, Manchester University Press, 1986.

5. For a fuller discussion of this process in Britain see A E Bottoms and R H Preston (eds), *The Coming Penal Crisis: A criminological explanation and theological exploration*, Scottish Academic Press, 1980. The introductory essay by Tony Bottoms is of particular value.

6. See, for example, Cressey, D R, *The Prison: Studies in Institutional Organisation and Change*, New York, 1961. Thomas, J E, *The English Prison Officer since 1850*,RKP, 1972.

7. Bottoms and Preston (eds) *op.cit*, p.11.

8. F H McClintoch, "The Future of Imprisonment in Britain", in Bottoms and Preston, *ibid*, pp.127-8.

9. See Currie, *op.cit.*, pp.60-61.

10. *Inquiry into Prisoner Grievances at HM Prison Peterhead*, HMSO, 1987, p.64.

11. *op.cit.*, p.65.

12. Chambers and Tombs, *British Crime Survey (Scotland)*, 1984, p.9.

13. *op.cit*, p.17.

14. This argument is dealt with in full in Kinsey *et al*, *Losing the Fight Against Crime*, Blackwell, 1986.

15. Andrew von Hirsch, *op.cit*, p.20.

16. *ibid*, p.21.

17. Sydney and Beatrice Webb, *op.cit*, pp243-4.

18. *Bail and Custodial Remand: Report of a Working Group*, SACRO, 1987. *Facing Reality: the Scottish Prisons Crisis in the 1980s*, Scottish Council for Civil Liberties, 1987.

THE GOVERNMENT CASE AGAINST NATIONAL PAY BARGAINING: AN ANALYSIS FOR SCOTLAND

P.B. Beaumont* and R.I.D. Harris**

The Conservative Government's 1985 White Paper, *Employment: The Challenge for the Nation* stated that 'the biggest single cause of our high unemployment is the failure of the jobs market, the weak link in our economy'.[1] This document went on to highlight four required areas of reform: (i) quality, 'so that businesses can find the increasingly demanding skills they need, now and in the future'; (ii) costs and incentives, 'so that people are neither prevented from pricing themselves into jobs nor deterred from taking them up'; (iii) flexibility, 'so that employers and employees adapt quickly to new circumstances'; and (iv) freedom, 'so that employers are not so burdened by regulation that they are reluctant to offer more jobs'. One of the most highly publicised, not to say controversial, individual proposals towards such ends emerged in the months of late 1986 and early 1987 in a series of statements by senior members of the Government (the Chancellor of the Exchequer, the Environment Secretary, and the Minister of Employment) that were highly critical of the continued maintenance of national pay bargaining arrangements in Britain. And with the Conservative Government entering a third consecutive term of office it is anticipated that tangible moves to break up national bargaining arrangements, particularly in the public sector[2], will be one of their more immediate industrial relations priorities. Indeed as this chapter was being prepared (June 1987) the industrial action by the two largest civil service unions in support of a 15 per cent pay claim entered its tenth week, with the Treasury demand for an acceptance of the principle of regional pay differentials being held to be a major factor in the continuation of the union-management deadlock.[3]

A major component of the Government's argument against national pay bargaining arrangements is that relatively high unemployment regions such as Scotland would gain in employment terms (through a resulting, increased inter-regional mobility of both labour and jobs) from the reduced existence and strength of such arrangements. For this reason it is the Government's case against national pay bargaining that is the subject of this chapter. Accordingly in what follows we initially outline the essence of the Government's argument, indicate some of the immediate reactions to and criticisms of their case, and highlight the key questions for which information is necessary in order to evaluate the likely impact of such a proposal in Scotland. The second, and more substantial, part of the chapter then presents a variety of empirical evidence concerning the possible implications for Scotland. The latter part of the chapter contains the following empirical material: (i) some evidence on the extent (and nature) of average *money* and *real* earnings levels in Scotland compared to that in some other regions of the country in recent years; (ii) an indication of the extent of national pay bargaining arrangements in Scotland compared to other regions, and the particular industries of Scotland most affected in this regard; (iii) an examination of the size of wage differentials for workers covered by collective bargaining arrangements in Scotland and the South of England, and their relationship to the extent of national bargaining in individual industries (and socio-economic groupings) in Scotland; and (iv) finally, we present the results of a preliminary examination of the view that national bargaining arrangements have been an important mechanism for transmitting wage increases from the South of England to Scotland through the course of time. A brief concluding section then draws together our major findings and identifies important issues for future research in the particular subject area.

The Government Case and its Critics

Before outlining the essential elements of the Government's case against national pay bargaining, there are one or two preliminary points that need to be made by way of introduction. The first is that this particular proposal is perfectly consistent with the Government's general philosophy of and position towards the operation of the labour market, and with other previously taken measures such as the abolition of both Schedule 11 of the Employment Protection Act 1975 and the Fair Wages Resolution of 1946 (these two measures sought to ensure the widespread adoption of industry-wide, collectively bargained wage rates) and their downgrading of the role and influence of wages councils. It is also important to make clear that when the Government is criticising national pay bargaining arrangements they are talking of *both* industry level bargaining arrangements and company level bargaining arrangements; their favoured bargaining structures would appear to be ones at the individual plant/establishment or regional levels. The sort of collective bargaining arrangements favoured by the Government are those associated with companies such as British Aerospace, Hoover and more recently Shell Oil and Brace Bros. where there are very definite regional or plant differences in wage settlement levels, based on factors such as local pay rates, local costs and plant profitability. And finally, as essential background information one needs to be aware of the major trends and changes in contemporary bargaining structures in Britain. These are essentially as follows.[4]

(i) The 1970s and '80s have seen a strong and sustained movement away from multi-employer, industry level bargaining structures to single employer arrangements at the plant and company level. The former only remain important in the public sector and in certain private sector industries such as footwear manufacturing and construction.

(ii) The early to mid-'80s witnessed a movement towards company level, as opposed to establishment level, bargaining, particularly for non-manual workers in the manufacturing sector.

(iii) Although they constituted the original basis of the collective bargaining system in Britain, regional and district level bargaining arrangements are currently few in number (see Table 1) and where they do exist, as in the road haulage industry, appear to be somewhat 'unstable' in nature. (For example, early in 1984, 7 of the 21 road haulage association regions failed to reach a pay agreement, while in an eighth region the employers' side negotiators all resigned.)

The essence of the Government's argument against national pay bargaining, as presented in Mr Kenneth Clarke's (the Employment Minister's) speech at the City University Business School on 17th February 1987 was that:[5]

We must move away from the belief that national pay bargaining is the right way to determine wages. It is remote and destroys jobs. It takes insufficient account of the different circumstances of individual enterprises, or of variations in the demand for workers and the cost of living in different parts of the country.

In support of a similar, earlier statement by the Chancellor of the Exchequer, the NEDC prepared a brief paper which made the following basic points:[6]

(i) Some 60 per cent of non-manual and 70 per cent of manual workers' pay rates are determined by collective bargaining. In the case of manual employees over half of this total have their pay rates determined through national agreements (and over 80 per cent have some element of national agreement influence), with the relevant figures for non-manuals being 75 (and 85) per cent respectively. The influence of national and company-wide bargaining has been growing in recent years.

(ii) Almost all public service workers, the majority of workers in the public trading sector, and many workers in the private sector have pay rates which are uniform throughout the country, except for London weighting.

(iii) Regional variation in earnings outside London is relatively small and much smaller than regional variations in labour market pressure, as measured by relative unemployment rates. Some of the regional variation that does occur will reflect differences in the occupational and industrial structures of the regions. This implies that differences due to variations in pay rates are probably even smaller.

In summary, the Government's case against national pay bargaining views such institutional arrangements as a wage transmission mechanism between regions which (i) limits the extent of inter-regional variation in earnings levels, (ii) makes such earnings levels relatively unresponsive to regional (and local) labour market pressures, and (iii) involves a loss of jobs in high unemployment regions as their wage levels are set artificially high due to reflecting the pressures of low unemployment regions such as the south-east of England. Accordingly any study such as ours will ideally need to be concerned to demonstrate the numerical extent of national pay bargaining, the extent of pay variation associated with such arrangements and the impact of such arrangements as a source of inter-regional earnings differentials. These particular questions and issues are pursued in the subsequent empirical work of this chapter which is, at least to our knowledge, the first, direct examination of the Government case against national pay bargaining.

The Government's particular criticism of national pay bargaining involves two *larger* issues or beliefs, namely that (i) wage increases in local labour markets are not responsive to local demand conditions and (ii) jobs are lost because pay levels are set too high. These two questions are not pursued here because they would take us well beyond the details of the particular case against national pay bargaining. It is, however, important to be aware of the extensive debate and criticism surrounding the latter point,[7] while a recent paper by a leading US labour economist concluded that wages are in fact more responsive to unemployment in the UK (by county areas) than is the case in the US (by states);[8] this latter finding would certainly appear to raise some questions about the strength of the former belief mentioned above.

The Government have claimed that their case against national pay bargaining has been distorted and over-simplified due to being caught up in emotive discussions about the North-South divide in the economic performance of Britain.[9] The theory of bargaining structures certainly supports the logic of the Government's case to the extent that it is generally held that centralised bargaining arrangements are less sensitive to demand conditions (and hence facilitate the exercise of union power in terms of the size of wage settlements), particularly in poor financial times and situations of weak labour markets.[10] This relationship is well documented in a recent study of the wage impact of a change in the level of bargaining in the coalmining industry in Britain,[11] while a number of studies in the early 1970s pointed to the role of national bargaining as a possible factor in the similarity of wage changes across regions.[12] However, the immediate reactions to this particular proposal of the Government have overwhelmingly ranged from indifference and scepticism through to outright criticism and hostility. For example, the Confederation of British Industry's major review of pay in the 1980s makes virtually no mention of the subject,[13] while the TUC have argued that the Government's case exaggerates both the extent of national pay bargaining arrangements and their role in determining actual pay rates.[14]

There have also been questions raised about the relevance of regional earnings and unemployment figures as the means of making a case against national pay bargaining,[15] while a number of employers associations have, perhaps not surprisingly, pointed to some of the advantages of continuing to maintain industry level bargaining arrangements;[16] it has, for example, been suggested that such arrangements have helped to hold down the level of pay settlements by ensuring that highly profitable companies cannot be 'targetted' by unions to settle high and set precedents for the rest of industry. And finally, most industrial relations researchers would be highly sceptical of any view or argument to the effect that there is one best (or least desirable) type of bargaining structure for the system of industrial relations as a whole. The point here is that the type of bargaining structure that is suitable for a highly competitive industry with a large number of small sized firms, for instance, will be very different to that which is suitable for an industry without such environmental and organisational characteristics. In short, the choice of an appropriate bargaining structure for a particular union-management relationship very much depends on the particular organisational characteristics of the parties concerned and the nature of their larger operating environment.[17] Moreover the very fact that the Government have exclusively couched their criticism of national bargaining arrangements in terms of the wage impact of such arrangements can be criticised for ignoring the *multiple* effects (e.g. on the various aspects of strike activity) of any change in bargaining structures.

This completes our initial discussion of the nature of the Government case against national pay bargaining, together with an indication of some of the criticisms that have been made of it. The remainder of the chapter presents our available empirical evidence for Scotland, along the lines indicated in the introductory section. Accordingly, the first matter we turn to consider now is the relative wage position of Scotland in recent years.

The Relative Wage Position of Scotland

The first set of evidence presented is that in Figure 1A below. This shows relative average male (full time, adults only) hourly earnings (GB = 100) for five regions for the period 1970-86.

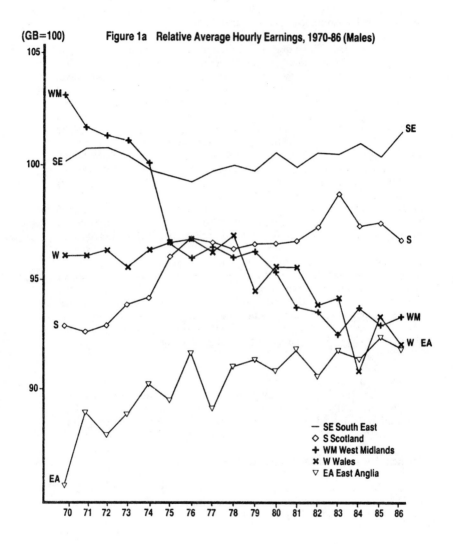

(GB=100)   Figure 1a   Relative Average Hourly Earnings, 1970-86 (Males)

— SE South East
◇ S Scotland
+ WM West Midlands
✕ W Wales
▽ EA East Anglia

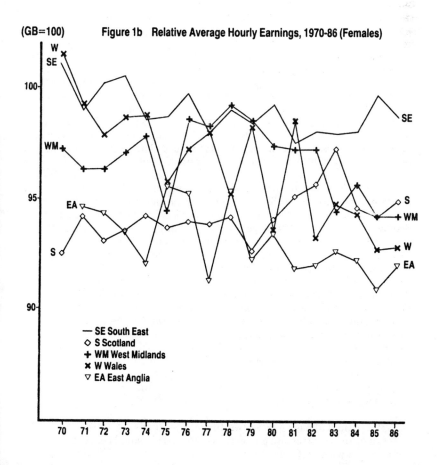

(GB=100)   Figure 1b   Relative Average Hourly Earnings, 1970-86 (Females)

— SE South East
◇ S Scotland
+ WM West Midlands
✕ W Wales
▽ EA East Anglia

In essence this graph indicates that Scotland started in a relatively low position (i.e. 92.9 per cent of the GB average), but experienced a steady improvement throughout most of the period, with the result that average male hourly earnings stood at some 96.7 per cent of the GB average in 1986. This relative improvement in Scotland contrasts strongly with the position in the West Midlands, for example, where a substantial relative wage loss occurred over these years. It is also worth noting here that East Anglia is the region with the lowest male earnings for any GB region; this fact is something that often appears to be missed in general discussions of the 'high wage south and low wage north'. To round off the overall picture here, Figure 1B presents exactly the same wage information for women workers for the same regions over the same period of time. And here we find that the average hourly earnings of women workers displayed less divergence from the GB average, although much greater variance from year to year. Again Scotland tended to show steady improvement over the period, although 1984 witnessed a quite substantial fall.

One of the standard contentions or explanations of the relative wage position of regions such as Scotland concerns the nature of their industrial structure, the argument frequently advanced being that a region like Scotland is a relatively low wage one because of its 'overdependence' on (i.e. a relatively high proportion of overall employment in) older, declining ('sunset') industries which are individually low paying industries. In order to investigate this possible explanation we constructed an *adjusted* relative earnings series by weighting national average hourly earnings by the Scottish employment structure across industries and occupations (the 10 Divisions of the 1980 Standard Industrial Classification were used, with the data split into manual and non-manual workers); this weighting procedure to measure the influence of structure is the basis of 'shift-share' analysis that has been so extensively used by urban and regional scholars.[18] The resulting series, which indicates what regional earnings would have been if workers had been paid national rates of pay (given the region's employment structure) are set out in Figures 2A and 2B, for men and women workers respectively.

The basic findings of these two figures are, firstly, that for Scottish males, the effect of structure is to depress earnings by some 2 per cent, and, secondly, for women (Figure 2B) the importance of structure is much less at around 1 per cent on average, although practically disappearing by 1981. In short, the influence of industrial structure in accounting for the relative wage position of Scotland is relatively limited. Finally we need to consider the relative *costs of living* in each region before we can fully talk about the extent and nature of the regional earnings gap. Figures 3A and 3B replicate Figures 1A and 1B respectively, but with earnings deflated by the regional cost of living (available from the Reward Regional Surveys from 1973).

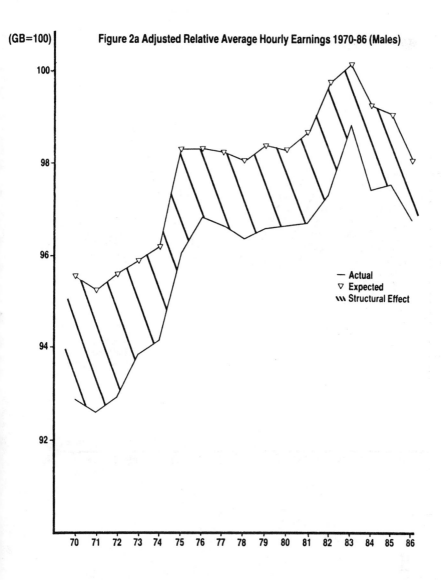

(GB=100)

Figure 2a Adjusted Relative Average Hourly Earnings 1970-86 (Males)

— Actual
▽ Expected
\\\ Structural Effect

(GB=100)　　Figure 2b Adjusted Relative Average Hourly Earnings, 1970-86 (Females)

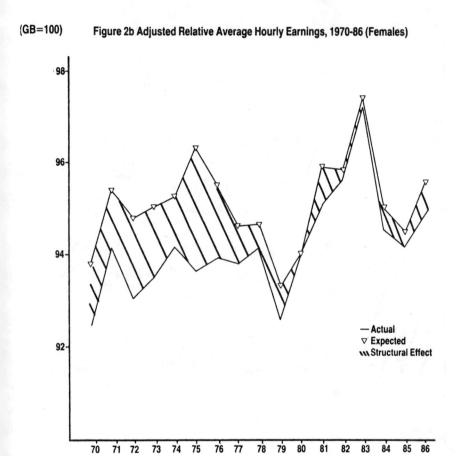

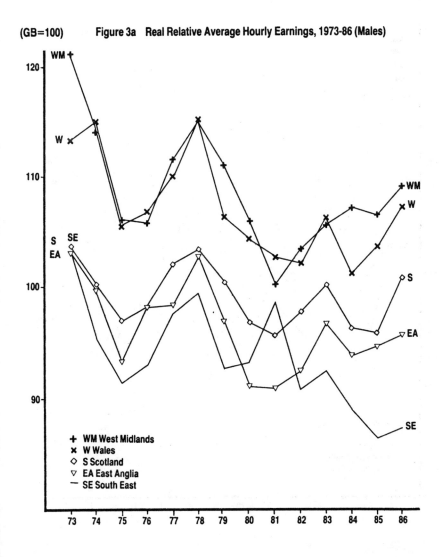

(GB=100)   Figure 3a   Real Relative Average Hourly Earnings, 1973-86 (Males)

+ WM West Midlands
× W Wales
◇ S Scotland
▽ EA East Anglia
— SE South East

(GB=100)　　　Figure 3b　Real Relative Average Hourly Earnings 1973-86 (Females)

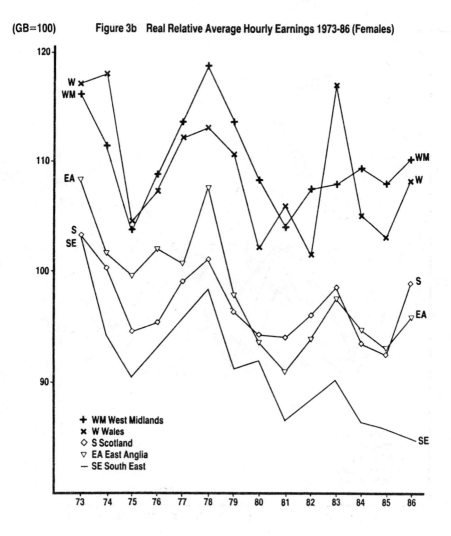

+ WM West Midlands
× W Wales
◇ S Scotland
▽ EA East Anglia
— SE South East

For Scotland, the regional cost of living was 99 per cent of the GB average in 1986 (e.g. in comparison to 133 per cent for the GLC and 88 per cent for Yorkshire and Humberside), and *real* relative earnings were generally at or fluctuating around the GB average in Scotland for male workers throughout the period 1973-86; if anything there is a very slight downward trend, with a similar picture also apparent for women workers. The major effect of deflating each relative earnings series would appear to be the effect on the *South-East* region (a similar pattern would also emerge for the GLC if we included it in the various diagrams, namely its ranking would drop from highest to lowest paid region). It is also interesting to note that while relative earnings in the West Midlands fell for male workers throughout the period (see Figure 1A), the effect on real earnings was lessened because prices increased at a somewhat slower rate (hence the region's position in Figure 3A). To investigate fully the substantial and important subject area of the extent (and nature) of the interaction between wages and prices would obviously take us well beyond the scope of this chapter, although it would seem to be the case that inter-regional wage differentials reflect, at least to some extent, the differing costs of living to be found in different areas of the country.

The aggregate information we have presented to date on relative earnings levels (in both monetary and real terms) for individual regions is, hopefully, of some interest in its own right. However, our basic purpose in presenting it was essentially to provide some relevant background for a more detailed examination of the possible implications for Scotland of the Government's position towards national pay bargaining arrangements. Our logical first step now is to consider the extent of such arrangements in Scotland, which is the concern of the following section.

The Extent of National Pay Bargaining in Scotland

In Table 1 below we utilise the largest and most representative set of survey data on workplace industrial relations structures in Britain to indicate the extent of national pay bargaining arrangements in Scotland compared to that in other parts of the country. This information is for the year 1980, and although there has been a similar, follow up survey in 1984, the latter data file is not yet readily available to researchers.

There are a number of interesting findings apparent in the Table, such as the generally limited extent of regional/district level bargaining arrangements in all areas of the country (as was commented on in an earlier section) and the fact that collective bargaining coverage is considerably higher in Scotland than is the case in the southern regions of Britain.[19] For present purposes, however, particular attention should be paid to the figures in columns (i) and (iii), which are the categories of bargaining that have been singled out for criticism by the Government. And here we find a somewhat mixed position for Scotland in that it has something of an *above*

Table 1: Coverage by collective agreement (manual workers) in Scotland and selected other areas, 1980

Areas[1]	Percentage Covered by:[2]						
	(i) National/ Industry-wide	(ii) Regional/ District	(iii) Company: All Plants	(iv) Company: Some Plants	(v) Single Plant	(vi) Other Miscellaneous	(vii) No Agreement
Scotland	42.5	4.4	12.3	3.6	22.1	1.5	13.5
Development regions	40.9	1.4	14.9	4.2	24.7	2.3	11.7
Southern regions	30.4	2.9	13.8	5.0	22.9	0.9	24.2
Other regions	31.9	1.8	15.7	4.9	33.0	1.3	11.4

[1] Development Regions =North, North West and Wales;
Southern regions = South East, East Anglia and the South West;
Other regions = Yorks-Humberside, East and West Midlands.

[2] Respondents were asked to choose the most important type of bargaining agreement. Hence, other (different types of agreement might also feature for some groups of workers.

Table 2: Coverage by collective agreement (manual workers) in Scotland by industry, 1980

Industry	(i) National/ Industry-wide	(ii) Regional/ District	(iii) Company: All Plants	(iv) Company: Some Plants	(v) Single Plant	(vi) Other	(vii) No Agreement
Agriculture	–	–	–	–	–	–	–
Energy and water	45.0	–	–	–	–	–	55.0
Metal and chemicals	10.0	10.4	30.1	–	34.1	–	15.4
Engineering and vehicles	15.4	–	–	13.3	66.2	–	5.1
Other manufacturing	38.9	8.9	18.9	4.0	25.0	–	4.4
Construction	83.1	8.6	4.8	–	–	–	3.6
Distribution	16.4	–	21.7	–	2.9	–	59.0
Transport and communication	51.7	–	14.4	–	11.3	11.5	11.1
Business services	6.5	2.0	–	–	–	–	91.5
Other services	73.5	–	7.8	0.8	–	5.2	12.7

average level of national/industry-wide bargaining, but a *below* average level of company (all plants) level bargaining arrangements. There is certainly a considerable difference between Scotland and southern regions in the extent of national/industry-wide bargaining coverage, although the difference in the extent of company level arrangements between Scotland and the south does not seem to be of the order of magnitude that some commentators have claimed to be the case.[20] In order to see which individual industries in Scotland are most (least) affected by these particular collective bargaining arrangements of which the present Government is so critical, Table 2 uses the same data source to present an industry level breakdown of the extent of these different levels of bargaining in Scotland.

Again concentrating on columns (i) and (iii) we find that national/ industry-wide collective bargaining in Scotland is most important in construction, other services, transport and communication and energy and water, while company (all plants) bargaining is most important in chemicals and metals, distribution and other manufacturing. Interestingly, the same industries do not have the same rankings in terms of the numerical importance of these different types of bargaining arrangements in the south, suggesting that the *overall* extent of different types of bargaining arrangements in individual regions is not simply a function of their particular industrial structure.

Wage Differentials and National Bargaining Arrangements

The question which we now pose is whether there is any evidence of a consistent, systematic relationship between the extent of national pay bargaining arrangements for individual industries (and different socio-economic groupings) in Scotland and the size of the wage differentials between Scotland and the South of England. In other words, do the particular industries (and socio-economic groupings) in Scotland which have relatively high levels of national bargaining coverage also have the least sizeable wage differentials when a comparison is made with the South of England? The wage information for different levels of bargaining that we present here does *not* come from the particular data source that was utilised in Tables 1 and 2. Instead we draw on information that comes from the annually conducted (in April) New Earnings Survey, which is the most important and detailed source of wage information in Britain (indeed it is one of the highest quality such data sets collected in the advanced, industrialised world). The particular figures that we present here come from specially prepared, *unpublished*, material contained in the 1973 and 1978 surveys which both contained a special question about various levels at which collective bargaining was conducted; the same question was repeated in the 1985 survey, although this information is not yet available to researchers in the same form as that for the years 1973 and 1978. The particular question included in these surveys distinguished between

138

workers not covered by collective bargaining arrangements and those who were covered by such arrangements, with the latter being subdivided into (i) national agreement only, (ii) national plus supplementary agreement and (iii) local agreement only.

There has in fact been considerable academic interest in this particular set of wage and collective bargaining coverage information. The existing studies based on this particular data source have generally tended to compare the level of collectively bargained wages with those for workers not covered by collective bargaining arrangements, across industries and for particular industries and socio-economic groupings, with the results tending to show (i) a positive wage return to collective bargaining coverage although the magnitude of this effect tends to vary quite considerably between individual studies, and (ii) something of a gradient of returns to the different types of bargaining arrangements, with the most (least) sizeable return being associated with local (national only) bargaining.[21] The approach adopted here is rather different to that of these existing studies in that we are interested in comparing the *collectively bargained* wage in Scotland with that in the South of England. Accordingly in Table 3 below we set out the average hourly earnings of male workers covered by collective bargaining arrangements for the different industries in Scotland and the South for both 1973 and 1978.

The contents of Table 3 indicate that for all industries the average hourly earnings of workers covered by collective bargaining arrangements in Scotland were some 9 and 7 per cent below that in the South of England in 1973 and 1978 respectively (the relevant figures in the case of workers *not* covered by collective bargaining arrangements were 15 and 10 per cent respectively). The largest sized negative differentials for Scotland were in transport and communications, and business services, while the most sizeable, positive differential was in the metals and chemicals industry. Table 4 presents the results of a similar exercise undertaken on the basis of socio-economic groupings, as opposed to individual industries.

The contents of Table 3 indicate that for all industries the average hourly earnings of workers covered by collective bargaining arrangements in Scotland were some 9 and 7 per cent below that in the South of England in 1973 and 1978 respectively (the relevant figures in the case of workers *not* covered by collective bargaining arrangements were 15 and 10 per cent respectively). The largest sized negative differentials for Scotland were in transport and communications, and business services, while the most sizeable, positive differential was in the metals and chemicals industry. Table 4 presents the results of a similar exercise undertaken on the basis of socio-economic groupings, as opposed to individual industries.

The key question raised by the figures in Tables 3 and 4 is whether there is any consistency when one ranks industries (and socio-economic

Table 3: Average hourly earnings, male workers covered by collective bargaining, by industry: Scotland and the South, 1973 and 1978.

Industry	1973			1978		
	Scotland	The South	Percentage Differential	Scotland	The South	Percentage Differential
Agriculture	0.64	0.59	+108.47	1.40	1.37	+102.19
Energy and water	1.00	1.03	− 97.08	2.29	2.31	− 99.13
Metals and chemicals	0.89	0.86	+103.48	2.11	1.93	+109.33
Engineering and vehicles	0.94	0.95	− 98.94	1.96	2.02	− 97.03
Other manufacturing	0.81	0.95	− 85.26	1.80	1.94	− 92.78
Construction	0.83	0.86	− 96.51	1.82	1.80	+101.11
Distribution	0.71	0.78	− 91.03	1.58	1.67	− 94.61
Transport and communication	0.82	0.96	− 85.42	1.81	2.05	− 88.29
Business services	0.99	1.21	− 81.81	2.35	2.66	− 80.34
Other services	1.07	1.14	− 93.86	2.30	2.48	− 92.74
All industries	0.90	0.98	− 91.84	2.00	2.13	− 93.90

Table 4: Average hourly earnings, male workers covered by collective bargaining, by socio-economic group, Scotland and the South, 1973 and 1978.

Socio-economic Group	1973			1978		
	Scotland	The South	Percentage Differential	Scotland	The South	Percentage Differential
Managers	1.37	1.59	−86.16	3.15	3.25	− 96.92
Professionals	1.44	1.52	−94.74	3.02	3.23	− 93.50
Intermediate non-manual	1.19	1.27	−93.70	2.50	2.65	− 94.34
Junior non-manual	0.83	0.91	−91.20	1.77	1.99	− 88.94
Foremen	0.97	0.99	−97.98	2.07	2.06	+100.49
Skilled manual	0.86	0.88	−97.73	1.87	1.83	+102.19
Semi-skilled manual	0.75	0.79	−94.94	1.66	1.70	− 97.65
Unskilled manual	0.70	0.72	−97.22	1.51	1.55	− 97.42

groupings) in Scotland by the extent of national bargaining coverage and the size of their wage differentials with the South of England. In other words, do industries (socio-economic groupings) with relatively high levels of national pay bargaining have the least sized wage differentials, *which is the relationship that should emerge if there is substantial validity in the Government's argument.* (In view of the possible interest in the full data set that has been used to undertake this particular exercise we set it out in the Tables that constitute the Appendix to this chapter.) The basic statistical results pertaining to this 'hypothesised' relationship are those set out below in Table 5.

Table 5: Pearson correlation coefficients between differences in earnings of covered workers and differences in coverage by national (and all) collective agreements, across industries and socio-economic groups, and by year, 1973 and 1978.

| | National Agreements | | All Agreements | |
	1973	1978	1973	1978
Across industries	−0.07	0.06	−0.45*	−0.08
Across socio-economics groups	−0.24	−0.04	−0.70**	−0.18

** Significant at the 5% level
* Significant at the 10% level

The contents of the above Table do not provide any obvious, strong support for the Government argument in that there is no statistically significant relationship apparent between the extent of national bargaining arrangements and the size of wage differentials, either across industries or across socio-economic groupings.[22] There is certainly some evidence for 1973 that relatively high levels of *overall* collective bargaining coverage (regardless of type) was correlated with the least sized earnings differentials, although even this relationship, which is a widely expected effect of collective bargaining in any system of industrial relations,[23] was not strongly present in 1978.

To take a fuller, more comprehensive look at the Government's argument one would ideally need to have the sort of information contained in Tables 3 and 4 available on a year to year basis for an extended period of time. Unfortunately, no such data set currently exists in Britain, but we nevertheless feel that it is essential to try and round off our work by considering, at least to a limited extent, the movement of wage differentials through the course of time. There were, as we mentioned in an earlier section, a number of studies in the 1970s which suggested that earnings changes in relatively prosperous, high demand labour market areas (e.g. the South-East) were passed on, in whole or part, to other, less prosperous areas of the country over the course of time through institutional mechanisms typically associated with the system of collective bargaining.[24] The more 'sophisticated' of these wage leadership or wage transmission studies (in terms of detailed data and statistical analysis) tended to be single industry studies (e.g. engineering).[25] However, in a preliminary exercise such as this it seemed more appropriate to adopt a rather broader inter-industry perspective, albeit one that would necessarily result in the use of a relatively simple, statistical technique. In view of the latter fact our final set of findings presented below should be regarded as no more than *suggestive* in terms of some pointers provided for further, more detailed research.

In essence we examined the extent to which changes in earnings were correlated over time between the South East (GLC and the rest of the South East) and Scotland for different sub-groups of workers. The resulting findings are those set out below in Table 6.

Table 6: Pearson correlation coefficients between changes in real average hourly earnings[1] in Scotland and the South East region (including the GLC), 1974-86

Industry	Manual Workers	Non-Manual Workers
Agriculture	0.57	0.26
Energy and Water	0.19	0.67
Metals & Chemicals	0.74	0.68
Engineering & Vehicles	0.76	0.87
Other Manufacturing	0.63	0.87
Construction	0.60	0.36
Distribution	0.74	0.78
Transport & Communication	0.78	0.73
Business Services	0.12	0.49
Other Services	0.85	0.86

[1] Deflated by regional retail prices.

The correlation coefficients are generally high, indicating that *real* earnings moved together quite closely over time. However, what is more important for present purposes is whether this tendency was greater for those sub-groups of workers most dependent upon nationally negotiated wage agreements. This is certainly the case for 'Other Services', but there are other instances where such a relationship does not hold. For example, national only bargaining is not especially high in Engineering and Vehicles (see the first Table in the Appendix), although changes in earnings were almost as highly correlated between the two regions as for Other Services. This was also true for Other Manufacturing, and Distribution, whereas for Energy and Water the correlation coefficient was lower for manual workers, despite the high level of nationally negotiated agreements. Generally, earnings grew at similar rates in both regions for the various sub-groups, although the latter displayed quite different levels of dependence upon national only agreements, so that there is no strong, obvious evidence of the clear cut, consistent relationships that might reasonably be expected on the basis of the Government's argument; but beyond this simple statement we again caution against reading too much into the findings of Table 6.

Conclusions

The major empirical findings to emerge in this chapter may be briefly summarised as follows:-

(i) the earnings of both men and women workers in Scotland tended to rise relative to the average(s) for Great Britain as a whole over the years 1970-86;

(ii) the particular industrial structure of Scotland accounted for only a relatively small proportion of the earnings differential between Scotland and Great Britain;

(iii) once allowance is made for differences in regional costs of living, real earnings levels in Scotland approximate those of Great Britain as a whole;

(iv) the coverage of industry level bargaining arrangements in Scotland is considerably greater than that in the southern regions of England, although the difference in the coverage of company level bargaining is much less between the two areas;

(v) the size of the wage differentials between workers covered by collective bargaining in Scotland and the South of England are not systematically related to the extent of national bargaining in Scotland at selected points in time;

(vi)   over time, real earnings levels in Scotland and the South East have moved closely together, although the extent of this synchronisation does not appear to be particularly related to the extent of national bargaining arrangements.

As to the nature and direction of further research in this subject area, we have indicated in the text of the chapter that new relevant data sources (i.e. the 1984 Workplace Industrial Relations Survey and the 1985 New Earnings Survey) will shortly become available to researchers. This will permit the contents of Tables 1-4 to be usefully updated so as to provide a more recent perspective on the issues considered there. In addition it will be important for researchers to undertake more systematic and sophisticated analyses of the question raised by the contents of Table 6, namely the extent and nature of relative wage movements through the course of time.

P.B. Beaumont, Department of Social and Economic Research, University of Glasgow.

R.I.D. Harris, Department of Economics, Queen's University, Belfast.

References

1. Department of Employment, *Employment: The Challenge for the Nation*, 1985, p.13-14.

2. P.B. Beaumont, "Industrial Relations in the Public Sector" in Brian Towers (ed), *Handbook of Industrial Relations*, Kogan Paul, London, 2nd edition, 1987.

3. *The Times*, 18th June 1987.

4. P.B. Beaumont and A.W.J. Thomson, "The Structure of Collective Bargaining in Britain" in A. Bowey (ed), *Handbook of Wage and Salary Administration* 3rd edition, Kogan Page, London, 1988.

5. Quoted in *IDS Report* 495, April 1987.

6. NEDC, "Regional Pay Variations", mimeographed paper, 25th November 1986.

7. D. Metcalf and S. Nickell, "Will Pay Cuts Bring More Jobs?", *New Society*, 28th February 1985.

8. Estimated Effects of Changes in Unemployment on Changes in Wages in Regions, US v. UK

| | UK, by County 1979-85 | | US, by State 1979-84 | |
	1	2	3	4
Change in unemployment rate	−.99 (.28)		−.43 (.30)	
Change in (log) labour force		−1.16 (.27)		−.14 (.30)
Change in (log) employment		1.00 (.24)		.39 (.35)
R-squared	.41	.46	.25	.39

Additional regressors: % manufacturing: % service (UK), education.

(Source: R.B. Freeman, *the Effect of Labour Market Institutions on Economic Performance*, Irish Economic Association, Kilkenny, May 1987.)

9. *Financial Times*, 4th March 1987.

10. P.B. Beaumont, A.W.J. Thomson and M.B. Gregory, "Bargaining Structure", *Management Decision*, Vol.18, No.3, 1980.

11. P. Cappelli, "Bargaining Structure, Market Forces, and Wage Outcomes in the British Coal Industry", *Industrial Relations*, forthcoming.

12. See, for example, A. Thirlwall, "Regional Phillips Curves", *Bulletin of Oxford Institute of Economics and Statistics*, Vol.31, No.1, February 1970, p.19-32.

13. "Pay in the 1980s", memorandum by the CBI to NEDC, 20th February, 1987.

14. "National Pay Bargaining", memorandum by the TUC to NEDC, 25th November 1986.

15. *IDS Focus*, 42, December 1986.

16. *IDS Report*, 495, April 1987.

17. Beaumont and Thomson in Bowey (ed), *loc. cit.*

18. See, for example, S. Fothergill and G. Gudgin, "In Defence of Shift

Share", *Urban Studies*, Vol.16, 1979, p.309-19.

19. P.B. Beaumont and R.I.D. Harris, "Sub-Systems of Industrial Relations: The Spatial Dimension in Britain", *British Journal of Industrial Relations*, forthcoming.

20. Howard Newby et al., "From Class Structure to Class Action: British Working-Class Politics in the 1980s", in Bryan Roberts, Ruth Finnegan and Duncan Gallie (eds), *New Approaches to Economic Life*, Manchester University Press, Manchester, 1985, p.93.

21. See, for example, M.B. Gregory and A.W.J. Thomson, "The Coverage Mark Up, Bargaining Structure and Earnings in Britain, 1973 and 1978", *British Journal of Industrial Relations*, Vol.19, No.1, March 1981, p.33.

22. The test on this particular data-set is only for the industry wide bargaining component of national pay bargaining, and not for the company (all plants) component thata has been attacted by the Government.

23. See, for example, Lloyd G. Reynolds, Stanley H. Mazters and Colleta H. Moser, *Labor Economics and Labor Relations*, Englewood Cliffs, New Jersey, 9th edition, 1986, p.573-76.

24. Thirlwall, *loc. cit.*

25. See D.J. Mackay and R.A. Hart, "Wage Inflation, Regional Policy and the Regional Earnings Structure", *Economica*, Vol.44, 1977, p.267-81.

Appendix 1

Coverage by Collective Agreement (full-time males) by Industry in Scotland and the South, 1973 and 1978

Industry (1980) Division	Average Hourly Earnings (£)		Percentage covered by:			
	Covered Workers	Not covered Workers	National plus Supplementary Agreement	National Agreement Only	Supplementary Agreement Only	No Collective Agreement
All Industries (0-9)	0.98 (2.00) / *0.90 (2.13)*	0.97 (2.13) / *1.14 (2.37)*	24.7 (19.1) / *19.0 (17.1)*	44.5 (42.1) / *38.8 (36.1)*	8.7 (10.9) / *9.7 (10.7)*	22.1 (27.9) / *32.4 (36.1)*
Agriculture etc (0)	0.64 (1.40) / *0.59 (1.37)*	0.57 (1.38) / *0.62 (1.34)*	15.7 (5.9) / *14.3 (8.3)*	17.3 (16.2) / *23.6 (25.7)*	3.6 (4.5) / *5.8 (2.4)*	63.5 (73.4) / *56.3 (63.3)*
Energy and Water (1)	1.00 (2.29) / *1.03 (2.31)*	1.26 (3.60) / *1.30 (3.63)*	12.6 (2.1) / *25.5 (12.7)*	81.8 (81.0) / *64.6 (76.2)*	2.1 (6.0) / *3.3 (3.9)*	3.4 (10.9) / *6.7 (7.2)*
Metals and Chemicals (2)	0.89 (2.11) / *0.86 (1.93)*	1.14 (2.70) / *1.23 (2.58)*	44.2 (29.5) / *18.7 (16.3)*	19.7 (27.7) / *18.8 (11.7)*	9.3 (20.6) / *13.5 (24.6)*	26.8 (22.2) / *48.9 (47.4)*
Engineering and Vehicles (3)	0.94 (1.96) / *0.95 (2.02)*	1.20 (2.45) / *1.16 (2.39)*	48.1 (41.6) / *35.4 (28.4)*	25.0 (15.0) / *17.3 (11.4)*	11.4 (17.9) / *14.8 (21.8)*	15.5 (25.5) / *32.5 (38.4)*
Other Manufacturing (4)	0.81 (1.80) / *0.95 (1.94)*	1.02 (2.26) / *1.14 (2.40)*	25.1 (22.4) / *23.2 (24.1)*	20.7 (17.6) / *23.8 (18.8)*	21.0 (24.1) / *15.6 (15.7)*	33.2 (36.0) / *37.3 (41.3)*
Construction (5)	0.83 (1.82) / *0.86 (1.80)*	1.19 (2.26) / *1.15 (2.22)*	19.7 (12.5) / *20.9 (16.9)*	64.6 (60.9) / *51.6 (46.8)*	2.3 (2.2) / *2.8 (3.2)*	13.5 (24.5) / *24.7 (33.2)*
Distribution (6)	0.71 (1.58) / *0.78 (1.67)*	0.77 (1.77) / *0.94 (2.00)*	10.6 (9.6) / *8.4 (9.7)*	28.8 (19.3) / *20.0 (16.3)*	10.3 (10.3) / *11.4 (9.2)*	50.3 (60.7) / *60.2 (64.7)*
Transport and Communications (7)	0.82 (1.81) / *0.96 (2.05)*	0.96 (1.84) / *1.09 (2.26)*	21.5 (18.5) / *9.6 (12.1)*	57.2 (54.4) / *66.6 (63.0)*	10.2 (10.0) / *10.4 (8.7)*	11.0 (17.1) / *13.4 (16.2)*
Business Services (8)	0.99 (2.35) / *1.21 (2.66)*	1.11 (2.40) / *1.45 (3.03)*	17.7 (9.5) / *9.8 (12.8)*	18.8 (31.0) / *16.1 (14.5)*	10.4 (12.2) / *11.0 (9.3)*	25.0 (47.3) / *63.1 (63.4)*
Other Services (9)	1.07 (2.30) / *1.14 (2.48)*	0.79 (2.06) / *1.08 (2.30)*	12.2 (10.9) / *13.7 (14.1)*	76.2 (75.9) / *68.4 (66.2)*	1.5 (1.7) / *2.4 (3.0)*	10.0 (11.5) / *15.5 (16.8)*

Source: New Earnings Survey

Note to Table: Figures in italics refer to the South (South East, South West and East Anglia). Figures in brackets refer to 1978.

Appendix

Coverage by Collective Agreement (full-time males) by Socio-Ecomic Group in Scotland and the South, 1973 and 1978

Values shown as: Scotland plain (1978 in brackets) / South in italics (1978 in brackets).

Socio-Economic Group (SEG)		Average Hourly Earnings (£)		Percentage covered by:			
		Covered Workers	Not covered Workers	National plus Supplementary Agreement	National Agreement Only	Supplementary Agreement Only	No Collective Agreement
All Workers	(1-8)	0.90 (2.00) / 0.98 (2.13)	0.97 (2.13) / 1.14 (2.37)	24.7 (19.1) / 19.0 (17.1)	44.5 (42.1) / 38.8 (36.1)	8.7 (10.9) / 9.7 (10.7)	22.1 (27.9) / 32.4 (36.1)
Managers	(1)	1.37 (3.15) / 1.59 (3.25)	1.50 (3.15) / 1.72 (3.35)	12.1 (7.9) / 7.6 (9.3)	30.9 (27.3) / 25.1 (20.5)	8.5 (8.7) / 9.6 (8.2)	48.5 (56.1) / 57.7 (62.0)
Professionals	(2)	1.44 (3.02) / 1.52 (3.23)	1.32 (2.88) / 1.51 (3.13)	15.9 (9.6) / 11.7 (10.0)	45.2 (50.6) / 38.2 (38.3)	6.4 (4.8) / 8.1 (9.1)	32.5 (35.0) / 42.0 (42.6)
Intermediate Non-Manual	(3)	1.19 (2.50) / 1.27 (2.65)	1.03 (2.14) / 1.15 (2.37)	9.2 (7.6) / 6.8 (10.3)	51.3 (52.4) / 44.3 (42.6)	7.8 (7.3) / 9.0 (9.9)	31.7 (32.7) / 40.0 (37.1)
Junior Non-Manual	(4)	0.83 (1.77) / 0.91 (1.99)	0.81 (1.69) / 0.90 (1.87)	16.5 (14.0) / 12.1 (11.5)	46.3 (49.6) / 40.8 (44.4)	8.7 (9.2) / 9.7 (8.5)	28.6 (27.1) / 37.4 (35.6)
Foremen	(5)	0.97 (2.07) / 0.99 (2.06)	0.91 (1.93) / 0.97 (1.95)	22.7 (17.2) / 19.5 (19.0)	46.2 (33.8) / 38.9 (28.0)	9.8 (19.9) / 11.8 (15.2)	21.3 (29.0) / 29.8 (37.8)
Skilled Manual	(6)	0.86 (1.87) / 0.86 (1.83)	0.78 (1.65) / 0.80 (1.72)	35.6 (29.2) / 29.4 (25.9)	45.2 (40.9) / 41.7 (35.1)	8.8 (11.3) / 10.0 (13.2)	10.3 (18.6) / 18.9 (25.7)
Semi-skilled Manual	(7)	0.75 (1.66) / 0.79 (1.70)	0.61 (1.42) / 0.70 (1.52)	26.7 (23.6) / 24.5 (23.1)	38.2 (34.0) / 36.9 (36.3)	11.3 (16.2) / 10.8 (11.0)	23.9 (26.2) / 27.7 (29.6)
Unskilled Manual	(8)	0.70 (1.51) / 0.72 (1.55)	0.60 (1.37) / 0.62 (1.37)	27.0 (19.0) / 26.1 (21.7)	52.5 (52.1) / 41.9 (42.4)	6.4 (8.9) / 9.4 (10.6)	14.1 (19.9) / 22.6 (25.3)

Source: New Earnings Survey

Note to Table: Figures in italics refer to the South (South East, South West and East Anglia). Figures in brackets refer to 1978.

SECTARIANISM IN SCOTLAND:
A CONTEMPORARY ASSESSMENT AND EXPLANATION

Steve Bruce

In November 1985 the Conservative government led by Margaret Thatcher signed an accord with the Irish Republic which gave Dublin a role in representing the interest of Catholics in Ulster. Ulster Unionists began a campaign of protest against what they saw as an important step towards a united Ireland. Some Scottish Protestants, offended by what for them was the Tory Party's abandonment of unionism, formed a Scottish Unionist Party and threatened to stand against Conservatives with thin majorities at the next general election. Had there been any great support in Scotland for Ulster unionism such splitting of the right-wing vote would have killed off the Conservative Party on Scotland. As it was, the SUP decided not to field candidates but to recommend tactical voting for the person most likely to beat the Conservative and that the recommendation made no difference to the result merely demonstrated the lack of interest in Ulster and illustrated the irrelevance of religion in Scottish politics.

My aim is to clarify an argument about the importance of sectarianism in contemporary Scotland, to evaluate evidence, and to present an explanation for the decline of the salience of religion in Scotland.

The Historical Background

Most Catholics in Scotland are descendants of Irish immigrants. Most of the native Scots were and are Protestants. The Lowlands embraced the Reformation. The Highlands remained Catholic or Episcopalian until the late eighteenth and early nineteenth century but then converted to evangelical Calvinism. Small pockets of Catholicism and Episcopalianism remained in the western highlands and in parts of the north-east lowlands, such as Banff and Buchan. However, Scotland became and remains a predominantly Protestant country. The vast majority of Roman Catholics in Scotland came from Ireland and settled, first in the western Lowlands, and then spread to Edinburgh and West Lothian and parts of Fife. The bulk of the settlement coincided with the industrialisation of Scotland.[1]

No-one doubts that the Irish in Scotland were initially the victims of both disadvantage and active discrimination. The same relative lack of economic and political power which led them to migrate in the first place caused them to enter the Scottish labour market at the bottom. Many were indigent. Others were willing to undercut the wages of Scottish workers and to act as strike-breakers.[2] There was considerable conflict between the Irish and the native Scots. Hardly surprisingly, the social and economic conflict fueled religious enmity. The poverty and low levels of education of the Irish were taken by Scots Protestants as evidence of the social evils of Catholicism. Interestingly, Protestants did not have a monopoly of anti-Irish prejudice and discrimination. As Handley's excellent histories demonstrate, the old Scots Catholics were barely less hostile.[3] Even long after the Irish had come to outnumber indigenous Scots Catholics, the hierarchy remained entirely Scottish.

In *No Pope of Rome*, I argued that sectarianism in Scotland has become an irrelevance: 'just a boy's game'. Why anti-Catholicism should have faded so quickly when it remains a powerful sentiment in Ulster will be explained shortly. Firstly, there is the issue of the salience of religio-ethnic conflict in contemporary Scotland. A number of scholars, either in published reviews or in private correspondence, have suggested that the assessment presented in *No Pope of Rome* is altogether too sanguine.[4]

The Evidence of Sectarianism

There is considerable superficial evidence of sectarianism, if by that rather loose journalistic term we mean the aggressive display in the public sphere of religious and ethnic differences which, in modern societies, are supposed to be confined to the private world as matters of 'personal preference'. City walls are still daubed with slogans such as 'Fuck the Pope'. Gangs of working class youths who identify themselves (and each other) as 'prods' and 'taigs' sometimes battle in the streets. Positions of support for the sides in the Ulster conflict are sympathetically struck and diluted forms of that conflict are replayed in Glasgow and Edinburgh. Some descendents of Irish Catholics march under 'Troops Out' banners and small numbers of young Orangemen organise counter-protests. Both Glasgow and Edinburgh have a Catholic and a Protestant football team. Until 1986, Glasgow Rangers refused to sign Catholics. Although Glasgow Celtic have had the odd Protestant on their staff, supporters continue to see the club as a Catholic club and the tricolour – the flag of the Irish Republic – is regularly displayed by Celtic supporters.

Bill Murray, the author of a recent book on Celtic and Rangers, sees such displays as evidence that sectarianism is still a force in Scotland.[5] It is my contention that these phenomena are of little importance (except to the small numbers of people who take part in them). If we adopt the metaphor of an iceberg, I contend that the relatively rare public displays of sectarian animosity are not the visible tip of a submerged mass of ice but are rather all that is left. My critics believe that there is still a sizeable piece of sectarian ice under the surface.

Evidence can be searched for in a number of places. We can begin with formal law. Since the 1829 Emancipation Act, Scottish Catholics have suffered only the most piffling legal disabilities and these were removed by the 1926 Relief Act. However, as the fortunes of American blacks have clearly shown, formal law may be no indicator of genuine equality. In any consideration of political equality. what matters is not so much the legal right to vote but the ability to turn the franchise into political power. Here the evidence seem clearly on the side of those who argue that the Irish who settled in Scotland have been successfully assimilated. Perhaps because they refrained from forming separate Catholic trade unions and parties, and instead became involved in the secular labour movement. Scottish Catholics have attained considerable power.[6] The Labour Party in the lowlands of Scotland (and especially in Strathclyde) is at least Catholic in proportion to the presence of Catholics and it has been in power in Glasgow since the nineteen thirties.[7]

This is not to say that religion was not a factor in Scottish politics; it was. In the early part of this century, many Protestants in the lowland urban areas supported first Liberal-Unionists, then Conservative and Unionists and, after the Catholic Church had dropped its opposition to 'moderate' socialist candidates, the majority of Catholics voted socialist. For a very brief period in the nineteen thirties, Protestant parties – Alexander Ratcliffe's Scottish Protestant League in Glasgow and John Cormack's Protestant Action in Edinburgh – enjoyed considerable success in municipal elections.[8] However, that success served only to break the hold of the Conservatives on Glasgow Corporation and to allow in a socialist administration. For a short period the Orange Order was able to deliver working class Protestant votes to Unionist and Conservative candidates but this has not been the case since the fifties. And even when the Orange Order could deliver the Protestant votes, it made very little difference because there were few locations in which this gave them power. Although the Order might still like to engage in sectarian politics, the Conservative Party has no interest in attracting or sustaining an anti-Catholic vote. Its electoral base lies in class politics and the South of England. Interest in Orangeism declined to the point that in 1970, the party nominated three Catholics and one, Michael Ancram, has since served as chairman of the Scottish Conservatives. There has been very little to distinguish the Conservative Party's Ulster policy from that of the Labour Party and its recent accord with the Dublin government has left the Orange Order talking about opposing Conservative candidates in future elections. Finally, the odd maverick, such as Pastor Jack Glass, who has tried to revive sectarian politics in Scotland has performed embarrassingly badly at elections.

To summarise the situation which has obtained at least since the second world war, religious affiliation has played no greater part on the politics of Scotland than it does in the politics of the United States or New

Zealand. It is certainly not, as those commentators who are struck by the behaviour of some football supporters would maintain, comparable to the situation in Northern Ireland. This is not to say that some Scots have not wished to pursue sectarian politics. It simply means that, irrespective of desire, the situation has not permitted it, and in the absence of success even those rhetorically committed to such politics have tended to lose heart.

Political power is important because it gives access to local resources such as employment in local government and council housing. I know of no evidence that Catholics now fare any worse than Protestants in either of these important areas. Given the already mentioned influence of Catholics in the Labour Party in Scotland, this is not surprising. Furthermore, the management of such resources has, since the war, become more and more the preserve of highly mobile middle-class professionals who may in their careers move from region to region and are thus very unlikely to share the particularist impulses of those local groups who might wish to see discriminatory policies pursued. However, this is clearly an empirical issue. If evidence of Catholic disadvantage does exist, then it should be published.

Although electoral politics are important, their study does not exhaust the search for evidence of disadvantage or discrimination. What of socio-economic position? Is there evidence that Roman Catholics are generally poorer and of lower status than non-Catholics, and, if so, does an explanation of any difference lead us to conclude that there is systematic disadvantage or discrimination? The first and most important thing to note is the dearth of data. Unlike the Northern Ireland census, the Scottish census does not contain a religion question and we are thus denied a vast amount of potentially illuminating data. However, the Scottish Mobility Survey (SMS) conducted in 1975 did record the type of school attended by respondents and thus permits some comparison of the educational performances and social mobility of those men who attended Catholic schools and those who did not.

It should be noted that the SMS data refers to people who attended school between 1925 and 1972 and is thus already a remembrance of things past. The main conclusion is that there are statistically significant but small differences between the two samples, which increase as one moves towards higher levels of qualification. 68.4% of Catholics obtained no exam passes at all, as compared with 63.4% of non-Catholics. 5.8% of Catholics obtained university entrance qualifications, as compared with 9% of non-Catholics. As Payne and Ford put it 'the differences tend to be more acute at the upper end of the range of qualifications, and since this only applies to about 1 in 10 of the sample, it seems unlikely that *most* pupils' educational chances were seriously impaired by religiously-segregated education'.[9] Surprisingly, controlling for class suggests that working-class Catholics actually perform slightly better than their non-Catholic counterparts, while middle-class Catholics seem at a disadvantage.

It is also possible to use the SMS data to compare rough rates of social mobility for the two populations. Credentials play only a relatively modest role in mobility. Almost all of those people with higher education qualifications attained middle class jobs, but 'the overwhelming majority of persons in the middle class both for Catholics and non-Catholics, pre- and post-1933, do *not* have a high level of education'.[10] The one highly significant finding concerns the upward mobility of those people with low levels of education: 'Whereas 22.2% of Catholics from working class backgrounds and born before 1933 were able to enter middle class jobs with low qualifications, 33.0% of non-Catholics with the same characteristics were able to do so and of those born after 1933 only 24.5% of Catholics achieved this against 30.0% of non-Catholics.[11]

Two points should be made about this considerable difference. Firstly, as Payne and Ford recognize, they are describing the past. Someone born in 1940 entered the labour market in 1956: thirty two years ago. Someone born in 1950, in 1966: still twenty two years ago, and so on. Secondly, even the very crude division around 'born in 1933' (hence entering the labour market between 1949 and 1952), shows a considerable improvement in the mobility of Catholics. Catholics born before 1933 enjoyed a rate of 'unearned' mobility which was only 67.3% of that of non-Catholics; for those born after 1933 it was 81.7%. Clearly one would need to be able to further sub-divide the age bands to see if such a trend continued.

It is far easier to describe the data than it is to explain it. It may well be that the different rates of mobility for the two populations were caused by discrimination. Other studies have identified the importance of informal contacts in securing jobs. Given that the Irish came into the Scottish labour market at the bottom, it only requires Protestants and Catholics to consistently favour co-religionists for inequality to persist. Informal aid in securing positions will perpetuate the pattern of advantage. The fact that the pattern has not been maintained and that non-Catholic advantage has been reduced (halved, according to the SMS data) suggests that informal discrimination has been diminishing. But this is to present the explanation which gives the greatest weight to discriminatory practices. There is another highly likely possibility which Payne and Ford describe as '"passive discrimination" against Catholics'.[12] The majority of Catholics are concentrated in the poorest areas of Scotland. In 1970, eight out of ten Catholic children were in schools in West Central Scotland: the part of Scotland with the least potential for social mobility. The pattern of settlement established in the nineteenth century thus has a restraining effect on Catholics, entirely irrespective of the behaviour of non-Catholics. Although Payne and Ford put 'passive discrimination' in inverted commas, the use of the term 'discrimination' to describe a disadvantage caused by the general decline of a region seems inappropriate. When 'discrimination' is the noun form of an active verb, how can it be 'passive'? Who is doing it?

What would be illuminating is evidence about the relative fortunes of Protestants and Catholics in West Central Scotland but such data are not presently available.

Clearly, the most obvious conclusion about the relative socio-economic status of Catholics and non-Catholics in Scotland is that the data required to say anything more than the above is missing. However, in the absence of anything better, anecdote is not without its place. In this respect, it is worth noting that a recent collection of studies of poverty and deprivation in Scotland makes no mention of religion. The words 'religion', 'sectarianism', 'Protestant' and 'Catholic' do not even appear in the index of *Scotland: the real divide*.[13] Although a desire to avoid what is a politically sensitive issue may have had some bearing on these omissions from a work edited by two Scottish Labour MPs, I cannot believe that 18 researchers studying the social distribution of income, educational opportunity, employment and wealth would all have conspired to completely pass over something of relevance to their findings. Similarly, one might note that, of the 385 items listed in the 1986 *Scottish Government Yearbook* bibliography of publications on Scottish politics and government, only two concern religion: one is my *No Pope of Rome*; the other is Bill Murray's *The Old Firm!*

Segregation as Sectarianism?

One commentator pointed to the degree of religious segregation which still exists in Scottish life as being evidence of the social importance of religious differences. The majority of Roman Catholic children are still educated in separate Catholic schools. There is still residential segregation and there is 'leisure' segregation. Protestants and Catholics support different (and often locally competing) football clubs. Especially in the larger lowland urban areas, there are Catholic and Protestant 'fraternal' associations and there are Protestant and Catholic drinking clubs and public houses. However, segregation is not necessarily evidence of discrimination (although it may be precisely that). The Roman Catholic Church may have begun its own school system because it felt that the public schools, having initially been Protestant church schools, would undermine the socialization of Catholic children in Catholic beliefs and culture. But since the end of the last century the public schools have been independent of the Protestant churches. From 1872 until 1927, they were managed by directly elected boards which had Catholic clergy members.[14] That a separate Catholic school system still exists is entirely due to the wish of the Catholic Church in Scotland to socialize Catholic off-spring in the culture and ethos of Catholicism. This can hardly be regarded as evidence of anti-Catholic discrimination.

It seems similarly inappropriate to take the voluntary segregation of leisure associations as evidence of discrimination. Some degree of segregation follows inevitably from the desire of orthodox Catholics and Protestants to maintain their own religious cultures. To see separation as a 'social problem' is to endorse improperly the view that religions should be liberal and ecumenical. Likewise, to regard membership of voluntary associations (such as the Orange Order or the Troops Out Movement) which support conflicting political positions as a matter of public concern, as something which modern democracies should have outgrown, is curious. It seems most sensible to confine the shorthand 'sectarianism', and the concern it connotes, to the maintenance or re-introduction into the public arena of religious particularisms which, in modern societies, are supposed to be confined to the private world.

The question of whether there is in Scotland a degree of sectarianism which is significant, either because it is a neglected part of the operation of the social system or because it should cause 'right-thinking' people disquiet, should not be answered by a measure which includes voluntary association as an index. More properly, what is at issue is the extent to which private prejudices are acted upon in the public sphere so as to affect the lives of those who do not wish to be affected. It should not be a matter of public policy concern that the Church of Scotland only permits those who can pass certain doctrinal tests to enter into communicant membership. Similarly, it should not be a matter of great concern that Scots of Irish Catholic ancestry are far more likely than non-Hibernian Scots to support Irish Republican and nationalist movements. What would be evidence of enduring sectarianism would be the operation in the public sphere of what we permit as private opinion. Hence we need to ask whether Catholics fare significantly worse than non-Catholics in educational provision and performance, in the exercise of political rights, in the consumption of public goods such as state-funded housing, welfare benefits, health provision, and in the general indices of socio-economic status. Furthermore, once such data are presented, we need to know to what extent any identified disadvantage results from active discrimination. And, presumably, we would be interested initially in anti-Catholic discrimination. It is altogether another question if a population remains relatively disadvantaged because it has performed the societal equivalent of shooting itself in the foot. It would be interesting if, as some radical Catholics have suggested, it was the case that the Church's insistence on maintaining its own school system was an own goal; interesting, but not what is conventionally thought of as evidence of sectarianism.

I do not wish to propose a simple infrastructure-superstructure argument but it is generally the case that religion only remains an important base for 'secular' association when it is underpinned by shared socio-economic characteristics. As Scottish Catholics have experienced upward mobility and come to spread themselves more evenly across the occupational spectrum their shared Catholicism has diminished as a source of identity and has, to a large extent, been superseded by class. More and more middle class Catholics send their children to non-Catholic schools. Catholic fertility rates have declined to approach the norm for Protestant Scots.[15] Most significantly, the Catholic Church in Scotland's own statistics show that by the 1970s 'mixed' marriages were almost half of the total of all marriages contracted by Catholics.[16]

Explaining the Failure of Scottish Anti-Catholicism

Some of the evidence which has been offered against the following argument misses the point and it is best to clarify the nature of the argument before the details are presented. That some Scottish Protestants and Catholics continue to dislike each other is neither here nor there. The argument is not that some time between 1850 and 1940 Scottish Protestants became tolerant, theologically liberal and ecclesiastically ecumenical. It is that some Scottish Protestants tried to act in a discriminatory manner but found that they lacked the wherewithal to act particularistically. However much some Protestants may have wished to maintain their economic, political, social and cultural advantages, a variety of forces outside their control radically reduced their ability to do so. Being unable to act on their world-view gradually led all but the most committed to abandon that world-view. The clearest way of presenting an explanation of the decline of religious politics in Scotland is to offer comparisons between Scotland and Ulster.

The first obvious difference between Scotland and Ulster is the greater secularisation of the former. Whether one considers the involvement of individuals in organised expressions of religiosity, or the impact of religious values on the general culture and polity, one has to conclude that Scotland is less religious than Northern Ireland.[17] But this suggests a tautology; we explain the decline of anti-Catholicism in Scotland by arguing that religion matters less. To avoid the charmed circle we need to explain why religion matters less in Scotland. Part of that will involve elements particular to Protestant-Catholic conflict but there is a more general element. It is well-recognised that modernization and pluralism undermine religiousity.[18] Scotland is far more integrated into the British economy and into European culture than is Northern Ireland. Thus, even if relations with Catholics had not been an issue in either context, one would have expected Scotland to be the more secular.

But if we concentrate on relations between Protestants and Catholics, a major difference between Scotland and Ulster can be found in the interaction between a high degree of internal fragmentation and the absence of external threat. I have argued in detail elsewhere that conservative Protestantism is inherently fissiparous.[19] However, the cohesion of Ulster Protestants suggests the point ably made by Durkheim, Simmel and Coser: cohesion may be created and maintained by the presence of an external threat.[20] I will first discuss the reasons why the

Irish Catholics in Scotland were not seen by Scottish Protestants as a threat of proportions similar to that posed by the Catholic majority in Ireland. I will then consider the roots of Scottish Protestant fragmentation. The interaction between these, the perceived threat to a group and its internal cohesion, explains the degree of anti-Catholicism. Having established that, I will turn to consider the ability of such anti-Catholics as remained to pursue their policies.

The Irish Catholics in Scotland

In the first place there were not all that many Catholics in Scotland. The best figures available suggest that the Catholics formed 9.2% of the population of Scotland in 1878, rising gradually to 13.7% in 1931 and 15.9% in 1977.[21] In contrast, if one takes Ireland as a whole, Catholics form the vast majority of the population and in Northern Ireland, as constituted since 1926, they form more than a third of the population.[22] The total impact of the Irish Catholic immigrants on Scotland was considerably reduced by the concentration of their settlement in certain regions. Basically, they concentrated where industry was developing: Ayrshire, Lanarkshire, Glasgow, Dundee, Dunbarton, the Lothians and Edinburgh. And even within these areas, distribution was uneven. While Catholics formed 25.3% of the population of Strathclyde Region in 1977, they were only 10.1% of Lothian.[23] Although Catholics were strongest in the most populous parts of Scotland, important organisations such as the Church of Scotland and the Free Church had a national structure which, although skewed towards population concentration, had been slow to adapt to movements of people. Thus in the period from 1890 to 1930 – the crucial time for the career of anti-Catholicism – relations with Catholics were not a practical issue for much of the Church.

The Irish Catholics in Scotland flirted with Irish politics, but generally they settled to regard themselves as Scots. While they acted to preserve their own religion and culture, they did not for long have a distinctive Catholic politics.[24] Unlike the Catholics of Ulster, Scottish Catholics were not intent on moving the Protestants of Scotland into another political formation. Hence the only way in which they could be seen as a 'threat' was to suppose that they would change dramatically the nature of Scotland from within and not many Scots, even those of a conservative Protestant faith, were convinced of that.[25] Although the idea was floated by some Catholic politicians, a specifically Catholic party, along the lines of the European Christian Democratic parties, was not formed. Instead Catholics became active in the secular Labour movement and in what became the Labour Party. This meant that a neat alignment of religion and politics could only be created if all or most Protestants supported the Unionist and later Conservative parties. But arguments between the supporters of the established Kirk, and the dissenting heirs to the Secession Churches (who were later joined by the Free Church) has caused elements of the urban bourgeoisie and the Highlands who supported the Free Church to support the Liberal Party. The re-union of the majority of Presbyterians reduced the salience of the church establishment issue and thus helped erode the links between Presbyterianism and Liberalism. Some Protestants followed Liberal Unionists into the Conservative and Unionist fold but many, especially among the more theologically conservative Presbyterians, remained Liberals.

The ability of the Conservatives to sustain a pan-class Orange vote was further undermined by them retaining far longer than their English counterparts an image of being a hunting, shooting and fishing party while the majority of Orangemen were members of an urban industrial proletariat.[26] The Tories' lack of responsiveness to Scottish concerns, the power of the Labour Party in local government, and the rise of Scottish nationalism all helped erode Protestant support. Any lingering attachment to the Conservative Party the Protestant working class might have carried into the nineteen eighties has been destroyed by the collapse of Scottish heavy industry which is, rightly or wrongly, blamed on the economic policies pursued since 1979 by the Conservative government. That government's Ulster policy has also offended many Orangemen.

To summarise these three points, the Catholic presence in Scotland did not offer good evidence of a significant 'threat' to the Scottish Protestants, and hence did not act as a counter to the fragmentation which already existed and which increased between 1870 and the present. In contrast, relations between Protestants and Catholics in Ireland caused an *increase* in Protestant cohesion. In the eighteenth and early nineteenth century, one had considerable conflict between the Ulster Presbyterians and the more 'Anglo' Irish of the Church of Ireland; reaction to Catholic demands for first emancipation and later home rule, brought Protestants in Ulster together into a homogenous political bloc.

Scottish Protestant Fragmentation

There were a number of sources of fragmentation in Scottish Protestant culture. The first major division was between Highlands and Lowlands. The topography of the Highlands delayed its development so that it was always out of step with Lowland Scotland. When the Lowlands were Protestant, the Highlands were Catholic and Episcopalian. By the time the Highlands had been converted to Calvinism, the Lowlands had become secularized and the dominant form of Protestantism, for those who still had any, was moderate, rational, and ecumenical. In language, custom, social relations, and economy, the two parts of Scotland have been so different as to challenge the usefulness of regarding the area north of the Solway sands and the Tweed as one country.

As was the case with England, social differentiation produced a fragmentation of the religious culture. In Scotland, the divisions were deeper and more far reaching. In part this was a result of the special place of the Christian Church in Scottish life. In the absence from Scotland of many of the institutions of a political system, the Presbyterian Church enjoyed an inflated importance for Scots. Furthermore, that the national church was Presbyterian, rather than Episcopalian, was important because the more 'reformed' Presbyterianism gave greater opportunities of factionalism and schism than did the English national church, with its considerably lower rates of lay participation. Scottish Protestants spent most of the nineteenth century arguing with each other, rather than with Catholics, and produced a de facto pluralism which hastened secularization.[27]

Political Impotence

Some reviewers seem to have misunderstood the argument which I and Tom Gallagher have advanced. Neither of us is arguing that the desire to discriminate on the grounds of religious or ethnic background is now entirely absent in Scotland. Rather we have argued that even those Scots Protestants who wished to maintain discriminatory practices were unable to do so. Even had they been united, their chances of success were undermined by their political impotence.

Protestant divisions might have been partly healed had there been a 'pork barrel' to bribe dissenters, and the power to punish those who could not be sweetened. But Scotland had few such resources. Since the Union of the Crowns, real power has lain in London. The elites therefore have tended to see London and cosmopolitan values as their main point of reference. The limited number of members of the elite who wished to maintain a Protestant ascendancy in Scotland did not have the power to fulfil their ambitions, and they had little to offer the Protestant working classes. In contrast, the Unionist elite in Ulster could make major concessions to the working class. They legalised the popular militias as the Special Constabulary[28] and they discriminated in housing and local employment policy.[29]

The Ulster Unionists were popular enough to resist being incorporated in a united Ireland and for almost fifty years they had considerable control over many areas of life in Northern Ireland. Although subordinate to the British parliament at Westminster, the devolved parliament at Stormont could make its own policy on local government, employment, housing, education and policing; precisely those areas which would best serve to alienate the Catholic minority. The continued alienation of the Catholic minority then acted as a constant local reminder of the dangers to Protestants of incorporation into a united Ireland and hence maintained the religious and cohesion of the Protestant population.

Scotland did not have that degree of control over its own affairs. The only Scottish institution that still had some influence was the Church and it was divided. The Scottish Unionists could not offer much to militant Protestants because they were a small part of a party which represented England and Wales as well as Scotland. An example of their powerlessness was the failure of two Scots Unionist members of parliament – Sprot (North Lanarkshire) and McInnes Shaw (Renfrew) – to have Scotland exempted from the provisions of the 1926 Catholic Relief Bill. Scottish matters generally, let alone relations with Catholics which were only a concern for part of Scotland, had little impact on the British parties. Taking the other side of the coin, voters in Scotland knew that there was little point in electing anti-Catholic politicians such as Ratcliffe or Cormack to Westminster. What could one or even ten militant Protestants in Westminster have achieved?

The devolution of some elements of public administration to the Scottish Office did not increase the ability of Scottish Protestants to discriminate against Catholics because the Office was controlled by the most cosmopolitan and 'anglicised' Scots. And the increase in 'planning' which has been characteristic of public administration in Scotland has been accompanied by the removal of power from local authorities through increased centralization.[30]

Desire and ability interact. The obdurate reality of impotence is, for most people, enough to cause a gradual shift in desires until the situation that obtains is endorsed as being what was really wanted all along. A small proportion of mostly working class Protestants continue to wish to act in a sectarian fashion but the majority of Scots Protestants have, since the turn of the century, come to endorse a liberal culturally pluralistic tolerant society as being the sort of society they want.

The Elements of Religio-Ethnic Conflict

One very simple generalization can be drawn from the comparison of religious politics in Ulster and Scotland. The survival of Protestant politics requires an ideological element – a theory of the virtues of one's own people and the vices of some other group – and actual competition between the two populations. This does not mean that one requires actual competition between every member of both populations. The proposition is not refuted by pointing out that racist attitudes can be held by people in parts of America that have hardly ever seen a black. The 'actual' conflict can be fixed and made real for members of a society who themselves have not participated in it by the transmission of experiences through various media. Nonetheless, a sustained absence of actual competition for a large part of a population will reduce the plausibility and importance of the experience of the rest. This simple proposition explains the collapse of anti-Catholicism in Scotland and, by simple reversal, the maintenance of anti-Catholicism in Ulster.

The Highlands of Scotland retained a Calvinist evangelical Protestant faith but did not engage in any of the expressions of practical anti-Catholicism. The Orange Order, the main organisation for popular anti-Catholicism, has never had any support from above the Highland line. The Highlanders had the right theology for anti-Catholicism but not Irish Catholic immigrants. The Lowlands of Scotland were already well on their way to being a secular society by the time the Irish Catholics arrived in any great numbers. The main churches had either abandoned evangelical Protestantism or, even if they maintained it, had accepted pluralism. Of crucial importance is the observation that, as in most other societies, the urban working class of the Lowlands, the very people who were in day to day competition with the Irish Catholics, were not 'theologically' Protestant. The proletariat of Glasgow had the actual competition with Catholics but it lacked the ideological element to legitimate and sustain the conflict. The consequence of this is best seen if one moves from large-scale generalization to actual individuals and social movement organisations. Militant Protestant leaders in Glasgow such as Jack Glass and David Cassells (an independent evangelical with close links to Ian Paisley's Free Presbyterian Church of Ulster) are constrained by the absence of a general evangelical culture amongst those 'Protestants' who are prepared to campaign against Roman Catholics. They are forced to distance themselves from the supporters of the Orange Order and the recently formed paramilitary Protestant groups because they know (and their critics are quick to remind them) that the average Orangeman is not an evangelical, is not 'born again', is not a total abstainer, and does not keep the sabbath. Lowland militant Protestant leaders are forced to distance themselves from the only constituency which shares their willingness to protest against Catholics because that constituency possesses none of the other characteristics of evangelical Protestantism.

Conclusion

The comparison of relations between Protestant and Catholics in Scotland and Ulster suggests that the factors important for the continuation of sectarian politics are: (a) the degree to which religion plays a part in the shared ethnic identities of the populations at the time they come into contact; (b) the extent to which conflict between the populations reinforces the part played by religious elements in the ethnic identity; and (c) the degree to which the populations involved have the power to act in support of their own interests. If one wishes to move beyond the already rather abstract notion of the interaction between internal fragmentation and external threat, the comparison of Scotland and Ulster suggest that the single simplest point that can be made concerns the degree of secularization. Confining ourselves to Protestantism, we can suppose that the internal dynamic of Protestantism is fission. Especially in the non-Lutheran cases, Protestant churches (until the modern era in which orthodoxy has been largely abandoned) have tended to divide. Protestantism inadvertently encourages pluralism. Exceptional circumstances are required to retard this dynamic and the classic exceptional circumstance is that of being confronted by a large population which shares a religious identity antithetical to that of the Protestants. In such a circumstance pluralism is not possible because it will mean not religious liberty for all but submersion and erosion. What is crucial then is the period in which the initial contact between the two populations occurred. The Protestants arrived in Ulster in the early eighteenth century. The Catholics arrived in Scotland in the nineteenth century.

Steve Bruce, Department of Social Studies, Queen's University, Belfast.

References

1. For a more detailed history of religion in Scotland, see S Bruce, *No Pope of Rome: militant Protestantism in modern Scotland*, Edinburgh, Mainstream, 1985, or J H S Burleigh, *A Church History of Scotland*, Oxford, Oxford University Press, 1960.

2. A B Campbell, *The Lanarkshire Miners: a social history of their trade unions, 1775-1874*, Edinburgh, John Donald, 1979.

3. J Handley, *The Irish in Scotland*, Cork, Cork University Press, 1945, and *The Irish in Modern Scotland*, Cork, Cork University Press, 1938.

4. For example, D Birrell's review of *No Pope of Rome* in *Sociological Review*, 1986, 34(3), pp.714-6, and C Brown, *The Social History of Religion in Scotland Since 1730*, London, Methuen, 1987.

5. B Murray, *The Old Firm: sectarianism, sport and society*, Edinburgh, Mainstream, 1984.

6. For a good discussion of the involvement of the Irish Scots in Irish poilitics, see I Wood, 'Irish immigrants and Scottish radicalism, 1880-1906', pp. 65-89 in I MacDougall (ed), *Essays in Scottish Labour History*, Edinburgh, John Donald, 1978.

7. T Gallagher, 'Catholics in Scottish politics' , *Bulletin of Scottish Politics*, 1981, Spring, pp.21-43. It should be noted that the community of interest shared by most of the Catholic councillors gave them more influence greater than their numbers.

8. See S Bruce, *op.cit.*, Chs 2 and 3. The Scottish Protestant League and Protestant Action are also described in T Gallagher, 'Protestant

Extremism in Urban Scotland 1930-1939: Its Growth and Contraction', *Scottish Historical Review* 1985, 64 (2), pp. 143-167, and *Glasgow: the Uneasy Peace*, Manchester, Manchester University Press, 1987.

9. G Payne and G Ford, 'Religion, Class and Educational Policy', *Scottish Educational Studies*, 1977, 9(1), p.90.

10. Payne and Ford, *op.cit.*, p.94.

11. *ibid*.

12. Payne and Ford, *op.cit.*, p.97.

13. G Brown and R Cook, *Scotland, The Real Divide: poverty and deprivation in Scotland*, Edinburgh, Mainstream, 1983.

14. J Scotland, *The History of Scottish Education; Volume 2: From 1872 to the present day*, London, University of London Press, 1969.

15. S Kendrick, F Bechhofer and D McCrone, 'Recent trends in fertility differentials in Scotland', pp.33-52, in H Jones (ed), *Population Change in Contemporary Scotland*, Norwich, Geo Books, 1984.

16. D McRoberts, *Modern Scottish Catholicism: 1878-1978*, Glasgow, Burns, 1979, p.237.

17. For the most recent figures for church membership and church attendance, see D Brierley, *UK Christian Handbook; 1987-88 Edition*, London, MARC Europe/Bible Society, 1987.

18. P L Berger, *The Heretical Imperative*, London, Collins, 1982; B R Wilson, *Contemporary Transformations of Religion*, London, Oxford University Press, 1976.

19. S Bruce, 'Authority and fission: the Protestants' divisions', *British Journal of Sociology*, 1985, 36(4), pp.592-603.

20. L Coser, *The Functions of Social Conflict*, London, Routledge and Kegan Paul, 1965; E Durkheim, *Suicide*, London, Routledge and Kegan Paul, 1975; G Simmel, *Conflict*, Glencoe, Ill., The Free Press, 1965.

21. McRoberts, *op.cit.*, p.228.

22. P A Compton, 'The demographic dimension of integration and vision in Northern Ireland', pp.75-104 in F P W Boal and J N H Douglas

(eds), *Integration and Division: geographical perspectives on the Northern Ireland problem*, London, Academic Press, 1982.

23. McRoberts, *op.cit.*, p.240.

24. Gallagher, *op. cit.*.

25. Those who wish to claim that anti-Catholicism remained strong in the main churches, even into this century, often point to reports such as *Report of the Committee to Consider the Overtures on Irish Immigration and the Education (Scotland) Act 1918* which the Church of Scotland's General Assembly formally accepted in 1923. Anyone with experience of large bureaucracies will appreciate the value of committees and reports in side-tracking enthusiasts whose views or enthusiasm are not shared by the majority. The image of the Kirk (and most other such organisations) built up from the committee reports it has considered (or even accepted) would be a wildly inaccurate one. What is more significant is an obvious lack of willingness to act. For all some ministers were willing to voice anti-Catholic sentiments (and more were unwilling to publicly oppose them), the Kirk did not campaign against the 1918 Education Act which incorporated Catholic schools into the state system on such favourable terms that 'Rome on the rates' is not an especially exaggerated description.

26. J Kellas, *The Scottish Political System*, Cambridge, Cambridge University Press, 1982, Ch.6; C Harvie, *No Gods and Precious Few Heroes: Scotland 1914-1980*, London, Edward Arnold, 1981, Ch. 4.

27. For a detailed account of the links between fission, pluralism, the rise of tolerance and secularization, see S Bruce, *A House Divided: a sociology of Protestantism*, Oxford, forthcoming.

28. M Farrell, *Arming the Protestants: the formation of the Ulster Special Constabulary and the Royal Ulster Constabulary, 1920-27*, Dingle, Brandon Press, 1983.

29. P Buckland, *The Factory of Greivances: devolved government in Northern Ireland, 1921-39*, Dublin, Gill and Macmillan, 1979.

30. On the Scottish Office and local government in Scotland, see J Kellas, *Modern Scotland*, London, George Allen and Unwin, 1980, Ch.8.

SCOTLAND AND CATALONIA: THE PATH TO HOME RULE

Luis Moreno

Introduction

Scotland and Catalonia share a somewhat similar configuration as sub-state peripheral nations with analogous perceptions, interpretations and aspirations for home rule within their respective British and Spanish frameworks. Nevertheless, Scotland and Catalonia have not followed parallel processes over the last decades, as far as the achievement of institutional forms of self-government is concerned[1].

The nationality of Catalonia at present enjoys a great degree of political autonomy within the quasi-federal Spanish *Estado de las Autonomias*. On the contrary, and although in Scotland there is a wide constellation of political and social forces favouring Scottish home rule, the task of translating this common concern into action has proved in the last years to be extraordinarily difficult.

It will be contended later on in this article than an inter-party political convention is the desirable option for the achievement of self-government in Scotland, although a change in the traditional political pattern of self-interest and party competition characteristic of British politics is required to achieve such a goal.

It must be emphasized, however, that not only is it an absolute requirement that the Scots have a vision of self-government but that this vision must also be brought into the realm of the possible/probable through social mobilisation.

Very similar to the approach of a majority of Catalans to the so-called "national question", non-secessionist self-government in Scotland bases its argument mainly on the following:

(1) Scottish cultural, economic and political differences with the rest of Britain, marked by an increased centre-periphery dichotomy in Britain.

(2) Scottish *dual nationality*: one being the result of a reinforcement of the pre-Union identity, and the other being the product of the national integration brought about by British state-building after 1707.

(3)   A desire for democratic political decentralisation related to a sense of national/regional consciousness.

Scottish and Catalan Affinities and Differences

In order to set out subsequent sections, it is first of all necessary to focus on the main historical, political, socio-cultural and economic affinities and differences between Scotland and Catalonia. They can be outlined as follows:

(A) Historical[2]

Affinities. In pre-capitalist Europe, Scotland and Catalonia exercised significant political independence as ethnically structured territories. This continued until their personal dynastic unions with England and Castile, respectively (ie. James VI & I in 1603 and the Catholic Kings in 1469). Nevertheless, both nations continued to preserve institutional forms of self-government until the coercive imposition of political standardization which occurred in the aftermath of a military defeat (ie. the failure of the Jacobites to reinstate the Stuarts in 1745 and the Catalans' setback in their support for Archduke Charles in the Spanish War of Succession in 1714). These events formed the basis of the origins of the processes of national integration and state-building which occurred in the United Kingdom and Spain during the 18th and 19th centuries.

In Scotland and Catalonia, during the second half of the 19th and the first half of the 20th centuries, there was a progressive reassertion of nationalist values with unfulfilled economic and social expectations, caused by the decline of the British Empire and the inability of the Spanish bourgeoisie to achieve its revolution nationwide. These political movements eventually forced concessions from the centre which, in order to accommodate them, granted a degree of administrative devolution, eg. the Secretaryship for Scotland in 1885 and the *Mancomunitat de Catalunya* in 1914. The creation of the Scottish Office in Edinburgh in 1939, and the achievement of the 1932 Catalan Statute of Autonomy, although different in political and institutional content, can be seen as outcomes of a similar political struggle for the gain of larger degrees of home rule.

In the 1960s and 1970s, with the progressive obsolescence of the centralist state apparatus in liberal Britain and despotic Spain, the peripheral nationalism of Scotland and Catalonia challenged the political legitimation of the corporatist forms of uniformity imposed on them from the centre of their respective polities. With the 1979 Referenda in Scotland and Catalonia, the desire for self-government of a majority of Scots and Catalans was expressed (51.6% cent in Scotland and 88.1% in Catalonia in the turn-out).

Differences. While throughout the Middle Ages the Catalan-Aragonese Confederation was one of the leading Mediterranean powers, Scotland continually struggled to overcome the "natural" expansionist interests of England in the Wars of Independence.[3] Both the out-looking Catalan and defensive Scottish psycho-social attitudes have somehow moulded the ancestral national character of the Catalans and Scots. More important, however, is the fact that when the nationalist movements emerged defiantly in the 1960s and 1970s, the ancestral detachment of their respective compound identities – ie. Scottish and Catalan, but at the same time British and Spanish too – reflected the assertive and reactive nature of their similar political aspirations for self-government.

The main historical dissimilarity between both political processes in Scotland and Catalonia in contemporary times is that, during the Second Spanish Republic, the Catalans achieved democratic institutions of self-government although the Statute of Autonomy and the *Generalitat* were later abolished by Franco in 1939 at the end of the Civil War. The Scots have not had any analogous experience.

These divergent realities undoubtedly conditioned not only social mobilisation in Scotland and Catalonia prior to the 1979 Referenda but, more importantly, the form and content of the political response from the centre of both centralist states.

It is, however, important to note that if the "memory" of the Republican Catalan Government and Parliament has counted as an extraordinary asset in the centre-periphery negotiation in the transitional period after the demise of Franco's dictatorship, the mere existence of an administrative Scottish Office since World War Two, in combination with the civil institutions preserved by the 1707 Treaty of Union, has also enhanced the subsequent salience of the Scottish dimension in British politics.

(B) Political

Affinities. Scotland and Catalonia have, in recent times, seen the rise of strong nationalist parties – the Scottish National Party and the coalition *Convèrgencia i Unió* – which have brought not only an element of hetereogeneity to the British and Spanish electoral scenarios but have also tested the adaptability of both liberal and post-despotic state apparatuses to profound institutional changes (see electoral results in Scotland and Catalonia in Tables 1 and 2).

The lack of major political violence in these two nationalities is, moreover, highly significant. It indicates the absence both of strong intra-communal social cleavages, as is the case in Northern Ireland, and of a considerable section of the population ready to support the fight for self-determination, by whatever means possible, as in the Basque Country. In any case, both forms of political nationalism share the perception that political violence would undoubtedly jeopardise social mobilisation and popular support for the cause of self-government. Moreover, the reformist character of such nationalisms is antagonistic to radical change. Neither have the policies of repression by their centralist states or the internal social climate reached the level of suffocating oppression or civil war as happened in the Basques Country and Northern Ireland in the 1960s and 1970s.

Differences. Setting aside electoral and institutional traditions, the stark difference between the Scottish and Catalan processes for gaining home rule rests upon their antithetical strategic approaches. The Scottish political class has tended to defend, in an inert manner, a political territorial pattern, a situation which did not exist in post-Franco Catalonia and which has also been greatly influenced by the dialectics of partisan competition and self-interest characteristics of British politics.

TABLES 1: Percentages of popular votes in General Elections in Scotland since the Second World War.

YEAR	LABOUR	CONSERVATIVE	LIBERAL (*)	SNP
1945	47.3	36.3	9.0	1.2
1950	46.1	44.8	6.6	0.4
1951	47.8	48.6	2.7	0.3
1955	46.7	50.1	1.8	0.5
1959	46.6	47.2	4.0	0.5
1964	48.7	40.6	7.6	2.4
1966	49.9	37.6	6.8	5.0
1970	44.5	38.0	5.5	12.8
1974(Feb)	36.6	32.9	8.0	22.7
1974(Oct)	36.3	24.7	8.3	30.6
1979	41.5	31.4	9.0	17.1
1983	35.1	28.4	24.5	11.8
1987	42.4	24.0	19.2	14.0

(*)   The 1983 and 1987 results correspond to the SDP/Liberal Alliance.

TABLE 2: Percentages of popular votes in General and Catalan elections since 1977.

YEAR	PSC-PSOE	CiU	PSUC	ERC	AP	UCD/CDS	OTHERS
1977 (General)	28.4	16.8	18.2	4.5	3.5	16.8	11.8
1979 (General)	29.2	16.1	17.0	4.1	3.6	19.0	8.8
1980 (Catalan)	22.3	27.6	18.6	8.8	2.3	10.5	8.3
1982 (General)	45.1	22.2	4.6	4.0	14.4	2.0/2.0	5.7
1984 (Catalan)	30.0	46.6	5.5	4.4	7.7	–	5.8
1986 (General)	41.0	32.0	3.9	2.7	11.4	4.1	4.9

PSC-PSOE: Catalan Socialist party federated to the Spanish PSOE
CiU: Centre-right Catalan nationalist coalition
PSUC: Catalan communists
ERC: Centre-left Catalan nationalist party
AP: Spanish conservative party
UCD: Centrist coalition which disappeared after the 1982 General Election
CDS: Centrist party created in 1982

Thus, the achievement of home rule, which has been the concern of a majority of Scots, has always been subordinated to the priorities of each party. The Catalan forces, on the contrary, not having to break a territorial pattern of institutional power in post-Franco Catalonia, have sought and negotiated the articulation of a common strategy to make the re-establishment of institutions of self-government after the demise of Francoist dictatorship possible. This pattern has followed the traditional inclination of the Catalan *seny* ("common sense") for negotiation and compromise, or *pactisme*[4].

(C) Social and Cultural

Affinities. The concept of dual nationality, or compound nationality, is a common element of identification for a majority of Scots and Catalans (see results of survey polls on national identification by Scots and Catalans in Tables 3 and 4). Both peripheral nations have preserved a national identity, or quasi-nationhood, from pre-Union times and have also assimilated a post-Union identity, a product of the process of malintegration in the British and Spanish state-building.

A consequence of such pre-Union collective consciousness is the employment of both Scottish mythology and the Catalan language as the main socio-cultural instruments in the forging of ethnical cohesiveness.

Differences. The diverse nature of socio-cultural instruments has reinforced the assertive and reactive character of Scottish and Catalan nationalism. Not surprisingly, many of the Scottish myths for popular consumption deal with heroes like William Wallace or Robert the Bruce, or events like the battle of Bannockburn, rather than the egalitarian values developed in Scottish civil society since the union with England. The former emphasises Scotland's successful defence against the external English adversary, and contributes to feed, in turn, a certain sense of defensive "hopelessness" in national Scottish values *vis-à-vis* the "powerfulness" of the English ones[5].

TABLE 3: National identification by Scots (1986).

Question: "We are interested to know how people living in Scotland see themselves in terms of their nationality. Which of the statements on this card best describes how you regard yourself?"

		%
(1)	Scottish, not British	39
(2)	More Scottish than British	30
(3)	Equally Scottish and British	19
(4)	More British than Scottish	4
(5)	British, not Scottish	6
	(Don't Know)	2
(*)	Those expressing a degree of dual nationality	54
(*)	Those expressing exclusive single nationality	46

(*) Percentages have been rounded. "Don't Knows" have been ignored.

Source: System Three Scotland, July 1986, see Appendix 2, Luis Moreno, (1986), *Decentalisation in Britain and Spain*. Ph.D. thesis, University of Edinburgh, pp. 439-441.

TABLE 4: National identification by Catalans (1985).

Question: "In which of these five categories do you include yourself?"

		%
(1)	I consider myself only Catalan	9
(2)	I consider myself more Catalan than Spanish	24
(3)	I consider myself as much Spanish as Catalan	47
(4)	I consider myself more Spanish than Catalan	7
(5)	I consider myself only Spanish	12
	(Don't Know)	1
(*)	Those expressing a degree of dual nationality	79
(*)	Those expressing exclusive single nationality	21

(*) Percentages have been rounded. "Don't Knows" have been ignored.

Source: ECO poll published in *Cambio 16*, no. 698. See Appendix 2, Luis Moreno (1986), *ibid*, p.442.

The Catalan language, on the other hand, provides the means for a permanent re-assertion of Catalan ethno-cultural distinctiveness. The external adversary theory has also played, and continues to play, an important role in the articulation of political mobilisation in Catalonia. However, the emergence in the last decades of new outward-looking cultural forms, not exclusively tied to the pre-Union signs of identity, has brought about an active socio-cultural Catalan role in concurrence with other Spanish values.

(D) Economic

Affinities. The regional economies of Scotland and Catalonia have similar economic indicators as regards population (5.15 and 5.96 million, respectively), location (peripheral regions) and production (EEC GDP: 1.5% and 1.4%). They have traditionally perceived themselves as discriminated by the core areas and political elites of their respective unitary states, ie. the Scottish perception of relative deprivation and the Catalan sense of comparative grievance. In other words, while a large sector of Scottish society is of the opinion that the English – especially those living in the South – are economically better off than the Scots, the Catalans' comparative grievance is based upon a feeling of being treated unfavourably by the centre, or receiving less than they have given. These two popular perceptions have greatly fuelled the rise of modern nationalism in both peripheral nations.

Differences. In relative terms, and taking into account both the British and the Spanish contexts, Scotland can be seen to be poorer and Catalonia richer. Growth of population, one simple indicator of the well-being of a country, illustrates this point. Whereas in 1931 the population of Scotland accounted for 12.1% of the UK total figures, in 1971 the percentage fell to 10.7%. Catalonia's population, by contrast, climbed from 11.2% of the Spanish total in 1940 to 15.6% in 1974.

However, as far as natural resources are concerned, the contrast is spectacular. North Sea oil, for example, provided £16bn of the gross revenue of the UK Treasury in 1982, while the very few natural resources in Catalonia amount to no more than some salt and lignite mines and a very small oil extraction off the coast of Tarragona.

Although both countries have shared the recent experience of the increased penetration of multinational companies, their regional economies show dissimilarities with respect to their economic structures: specialised, in the case of Scotland, with large "uncompetitive" heavy industries which are in the gradual process of closure; and diversified, in the case of Catalonia, with production based on small firms and businesses. Paradoxically, the financial sector based in Edinburgh is very strong in comparison with the feebleness of Catalan local finances.

In general terms, the "productive" sector of the Scottish regional economy relies upon the implementation of policies from above, basically through the provision of jobs and the creation of economic activities via British public expenditure. On the other hand, an entrepreneurial vocation developed by a *petite bourgeoisie* mentality makes the Catalan industrialists more likely to develop initiatives from below. These are on a small scale and are very adaptable to changing economic scenarios.

Catalan experiences, future variables and the quest for Scottish Home Rule.

The task of putting forward a systematic pattern of predictions is factually inaccessible rather than methodologically problematical. In this section we will seek to induce a political situation through which self-government in Scotland can be achieved and exercised in the foreseeable future and which has proved to be effective in the light of the Catalan experience. In any case, a climate of political consensus is the *sine-qua-non* requirement prior to any further development.

It needs to be said, however, that the prospect of political agreement between the different representative political parties operating in Scotland is rather unfamiliar in the competitive complexion of the British political system. Perhaps the whole idea of a political convention is regarded as strange in Britain because of the preoccupation with *parliamentary sovereignty* – itself evidence of the archaic nature of the British state – and the failure to develop a doctrine of *popular sovereignty*.

However, some variables are considered to be highly important in any future development concerned with Scottish self-government:

(1) *SNP electoral revival*. This is a "compelling" variable which could provoke an expedient response by the British parties to the rapid setting up of a Scottish Assembly or Parliament. This new hypothetical electoral upsurge of the SNP in a medium-term future would need the concurrence of two other main sub-variables:

(1,a) An increase in both the *economic decline of Britain* and in the *sense of relative deprivation* felt in Scotland.

In general, the trend of relative economic decline in Britain has been steady since the end of World War Two. This decline has taken place amidst a rapid increase in the economic expansion of other industrial countries. In 1955, for instance, the United Kingdom was fifth in the world league of income per head. In 1981 the UK GNP per capita was $9,000, 26th in the world behind countries like the Federal Republic of Germany ($13,450 and 9th), France ($12,190 and 16th) or Japan ($10,080 and 25th).

Some authors predict that if present trends continue, Britain will be overtaken by countries like Spain in the mid-term future and that the British economy will not reach the present level of the national income in the Federal Republic of Germany until 2051[6].

The classical free-liberal market and supply-side monetarist policies developed by the Thatcher Governments have severely damaged the traditional "lameduck" heavy industries located in Scotland, but have served very appropriately the ethnocentrist interest of British capital based in the City. This financial industry has simply disregarded investments in the North of Britain and has concentrated mainly on speculative operations overseas – namely, US financial markets – or in investment ventures in the South East of England.

This sense of relative deprivation could certainly be channelled in electoral terms through an instrumentalist vote for the SNP, together with a wide support for Labour which, as the 1987 General Election has proved, also receives in Scotland a large proportion of the so-called "protest vote" articulated against the English Tory policies which are aimed at favouring the Conservative strongholds in the South of England.

(1,b) *An SNP effective strategy and charismatic leadership.* The lack of charismatic leadership has been a feature universal to all the parties operating in Scotland at least in the last twenty years – with the quasi-exception perhaps of the cases of John Mackintosh, Jim Sillars and Winnie Ewing. This lack of leadership is an element which highly conditions the nature of social mobilisation for self-government in Scotland.

In this respect the "Billy Wolfe affair" can be cited as a very illustrative one. The fact that the chairman of the SNP was "able" to alienate, with his comments in 1982, the important Catholic minority in a country where religious bigotry still exists in some areas causes more than perplexity. The view that a democratic and participatory structure, combined with the strong commitment of the SNP membership, does very little to compensate for the absence of charismatic leadership and the tactics-strategies confusion over Party goals has to be stressed.

Indeed, the passive political attitude of the Scots might be galvanised by the presence of a charismatic political leadership like that of Jordi Pujol in Catalonia. This factor is essential for the breaking of the ingrained attitude of political defeatism and institutional solidarity so characteristic of some Scottish political culture.

(2) *The "conversion" of Scottish Labour to self-government.* Labour has traditionally failed to assimilate the fact that political decentralisation mounts *per se* a democratic challenge to the structure of a capitalist state which, in the case of Britain, uses the practices of economic corporatism and political centralisation to maintain its supremacy. Labour, on the other hand, should no longer hold the populist view of attacking the self-interest of Welsh and Scottish nationalisms while, at the same time, deploying the same kind of English-British nationalist self-interest in attacking the EEC in the European Parliament.

The alleged defensive mood of Scottish politics finds in the case of Labour the compliance of a political leadership most unwilling to use political mobilisation to pursue the democratic principle of self-government.

In any possible future, however, the political fortunes of Scottish home rule would very much depend on the attitude of the Labour membership in Scotland and, as a result of this, on the willingness of Scottish Labour leaders to operate also in the Scottish dimension of British politics, rather than exclusively aiming their territorial interests at gaining institutional power in London.

In Catalonia, the label "national" or "nationalist" cannot be claimed solely by the parties which explicitly define themselves as such. Both socialist PSC and communist PSUC are not only Catalan national organisations but were also main catalysts and protagonists in the process of political negotiation aimed at the re-establishment of home rule in Catalonia.

In contrast with some of their European counterparts, notably the British Labour Party, the Spanish socialist PSOE has traditionally had a strong anti-centralist tradition and federalist vocation.

(3) *The transformation of the British state.*. The issue of Scottish self-government is very closely related to the content and form of any future social transformation in the British state. The trend of political backwardness in Britain, which has encompassed the loss of the Empire and progressive economic decline, has seen an increased paternalist centralisation in the last decades since World War Two. This situation has been described as follows:

> "We live in an archaic political society...The British state is to be defined as an *ancien régime* closer in the spirit to the monarchy overthrown in 1789 than to the republican constitutions which followed in France and elsewhere in Europe... The reason that the British economy does not work is that British institutions are in terminal decay"[7].

The failure of the democratic parliamentarian system in the industrial state has been caused, amongst other factors, by its problems to function spatially in large communities (ie. nation-state).

The fate of any social transformation within the British state is closely related to the creation of geographical, political and cultural communities through which civil society can determine the mechanisms of participation. This opposition to centralist corporatism, a feature common to other Western European states, cannot simply rely on the appearance of spontaneous "unhistorical" upsurges of social mobilisation (eg. May 68), but must rely on the developments of self-governed activities which reject the technocratic solutions and the tutelar role of the "paternalist" industrial state.

(4) *A political convention for Scottish Home Rule*. The means by which an institutionalised form of self-government can be achieved in Scotland from the point of view of its "desirability" takes into account two crucial premises:

(a) The product of broadly agreed proposals of home rule will inevitably respond to a broad desire for self-government expressed by the Scots.

(b) The social mobilisation which would follow the political agreement by the political parties in Scotland on the form and content of the home rule proposals would confer a character of irreversibility to the whole political process.

The most desirable and workable form of self-government in Scotland is provided by the process of negotiation and agreement among those parties representing the broad majority of the Scottish electorate. A political convention, encouraged by a cross-party organisation like the *Campaign for a Scottish Assembly*, or another of similar characteristics, would provide the means for discussion and agreement on the kind of assembly/parliament to which the Scots aspire.

In Catalonia, the *Assemblea de Catalunya*, set up in 1971, genuinely reflected the struggles against both dictatorship and centralist rule. Its activities followed a simple four-point programme which included the recovery of Catalan Home Rule. This Assembly of Catalonia gathered together Liberals, Social Democrats, Christian Democrats, Socialists, Communists, trade unionists, urban community associations, university groups, intellectuals and ordinary people in a clandestine and highly representative movement of opposition to Franco's regime in Catalonia. More importantly, it started the practice of inter-party discussion and negotiation which subsequently proved to be essential in the task of wording the Autonomy Statute for Catalonia.

In Scotland, some Scots still believe that devolution has something to do with the total secession of Scotland from the rest of Britain. So, the constitutional convention would have the goal, among others, of publicly debating the differing views of the various parties on the home rule issue. Were the SNP to put forward the claim "independence-nothing-less" in the negotiations of the political convention, the Scottish population at large would be able to distinguish more clearly between the arrangements for home rule and those for complete secession.

Once the content and form of the proposals had been broadly discussed and agreed to in the Scottish convention, the legislative procedure *should* start in Westminster. At this point the biggest question would be raised: Would MPs at Westminster, with their "own" territorial constituencies, allow the Scots whatever they wanted?...

In such a situation, the role of the Scottish Labour MPs would be crucial. As was said before, any form of home-rule to be achieved in Scotland very much depends on the "Scottishness" of the Labour MPs elected in Scottish constituencies.

Proceeding to a Scottish Convention

The best-positioned body to call on for political negotiations over the setting up of both a Scottish Assembly and an Executive would be a cross-party organisation. Once a cross-party organisation like the CSA was accepted as convener body by the representative parties, the next step would be a constituent meeting with the political representatives of their respective parties. This aspect is not merely formal: in order to avoid pre-judgements about the way the Convention should operate, the constituent parties would be the ones who decided upon the working methodology to be adopted. The role of the convener would subsequently be that of taking charge of the provision of the material elements needed for the proceedings of the Convention. The convener would, consequently, become the instrumental body which would put into practice the decisions taken by the Scottish Convention.

To say that the political parties should be the constituent parts of the Convention is not to deny their own prerogative to consider the inclusion or not in the Convention of other representative Scottish "voices" (eg. Local Authorities, STUC, Chambers of Commerce and Industry and/or representatives of the major religious organisations). The parties, by the very expression of their political will, would accept the "operational" legitimacy of the Convention and so, the result of the negotiations would be one of a tacit consensus assumed by the parties involved.

The goal of a Scottish Convention can only be realized by the prior assumption made by the political parties that an institutional form of self-government for Scotland can be achieved by consent and, in so doing, reflecting the electoral preferences of the Scots for those parties advocating home rule for Scotland. If we take into account the 1987 General Election results we should stress the fact that 85% of all MPs elected in Scotland are members of political parties advocating some form of Scottish self-government (ie. Labour, Alliance and SNP).

In the eventuality of political agreement being reached, and being widely embraced by the parties involved in the Convention, the next step would be constituted by the formal acceptance of the constitutional proposals by the Scottish Grand Committee.

Finally, and in order to make the whole process workable, the political agreement reached within the Scottish Convention would accomplish one priority goal:

– The constituent parties would agree not only on the content and form of the proposals, but would explicitly pursue social mobilisation in order to implement them. That is, a new popular referendum on the text containing the proposals agreed in the Scottish convention would be held before the implementation of such legislative provisions.

Catalonia, a referential example and a precedent.

The afore-mentioned proposals are not original *per se*. This is to say, they have already been attempted succesfully in Catalonia, a country with a context similar to that of Scotland. Indeed, the process in Spain of decentralisation and regional autonomy in which nationalities and regions participated in the framing of their own statutes offers a remarkable example.

In Spain, after the 1977 Spanish General Election, 80% of the Catalan elected candidates to the *Congreso de los Diputados* (Lower House of the Spanish Parliament), and all but one of the elected candidates to the *Senado* (Upper House) were committed to Catalan Home-Rule.

Most certainly in post-Franco Catalonia the achievement of home rule was a political priority for all major political parties, regardless of other ideological cleavages. A few days after the 1977 General Election, the *Assemblea dels Parlamentaris* (Assembly of Parliamentarians) first met in Barcelona to start on the wording of the Statute of Autonomy. On 29th December 1978, during the final vote on the draft of the Statute Bill finalised in the town of Sau (Girona), there were no votes against the drafted text in the *Assemblea dels Parlamentaris* and only one abstention.

Very significantly, the drafted Catalan Autonomy Statute involved the active presence of the Conservative MP, Laureano López Rodó, a prominent minister in Franco's government during the 1960s.

The Bill of the Autonomy Statute for Catalonia was debated in the Spanish Joint Parliamentary Committee which was composed of the members of the Constitutional Committee of the *Congreso de los Diputados* (34 votes in favour, 1 against and 1 abstention) and the Catalan Assembly of Parliamentarians (21 affirmative and 1 abstention). On October 25, 1979, 88.1% of the Catalan vote (52.6% of the registered electorate) voted affirmatively for the implementation of the Autonomy Statute. The turnout was 59.7% of which 7.7% were "No" votes, 3.5% Blank votes and 0.5% spoiled votes. On 30th November and 12th December, respectively the Spanish *Congreso de los Diputados* (317 MPs in favour, 1 against and 13 abstentions) and the *Senado* (168 MPs in favour, 1 against and 3 abstentions) ratified the provisions of the Catalan Autonomy Statute. The Royal Assent was given on December 18, 1979. On 17th January 1980, the provisions of the Statute of Autonomy for Catalonia were fully put into effect, after their publication in the Spanish Official Gazette *BOE* on December 22 , 1979.

Conclusion

It is simplistic to believe that historical events and processes can operate in the same way and with the same results in different countries but, having said that, Scotland and Catalonia have so many features in common that it would also be unrealistic to deny beforehand a similar result in their respective paths to home rule.

There are global trends to decentralisation in the Western world. In fact, the centralisation/decentralisation debate has usually remained isolated on the political fringe of the discussion of the efficiency versus inefficiency of state institutions in the provision of public goods. Such marginal treatment minimises the comprehensive study of the formation (state building and national integration) of the modern states, the intergovernmental relations within its boundaries, the crisis in the legitimacy of its political institutions (eg. Parliament and representative democracy) and the impact of the internationalisation of capital in the "post-industrial" state.

Power has an inherent territorial dimension: it cannot be abstracted from its geographical component. The development of industrial society inevitably involved a reallocation of the spatial division of power. Since the Industrial Revolution, and due mainly to a marked increase in the volume and scope of government activity, power has been progressively allocated according to meaningful geographical criteria. As a consequence, the issues "dispersion-concentration", "central-local relations" and "state homogenization-regional diversity" have become crucial for both the configuration of the state institutions and the social transformations which can take place within the state.

Diverse economic, cultural and political factors are leading to the recognition of pluralist centres of decision-making. In this respect, Scotland and Catalonia may represent the future of decentralised political structures. In other words, decentralisation needs to provide a deepening of democracy by means of a more effective access by civil society to political decision-making, something which in the case of minority nations like Scotland and Catalonia overlaps with their ethnic/cultural/economic dimension.

References

1. This article is a revised version of different sections of the Ph.D. thesis written by the author under the title, *Decentralisation in Britain and Spain: The cases of Scotland and Catalonia* (1986, University of Edinburgh).

2. For a chronological account of both Scottish and Catalan contemporary processes of home rule see Appendix 3, *ibid*, pp. 443-453.

3. The Catalans also fought Castilian/Spanish assimilation in revolts and wars of independence from 1640 to 1714: ie. "War of Reapers" 1640-1652 with the result of Catalonia's loss of Roselló and Cerdanya to France in 1659 (Peace of the Pyrenees) and War of Succession which ended with the surrender of the Catalans after the forces of Philip V entered Barcelona on September 11, 1714.

4. *Seny* is a word which implies common sense, prudence and wisdom rather than intelligence. *Pactisme* establishes "that rules are made by parties entering into contracts of their own accord, and also that social life is the result of bargaining among people, and not unilateral violence or imposition" (Giner, S, 1980, *The social structure of Catalonia*, Sheffield University, pp.5-6).

5. Authors like Paterson, L (1981, "Scotch Myths – 2" in *The Bulletin of Scottish Politics*, no.2, p.71) argues that Tartan's principal legacy is a "cancerous national inferiority complex: the quite unmistakably psychological end-product of two centuries of tawdry palliatives – of escaping from social problems into wishful fantasy".

6. Cf., for instance, Pollard, S (1982), *The Wasting of the British Economy*. London: Croom Helm, and Gamble, A (1985), *Britain in Decline*, 2nd ed. London: Macmillan.

7   Ascherson, N (1985), "Ancient Britons and the Republican Dream", John P Mackintosh Memorial Lecture (November, 16th), reproduced in *Radical Scotland*, 18th issue, Dec/Jan.

*T*H E · W A Y · T O · A
BRIGHTER FUTURE

WITH
SCOTVEC'S NATIONAL CERTIFICATE

Go for the National Certificate — the alternative way to modern skills.

You choose the place — over 500 schools and colleges in Scotland

Your pace — full time? part time?

Over 2,000 modules available.

Scotvec's National Certificate modules prepare you for a career in catering, business and public administration, science, technology and many other areas — meeting the objectives set by industry and commerce.

Find out more; contact your local Further Education college, careers service or Scotvec.

SCOTVEC
Scottish Vocational Education Council

SCOTVEC HANOVER HOUSE 24 DOUGLAS STREET GLASGOW G2 7NG

182

THE PRICE OF PRIVATE PLANNING[1]:

A REVIEW OF URBAN PLANNING POLICY IN SCOTLAND

Robin Boyle

In August 1987, not many people in Scotland – or in England for that matter – celebrated what in effect was the fortieth anniversary of Town and Country Planning. In its day, this complex framework of legislation was considered to be the most far-reaching of the post-war "reconstruction" Acts. Lewis Silkin, then Minister of Town and Country Planning, was champion of a system that would be the bedrock for the rebuilding of Britain's ageing towns and cities. His legislation imposed sweeping controls over the development and use of all urban land and introduced an effective nationalization of development value through the imposition of a Betterment Levy. What's more, the 1947 Act empowered local government to take a leading role in the redevelopment of towns and cities, building a new Jerusalem on the basis of positive urban intervention, promoting the wider public interest through development planning and regulating the excesses of the private sector through a system of development control.

In 1987, the planning system is still on the statute book, but the aspirations of its Founding Fathers – of Silkin, Uthwatt, and Reith in the 1940's and the earlier ambitions of Burns, Addison or Wheatley in Scotland – seem long forgotten. This is therefore an appropriate occasion to take stock and to examine how planning has changed in the 1980's and what this means for Scottish towns and cities. It is also apposite, after more than eight years of a Thatcher government – antipathetic, at best, towards planning's traditional values of regulation and selective intervention through local public control – to ask who now controls the type and pace of urban change and to examine the future of Town and Country Planning in the 1990's, and indeed the extent to which it still has one?

With reference to changes in British planning policy and selecting examples from Scotland, two central questions bind this discussion together. First, how has planning been affected by *deregulation*? What role is left for the planning system in a society that is being increasingly led away from the collective, public domain of post-war Britain into the private, personal world of the late 20th century. Indeed, if regulatory planning is anathema to a Conservative administration why retain the legislation, why keep the machinery going? Does the post-war evolution of planning offer clues as to this apparent contradiction?

Second, who then becomes *responsible* for urban change, who determines the future of urban Scotland? Gone is the thirty year-old relationship between central and local government that planned, controlled and re-built contemporary urban Scotland. Between the 1940's and the 1970's two distinct phases of sub-regional planning introduced extensive urban change: new town construction; overspill agreements; suburban housing development; infrastructure projects; inner city comprehensive redevelopment; urban motorway construction; industrial relocation; regional parks and more. Planned state intervention has been *the* dominant architect of modern Scotland.

This legacy of public planning has been replaced by support for the activities of the private sector and a rearrangement of the balance between public control and private development. The terms privatism and privatisation have been applied in this context but they need to be placed in a policy framework that has seen a centralisation of authority and a commensurate weakening of the local state. Urban planning in the 1980's is therefore no longer to be directed by local government under the guidance of central government but is to become the product of a new public-private partnership. The issues of deregulation and the transfer of responsibility cannot be avoided in an assessment of this new partnership.

Deregulating Town and Country Planning

During the 1970's Keith Joseph, and others in the Conservative Political Centre, launched a sustained attack on the planning system. Despite the support given to Town and Country Planning by successive Tory Secretaries of State[2], and often disregarding the views of the property industry[3], the New Right was eager to see an in-coming Conservative government sweep-away much of the statutory planning system. Frank (later Lord) Harris's Institute of Economic Affairs and other free-market pressure groups had long been critical of the planning system, claiming it had merely served to crowd-out the private sector, distorting and delaying the market and imposing additional costs on development. They were joined by what Greg Lloyd[4] convincingly refers to as the "libertarian planning school". Critical of the over-extension of the planning system, Sorensen and others, argued that the planning system should return to its rightful role as a mechanism for controlling and minimising the externalities associated with development.[5]

These opinions were most forcibly articulated in a report by Robert Jones[6], entitled "Town and Country Chaos". His recommendations were to surface again as an important chapter in the "Omega Report", a blueprint for privatization produced by the right-wing Adam Smith Institute.[7] Jones found little to commend the statutory planning system in

Britain. His conclusion was that public planning, directed towards the best interests of the community, was a demonstration of collective failure. In contrast, the best examples of town planning were to be found in the private domain, citing Belgravia in London and Edinburgh's New Town as good examples. The conventional wisdom that public planning had secured lasting social and environmental improvement was questioned: rather than improving cities, the control of non-conforming uses had instead resulted in rigid partitioning and served to stifle new development; the imposition of planning control and conditions on development far from achieving civic improvement led instead to intolerable delay, increased building costs and bureaucratic architecture: "what looks to middle-class eyes as the protection of a city's character and the imposition of order instead of chaos, might seem to working class eyes as the denial of opportunity and convenience. A bustling, growing and thriving city, changing and mushrooming with all kinds of vigorous developments, might seem more attractive than a quiet and planned stagnation".[8] And the ASI Report concludes that, "(t)here is no doubt at all that the removal of most of the planning restrictions and controls which are applied in Britain would bring major and lasting benefit to the community".[9]

Not that an unfettered market place or untrammelled laissez-faire is the complete answer. Greg Lloyd again shows that often Libertarians argue that "there is a role for the state in improving the conditions in which markets operate and in maintaining certain minimum social standards ... with land being allocated firmly through property markets".[10] They also contend that private solutions to land and property disputes, with possible redress to the courts, are far superior to state regulation. The ASI recommended the setting-up of land use tribunals, replacing official planning controls with private covenants and using private building codes to ensure minimum acceptable construction standards.

It was this criticism from the Right that played some part in the concept of using deregulation – including removing planning restrictions – as a means of attracting industry into Enterprise Zones first announced in 1980. Alongside the financial inducement of exemption from the payment of rates for 10 years, firms were also offered the incentive of being able to avoid land-use and environmental controls imposed through the planning system. As is now quite clear, the rhetoric of deregulation in the EZ's has not been matched by real change. Indeed, the Planning Schemes drawn-up for some of the zones has strengthened, not weakened, environmental control. In the Tayside Enterprise Zone, using landlord approval and Section 50 Agreements, the SDA and the local authorities concerned have applied strict control over the type of development permitted. Even where retailing has been allowed inside Enterprise Zones – as in Swansea, Dudley, Gateshead and others[11] – development has been "hedged round with a list of exclusions,conditions and limitations".[12] Moreover, Roger Tym and Partners reached the conclusion that:

"It is not possible to say with confidence ... on the basis of experience in EZ's that the (planning) scheme approach could necessarily be extended without difficulty to different types of area, where there might be, for instance, a more intricate and mixed pattern of land uses, more at stake environmentally, and consequently, more problems safeguarding third party interests".[13]

As we shall see, this warning was not heeded by government.

Following their election victory in 1983, the Conservative government placed renewed emphasis on the benefits to society – an increasingly private society – of further deregulation, especially the removal of control over business. And it was not coincidental that assistance for industry, especially small-business, was given a new priority, nor that David (later Lord) Young, one-time Chairman of the Manpower Services Commission was given a key co-ordinating position in Cabinet. The policy process began with the publication of two reports that sought to inform and elicit opinion on the problem and on solutions that could be promoted by government. In 1984, a consultation report was released proposing the introduction of "simplified planning zones" – areas, designated by local authorities, where there would be the minimum of planning controls, especially over business.[14] The justification for this experiment in deregulation was supported by a report from the Department of Trade and Industry, "Burdens on Business"[15], that catalogued the costs on business of "complying" with government regulation. Supported by other studies, especially from the CBI, the report argued that planning controls were a burden on small business and that their profitability was hampered by petty controls and restrictions. The speed at which planning decisions were made (or not made) was seen as the key issue, and hence the concept of introducing a form of automatic planning consent in particular areas was an attractive alternative.

These ideas were then translated into a White Paper, entitled "*Lifting the Burden*"[16], which articulated the government's position very clearly:

"The amount of regulation which new and established firms face acts as a brake on enterprise and the wealth and job creating process. Deregulation means two things. First, freeing markets and increasing the opportunities for competition. Second, lifting administrative and legislative burdens which take time, energy and resources from fundamental business activity" (par 1.5).

The White Paper examined deregulation across a range of topics but "Planning and Enterprise" was singled-out for detailed analysis and the most comprehensive recommendations for legislative reform. Amongst a range of detailed proposals, the principle measures included:

(1) establishing simplified planning zones where certain forms of development could take place without the need for planning permission;

(2) introducing changes to the General Development Order specifying types of development that may occur without planning permission; and

(3) reviewing the Use Classes Order in order to extend the use of land and buildings without the need to obtain formal approval.

These and other measures were seen in the context of a general simplification of bureaucratic control over development:

"while deregulatory measures ... are important, the key objective must be to keep the planning process simple – to avoid over-elaboration and unnecessary detail in development plans, and to concentrate on the essentials in dealing with applications ... Deregulation does not imply only the abolition of unnecessary controls. It also means achieving simplicity and efficiency in the way that necessary control is carried out". (par 3.14)

The proposal to introduce simplified planning zones (SPZ) and other modifications to the statutory planning system reached Parliament in April 1986, and were codified in the *Housing and Planning Act* of November the same year. Draft regulations on the detail of SPZ's were circulated in the early summer of 1987, with the expectation that the first zones would be introduced by the end of the year.[17]

The Act gives planning authorities the power to prepare SPZ schemes for all or part of the planning authority's area, to be effective for 10 years after the date of receiving approval from the Secretary of State. The most contentious part of the legislation gives the Secretary power to impose a simplified planning zone on a reluctant authority. He may do this after a member of the public – an individual or company – has sought and been refused SPZ designation by a planning authority. Furthermore, the Secretary of State has extensive call-in powers and may amend SPZ proposals as he sees fit.

These changes effectively shift responsibility for certain types of environmental change on to the developer, the property-owner, the individual; a higher priority is thus given to private (often commercial) interests with a commensurate diminution in collective or community (often welfare) interests. Furthermore, these changes represent a general relaxation of the land and property market and, as Lloyd argues, "(s)implified planning zones are likely to be located according to market pressures, that is, areas which offer the greatest potential return for property developers".[18] This then has implications for urban communities. Specific planning policies are liable to encourage private property development yet at the same time may create the conditions of imposing environmental and social costs on communities least able to respond.

The performance of Enterprize Zones would suggest that SPZ's may not effect as great a degree of deregulation in the planning system as originally intended. Indeed, throughout urban Scotland they may initially have little noticeable spatial impact. But they are likely to become important symbols of change and in the long run will alter attitudes to environmental and land-use control. Simplified planning zones offer evidence that government is committed to achieving a shift in the responsibility for determining urban change and at the same time is prepared to offer further inducements to the private process of urban development. In case there was any doubt as to the direction of urban planning policy, government reaffirmed its belief that deregulation is the key element in achieving urban regeneration:

> "'Simplified planning zones are based on the planning regime successfully pioneered in the Enterprise Zones. They provide planning authorities with a new method of attracting private investment to areas in need of development or regeneration. For developers and landowners, they provide the certainty of knowing what types of development can be carried out in an area. They save the authority and developers the work and expense involved in making and processing individual planning applications".[19]

Public-Private Partnerships

Planning frequently succumbs to the ephemeral attractions of fashion. Be it the physical determinism of the 1950s, the worship of a technological panacea in the Sixties, or the naive support for participation and social planning in the early 1970's, the practice, the profession and the politics of planning has lurched from one paradigm to another, vainly searching for the Holy Grail of the urban solution.[20] And the urban answer of the 1980's appears to be the public-private partnership. But unlike earlier support for mathematical modelling or corporate planning, this latest fashion is likely to be more enduring. Beneath the slogans and the rhetoric of a new approach lies a consistency and coherence that can be traced back to 1947, and even further into the history of public support for market-led property development.[21]

Reaffirmation of support for the public-private partnership dates back to the emergence of inner-city policy during Peter Shore's tenure in the Department of the Environment. The 1977 White Paper – *Policy for the*

Inner Cities[22] – and the *Inner Urban Areas Act* the following year launched an "enhanced" urban policy that concentrates public expenditure on the Inner Area Programmes. Running in parallel, policy focussed on urban economic development supported by a search for initiatives that could stimulate an increased level of activity by the private sector in selected parts of British cities. Labour therefore prepared the way for the public-private partnership; the in-coming Conservative government grasped the model with both hands:

> "In September 1979 the then Secretary of State for the Environment, Michael Heseltine, announced that Partnership and Programme arrangements and the powers available under the Inner Urban Areas Act would be retained, but there would be a greater emphasis on the role of the private sector as an essential factor in securing the long-term revival of inner city areas....."[23]

And by 1987:

> "The Government's aim is to help cities to adjust to change and to restore confidence in their future. There is no single solution, but a mix of well-targeted programmes to stimulate development and investment, widen housing choice, tackle dereliction and foster new opportunities for local businesses and local people.

> None of this can be realised by Government or local authorities acting alone. Cities grew and flourished because of private enterprise. It is private enterprise, backed by well-directed Government action, that will renew them. The emphasis is on co-ordinated effort to involve local communities and the private sector in the task of regeneration, and to build on their initiative."[24]

Despite frequent Ministerial changes at the DoE and the Scottish Office this policy focus was maintained throughout the mid-eighties with numerous amendments to existing programmes and initiatives introduced through guidelines and new legislation.

For example, in 1983 the Property Advisory Group reported to the Department on *"The Climate for Public and Private Partnerships in Property Development"*.[25] They advocated the introduction of policy that measures success in terms of private property development, and urged:

> "local authorities to concentrate much more attention on the benefits to their localities of successful private development ... If they see their tasks in this context, local councils will the more readily identify their role in 'partnership' as helping to create the circumstances in which the private development industry, while still satisfying its own commercial criteria, can contribute to an area's economic, physical

and social improvement". (par 12).

Government listened to this advice.

The 1986 *Housing and Planning Act* is a case in point. Not only did this piece of legislation introduce the simplified planning zone but also brought the Urban Regeneration Grant (URG) to the lexicon of urban policy. This new grant, to be paid from central government direct to private property developers undertaking projects in areas suffering from dereliction, is applicable in Scotland, but the indication is that the Scottish Office will continue to operate the LEG-UP scheme, an existing property subsidy managed by the SDA that already by-passes local government. In a sense, therefore, URG represents the "maturing" of urban policy, returning once more to a focus on property development, enabling direct central government subsidy for urban regeneration, providing financial support for the promotion of public-private partnerships – and not necessarily in the most acutely deprived urban areas.

It is similarly possible to trace the growing importance of the public-private partnership in various sections of housing policy. This co-operative model is now viewed as the solution to a whole range of difficult issues in urban Britain: the rehabilitation of private inner-city stock and promotion of Agency Services; further extension of owner occupation through shared ownership and young-persons schemes; the private financing and construction of housing to satisfy special needs of, for example, the elderly, the young, the mentally ill; newbuild for private rental; and, notably, the physical renewal and subsequent management of difficult-to-let council stock.[26] The concept of incorporating the private sector into Scottish housing policy also lies at the heart of the proposal to create a new single housing agency "Scottish Homes". Hence, URG, the Urban Development Grant (UDG) and LEG- UP, as well as changes to the future planning and management of public housing are all components of the same refocussing of urban planing policy.

If the public-private partnership has long been part of the established planning process, what, if anything, is different in the 1980's? Returning to the theme of transferring responsibility for planning and urban policy, the new partnership not only places a premium on the generation of property development but directly uses the private sector as the vehicle to determine and implement policy. At the UK scale, the activities of the Phoenix Initiative exemplify this redirection of policy. With financial backing from the National Council of Building Material Producers, the Policy Forecasting Unit prepared a manifesto entitled "The Phoenix Partnership" sub-titled "Urban Regeneration for the 21st Century". With evangelical fervour, the Report[27] begins:

"Throwing money into inner cities would not by itself halt the decline. Cities are living organisms. ... Before change can take place there has to be vision of the future in which the local community participates and believes. ... There is an alternative to the present apathy which exists in too many of our towns and cities."

That alternative, according to the Report, is to be found in the USA, in the success stories of Baltimore, Pittsburgh, Oakland and Minneapolis. Not only are these locations cited as exemplars of urban renaissance through the public-private partnership but that the national policy framework operating in the USA – of UDAG, of municipal bonds, of tax increment financing – is a model for the UK. Moreover, drawing on evidence from a US case study, the Report argues that the strength of the public-private partnership lies in the "de-politicisation" of the development process: "(p)ublic agencies are singularly ill-equipped to play a supporting role in the development process. ... their role in comprehensive development projects is counter-productive".[28] The social component of urban planing policy they argue is best left to the "impressive commitment" of British commercial and financial companies.

Since 1985, support for the Phoenix Partnership has been widened to include an array of organisations from the property development sector: the Building Employers Confederation, the British Property Federation, Business in the Community, the Urban Investment Review Group, the Association of British Insurers and the Building Societies Association. Phoenix also received political support from the SDP, when David Owen used the Report in his prescriptions for urban Britain. With the approval of the DoE, the renamed Phoenix Initiative is now actively pursuing public support for the development activities of its members. Hence the concept of the urban partnership has effectively been reversed. Instead of exploring ways in which the private sector could assist the public process of urban regeneration, the Phoenix Initiative seeks the modification of policy – national and local – to subsidise private development. Increasingly it would appear that at least one purpose of urban policy is to support the objectives of the Building Material Producers and the British Property Federation.

PROBE, Partnership Renewal of the Built Environment, is another example of a private initiative that has received the support of government. This organisation, funded by the Halifax and Nationwide Building Societies and the Lovell Group, offers expertise and skills "which can complement and work in harmony with public authorities to help solve local problems"... "can assist by taking a totally independent view of the problems of a specific authority, and attempt to find solutions to those problems within their own policy guidelines"...and..."is therefore able to work with a local authority to present a case that accords with the requirements of the building societies and other financial institutions"....
"PROBE is proving that good business and a social perspective can mix successfully".[29] Neither Phoenix nor PROBE has started work in

Scotland, but both are known to have explored developments north of the border.

Solesbury[30] addresses some of the dilemmas inherent in this policy shift, but suggests that the simple public-private distinction needs to be widened into an examination of how business, government and the not-for-profit sector can implement urban policy. Moreover, he argues that "(t)he concept of partnership implies equality and reciprocity. Both are rarely evident in the arguments...between sectors and interests in urban policy. A whole array of alternative arrangements are being suggested for which a new vocabulary is needed".[31] This, and other assessments, will be further examined in the concluding section, illuminated by comment on how Glasgow has adapted to this new, very different style of planning.

Glasgow's Private Partnership

An initiative in the city of Glasgow demonstrates how a public-private partnership works in practice. With the support of the Scottish Development Agency, Glasgow Action – a public-private partnership based in the city-centre – now occupies a key position in the promotion of the city's economic profile and acts as a catalyst for city-wide property developments. While Glasgow Action may have the ear of the SDA, it maintains that it has no direct access to major public resources, relying instead on generating investment from the private sector. This initiative therefore represents a radical departure from the substance and style of urban planning policy in the 1970's where the SDA played a key role in funding a series of Area Projects throughout Scotland.[32] This policy shift was first introduced by the SDA in 1984, implemented in Glasgow and then extended to the Inverclyde Project, based in Greenock.

Glasgow Action – formed around a group of prominent city businessmen that includes Sir Norman Macfarlane, chairman of the Glasgow-based Macfarlane Group (Clansman) plc before becoming chairman of Guinness – was one of the products of a major study of development potential in the city centre, funded by the SDA and conducted by consultants, McKinsey and Company. They recommended that public action should seek to strengthen Glasgow's role as a major service sector and that such a strategy should be led by a private organisation.[33] Although senior politicians from both Glasgow District and Strathclyde Regional Councils are represented on the board, leadership, control and direction is firmly located in the private sector. Glasgow Action's strategy is unashamedly based on economic boosterism, clearly reflecting the aspirations of the business community in the city.

Glasgow Action – like the Phoenix concept in England – is closely modelled on the US public-private partnership.[34] The glistening hotels, convention centers and Festival Markets in older industrial cities such as

Baltimore, Boston and Detroit proved irresistible to city politicians from Scotland seeking a solution to their urban economic problems. Moreover,the SDA and others promoting a different approach to urban regeneration were influenced in no small way by the attractive combination of private leadership and private investment they found in Minneapolis, Minnesota. The model for Glasgow then, is to combine the strictly commercial goals of the downtown develoment committee with the somewhat more altruistic objectives promoted through the private sponsorship of community develoment. Perhaps most important of all, Glasgow Action came to inherit the American belief that urban regeneration depends first and foremost on creating the correct conditions for private investment. To quote from their first brochure:

"Glasgow Action is the name of a group of leading business people and politicians – and of the visionary plan they have for Glasgow's future, for the Glasgow of the 21st Century. The thinking behind the plan is that the development of a strong business and consumer service industry base will stimulate the regeneration of the city as a whole ...; it aims to recreate Glasgow's entreprenurial spirit".[35]

Based on the McKinsey study, six targets have been selected as the focus of activity: attracting company headquarters or at least HQ activities to the city; developing a range of exportable services; expanding the city's facilities for specialised education; building Glasgow's tourist industry; improving the image of the city and, last, continuing to upgrade the environment. Glasgow Action has been particularly active in its promotion of "events" in the city, including a Jazz Festival and an annual fashion exhibition. It has also claimed some credit for the selection of Glasgow as the "European City of Culture 1990". Its principle role, however, is to select and back "project champions".[36] Most have been property related: a Legal Services Centre, retail schemes, inner-city housing and hotel developments. This began in the Merchant City area to the east of the main retail core, and has been extended into other central city locations such as the Broomielaw and further along the Clyde, linking into the Scottish Exhibition and Conference Centre and the site of the 1988 National Garden Festival.

There is perhaps a danger in reading too much, too early into the activities of Glasgow Action. Nevertheless, the acceptance of this private forum by the city council, its involvement with major development projects in the city centre and the significance given to it by the SDA suggests that Glasgow Action may become a permanent feature in Glasgow's policy community and may lead to similar initiatives in other urban centres. Already studies in Edinburgh and the report "Aberdeen 2000" suggest that planning policy for Scotland's largest cities will be influenced by emerging forms of public-private partnership. And even at the local scale, in difficult economic circumstances, the same model is being pursued. After ten years, the GEAR Project in Glasgow is being replaced by the East End Executive – a "joint private/public sponsored organisation which draws upon the combined resources, commitment and expertise of both sectors, including the active involvement of a range of companies in the area".[37]

The aspirations and activities of Glasgow Action sit quite comfortably alongside the planning framework now operating in the city, particularly in the city-centre. The Central Area Local Plan, various housing policies – not least support for private sector residential conversions and new build construction – and the increasing importance given by the SDA to property development can effectively be considered as a coherent policy framework. Together, they induce private investment into the city, greatly improve the appearance of the city-centre, encourage modest increases in home ownership (especially in the Merchant City), and fuel the symbolic regeneration of the city.

But this is a very different style of planning to that of the 1960's and 1970's. Public policy towards the "renaissance" of the Merchant City is a good example. Building on the "Alternative Strategy" introduced by the Housing Department in 1980, and the City's Planning Department began to relax certain constraints on private development within the city centre. This coincided with the availability of grant aid from the Housing Department and the introduction of LEG-UP support from the SDA. The report on "Private Housing Opportunities within the Merchant City"[38] followed by a series of "developer's briefs" was instrumental in creating a sympathetic policy and the appropriate financial framework for the conversion of empty warehouses and factory units in the Merchant City area. Although the City Centre Local Plan took more than 10 years to reach the stage of approval by the District Council, the city planners were able to effectively ignore this bureaucratic mechanism, instead they promoted development through a combination of selectively releasing parcels of land (the city owned 40 per cent of the vacant sites in the Merchant City), selling or giving away empty property (60 per cent of which was in Council ownership) and packaging available grants and loans for the private sector.

Conclusion

One of the central weaknesses of pursuing a private-led approach to planned urban change is the assumption that the market is willing and capable of financing and implementing the necessary development. Certainly in comparison with the US, and also in contrast to the level of market demand in the south of England, the private sector infrastructure in much of urban Scotland is substantially less well developed. Moreover, the spatial distribution of the private infrastructure that does exist is very uneven. The older inner-city areas and the equally deprived local authority-owned housing estates on the periphery lack local business networks that are essential to any strategy that seeks to invigorate local economic development. In these areas moreover, the opportunity for external private investment has been limited, and the levels of indigeneous poverty mitigate against the accumulation of household savings and the possibility of local capital investment.[39]

Private sector-led regeneration depends on key individuals and companies being present or at least able and willing to come forward. In the city centre, even in Glasgow, it is perfectly possible to identify and utilize a business elite capable and motivated to help implement such a strategy, given the necessary public support. But in the inner-city, such as Glasgow's Woodlands or Dalmarnock, out in the peripheral housing estates of Possil or Easterhouse, and throughout older industrial towns facing the worst consequences of economic decline there is little evidence of this private infrastructure. Yet it is precisely in these areas – communities facing high levels of unemployment, declining job opportunities and falling wages – that government seeks to expand its policy of using private-led urban economic development.

Moreover, the related policy of attracting private resources into such areas to fund physical regeneration of the environment and replace the housing stock assumes a supply of indigenous local capital that can replace public investment. The reality is different. Instead of local investment in the physical environment, privatization policy becomes an attempt to create a middle-class in these areas by importing capital. And the consequences are mixed. In the short-term, this policy transfers the resource costs of improvement from the public to the private sector and alters the tenure balance of the housing stock. But the long-term benefits of this policy – and the substantial public subsidies involved – are selective. Income levels in these areas may not be able to support the whole cost of home-ownership. While mortgage repayments may be little more than the existing rental change, the additional costs of ownership can be crippling. Thus, the creation of a middle-class in the peripheral estate or in refurbished inner-city high-rise blocks results in a displacement of poorer residents hence shifting, not solving urban problems.

The evolution of urban planning policy in Scotland and support for the public-private partnership has shifted attention from the social problems of the inner city to a concern with managing economic adaptation. Having secured support from government for this shift, policy-makers then turned their attention to the commercial opportunities available in the city-centre, pursuing objectives that reflect the needs and aspirations of the business community. This in turn changed the agenda of urban policy: what is good for the business community becomes the goal for the city as a whole. What may be more important for residential neighbourhoods in the city may not figure at all on the urban audit prepared by financiers and industrialists who sit on the new urban action committees. And the long-term implications are even more serious. Evidence from the US demonstrates that where the private sector sees commercial advantage they retain interest and commitment. When they are then asked to support activities that are not part of their agenda they are quick to withdraw, leaving behind a political, organisational and fiscal vacuum. Moreover, an explicit acceptance of commercial objectives can effectively redirect public policies and programmes away from areas most in need, further reducing the resources available to communities that have no part to play in the pursuit of private interests.

Not only has the planning system been weakened by the past decade of public neglect and the reallocation of public expenditure, but the insidious process of deregulation has effectively narrowed the definition of Town and Country Planning. Professional support of the public-private partnership is understandable as practitioners seek a new role in the process of urban change. And in the absence of public resources, private sources become the only available means of realising planning objectives, albeit at the price of accepting the rules laid down by the private development industry.

Herein lies one answer to the questions posed at the beginning of this chapter. A slimmer Town and Country Planning has been retained because it offers advantages to the development industry. Public planning now directly benefits developers: it enables land-use change, provides overall direction and acts as a conduit for the regulated delivery of the necessary infrastructure. But in a climate of private – increasingly personalised – urban change, planning needs to face up to the costs of supporting the public-private partnership.

Robin Boyle, Centre for Planning, University of Strathclyde.

References

1. This chapter is based on presentations made by the author to the Political Studies Association Annual Conference, Aberdeen 1987 and to an International Housing Conference, Glasgow, 1987.

2. see David H McKay and Andrew W Cox *The Politics of Urban Change*, Croom Helm, London, 1979.

3. Andrew W Cox *Adversary Politics and Land*: conflict over land and property policy, Cambridge University Press, Cambridge, 1984.

4. M G Lloyd "'Privatisation, Liberalisation and Simplification of Statutory Land Use Planning In Britain", *Planning Outlook* 28: 1, 1985, pp.46-49.

5. A D Sorenson "Towards a Market Theory of Planning", *The Planner*

69: 3, 1983, pp.78-80.

6. Robert Jones *Town and Country Chaos*, Adam Smith Institute, London, 1982.

7. Adam Smith Institute *Privatisation*, Adam Smith Institute, London, 1985.

8. Jones, 1982, *op cit*, pp.12.

9. Adam Smith Institute, 1985, *op cit*, pp.83.

10. M G Lloyd "Releasing Private Enterprise: Lifting the Burden of Planning", *Strathclyde Papers on Planning* No. 8, University of Strathclyde, 1986.

11. see, Colin J Thomas and Rosemary D F Bromley "The Growth and Functioning of an Unplanned Retail Park : The Swansea Enterprise Zone", *Regional Studies*, 21:4, 1987, pp.287-300.

12. Roger Tym and Partners *Monitoring Enterprise Zones : Year Three Report*, Department of the Environment, London, 1984, pp.139.

13. *ibid*.

14. Department of the Environment *Simplified Planning Zones*, DoE, London, 1984.

15. Department of Trade and Industry *Burdens on Business : Report of a Scrutiny of Administrative and Legislative Requirements*, DTI, London, 1985.

16. Her Majesty's Stationary Office *Lifting the Burden* Cmnd. 9571, HMSO, London, 1985.

17. Scottish Development Department *Housing and Planning Act 1986: Simplified Planning Zones* – draft regulations, SDD, Edinburgh, 1987.

18. Lloyd, 1986, *op.cit*.

19. William Waldegrave "Simplified Planning Zones to Assist Urban Regeneration", *The Planner* 73:8, 1987, pp.6.

20. Alison Ravetz *Remaking Cities: Contradictions of the Recent Urban Environment*, Croom Helm, London, 1980.

21. Peter Ambrose *Whatever Happened to Planning?*, Methuen, London, 1986.

22. Her Majesty's Stationary Office *Policy for the Inner Cities*, Cmnd 6845, HMSO, London, 1977.

23. Department of the Environment *The Urban Programme 1985*, DoE, London, 1986.

24. Department of the Environment/Department of Employment *Action for Cities*: Building on Initiative, DoE/DTI, London, 1987.

25. Department of the Environment *Report by the Property Advisory Group: "The Climate for Public and Private Partnerships in Property Development"*, HMSO, London, 1983.

26. Tim Brindley and Gerry Stoker "Housing Renewal Policy in the 1980's", paper presented to the Political Studies Association, Aberdeen, 1987.

27. Harry Cowie *The Phoenix Partnership: Urban Regeneration for the 21st Century*, National Council of Building Material Producers, London, 1985.

28. *ibid*.

29. PROBE "Partnership Renewal of the Built Environment", publicity material, Swindon, 1987.

30. William Solesbury "The dilemmas of inner city policy", *Public Administration*, 64:4, 1986, pp.389-40.

31. William Solesbury "Urban Policy in the 1980's: The Issues and Arguments", *The Planner* 73:6, 1987, pp.18-22.

32. see, Robin Boyle "Urban Initiatives in Scotland – Measuring the Tartan Factor", *The Planner*, 73:6, 1987, pp.27-30. and, Michael Keating and Robin Boyle *Remaking Urban Scotland*: Strategies for Local Economic Development, Edinburgh University Press, Edinburgh, 1986.

33. McKinsey and Co. *Glasgow's Service Industries – Current Performance : a report to the SDA*, SDA, Glasgow, 1984; and McKinsey and Co. *The Potential of Glasgow City Centre*, SDA, Glasgow, 1985.

34. Timothy Barnekov, Robin Boyle and Daniel Rich *Privatism and*

Urban Policy in Britain and the United States, Oxford University Press, London, forthcoming.

35. Glasgow Action "Glasgow – the need for action" – publicity material, SDA, Glasgow, 1985.

36. Scottish Development Agency *Annual Report 1987: Agency of Challenge*, SDA, Glasgow, 1987.

37. *ibid.*

38. Department of Planning (Glasgow District Council) "Private Housing Opportunities Within the Merchant City", GDC, Glasgow, 1983.

39. Andrew Little "Personal Finances in Deprived Areas", unpublished MSc Thesis, University of Strathclyde, Glasgow, 1987.

POWER POLITICS

Steve Martin

A current important issue in environmental politics is nuclear power; and we in Scotland are as involved as any community in Britain. Scotland has three commercial electricity generating nuclear power stations run by the South of Scotland Electricity Board (SSEB), two at Hunterston in Ayrshire and one at Torness in East Lothian; in addition the UK Atomic Energy Authority (UKAEA) also run the Dounreay fast reactor research establishment in Caithness, and British Nuclear Fuels plc (BNFL) operate the Chapelcross plutonium production reactors near Annan in the south-west. In the past parts of Scotland have been earmarked as nuclear waste disposal sites, proposals which appear to be gaining currency again, and Orkney and Deeside have been suggested as possible uranium mining areas.

This article will discuss the nuclear power debate in Scotland with particular reference to the waste dumping controversy, the Torness nuclear power station campaign and recent proposals for a new fast reactor reprocessing plant at Dounreay. These issues have all generated public resistance, and have contributed to the widely held opposition to nuclear developments in Scotland.

INTRODUCTION

In the nuclear debate there is no issue more likely to anger and activate people than nuclear waste. Local communities perceive proposals for a nuclear 'dump' – or indeed even vague and unsubstantiated rumours of one – as a violation of their environment; they imagine poisoned water, children dying of cancer, and a wholesale destruction of their life-style. Their first impulse is to say "No: we don't want your radioactive refuse dumped in our backyard."

Once the initial emotions have subsided the threat of nuclear dumping serves to make people think. Ironically, the spokespeople from the nuclear industry who come to reassure the locals usually make matters worse. They claim that it is perfectly safe, and that nothing can go wrong. For many local people, this is the first time they have had to consider the nuclear industry. They gradually realise that nuclear dumping is but the final phase in a long process. They begin to question the whole process; they research and learn; they contact bodies for information. They become opposed to the whole

200

nuclear process, from uranium mining, through fuel production and generation, to reprocessing and waste disposal. They also make contacts with other communities facing the same threat. It is no longer "not in my backyard", it has become "nowhere at all".

And what is it these people learn which makes them so against the nuclear industry? It is not so much what they learn as how they learn it. Official spokespeople are seen as trying to hide information. Circuitous routes have to be taken to achieve an overview. Information from the industry often conflicts with that from other agencies, whether they be anti-nuclear groups or independent bodies. Opinion polls show that the public are likely to believe pressure groups before they believe government officials or nuclear industry spokespeople.[1] Therefore, information pieced together from various sources becomes more 'real' than that spoon-fed from government officials.

So what are the issues which make people so opposed to the nuclear power industry? In Scotland we have more than our share of the nuclear industry. The Hunterston nuclear power stations supplied 45% of Scottish electricity needs in 1986/7,[2] and Torness could increase this proportion to over 60%, making Scotland one of the most nuclear-dependent countries in the world. On top of this Scotland also plays host to the Dounreay fast reactor research establishment and the Chapelcross plutonium production reactors, and has been threatened in the past with uranium mining and nuclear waste disposal. And the nuclear dumping threat is about to rear its ugly head again.

TORNESS – THE BEGINNING OF NUCLEAR POLITICS

Nuclear politics began in Scotland in 1974 with a public inquiry into the SSEB's plans to build a nuclear power station at Torness Point near Dunbar in East Lothian. The inquiry lasted nine days in June and July of 1974. The then East Lothian and Berwick County Councils objected on amenity grounds; local farmers, anglers and residents gave evidence against the plant; and Friends of the Earth and the Edinburgh branch of the Conservation Society led a comprehensive case on safety and energy policy. Torness was the first public inquiry at which any comprehensive case was delivered against an application to build a nuclear power station; since then there have been inquiries into nuclear dumping, the Sizewell B nuclear power station, the Windscale Thermal Oxide Reprocessing Plant (THORP), and the Dounreay European Demonstration Reprocessing Plant (EDRP). All of these inquiries lasted much longer than Torness – EDRP and THORP lasted 95 and 100 days respectively, and Sizewell lasted over 2 years.

At the inquiry the SSEB said they needed Torness to fulfil a future electricity demand, and it would be good value for money. Permission was applied for to build up to eight reactors of any of four types. In his report of 12 November 1974 the Reporter, Mr A G Bell, recommended permission be granted.[3] The go ahead was given in February 1975, by William Ross (the then Secretary of State for Scotland), to build a Steam Generating Heavy Water Reactor (SGHWR), which was the reactor design then favoured by the Government.[4]

According to the Scottish Economic Planning Department, if the SSEB wanted to build a different type of reactor it would be up to the Scottish Secretary to decide "what additional processes, if any should be put in hand to assist him to decide"[5] whether consent should be granted. In 1978 the SSEB decided to build an Advanced Gas-cooled Reactor (AGR) at Torness because the SGHWR had fallen out of favour. Bruce Millan, the then Scottish Secretary gave the go ahead on 25 August 1978, without recourse to a further public inquiry.[6]

Wide-scale opposition to the development grew. Thousands of people gathered at demonstrations at the site in 1978 and 1979, and a Systems Three Scotland opinion poll published in 1978 showed 42% of those questioned were against the plant.[7] A poll by the same company published in May 1987 showed 53% would like the project to be abandoned.[8] Over nine years, despite an enormous propaganda effort by the SSEB and the near completion of the plant, more people are against Torness than when the go ahead was given.

The case against Torness is simple: there is no need for further electricity generating capacity in Scotland. At the 1974 inquiry the SSEB based their case on a 6% per annum compound growth in electricity demand until the end of the century; they expected demand to double by 1985.[9] Demand in 1986/7 was 21,032 million units compared with 19,220 million units in 1974 – an increase of only 9.4% over 12 years.[10] On top of which, the newest non-nuclear power station on the grid in Scotland, Inverkip oil-fired plant, "was placed on a care and maintenance regime from 1 April 1987"[11]: that is 2,000MW of plant in 'mothballs' compares with only 1,400MW which Torness represents. The SSEB's forecast was therefore wildly inaccurate, optimistic and deceptive.

Another way of looking at this argument is to consider the total generating capacity available on the grid. On 13 January 1987 there was a 'simultaneous maximum demand' in the SSEB area of 5,111MW; at the time the power stations were able to send out about 7,500 MW, 47% more capacity than required on the coldest day.[12] Furthermore, since the time of the Torness inquiry the number of thermal power stations on the grid in Scotland has been reduced from 13 to 7, but the installed capacity has increased from about 6,000MW to 7,700MW, thereby concentrating power production in a smaller number of larger stations with the consequent requirement for a large overcapacity to cope with plant which is closed for repair etc.[13]

An important consequence of concentrating electricity production in few, large, nuclear stations is the effect on employment. The nature of nuclear power stations means that they must be run continually as 'base load' supply. There are two reasons for this: first, the much larger capital versus fuel cost of a nuclear station requires constant use to recoup investment; and second, safety and efficiency may be compromised if the station is turned on and off to suit demand. Therefore, nuclear stations displace coal and oil stations from their previous role as base load capacity – with Torness and the two Hunterston stations operating to full capacity almost two thirds of the winter peak demand can be met. The employment effect of nuclear generation is twofold: it is a highly capital intensive industry clearly shown by the 9.5% decrease in the number of SSEB employees over the last 10 years (from 13,632 in 1978 to 12,339 in 1987) compared with the 320% increase in fixed assets per employee over the same period (from £49,039 to £207,744)[14]; and the knock-on effect on the coal and supply industries means that workers will be laid off as coal-fired stations and their associated pits have to close – bringing on Torness could mean up to 5,000 redundancies in the Lothians with the closure of Cockenzie and the Monktonhall and Bilston Glen pits.[15]

Torness is planned to have a 30 year operating life, during which time it will generate electricity by 'burning' uranium fuel. Periodically spent fuel rods will be removed from the reactor and 2 or 3 'flasks', each containing 20 spent fuel elements, will be sent to Sellafield by rail "not more than one train in any one week" for reprocessing. "The most probable route would be from Torness via Edinburgh-Carstairs-Carlisle to Sellafield, but other routes are available."[16] There is great concern among local authorities and the public about transport of nuclear materials through their communities, but the regulations covering such transports are Government policy and, as such, are not open for consideration at public inquiries.

At the end of that time the station will have to be decommissioned. No realistic costs have ever been proposed for decommissioning; indeed the procedures and method have not yet been worked out, after 30 years of nuclear power generation in the UK. Estimates for costs vary, but could be as high as the construction cost of the station.[17]

GOVERNMENT NUCLEAR WASTE POLICY CHANGES

Government nuclear waste policy has been subjected to severe criticism, both from environmental groups and from government advisory bodies. The policy reflects political pressures rather than technical, scientific developments. When the nuclear industry began in Britain in the 1950s no thought was apparently given to what would be done with the long-term waste products. Low level solid wastes have been disposed of on site at Sellafield and Dounreay, and a national dump exists at Drigg in Cumbria. More bulky and longer-lived radioactive materials used to be dumped in the north Atlantic Ocean, 500 miles south west of Lands End, but this route was abandoned in 1983 because of industrial action by the National Union of Seamen and international pressure.

Investigations began in the late 1970s to find a site for a deep depository for high level nuclear waste. This material is the concentrated liquid generated by reprocessing spent fuel. It is currently stored in steel-lined tanks at Sellafield. Almost 1,500 cubic metres of this material is awaiting disposal, and it remains radioactive for thousands of years.[18] It is intended that this liquid will be vitrified – turned into glass – but a commercial scale plant has not yet been built.

In February 1980 a public inquiry was held into an application by the UKAEA to carry out test drilling on Mullwharchar hill, in the Galloway Forest Park in south west Scotland, to discover if the rock was suitable for high level waste disposal. A further inquiry, looking at the Cheviots, took place later that year. Following great public opposition to the plans, and a report from their Radioactive Waste Management Advisory Commitee (RWMAC), the Government abandoned the high level waste programme in December 1981, and decided that the waste should be stored for 50 years before disposal.[19] However, Dr Stanley Bowie, a member of RWMAC and one of the country's leading nuclear geologists, resigned the following year because he believed the Government had taken the Committee's advice out of context: they had given in to political pressure.[20] A new disposal policy was announced in 1983: low and intermediate level wastes were to be disposed of on land. A deep anhydrite mine under Billingham in Cleveland, was proposed for intermediate level waste, and Elstow in Bedfordshire was proposed for low level waste.[21] Opposition groups were formed in the threatened areas. Billingham was abandoned in January 1985; one reason given was that ICI (the mine's owners) had refused access to the survey team because of huge pressure from the local community.[22]

Three further sites joined Elstow on the short list for a low level waste dump in February 1986 after a year of procrastination by the Government.[23] To avoid another embarrassing public inquiry, Special Development Orders were granted in Parliament to permit survey engineers access to the sites.[24] Local opposition grew, the sites were blockaded, injunctions were served, objectors were arrested, mistrust developed. On 1 May 1987 the Government abandoned the sites in response to a letter from John Baker, the head of NIREX (the company responsible for nuclear waste management). Mr Baker suggested "a major change of approach." The low level sites should be abandoned and efforts should be concentrated "on the development of options for the deep disposal of intermediate level wastes with the additional intention to piggy-back low level wastes in the same facility."[25] In response to the announcement David Clark MP, Labour's environment spokesperson, described the decision as "a squalid attempt to save themselves from electoral embarrassment" because the areas included constituencies of three Government ministers and unpublished internal opinion polls showed Conservative support waning in the constituencies, and a general election was due.[26]

Which brings the nuclear waste controversy back to Scotland. The merging of the intermediate and low level repository investigations gave cause for alarm to Scottish observers. During late 1987 rumours began to circulate among Scottish island communities. The islands of Jura, Raasay, Orkney and Shetland were the first to be suspected, although many more will follow. There is also suspicion that Mullwharchar may again become a possible site, along with an area of moorland in Caithness called Altnabreac which has already been surveyed as part of the 1970s high level programme. Anti-dumping groups have been formed in many parts of Scotland, and a national umbrella organisation – Scotland Against Nuclear Dumping (SAND) – was formed in June 1987. SAND will help to co-ordinate opposition to local dumping plans, will circulate information between groups, and will liaise with anti-dumping groups in England and Wales.[27]

FAST REACTOR DEVELOPMENT

During this period of nuclear waste policy changes, another nuclear initiative was being developed. In January 1984 Peter Walker, the then Secretary of State for Energy, signed a 'Memorandum of Understanding' with Energy Department representatives of Belgium, France, Italy and West Germany. This agreement marked Britain's entry into the European collaboration on fast reactor development.[28]

The fast reactor is the 'philosopher's stone' of nuclear power enthusiasts; it is a reactor system which is theoretically capable of 'breeding' its own fuel. The core of the fast reactor contains a fuel mixture of plutonium and uranium oxides, and is surrounded by a 'blanket' of 'fertile' uranium which is not itself capable of sustaining a chain reaction but can 'capture' neutrons which escape from the core reaction; this converts the uranium into plutonium which can then be used as a fuel. An essential component of this reactor system is reprocessing – the unburnt plutonium and uranium from the core, and the bred plutonium from the blanket, must be chemically separated and recycled to meet a return on the vast capital investment required for the system. The declared advantage of fast reactors over 'conventional' reactors is their ability to extract 60 times as much energy from a given amount of uranium by this breeding and reprocessing system.[29]

To date more than £2,500 million has been spent on fast reactor research and development in this country, much of the work being carried out at the UKAEA's Dounreay establishment near Thurso in Caithness.[30] The other European countries have also spent large sums on fast reactor research and development. The collaboration grew out of their objective to continue the fast reactor development but reduce the individual countries' financial commitment. Hence, the proposed programme is to include three full sized commercial demonstration reactors, a fuel fabrication plant and a reprocessing plant. However, because of the collaborative nature of the programme each of these plants could be in a different country.

In May 1985 the Government announced their support for an application for outline planning permission by the UKAEA and BNFL to construct the reprocessing plant component of the collaboration – the European Demonstration Reprocessing Plant (EDRP).[31] This plant was to take spent fuel from the three European collaborative reactors, reprocess it to extract the plutonium and uranium, and send those materials to the fuel fabrication plant. No decision has yet been taken as to where the reactors will be built, so until there is fuel to be reprocessed from them the Dounreay EDRP is proposed to reprocess spent fuel from the existing French Superphenix fast reactor, and the German Kalkar plant which is not yet operating. Highly radioactive plutonium spent fuel will therefore have to travel by sea and rail to Dounreay from up to 1,000 miles away; and pure plutonium oxide will be flown back to a fabrication plant whose site has not yet been decided.

THE EDRP PUBLIC INQUIRY

A public inquiry into the EDRP application began at Thurso on 7 April, and ended on 19 November 1986. The terms of reference of the inquiry were seriously questioned before the inquiry opened, and many major objectors decided not to participate because of the restrictions imposed on what evidence could and could not be heard.[32] The form of inquiry – a public local planning inquiry under the Town and Country Planning (Scotland) Act 1972 – meant that matters of Government policy could not be examined;[33] objectors had demanded a Planning Inquiry Commission which could have looked at all aspects of the application and which could have questioned government policy. Also, the Scottish Secretary refused to allow objectors to be financed from the public purse; the UKAEA/BNFL resources far outstripped those of the objectors, and they had access to public funding from the tax payer.

The major issues which arose during the inquiry were: transport plans, plant safety and management, nuclear waste management, radioactive discharges, health effects, economic effects and the threat of proliferation of nuclear weapons materials.

Transportation

The objectors argued Dounreay was the worst possible choice for a European reprocessing plant because of the distances involved in transportation – the greater the distances involved the greater the risk of accident or terrorist intervention. At the same time as dismissing such accusations, the Applicants would not openly discuss security arrangements for the transports, and the Reporter refused to accommodate detailed discussion of the links between nuclear weapons programmes and the fast reactor programme although the Applicants were allowed to say that fast reactor plutonium is not suitable for nuclear warheads.

One aspect of transport which angered objectors was the Applicants refusal to specify which port they intended to use to bring the spent fuel into the country, and from which the spent fuel will be taken by rail to Dounreay. At a pre-inquiry meeting in December 1985 the Applicants agreed to supply a short list of possible ports.[34] At the time of the inquiry this list contained four ports, three on the Cromarty Firth and Scrabster near Dounreay. During the inquiry it transpired that they were still considering other ports, and in his Part 1 report on the inquiry the Reporter discounted the Cromarty Firth options because "there is no indication of any support from the (Cromarty Firth) port authority" narrowing down the options to "the use of Scrabster as the port of entry or the use of a link to the national rail network permitting access to a wider range of ports."[35] In short, the Applicants are now free to choose any port, from the south coast of England to the north of Scotland, through which to bring in the spent fuel even though they were ordered to produce a short list for consideration at the inquiry and the objectors could therefore only present evidence and cross examine on that basis. It means that, if the proposal goes ahead, spent fuel could now travel up the length of the country.

Plant Safety and Management

Safe operation of the proposed plant, and the management's ability to ensure such, was also a subject of criticism. The Applicants claimed the record of BNFL at Sellafield was irrelevant to the application, although there have been over 300 incidents there over the past 30 years, and this application was jointly lodged by the UKAEA and BNFL.[36] BNFL were found guilty and fined £10,000 for four breaches of nuclear safety following discharge of a radioactive slick into the Irish Sea in 1983.[37] Also, an investigation by the NII, following a spate of accidents in early 1986, gave BNFL 12 months to overhaul plant safety or face closure: a month after their report was published another incident, similar to the one which prompted the investigation, occurred – the plant is still operating.[38]

The UKAEA's record at Dounreay is not as unblemished as they claim. In the run up to the EFRP inquiry the UKAEA were forced to release previously restricted minutes of the health and safety sub-committee which revealed a record worse than Sellafield's on a fuel throughput basis – 194 incidents occurred in 1984 alone.[39] Radioactive particles have been discovered on a beach near the plant, and contamination has been detected on buses used by workers which are also used by school children.

Nuclear Waste Management

Throughout the inquiry the Applicants, and Government policy witnesses, asserted that nuclear waste will be disposed of as according to government policy; for low level waste this meant in the shallow repositories proposed for the southern English sites. But, these sites have now been abandoned, so again the objectors found themselves arguing in an area which was subsequently changed. It was accepted by the Applicants that high level nuclear waste resulting from reprocessing overseas spent fuel will be stored at Dounreay pending construction of sites to take it. The logistical difficulties of transporting large volumes of low level wastes back to the country of origin, as is government policy, means that "it may be sensible to substitute an equivalent quantity, in radiological terms, of higher level waste" according to Mr Morphet of the Department of Energy – Britain will have to dispose of large volumes of low level European radioactive wastes as well as store high level wastes pending their return.[40]

Radioactive Discharges

Although the final design of EDRP is not yet certain it is clear it will incorporate the deliberate discharge, of low level liquid and gaseous wastes. These discharges will be "as low as reasonably achievable"; this does not mean that they will be safe. Considerable concern was expressed by the objectors about levels of discharge, and their effects on fishing, farming and tourist industries. Local produce could be 'tainted' in the public mind by the mere threat of discharges.[41]

The annual discharges will be about the same as from the French Cap de la Hague reprocessing plant which is a large commercial plant with a much greater throughput. It is clearly unsatisfactory that a demonstration plant not expected to be operational for over 10 years will discharge almost as much as an existing French commercial scale plant.[42] There are no proposals for the capture of krypton-85 gas, despite a greater amount of its discharge from EDRP than from the existing plant at Dounreay and Mr Justice Parker's (the Inspector at the 1977 Windscale Inquiry) comments that he was "satisfied" that krypton removal plant should be incorporated into THORP.[43]

Health Effects

A special 13 day session was set aside at the inquiry to consider evidence on the health effects of radioactive discharges. The basis of medical evidence from the Thurso area was a study prepared by Dr Heasman, a medical statistician with the Scottish Health Service, which showed an increased incidence of leukaemia in the 0-24 age group within 12.5km of Dounreay between 1979 and 1984.[44] When asked his opinion on the possibility of the increased leukaemia incidence occurring by chance, Dr Heasman replied: "It is more likely to have had some other cause."[45] This led him to conclude that some causal connection must exist, and Dounreay should not be excluded as the cause – a possibility strengthened by similar evidence which exists around Sellafield and other nuclear establishments.

In the conclusions to his Part 1 Report, Mr Bell turned this evidence on its head and declared: "the cluster identified within 2.5km of Dounreay in 1979/84 could have emerged by chance."[46] However, because of the continuing debate over whether or not a link between nuclear plants and leukaemia exist, he accepted that further work, including case studies, needs to be carried out. The unresolved nature of the controversy was highlighted by Andrew Hardie QC, the independent Counsel to the inquiry. He argued that a decision on the application should be postponed until the Committee on the Medical Aspects of Radiation in the Environment (COMARE) had published their major report providing new evidence on the Dounreay leukaemias.[47]

Economic Effects

No study of the socio-economic effects of the EDRP proposal have been made. The Applicants stated that between 600 and 800 jobs will be created during the construction phase, but labour required for operation will be redeployed from the existing workforce. The estimated cost of £200 million, about £250,000 for each temporary job, could be used more productively to create permanent jobs in the local area. For example, the tourist industry has below average costs per now job generated, is largely labour intensive and can expand rapidly.[48] It is important to study the lost opportunity cost of EDRP in terms of what effect the injection of a similar amount of capital into the tourist industry would have. As EDRP is to be funded from the money markets, with the Government underwriting the borrowing, there is no reason why the Government should not be willing to extend the same facility to some other agency. The alternative of funding other energy projects should also be examined, both in terms of return of capital and employment potential. Scotland, and particularly the far north, is well suited for the development of renewable energy technologies. Such an examination would be in the public interest.

It is also important to note that the usual practice in such projects is to import construction labour. A study for Gwynedd County Council, which covers an area containing two nuclear power stations, showed that unemployment actually rose after construction had finished because there was no work for those workers who chose to stay in the area.[49] The Council concluded that major construction schemes help prevent the growth of employment in more stable industries as a result of their impact on local wage levels and labour supply. Short term advantages need to be set against long term disadvantages.

As mentioned above, EDRP is but one component of a European collaborative venture, and until the collaborative reactors are operating it will be reprocessing fuel from the French and German fast reactors. The Applicants stressed the urgency of receiving outline approval for EDRP at this stage to allow them a bargaining counter in negotiations with the French who are also interested in building the plant.[50]

However, Superphenix, their reactor, is currently out of operation because of persistent leaks from its sodium secondary circuit; a problem which the French nuclear industry regard as presenting serious doubts for the future of the fast reactor programme. German involvement in the programme is also in doubt as their Kalkar reactor project is stricken with local political problems. After Chernobyl the Italian commitment to the collaboration wavered significantly when ENEL (their electricity utility) voted to withdraw from Europe's second fast reactor project.[51] Confidential documents leaked from the UKAEA in 1987 indicate that their is little support in this country for the fast reactor, and the countries in the collaboration are unable to agree on how the programme should proceed[52] – the whole venture could still fail; at any rate, the urgency implied by the Applicants is now retreating rapidly into the distance.

Nuclear Weapons Proliferation

As described above, the purpose of EDRP is to separate plutonium from spent fuel for future use as fast reactor fuel, but there is no technical reason why it could not find its way into nuclear warheads. In 1978 General Jean Thiry, an adviser to the managing director of the CEA (the French Atomic Energy Authority), wrote:

> "France will be able to build atomic weapons of all kinds and within every type of range. At relatively low cost, she will be in a position to produce large quantities of such weapons, with fast breeders providing an abundant supply of the plutonium required."[53]

France has refused to sign the Nuclear Non-Proliferation Treaty, although they have said that they will act as though they are a party to it. It is surely inappropriate for France to be bidding for a central role in a nuclear trading system whilst remaining outside the NPT and other multilateral control treaties. Britain should be urging France to sign the NPT, not aiding and abetting their nuclear ambitions.

Past British statements and practices also cast doubt on the uniquely civil role of EDRP. At the Sizewell inquiry every effort was made to convince the public that no plutonium from CEGB reactors had been diverted to military uses.[54] Three years later Lord Marshall, the CEGB Chairman, admitted plutonium had indeed been moved from civil to military stockpiles.[55] The CEGB were prepared to deliberately and grossly mislead a public inquiry on a point which was absolutely crucial to the debate. It is well known that BNFL practice "co-processing" at Sellafield – spent fuel from civil and military reactors is reprocessed together. The definition of civil or military material is also confused. One might reasonably expect that military plutonium comes from a military reactor, and civil plutonium from a civil one; but BNFL define the material by final destination not source.[56] So, if high purity (weapons-grade) plutonium comes from the co-processing it is classified as military material, whereas impure plutonium is called "civil". BNFL's contention that civil plutonium is not used in warheads can only be justified by this sleight of hand.

There is a great grassroots feeling in Scotland against nuclear weapons, so the proposal to build a reprocessing plant capable of providing material for not only British, but also French nuclear weapons, has been greeted with condemnation. There is nothing in the Applicants' case, or official statements, which gives absolute confidence that plutonium will not find its way into nuclear warheads; in fact there is good reason to suspect that it will.

POLITICAL RESPONSES

At the 1987 General Election the great majority of Scottish voters cast their ballot in favour of Parties against further nuclear expansion, but the elected British Government is fully committed to the expansion of the nuclear industry. The abandonment of English dump sites, the expanding reactor programme announced by the Central Electricity Generating Board, and rumours of nuclear dump sites all suggest that Scotland could be earmarked for further nuclear developments.

Scotland has been threatened by the nuclear industry in its many guises over the past decade, and people have learnt to be suspicious. At the time of the Torness inquiry there was little opposition to nuclear power, but as the campaign has developed a small group of protestors has become the majority. This popular opposition to nuclear power now has the support of political parties, trade unions, and local authorities. The Scottish National Party and the Liberals have been against nuclear power for a long time, and were joined by the Labour Party in 1986 following a successful anti-nuclear motion at their Conference.[57] At their 1987 Congress the Scottish TUC passed a motion calling for a moratorium on further nuclear stations,[58] after many years of supporting nuclear power, and the TUC nationally are currently reviewing the whole question of nuclear power.[59] Local authorities are now opposing Torness, Dounreay and proposed nuclear dumping; the Nuclear Free Zones Scotland Steering Committee have spent a lot of time researching and discussing these issues, and they have produced a booklet and other material on the EDRP proposal. There is no doubt that any future nuclear plans will be met with a strong and united opposition.

Steve Martin, Scottish Campaign to Resist the Atomic Menace, Edinburgh.

References

1. Donald McLeod, "Poll majority opposes new N-plants", *Scotsman*, 25.1.1987.

2. SSEB, *Report & Accounts 1986/87*, SSEB, Glasgow, 1987, p.15.

3. A G Bell, *Report into the inquiry into an application for consent under Section 2 of the Electric Lighting Act 1909 to the construction of a nuclear power station at Torness, East Lothian*, Edinburgh, 1974, p.67, para.1.

4. SCRAM, *Torness Nuclear power Station – From Folly to Fiasco*, Edinburgh, 1983, p.3.

5. Letter from Scottish Economic Planning Department to SCRAM, 21 September 1977.

6. Margaret Harker 'Millan presses Torness button', in *Evening News*, 25.8.1978.

7. *Attitudes to Torness nuclear power station*, System Three Scotland, 4.12.1978.

8. *Report of a survey on nuclear power*, System Three Scotland, 29.5.1987.

9. *op.cit.*, (3), p.6, para.14-16.

10. SSEB, *Report & Accounts 1974/75*, Glasgow, 1975, p.48, compared with SSEB, *Statistical Supplement & Tariffs 1986/87*, Glasgow, 1987, p.23.

11. SSEB, *Statistical Supplement & Tariffs 1986/87*, Glasgow, 1987, p.25.

12. *ibid.*, p.22 and p.25.

13. *op.cit.*, (10), p.49 compared with p.25.

14. *ibid.*, p.69 compared with p.24.

15. John Home Robertson MP, *Hansard*, 1.2.1982, col.81-84.

16. G W Maycock, *Appeal by SSEB against a refusal to permit the erection of a railhead facility at Skateraw, Dunbar*, Edinburgh, 1985, para.4.34- 4.35.

17. R Bullock, *Decommissioning of the Maine Yankee nuclear power plant, Maine, USA*, Environmental Action Foundation, Washington, 1984, p.66.

18. Environment Committee First Report, Session 1985/86, *Radioactive Waste, vol.1*, HMSO, London, 1986, Table 5, p.xxv.

19. P Hetherington, "Government halts nuclear waste tests", *Guardian*, 17.12.1981.

20. "Scientist revives row over nuclear waste", *Glasgow Herald*, 1.3.1982.

21. David Fairhall, "Two sites on short list for N-waste dumps", *Guardian*, 25.10.1983.

22. Maurice Samuelson, "Billingham rejected as nuclear waste dump", *Financial Times*, 25.1.1985.

23. Kevin Brown, "Tories in angry protests over N-waste sites", *Financial Times*, 26.2.1986.

24. John Carvell, "Nine rebels defy Government over N-waste sites", *Guardian*, 23.5.1986.

25. Letter from John Baker (NIREX) to Nicholas Ridley MP (Environment Secretary), 30.4.1987.

26. Alan Travis and John Ardill, "Ridley dumps N-waste sites", *Guardian*, 2.5.1987.

27. "Scotland unites against nuclear dumping", press release from Scotland Against Nuclear Dumping (SAND), 22.6.1987.

28. "Peter Walker signs a European Agreement for the fast reactor", Department of Energy press release, 10.1.1984.

29. UKAEA, *Annual Report 1986/87: special Dounreay supplement*, London, 1987, p.2.

30. Nuclear Free Zones Scotland, *Dounreay Expansion: the case against*, Glasgow, 1987, p.3.

31. Martin Dowle, "Dounreay picked for Euro waste plant", *Scotsman*, 25.5.1985.

32. David Fairhall, "Dounreay protestors in boycott", *Guardian*, 4.4.1986.

33. Letter from A G Bell to objectors to EDRP application, 9.1.1986, para.2.

34. *Transcript of pre-inquiry meeting held into the EDRP application*, 12.12.1985, p.98E.

35. A G Bell, *Report of Dounreay EDRP public local inquiry, part 1 draft*, Edinburgh, 1987, p.135, para.7.76(17).

36. *op.cit.*, (30), p.9.

37. Raymond Hughes, "BNFL fined £10,000 over Sellafield N-waste leaks", *Financial Times*, 24.11.1985.

38. *op.cit.*, (30), p.10.

39. "Dounreay hit by 194 radiation incidents", *Glasgow Hearld*, 3.2.1986.

40. *Transcript of EDRP inquiry*, 1986, day 1, p.25F.

41. *op.cit.*, (30), p.15.

42. *ibid*.

43. Hon. Justice Parker, *Windscale inquiry report, vol.1*, London, 1978, p.49, para.10.52.

44. M A Heasman *et al*, "Childhood leukaemia in northern Scotland", *The Lancet*, 1.2.1986, p.266.

45. *op.cit.* (40), day 69, p.17A.

46. *op.cit.* (35), p.197, para.10.84(10).

47. *op.cit.* (40), day 69, p.3A.

48. *op.cit.* (30), p.21.

49. Gwynedd County Council, *The impact of a power station on Gwynedd*, 1976, para.2.5.8.

50. UKAEA/BNFL, *Supplementary information relating to the outline planning application for a European Demonstration Fast Reactor Fuel Reprocessing Plant at Dounreay, Caithness*, London, May 1985, para.1.2.

51. *op.cit.* (30), p.22.8.

52. Confidential memorandum from J E Sanders (UKAEA fast reactor liaison officer) to Dr J E R Holmes (Director, UKAEA Winfrith), 9.4.1986.

53. *op.cit.* (30), p.24.

54. Rob Edwards, *Nuclear Power, Nuclear Weapons – the deadly connection*, CND Publications, London, 1985, pp.15-20.

55. Rob Edwards, "Official: CEGB plutonium did go to the Military", *New Statesman*, 21.3.1986, p.6.

56. Fred Pearce, "More clues in the plutonium puzzle", *New Scientist*, 19.9.1985, p.19.

57. Peter Riddell, "Labour votes to phase out N-plants", *Financial Times*, 2.10.1986.

58. "Power unions bypass differences", *Guardian*, 23.4.1987.

59. Nuclear Energy Review Body, *Review of Nuclear Energy – progress report*, TUC, 1987.

THE NORTH SEA: POLITICS AND THE ENVIRONMENT

Jonathan Side

In November 1987 the second International Conference on the Protection of the North Sea was held in London. The first ministerial conference, at least partly a response to growing pressure from environmental groups (and their electoral successes on the continent) was held in Bremen in 1984 and led to a declaration of general principals on the protection of the North Sea environment, which was supplemented by a set of specific actions and initiatives to be pursued by North Sea governments.

Much effort has now been directed towards assessments of the health of this sea area and 1987 provided a focus for a variety of publications and conferences to make pronouncements which could be considered by the ministers at their November meeting. This paper briefly reviews this unique international initiative and comments on some of the contributions to the discussion of the health of the North Sea.

Against this background the paper examines three environmental protection measures adopted unilaterally by the UK in 1987 which have a particular significance to Scotland and Scottish industry. The first is an account of the introduction of a ban on the retail sale (and hence general use) of anti-fouling paints containing tributyl tin (TBT) compounds. This was originally attempted in 1985 but thwarted by the aggressive response of paint manufacturers, the Paintmakers' Association and yachting interests. The second example examines the decision by the Government to ban the use of diesel base drilling muds on the UK Continental Shelf. The discharge of drill cuttings contaminated by oil base drilling muds continues to be a major source of oil entering the North Sea from offshore oil and gas operations. While this has received relatively little media attention the problems associated with the removal of the giant North Sea structures once their oil and gas producing lifetimes are at an end has been constantly in the news. The final example chosen is that of the Petroleum Act 1987 which establishes the legislative framework for controls over the decommissioning, dismantling and removal of oil and gas installations on the UK Continental Shelf.

Each of these examples illustrates different approaches and responses to environmental protection measures and provides some insights into the part played by vested interests in influencing specific environmental protection policies and public perceptions of the seriousness of particular pollutants.

THE NORTH SEA CONFERENCE

The 1984 North Sea Conference emerged as the favoured option for a new international initiative in response to growing criticisms of the effectiveness of the multifarious collection of international conventions and agreements governing North Sea environmental protection. The Governments bordering this sea area organised and participated in the Conference, not as a response to a particular pollution incident, or identifiable set of circumstances which serve to show the inadequacy of existing environmental controls – factors which characterised much of the earlier international marine pollution control initiatives (see Table 1) – but rather as a response to a growing and more evenly spread public and pressure group concern over numerous aspects of marine pollution and the general health of the marine environment. The nature of the shift in public perceptions is difficult to determine in a more precise manner, but has manifest itself in a variety of ways, perhaps most evidently in West Germany with the electoral successes of the green movement. The German Government was in many ways instrumental in the establishment of the first North Sea Conference.

In 1980 the German Council of Environmental Advisors published a report entitled "Umweltprobleme der Nordsee".[1] This presented an ecological inventory of the North Sea that attempted to identify pollutant sources and relate these to observed effects in the marine environment. One of the conclusions of the report suggested that while no convincing evidence of pollutant effects in the central and northern North Sea exists, there was a growing body of scientific evidence that many estuarine and coastal areas were manifesting signs of pollution. The Wadden Sea was an area of particular concern. In its deliberations the Council stressed the concept of "Vorsorgepricip" or principle of precautionary action as an essential element of marine environmental protection policy. The following year a German MEP presented a draft resolution to the European Parliament calling for a conference to discuss the pollution problems of the North Sea, and to draft a comprehensive convention for the protection of the aquatic environment of this sea area.[2]

Much of the subsequent discussion in the European Parliament focussed on the option of replacing the existing international conventions and agreements (and by implication their associated institutions) with a single convention which would provide a more effective legal regime. This proposition, which has a great deal of logic in its approach, and other advantages to commend it but also many drawbacks, was finally put in abeyance by the action of the West German Government which announced on 3 June 1982 that it would organise an international ministerial conference on the protection of the North Sea. The German Government's position was clear:

"The aim of the conference will not consist in the preparation and adoption of yet another convention or the establishment of new bodies. By means of political decisions, clear guidelines should be laid down for the practical solution of problems in areas where there are no sufficient decisions to date."

"In as far as omissions are found to exist in international conventions, it should be classified whether regulatory action is needed and the competent bodies should be requested to take action accordingly".[3]

The First North Sea Conference duly assembled in Bremen, and between 31 October and 1 November 1984 the Environmental Ministers of the North Sea states and representative of the Commission of the European Communities (see Table 2) reached agreement on a Declaration of General Principles and an extensive series of undertakings with regard to the pursuance of new measures for the protection of the North Sea and to strengthening and increasing the effectiveness of existing controls.

The final conference document[4] embodying the conclusions, agreements and declaration of the ministerial conference is structured in ten parts most of which itemise specific actions and undertakings made by the ministers for the improved protection of the North Sea:

A.   Introductory preamble

B.   General declaration

C.   Rivers and coastal waters – black and grey lists

D.   Pollution of the North Sea through the atmosphere

E.   Prevention of marine pollution due to the operation of ships

F.   Waste disposal at sea

G.   Airborne surveillance of the North Sea

H.   Measures to prevent or reduce oil pollution from offshore platforms

I.   Research and development on environmentally sound technologies, products and substitutes

J.   Further development of environmental monitoring programmes

The specific measures envisaged under each of these categories, which are often supplemented by supporting Annexes in the declaration, have been reviewed in detail[5], and only the Declaration of General Principles is reproduced here in Table 3. The Declaration embodies several striking and indicative features. Firstly it is a unique regional initiative and is probably the most systematic and detailed international undertaking on marine environmental protection ever entered into. Secondly the ministers of the North Sea states make in it a commitment to work within the existing international legal framework and associated institutions where necessary strengthening these and the links between them. Although not accepting the precautionary principle the ministers recognise that the marine environment is best protected against pollution by "timely preventive measures". Finally, as with several agreements struck within the relevant international fora the wording of a number of individual undertakings is a compromise designed to be acceptable to all parties though not necessarily reflecting the precise view of any.

Throughout 1987 the planned second meeting of the North Sea Conference (held in London in November 1987) provided a focus for the activities of environmental pressure groups and scientific meetings which digested and analysed data on the health of the North Sea. Much disagreement emerged.

Greenpeace issued an unusually glossy brochure summarising the pollution of the North Sea entitled "The Tide Must Turn". Not surprisingly the most competent assessments made in its 39 pages are for those instances where this organisation has had a history of campaigning on specific issues. Other parts are notably thin and lacking in the scientific understanding which has previously characterised much of this organisation's work. Greenpeace, or at least the authors of "The Tide Must Turn", see little hope in the 1984 Declaration of the North Sea Conference or the progress made since then:

> "Examination of the declaration and its many statements of intent reveals a string of broken promises and a complete lack of action to make any substantial moves towards staving off the threat that ecological changes in the North Sea will become irreversible".[6]

The major weakness, however, in "The Tide Must Turn" is that on some matters (most notably where there is little history of Greenpeace activity) science is put to one side in favour of what many may see as an alarmist misrepresentation of the effects of pollution:

> "Almost 50% of all Dabs caught in the southern part of the North Sea in 1984 were diseased".[7]

The principal focus for the scientific community was provided by the

Water Research Council's (WRc) Conference on Environmental Protection of the North Sea (24-27 March 1987).[8] The objectives of the conference were to provide, in so far as present knowledge allowed, a definitive appraisal of potential pollutants in the North Sea and an opportunity for discussion among scientists, industrialists, environmentalists and the regulatory agencies of North Sea governments. Apart from some notable examples of disagreement[9] the conference was generally in accord on the assessment of levels of pollutants entering the North Sea and on attributable biological effects. The Summary Report of the Conference, however, suggests numerous areas where there are deficiencies in scientific knowledge and highlights areas where further research work and in particular international collaboration is required. It is neither alarmist nor particularly reassuring, suggesting with polite understatement that, for example, "there are important differences in interpretation of present evidence on the incidence of fish diseases and possible causes".

An interesting contribution to the discussions preceding the 1987 ministerial conference was provided by the Report of the North Sea Forum[10], an *ad hoc* group comprising interested individuals from conservation bodies, environmental pressure groups and research scientists. The report is a collection of papers each of which largely reflect the emphasis of the author concerned but which have been collated in such a manner as to provide a holistic and thought provoking review of the health of the North Sea. To the non-specialist it is a much more accessible document than the several volumes containing the papers given at the WRc conference and contains a constructive attempt at an overview of the health of the North Sea. It is not by any means comprehensive and while it notes for example the serious state of depletion of the several North Sea fish stocks there is no discussion of the recent records on the incidence of diseased flatfish.

This year will no doubt provide ample opportunity for criticisms of the lack of progress made at the second North Sea Conference and during the intervening years since the first conference. If the criteria, however, is that in these years North Sea states have achieved more than in any comparable time period in the last decade then the conference initiative will almost certainly be judged successful. If, however, one has the view that the clock stands at five minutes to midnight for the survival of the North Sea then whatever progress has been made it will not have been sufficient.

The North Sea Conference and UK preparations to host it was only one item on the 1987 agenda of UK environmental protection policy. The following three examples of other measures adopted in 1987 have been selected partly because they have a special relevance to Scottish industry, partly because environmental pressure groups were not particularly involved in drawing attention to them, but also because of the differences in approach and response to environmental protection measures that they represent.

TBT – SOME BAD RELATIONS

The introduction of UK controls over the use on yachts and other small pleasure craft of anti-fouling paints containing tributyl tin (TBT) compounds followed many months of intense opposition from the manufacturers of marine anti-fouling paints and yachting enthusiasts. For several years the scientific evidence had been accumulating and suggested that these paints not only prevented the growth of marine fouling organisms on the hulls of treated vessels but also, in areas of intense boating activity, were responsible for damaging effects observed on a variety of marine organisms.

Scientific studies on the Pacific Oyster in Arcachon Bay in France had in the early 1980's begun to demonstrate a relationship between the occurrence of marinas and pleasure craft moorings and shell deformations in nearby commercial oyster fisheries.[11] It was shown that this could be reversed by transplanting affected oysters to areas devoid of boating activity, and that the spatfall (of juvenile oysters) was low and sometimes failed in areas where pleasure craft activity was high. Concerned at the correlation between these observed effects and the increasing use of TBT based anti-fouling paints on such vessels the French Government banned the use of organotin compounds in anti-fouling paints on vessels under 25 metres in length in January 1982. By 1985 scientific studies were demonstrating a substantial improvement in the state of the oyster fisheries in Arcachon Bay. A series of scientific studies in the UK were also suggesting that a variety of observed effects on the growth of marine organisms could be attributed to the presence of organotin compounds.[12]

The UK Government had been considering this evidence for some time and in 1985 proposed to adopt regulations under Section 100 of the Control of Pollution Act 1974 to prohibit the retail sale of any paint containing more than a trace booster of organotin compounds.[13] This proposal generated a dramatic response. Within months of the Consultation Paper being issued the Environment Minister, William Waldegrave, had received over 1000 objections accompanied by protestations in the yachting press. The scientific journal *Marine Pollution Bulletin* reported:

"The Paintmakers' Association (PMA) has launched a campaign opposing proposed regulations....which are designed to prohibit the use of anti-fouling paints containing organotin compounds on yachts and other small craft. In a leafleting campaign aimed at yachtsmen the PMA claim that the case against the use of tributyltin oxide as an anti-fouling agent in paint is unproven and that the proposed regulations would put anti-fouling technology back 15 years."[14]

The players and their roles were easily identifiable but the full extent of this drama's plot was only revealed some months later, in the unlikely guise of an article in British Rail's commuter magazine InterCity. International Paint, one of the PMA's leading members, had appointed a specialist firm of parliamentary lobbyists to take up the campaign against the proposed regulations:

"The job was one which called for a deft touch. The problem was that the company (International Paint) was marketing an anti-fouling paint for yachts which, its critics maintained, was not only poisoning the sea but killing off the oysters. When Good Relations was appointed, International Paint had few friends and lots of enemies – notably the oyster fishermen and the Ministry of Agriculture and Fisheries, which had persuaded the Department of the Environment to ban the product.

"The first thing the lobbyists did was to see if the scientific evidence held water, so to speak. On discovering that the case against its client was not overwhelming, Good Relations moved to the second stage. More than 1000 yachtsmen were invited to write to the Department of the Environment, the yachting press was mobilised and the support of the Royal Yachting Association was obtained."[15]

Good Relations has top political contacts: its chief executive is Paul Tyler former MP and Chairman of the Liberal Party. Among those on its payroll were Peter Archer MP, David Atkinson MP, Sir Anthony Grant MP, and Michael Mates MP. Good Relations had regarded this campaign as one of their most recent successes. The then Environment Minister, William Waldegrave denounced their actions as one of the worst cases of single issue lobbying he had ever encountered. In response Peter Luff – Deputy Managing Director of Good Relations and former political advisor to both Edward Heath and Peter Walker – remarked "when he said that I knew we were getting somewhere".

The Government's resolve weakened and in 1985 a compromise package was adopted.[16] This was amended in January 1987 to reflect advances in paint technology but shortly afterwards new scientific evidence prompted a rapid reassessment. Firstly there was concern over the possible contamination of Scottish salmon farmed in sea cages whose net panels had been treated with certain anti-fouling paints; some fish farmers had not adhered to a voluntary ban suggested in 1986. The closure of one Scottish oyster hatchery and severe problems encountered by another seemed only attributable to the presence of TBT. Finally evidence emerged that the UK's environmental quality target was not only being greatly exceeded in some estuaries and in areas such as the Norfolk Broads but was probably an order of magnitude too high to protect most aquatic organisms. The ban was finally introduced in May 1987[17]; scientific studies published since then have so far consistently reinforced the contention that TBT is capable of causing environmental damage at levels far below those reported for any previously studied marine pollutant.[18]

DIESEL OIL-BASE DRILLING MUDS BANNED

At the beginning of offshore oil and gas development several potential sources of pollution from offshore installations had been recognised and examined by UK regulatory agencies. In addition to the risk of spillage two routine sources of oil contaminated discharge were identified. These comprised the oily water discharges of production water (water recovered from the oil producing wells, separated from the oil on the platform, but discharged with an inevitable trace contamination of oil) and displacement water (water used in the large oil storage cells on some North Sea platforms which is displaced by the stored oil).

The controls introduced over these routine discharges of oily waters from offshore installations were anticipatory. In advance of the majority of discharges occurring the the North Sea the pollutant potential of these discharges had been examined and a uniform emission standard of 40 parts per million oil in water had been adopted.[19] This reflected the potential reduction in oil content achievable by the available treatment technologies. At this time the offshore industry was using water based drilling muds as lubricating fluids during drilling operations, and the discharge of these to the sea in conjunction with the drilled (rock) cuttings obtained from the drilling of wells was considered acceptable by North Sea governments. By the early 1980's, however, the industry began to switch from water based drilling muds to oil based alternatives (initially those based on diesel oil). The corresponding discharge of oil associated with the disposal of the contaminated drilled cuttings, the increase in which is shown in Table 4, was not subject to any statutory controls in the UK.[20] There was something of a legislative gap and, by the time it was realised that substantial amounts of oil were being discharged in this way, field survey data had already begun to demonstrate a clear impact on the seabed environment at sites close to some of the platforms making these discharges.[21] Thereafter any regulatory approach was inevitably reactive.

Following the findings of a joint government/industry working group the UK government simply amended existing legislation so as to prohibit such discharges.[22] Exemptions from this prohibition were then granted to individual platform operators subject to certain specified conditions. Even this attempt at introducing controls suffered an administrative setback and a delay of one year in introducing the amendment occurred.[23]

The conditions stipulated when granting an exemption from this prohibition did not seek, however, to minimise the amounts of oil entering the North Sea from this source. Instead the controls distinguished between so called "low toxicity" oil based drilling muds and their more toxic (diesel) counterparts and required special treatment facilities where the latter were used in production drilling operations. As Table 4 demonstrates the offshore industry switched rapidly to the less toxic option and the eventual ban[24] on the use of diesel based muds on 1 May 1987 caused little or no difficulties to offshore operators.

When compared to the pollution damage associated with the use of TBT paint products the environmental significance of the piles of oil contaminated drill cuttings surrounding many North Sea installations is of only minor significance, and no doubt most people are oblivious of their existence. The principal contamination occurs largely within the 500m safety zones surrounding offshore installations, threatens no-ones livelihood or health, and as these residues are subject to natural degradation these areas will recover in comparatively short biological timescales. The really important questions only arise if one considers the possibility that this might not have been the case.

THE ABANDONMENT OF OFFSHORE INSTALLATIONS

The North Sea oil and gas industry will continue to flourish for many decades to come but already the end of the lifetimes of a few producing oil and gas fields is in sight. The Geneva Convention on the Continental Shelf 1958, the international convention which provided coastal states with the right to explore and exploit hydrocarbon deposits beneath the seabed of their continental shelf and place installations offshore for this purpose, requires:

"Due notice must be given of the construction of any such installations, and permanent means for giving warning of their presence must be maintained. Any installations which are abandoned or disused must be entirely removed."[25]

and there was a general assumption, indeed as far as the fishing industry was concerned a promise[26], that at the time of decommissioning offshore installations the structures would be entirely removed. Although only certain of its provisions can be considered to have become international law the text of the United Nations Convention on the Law of the Sea 1982 embodies a less stringent requirement for platform removal:

".....Any installations or structures which are abandoned or disused shall be removed to ensure safety of navigation, taking into account any generally accepted international standards established in this regard by the competent international organisation. Such removal shall also have due regard to fishing, the protection of the marine environment and the rights and duties of other States. Appropriate publicity shall be given to the depth, position and dimensions of any installations or structures not entirely removed."[27]

The International Maritime Organization has acknowledged that it is the competent international authority referred to and in 1987 produced a set of Preliminary Draft Guidelines and Standards for the Removal of Offshore Installations and Structures in the Exclusive Economic Zone and on the Continental Shelf. The Preliminary Draft Standards propose two situations where the coastal state may decide that an offshore installation need not be entirely removed. These cases would occur, firstly, where an installation or part of it may serve a genuine new purpose if permitted to remain wholly or partially in place on the seabed (such as an artificial fishing reef), or can be left there without causing unjustifiable interference with other users of the sea; or, secondly, where entire removal is not technically feasible or would involve extreme cost or an unacceptable risk to personnel or the marine environment even though no genuine new purpose can be identified.[28]

The fishing industry argues, however, that until the LOS Convention enters into force, or these provisions are accepted as customary international law, coastal states which are party to the Geneva Convention must adhere to the requirement for complete removal of offshore installations.[29]

In April 1987 the Petroleum Act was enacted. This is a general enabling Act which establishes a broad legal framework for the abandonment of offshore installations on the UK Continental Shelf. The Act provides the Secretary of State with the power to require offshore operators to provide abandonment programmes for specific fields. These are to include an assessment of the cost of work to be carried out and any continuing maintenance that may be necessary where either an offshore installation or a pipeline is not completely removed. The abandonment of an offshore installation is thus governed in the first instance by the approval (or rejection) of the plan submitted by the offshore operator concerned. The Act, however, provides little indication of the specific measures that may be required to protect the marine environment and safeguard fishing interests. The Act enables the Secretary of State to prescribe regulations which may establish standards for removal and safety requirements for the dismantling, removal and disposal of offshore installations. However, while there is nothing in the Act that would prevent future governments from requiring complete removal the provisions clearly envisage that some installations or parts of them may be allowed to remain. Indeed as a basis for further discussions with the offshore industry, maritime and fishing interests the Government has suggested that one approach might be the establishment of stipulated clearance depths.[30]

The fishing industry continues to pursue its claim that its vessels have suffered a loss of access as a result of offshore oil and gas development. In 1987 the Scottish Fishermens' Federation, in conjunction with the National Federation of Fishermens' Organisations commissioned an update of an earlier study which attempted to evaluate the financial loss incurred by the fishing industry as a result of offshore oil and gas operations. The methodology of these studies, as even their authors would acknowledge, is far from satisfactory and depends on translating a per cent loss of geographical access into a corresponding proportional loss of catch. Fishing is not permitted in the 500m safety zones which now surround nearly every North Sea installation, and additionally fishermen claim a *de facto* loss of access around pipeline routes where there may be risks of damage to their fishing gear. The 1987 updated report concluded that "the fishing industry has a strong case for claiming compensation to the value of £446,600 for lost catches in 1986. This figure will increase as more platforms and pipelines are installed in the North Sea and is forecast to rise to about £600,000 per year by 1995."[31]

The UK Government has never accepted such a claim, but clearly in the context of abandonment, were it envisaged that some structures or their residues may be allowed to remain on the seabed, such a claim is no longer for a *temporary* loss of access. Both the UK Government and the offshore industry, however, have a common interest in minimising the costs of abandonment of North Sea installations. The estimated costs associated with various removal options are given in Table 5. Depending on the circumstances, however, up to 70% or more of the maximum cost of £6 thousand million will be met by the government in the form of corporation and petroleum revenue tax relief. Against the background of costs of this scale the cash value of the fishing industry's claim might be considered trivial.

Even were an acceptable financial arrangement to be struck between the parties involved one major concern of the fishing industry will need to be carefully addressed. It is essential that any residues allowed to remain in the North Sea do not degrade, break up or spread around the seabed. There is a very significant difference between such a potential obstacle course and a discrete pile of accurately charted debris. In the short term at least there is also some concern that if fishing is to be permitted again in areas presently designated 500m safety zones that there is no contaminatiion of fishing gear and nets as a result of the residue of oily drill cuttings remaining on the seabed.

DISCUSSION

At first sight it might seem that the approach to the development of legislation on the abandonment of offshore installations has been a precautionary one. Enabling legislation has been enacted well in advance of the decommissioning of the first structures (even though the standards necessary to ensure the protection of the marine environment and safeguard the interests of other users of the sea may be some time in the drafting). Such a view, however, would be misleading. Earlier drafts of the Law of the Sea Convention had reiterated the requirement of the Geneva Convention for complete removal. It was the intervention of the UK delegation at the tenth session of UNCLOS III which resulted in the rewording of this provision and which led to the acceptance of the possibility of partial removal.

This was certainly anticipatory but was driven not by a desire for environmental protection or the safeguarding of other maritime interests but rather a realisation of the costs involved in complete removal. If the latter had remained the norm the environment and the interests of other users of the sea, in particular the fishing industry, would, arguably have been better served – but at what would have been an extraordinary cost to the taxpayer.

In contrast to the development of environmental protection measures for the control of discharges of oily waters from offshore installations the introduction of controls over the use and associated discharge of oil based drilling muds was neither anticipatory nor a "timely preventive measure". Although the present environmental effects of this source of pollution are only minor when contrasted against pollutants such as TBT, there must still be some doubt as to the adequacy of the regulatory approach which permitted around some offshore installations:

1. Within a zone of 500m, "major deleterious biological effects" and contamination such that "seabed recovery in this zone is likely to be a very long process";

2. Within a zone of up to 2000m, "subtle biological effects" with a more rapid recovery on cessation of drilling and elevated hydrocarbon levels being detected beyond the area of biological effects.[32]

without any statutory mechanism being in existence to control the source of the contaminatioin. The switch by the offshore industry to the use of oil based muds could not have been predicted when the first examination of the potential environmental effects of offshore oil and gas operations was made, but industries frequently make such changes and the regulatory approach should allow for such occurrences.

In the example of the ban on anti-fouling paints containing TBT there are some important lessons to be learned. Firstly the use of these paints was fairly ubiquitous – there were no obvious centres of discharge associated with the manufacturers on which environmental pressure groups could focus activities. But the lack of environmental pressure group activity meant that even some environmentally conscious yachting enthusiasts continued to use anti-fouling paints containing organotin and opposed the ban. Science was slow in producing incontrovertible evidence, but then this is very much in the nature of scientific research which is usually led by a desire to improve the understanding of environmental processes rather than a need to produce water-tight evidence in support of a particular case. Furthermore scientists are not generally used to defending their work against aggressive campaigns led by vested industrial interests. It seems easy to criticise the government for lessening its resolve and accepting a compromise, but it is difficult for any minister to ignore such concerted opposition to proposed regulations. The Government finally got the controls it needed but if environmentalists, scientists and those involved in fish farming had been more vocal in 1985 this might have tipped the balance sooner.

If it is possible to identify any trend then it would seem to be one of polarisation. Scientists are possibly becoming more cautious, at least some industries more aggressive in the defence of their products and practices, environmental pressure groups more alarmist, with some pronouncing a threat to the survival of the North Sea on almost every environmental issue – perhaps at the expense of a focus on specific issues where they can most importantly play a valuable role. That focus, however, is still evident on matters concerning the nuclear industry in Scotland as the following paper testifies.

Jonathan Side, Institute of Offshore Engineering, Heriot-Watt University.

References

1. Council of Environmental Advisors (Der Rat von Sachverstandigen fur Umweltfragen), 'Umweltprobleme der Nordsee'. Verlaf, W Kohlhammer, Stuttgart and Mainz, 1980.

2. European Parliament Document 1-298/81, 16 June 1981.

3. Announcement by the German Minister of the Interior, issued as a press release by the Government of the Federal Republic of Germany on 3 June 1982.

4. *Declaration of the International Conference on the Protection of the North Sea – Conclusions of the Conference*. Bremen, 31 October/1 November, 1984.

5. J Side, 'The North Sea Conference: Bremen 1984 – London 1987', *Marine Pollution Bulletin*, 1986, 17, pp 394-399.

6. Greenpeace, 'The Tide Must Turn'. Greenpeace, London, 1987, p

31.

7. *Ibid*, p 39.

8. The International Conference on Environmental Protection of the North Sea, 24-27 March 1987, London. Preprints of papers presented at the conference are available together with a Conference Summary from the Water Research Council, Henley Road, Medmenham, Marlow, Bucks. The complete Conference Proceedings will be published in 1988.

9. The amounts of oil spilled from offshore installations was a subject of some controversy with a strong rebuttal to a Dutch claim being made by a representative of the UK Department of Energy (*Marine Pollution Bulletin*, 1987, 18, p 258). Other matters on which the UK was criticised are summarised in a general review by R Jenkins, 'North Sea Protection', *Marine Pollution Bulletin*, 1987, 18, p 251.

10. The Report of the North Sea Forum. The North Sea Forum, Council for Environmental Conservation, London,March 1987.

11. C Alzieu, Y Thibaud, M Heral & B Boutier, 'Evaluation des Risques dus a l'Emploi des Peintures Anti-salissures dans les Zones Conchylicoles', *Rev. des. Trav. Inst. Pech. Marit.*, 1980, 44, pp 301-349.

12. See for example M Waldock & J Thain, 'Shell Thickening in *Crassostrea gigas*: organotin antifouling or sediment induced?', *Marine Pollution Bulletin*, 1983, 14, pp 411-415.

13. The regulations originally proposed made it an offence to sell or offer for retail sale any paint containing organotin compounds where the total tin content exceeded 0.4 g (elemental tin) per 100 ml of paint. These would have permitted the continued sale of copper-based anti-fouling compounds which used a small booster of organotin compounds.

14. *Marine Pollution Bulletin*, 1985, 16, p 261.

15. S Aris, 'Political Fixers', *InterCity*, November/December 1986, pp 14-17.

16. *The Control of Pollution (Anti-Fouling Paints) Regulations 1985* was a compromise which prohibited the retail sale of paints containing more than 7.5% organotin in copolymer formulations, and 2.5% organotin in copper or other anti-fouling systems, thus setting an upper limit to the amount of organotin in the paint formulations.

17. *The Control of Pollution (Anti-Fouling Paints and Treatments) Regulations 1987* effectively prohibit the retail sale and hence general use of any paint containing a tri-organotin compound, and the retail or wholesale supply of treatments containing a tri-organotin compound for use on fish cages.

18. See for example I Lawler & J Aldrich, 'Sublethal effects of Bis(Tri-N-Butyltin) Oxide on *Crassostrea gigas* Spat', *Marine Pollution Bulletin*, 1987, 18, pp 274-277.

19. For a recent general review of this and other environmental protection measures of relevance to the offshore industry, see C Johnston, J Side & S Davies, 'The Use of Environmental Audit in Offshore Operations' in E Hill, J Shennan & R Watkinson (eds), Microbial Problems in the Offshore Oil Industry, An International Conference organised by the Institute of Petroleum, Aberdeen, April 1986. Published John Wiley & Sons, Chichester, 1987, pp 147-164.

20. J Side, 'Oil Based Muds – Understanding the Legislation', *Marine Pollution Bulletin*, 1986, 17, pp 88-91.

21. See for example, J Addy, R Blackman, J Blanchard, J Davies, J Ferbrache, D Moore, H Sommerville, A Whitehead & T Wilkinson, 'Environmental effects of oil-based mud cuttings', Offshore Europe Conference, Aberdeen, 10-13 September 1983, Society of Petroleum Engineers, SPE 11890.

22. The was accomplished by *The Prevention of Oil Pollution Act 1971 (Application of Section 1) Regulations 1984* for a fuller explanation see J Side, 'Oil Based Muds – Understanding the Legislation', *op.cit.*

23. A delay of one year (October 1983 – November 1984) occurred; industry had geared up to compliance from October 1983 and the effect of this was unlikely to have been significant.

24. This was brought about by the introduction of new exemption conditions issued by the Department of Energy in April 1987 (ref 80/729/12).

25. Article 5(5) of the Geneva *Convention on the Continental Shelf 1958.*

26. This view is given for offshore installations in R Allan, 'Abandonment – A Fishing Industry Perspective', Offshore Decommissioning Conference, London, 25/26 November 1986; and specifically for offshore pipelines in W Hay & R Allan, 'The Fishermen's View of Pipeline Removal', Conference on the Commissioning and

Decommissioning of Pipelines, Aberdeen, 9-11 June 1987.

27. Article 60(3) of the United Nations *Convention on the Law of the Sea 1982*.

28. For a more detailed treatment of the draft Standards and Guidelines and their development see J Side, 'IMO Drafts Platform Removal Standards', *Marine Pollution Bulletin*, 1987, 18, pp 474-476.

29. *op.cit.*, but for a full exposition of this legal argument see P McDade, 'The International Law of Abandonment of Offshore Installations: A Reassessment', *Oil and Gas Law and Taxation Review*, 1986, 11, pp 291-296.

30. J Side, *op.cit.*, p 475.

31. Mackay Consultants, 'Loss of Access to Fishing Grounds from Offshore Oil and Gas Activity', A Report for the Scottish Fishermen's Federation and the National Federation of Fishermen's Organisations, May 1987.

32. This summary statement of the zones of effect has been adapted from the findings reported in Addy *et al.*, *op.cit.* It is interesting to ask the question whether this would have been an acceptable environmental quality objective were one to have been established in the vicinity of platform discharges. While the statement, based on Addy *et al.*, implies long recovery times these are likely to be comparatively short compared to those of more persistent pollutants.

TABLE 1: Brief Summary of Some of the Principal International Conventions and Agreeements Providing for the Protection of the Marine Environment of the North Sea

REGIONAL:

The Bonn Agreement for Cooperation in Dealing with Pollution of the North Sea by Oil and Other Harmful Substances 1983. Originally adopted in 1969 as one of several initiatives drafted in response to the Torrey Canyon oil spill in March 1967, it was extended in 1977 to cover spills from offshore installations following the Ekofisk Bravo blowout and updated in 1983. It establishes governmental arrangements for dealing with an actual or anticipated spillage of oil or other harmful substance.

The Oslo Convention for the Prevention of Marine Pollution by Dumping from Ships and Aircraft 1972 was adopted following a major diplomatic incident when a Dutch vessel, the Stella Maris, tried unsuccessfully to dump 650 tonnes of chlorinated hydrocarbons in the northern North Sea in July 1971. Now extended to include incineration of waste at sea it establishes in its Annexes lists of substances the dumping of which is either prohibited (Annex 1) or can only be carried out under special permit (Annex 2). The dumping of any materials not appearing in these lists still requires the approval of the appropriate national authority.

The Paris Convention on the Prevention of Marine Polution from Land-Based Sources 1974 establishes provisions for particular pollutants emanating from land-based sources, pipelines and offshore installations. Pollutants are allocated to different lists depending on their toxicity, persistence and tendency to accumulate in marine organisms. Contracting Parties to the Convention agree to eliminate marine polltuion from land-based sources of List 1 substances (black list) and to strictly limit pollution from List 2 (grey list) substances. The need for such a convention was recognised by the signatory governments during the drafting of the Oslo Convention.

INTERNATIONAL:

The London Convention on Dumping of Wastes at Sea 1972 is broadly similar to the Oslo Convention. Among the major differences are the geographical areas covered by the Conventions with the London Convention applying world-wide.

MARPOL 1973/78 or the International Convention for the Prevention of Pollution from Ships as amended by the Protocol of 1978, controls the discharge from ships of oil (Annex I), noxious liquid substances carried in bulk (Annex II), sewage (Annex IV) and garbage (Annex V). Annex III contains provision for the marine transportation of harmful substances carried in packages.

TABLE 2: Governments and International Organisations Involved in the First North Sea Conference

---

PARTICIPANTS: Belgium, Denmark, The Federal Republic of Germany, France, The Netherlands, Norway, Sweden and the United Kingdom. France, although not strictly a North Sea state was a full participant because of its geographical proximity. Additionally the Commission of the European Communities was a full participant in the Conference.

OBSERVERS: Non-riparian EC states (Luxembourg, Greece, Italy), the Contracting States which were party to the relevant international conventions (see Table 1), the secretariats of international organisations, including the Paris and Oslo Commissions, the International Maritime Organization, the United Nations Envirnoment Programme, and the World Health Organisation.

TABLE 3: Part B: Declaration of General Principles

The Ministers declare their firm determination

– to make every effort at national and international levels as well as at EEC level to protect the marine environment of the North Sea effectively and permanently, and for this purpose to prevent, reduce and control adverse effects on the marine environment which result or are likely to result from human activities,

– in view of the impairment of parts of the North Sea and the possible impairment of the ecosystem of the North Sea as a whole, to continue the efforts made in the past few years at national and international levels as well as at EEC level in order to urgently further reduce existing contamination, in particular through rivers, coastal waters and the atmosphere and to prevent additional contamination or the risk of contamination and to pay increased attention in particular to the protection of the Wadden Sea which is of importance for the whole North Sea,

– to implement the existing international agreements for the protection of nature with a view to the conservation of the ecosystem of the North Sea – above all of the Wadden Sea and similar particularly sensitive coastal areas – without delay, and to make use of the instruments provided therein and intensively to continue existing co-operation for the protection of these areas,

- to set clear objective to be met within specific time-limits, taking account of economic conditions, and to use efficient instruments to achieve them,

- to lay down emission and environmental quality standards for preserving or restoring the marine environment,

- to bring closer together the uniform emission standards and environmental quality objectives approaches,

- to prevent waste from production and consumption as far as possible or to at least reduce it, and where this is not practicable, to recycle unavoidable waste as far as possible; the disposal of wastes which cannot be recycled should be in accordance with the best possible protection of the environment – in particular wastes which are or could be harmful to the marine environment and which cannot be recycled shall be disposed of on land in a controlled manner instead of discharged into the North Sea,

- to ensure that measures adopted by coastal states and the EEC to protect the North Sea are applied in such a way as to prevent the dumping in other seas of wastes including sewage sludges, which could do harm to the marine environment,

- to prevent or at least to reduce the input of hazardous substances into waste water as far as possible, and where this is not practicable, waste waters contaminated by such substances are to be treated, aiming at preventing or at least reducing, as far as possible such discharges into the aquatic environment,

- to intensify research and development for the improvement of knowledge relating to forms of marine pollution and for enhancing water quality in the North Sea, for example with the aim of using new low or non-waste and low-emission or emission-free technologies and to exchange internationally the information thus obtained,

- to ensure that, with regard to the North Sea, information on licensing practices is exchanged and arrangements for monitoring discharges are compatible,

- to develop existing monitoring programmes in order to secure a coherent system indispenable to the protection of the North Sea,

- to analyze and assess likely effects of projects and measures on the marine environment in the earliest possible stage of decision-making processes in relation to programmes and plans as well as the permissibility of individual projects,

- to make highly effective use of the possiblities offered by international agreements on the prevention of marine pollution and to develop them to the extent required, as well as to strengthen existing co-operation to lasting effect in order to achieve co-ordinated implementation of the Oslo and Paris Conventions and the EEC environmen programme,

- to take initiatives in international bodies to ensure that appropriate measures for the prevention of marine pollution are indicated and implemented as soon as possible, taking into account all economic and technical aspects,

- to review at regular intervals whether measures and programmes to maintain the quality of the marine environment of the North Sea adopted by the competent international bodies and implementing measures taken by national authorities in the coastal states that are member of those bodies, are sufficiently effective and to take further decisions at political level, as appropriate, with regard to the prevention and further marked reduction of marine pollution,

- to call upon other States which use the North Sea or whose activities adversely affect the marine environment of the North Sea to accede to the relevant international agreements for protection of the marine environment, to implement the provisions thereof, to monitor compliance with these provisions and to take further necessary measures at national and internaitional level as may be required,

- to use their best endeavours so as to make available appropriate financial means for the implementation in good time of the foregoing principles of environmental policy for the North Sea,

consider it necessary to make the results of this conference the basis of their environmental political action for the North Sea on the national level and within the EEC,

and resolve in order to bring about a comprehensive set of protective measures for the North Sea, to take the conclusions of this Conference as a basis for concerted action in the competent international bodies.

TABLE 4: Use of Oil Based Muds in Drilling Operations and Associated Discharges on the UK Continental Shelf

YEAR	1981		1982		1983		1984		1985		1986	
Number – No.; Per cent (%)	No	(%)	No	(%)	No	(%)	No	(%)	No	(%)	No	(%)
Exploration Wells	48	(23)	68	(30)	77	(34)	106	(34)				
Appraisal Wells	26	(12)	43	(19)	51	(23)	76	(26)				
Development Wells	137	(65)	118	(51)	95	(43)	108	(37)				
Total Wells Drilled	211		229		235		291		290		198	
Drilled Using:												
–water based mud	135	(64)	115	(50)	82	(35)	70	(24)	79	(27)	59	(30)
–diesel based mud	72	(34)	80	(35)	61	(26)	15	(5)	negligible		negligible	
–"low toxicity" oil based mud	4	(2)	34	(15)	92	(39)	206	(71)	211	(73)	139	(70)
Amounts of Oil discharged (tonnes):												
–diesel oil	6,900		7,400		7,700		1,400		negligible		negligible	
"low toxicity" oil discharged	350		3,200		10,400		18,400		20,200		13,000	
–total oil discharge from muds	7,250		10,600		18,100		19,800		20,200		13,000	

Source: compiled by the author from Department of Energy data; some figures are slightly at variance with the most recently published Department of Energy data by the latter do not allow such a detailed breakdown.

TABLE 5: UKOOA Estimates of Platform Removal Costs
£ million, including ancilliary structures

Area	Type & No.	Method and extent of removal							
		Topple			Partial Removal			Complete Removal	
		All	Av	S.(%)	All	Av.	S.(%)	All	Av.
	Steel								
North	14	600	43	(70)	1,320	94	(34)	2,015	114
Central	18	695	37	(66)	1,464	81	(29)	2,049	114
N & C		1,295			2,784			4,064	
South	99							1,157	12
	Concrete								
	8	265	33	(69)	265	33	(69)	859	107
Totals	(£ million)	2,717			4,206			6,080	

KEY

Av. – Average cost for the type of structure in the area concerned

N & C – North and Central North Sea areas combined

S. (%) – % saving on cost of complete removal by toppling or partial removal

Source: United Kingdom Offshore Operators' Association.

SCOTTISH ECONOMIC PERFORMANCE AND GOVERNMENT POLICY:

A NORTH-SOUTH DIVIDE?

Brian Ashcroft

1. Introduction

The recent performance of the Scottish economy has been variable. After the recession of 1979 to 1981 both the Scottish and UK economies exhibited positive growth, with the index of industrial production and construction rising by 8.7% and 11.8%, respectively, to the end of 1985. However, in 1986 the relative performance of the Scottish economy deteriorated. The index fell 3% below that achieved in 1985 while in the UK the same industries managed to increase their output by 1.8% over the year. The principal reason for the reversal in Scotland's economic fortunes lay in the sharp fall in the price of oil during late 1985 and early 1986. The collapse of the oil price had obvious consequences for the UK oil supply industry which being largely located in Scotland inevitably affected Scotland more than the rest of the UK. As output and employment fell so the Scottish unemployment rate eventually began to rise at a time when unemployment in the UK was beginning to fall, reflecting the strong growth in consumer spending and improved export performance as sterling depreciated significantly against the D-Mark during 1986.

With the publication of the delayed 1984 Census of Employment in January 1987, media concern about the performance of the Scottish economy shifted away from short-term developments to the longer run. The Census provided new estimates of the level and composition of the civilian employed labour force. Revised projections based on the Census suggested that the employed labour force in Britain had fallen by 3% between June 1979 and June 1986. Yet, in the Scottish, North, North West and Welsh Standard Regions there had been a fall of 8%, 10%, 12% and 13%, respectively, over the same period. The three southern Standard Regions, on the other hand, all exhibited positive employment growth. East Anglia recorded a 13% rise, while the South West and the South East posted increases of 5% and 2%, respectively.

For many commentators these figures were clear evidence of a "divide" in economic, and particularly employment, opportunities between the economies of the north and south of Britain.[1] In addition, several responsible non-governmental bodies such as the Scottish Council, the STUC, and the Fraser of Allander Institute, argued that the unfavourable imbalance between north and south had worsened over the past eight years.[2] Further deterioration was expected unless positive policies were introduced to reverse the trend. The Government responded by characterising such views as "facile", "simplistic" and "absurd".[3]

By the middle of 1987, and at the time of writing, the short-term outlook for the Scottish economy had become much more favourable.[4] Both the Scottish Business and CBI quarterly surveys had shown a progressive increase in business confidence from the beginning of the year. Prospects for employment were more encouraging. Seasonally adjusted unemployment had fallen by 3,100 a month on average over the six months to July. The rate of decline in Scottish unemployment during this period was, however, only about two thirds of that in the UK, reflecting the residual effects of the oil price fall in 1986 and, arguably, lags in the transmission of growth from the centre to the peripheral regions of the UK. Nevertheless, with the British economy enjoying faster growth than most of its international competitors and the signs of the upturn also clearly evident in Scotland, the question of the existence of a divide in economic opportunities between the north and south of Britain slipped from the headlines. But for those who believed in the existence of the division the recent improvements had simply drawn a temporary veil over the fundamental imbalance.

This chapter first considers the arguments for and against the proposition of a north-south divide. A consideration of the performance of key economic indicators in the British Standard regions going back to the 1960s, suggests that there is no simple dichotomy between the economic performance of the "north" and the "south" of Britain. Nevertheless, in those regions including Scotland that are traditionally assigned to the "north" there would appear to be a persistent lack of employment opportunities compared with the "south". The performance of the "midland" regions does, however, complicate the picture and it is arguable whether they should be considered separately from the rest. Moreover, variations in economic performance both within and between regions over time, should not be ignored.

The second section examines the economic forces that may be contributing to the division and the extent to which central government policies may be having a deleterious effect. It is suggested here that the imbalance may be viewed as a long-run phenomenon. Comparative regional economic performance is governed by the spatial distribution of economic activities and the national and international competitive pressures for industrial restructuring which are occurring against the background of a more permissive policy environment. The rigidity of regional wages may be a contributory factor.

Finally, the chapter concludes by asking whether government can play a positive role in restricting the tendency to economic polarisation between the north and south of Britain while preserving an environment favourable to national economic growth.

2. A North-South Divide?

The Arguments

In general terms, it has been suggested that the regional problem in Britain can be viewed as one of fundamental imbalance in economic opportunities between the Standard regions of East Anglia, the South East and the South West – the "south" – and the rest of Britain – the "north". For example, a 1983 report from the Regional Studies Association put it this way:

> "the evidence .... supports the identification of a basic regional dualism in the UK (consisting) on the one hand of a 'Greater South East England' zone of relative prosperity and, on the other, most of the rest of the country, characterised in general by economic debility and decline."[5]

Against this must be set the quite reasonable argument that Britain's urban and regional problems are complex. Areas of prosperity and promise exist in both the so-called "north" and "south". Differentiating between economic opportunities above and below a line drawn from the Wash to the Severn is therefore a crude and oversimplified way to categorise the economic geography of Britain.[6]

Proponents of the proposition go further, arguing that following the publication of the Census of Employment the imbalance is most clearly seen in, and therefore caused by, a lack of employment opportunities. A division which must eventually affect average incomes. However, those who would dismiss the notion of a north-south divide point to the recent more rapid improvement in unemployment in some northern regions such as the North and Wales compared with the rest of Britain. Other regions in the north particularly Scotland have higher levels of income per head than some southern regions and high rates of growth of manufacturing productivity.

The Evidence

Economists conventionally use the net value of output produced within a region per head of population as an index of living standards. Table 1 presents the most recent data for the Standard Regions of the UK, comparing gross domestic product (GDP) per head as a percentage of the

UK average over the ten year period 1975 to 1985. In terms of GDP per head it is clear that there is no simple division between north and south. In 1975, East Anglia and the South West ranked 8 and 9, respectively, with the South East pre-eminent. However, over the period all three southern regions exhibited the fastest rates of growth, resulting in East Anglia and the South West moving up the rankings to second and sixth, respectively, while the South East retained its premier position. The other "northern" regions, in contrast, all either retained their relative position or lost ground. The most obvious example of deteriorating relative fortunes is the West Midlands. This region, traditionally one of the prosperous UK regions, experienced significant relative decline, moving from second to eighth in the rankings, as manufacturing and the car industry in particular contracted.

Table 1:   Gross Domestic Product per Head in UK Regions, 1975-85

Region	GDP per head as % of UK average				Change in GDP per head as % of UK average	
	1975		1985		1975-85	
	%	Rank	%	Rank	%	Rank
East Anglia	92.8	8	100.8	2	+8.0	1
South West	90.3	9	93.8	6	+3.5	2
South East	112.9	1	114.8	1	+1.9	3
Greater London	125.8		125.8		0.0	
Rest of SE	103.6		107.7		+4.1	
Scotland	97.1	3	97.3	3	+0.2	4
Wales	88.7	10	88.8	10	+0.1	5
North West	96.2	4	96.0	4	−0.2	6
East Midlands	96.1	5	95.7	5	−0.4	7
North	93.6	7	92.9	7	−0.7	8
Yorks & Humber	94.1	6	91.8	9	−2.3	9
N. Ireland	80.0	11	74.8	11	−5.2	10
West Midlands	100.0	2	92.3	8	−7.7	11

Note: Ranking is by Standard Region

Source: Regional Trends, 1987 (HMSO)

The position of Scotland clearly differs from the other peripheral regions of the UK such as the North, Wales and Northern Ireland. Throughout the period Scotland retained its high third position in the rankings and GDP per head actually grew somewhat more quickly than the UK average. Figure 1 charts GDP growth in Scotland and the UK over four periods between 1966 and 1985. The four periods roughly correspond to the tenure of successive governments. It is clear from figure 1, that in the second decade the growth of GDP alone was lower in Scotland. The relative improvement in GDP per head in the Scottish economy must therefore have been due to a slower population growth and faster rate of outmigration than in the UK as a whole. Nevertheless, in the decade to the mid 1970s the growth of GDP was greater in Scotland than in the UK, reflecting the vigorous regional policy of the period, diversification towards more quickly growing industries and, of course, the discovery and exploitation of North Sea oil. Furthermore, while the growth of GDP was lower in Scotland in the seven years to 1985 than in the UK, the differential did narrow compared with the period 1974 to 1979. The narrowing of the differential can largely be explained by the success in attracting inward investment, resulting in significant output growth in the electronics and pharmaceutical industries and rapid productivity growth. But, sadly, the comparative buoyancy of GDP growth in Scotland did little to stem employment decline.

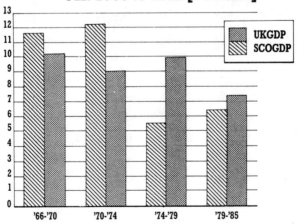

Fig. 1 GDP Change in Scotland and UK: 1966 to 1985 [Percent]

Source: Scottish Economic Bulletin, No. 33, 1986 and unpublished data.

Fig. 2 Employment Change: Scotland and Britain: 1966 to 1986 [Percent]

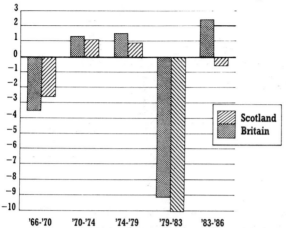

Source: Regional Trends and Employment Gazette, Vol. 95 No. 2, Historical Supplement No. 1, February 1987.

Figure 2 compares the change in employees in employment in Scotland and Britain during the tenure of successive governments over the period 1966 to 1986.[7] What is clear from the figure is that the gap between the employment performance of Scotland and Britain has progressively deteriorated under successive governments. From a favourable difference of 0.9 percentage points between 1966 and 1970, the performance gap became negative and increasingly so, with shortfalls of −0.2, −0.6, −0.9 and −3 percentage points, in 70-74, 74-79, 79-83 and 83-86, respectively. The figures for Scotland during the period from June 1983 to June 1986 will have been affected to some extent by the effects of the oil price collapse during the first half of 1986. Nevertheless, it is not unreasonable to suggest on the basis of this evidence that Scotland has been experiencing a long-run decline in employment opportunities compared with Britain as a whole.

For northern Britain the picture is less clear cut. Figure 3 charts the employment change in the north and south of Britain over the same period. Regions were assigned to the "north" if their employment performance was at least 10% worse than the GB average in a majority of the five periods. While this procedure is somewhat arbitrary it results in a clear geographical division. The East Midlands are included with East Anglia, the South East and the South West in the "south", while the West Midlands are assigned with the remaining regions to the "north". The north and south are therefore divided by a line running roughly from the Humber to the Severn.

Fig. 3 Employment Change: North and South 1966 to 1986 [Percent]

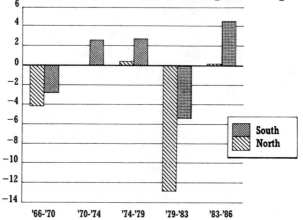

Source: Regional Trends and Employment Gazette, Vol. 95 No. 2, Historical Supplement No. 1, February 1987.

Several conclusions about the so-called "north-south divide" can be drawn from figure 3. First, employment performance has been consistently worse in the north under successive Labour and Conservative governments. Secondly, when the national economy experiences an upturn the differential appears to narrow,[8] although the evidence noted above suggests that this may be less true for Scotland. Thirdly, the figure does not provide conclusive evidence that the gap is widening. Yet, it is interesting to note that when the two consecutive upturns, 74-79 and 83-86, are compared, employment growth in Britain was greater by 0.9 percentage points in the latter period but the north-south differential was *worse* by 2 percentage points. This was the case even though the diferential had narrowed compared with that in the recession of 79-83. Whether the differential will continue to widen is an open question but what appears to be beyond doubt is that the division between north and south became more acute in the 1980s.

Much the same conclusions can be drawn from a consideration of regional unemployment rates, where differences between the northern and southern regions have tended to narrow with an upturn in the national economy and widen during national recession. Moreover, in the first five years of the present decade the differential widened appreciably.[9] It should be remembered, however, that the unemployment rate may prove to be an inadequate guide to the absence of job opportunities in an area. Supply-side responses to job loss such as migration and the failure of some groups, particularly women, to register their unemployment when no benefit is due, may limit the unemployment increase.

The gap between the employment performance of the north and the south is clearly sizable. Yet this is not to deny that there is an increasingly complex geographical pattern of economic advantage and disadvantage at sub-regional and urban levels in Britain. For many years more urbanised areas throughout the UK and other industrialised countries have performed less well than the urban periphery and more rural locations.[10] The north- south division in employment performance simply overlays that urban-rural shift. Recent research by J B Goddard and M G Coombes[11] makes this point clear. When an index of local economic performance[12] was constructed for the 280 local labour market areas in Britain the authors concluded:

"....within each region the variation between best and worst performing places spans a very wide range. Here, an emphasis on extreme cases would stress the substantial overlap between regions. However, more robust analysis relates to the interquartile range (excluding the extreme quartiles for each region). The interquartile ranges for the three south and east regions hardly overlap at all with those for the five northern and western regions, with the two Midland regions fittingly straddling this divide. ...... The conclusion must be that the clear existence of strong local contrasts in economic well-being are in no way a disproof of a substantial, and probably widening, north-south divide."[13]

3. Polarising Influences

The causes of the relative lack of job opportunities in the north are complex. In essence, the imbalance may be viewed as a long-run phenomenon reflecting the existing spatial distribution of economic activities, wage rigidity in northern labour markets, regional myopia and metropolitan bias on the part of UK companies aided by national and international competitive pressures for industrial restructuring, and an increasingly permissive policy environment.

As figure 4 indicates there is a long-run decline in the provision of manufacturing jobs, although not in manufacturing output. The job losses in manufacturing are heavily concentrated in the north because as manufacturing industry grew it largely favoured northern locations. Figure 5 shows that for most of the period the north's share of manufacturing employment has been in decline. After reaching a peak during the period of 57.2% in 1973 it had declined to 52.1% by 1986. Scotland's share also declined but at a slightly greater rate, falling from a peak during the period of 8.8% in 1974 to 8% in 1986. The decline in Scotland's share of manufacturing employment has occurred despite employment growth in some sectors such as electronics, instrument engineering, parts of food,

Fig. 4 Manufacturing & Service Employment Britain: 1971 to 1986 [000's]

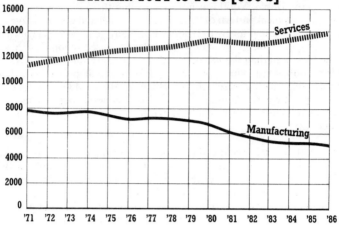

Source: Employment Gazette, Vol. 95 No. 2, Historical Supplement No. 1, February 1987.

Fig. 5 Manufacturing Employment in North and South: 1971 to 1986 [000's]

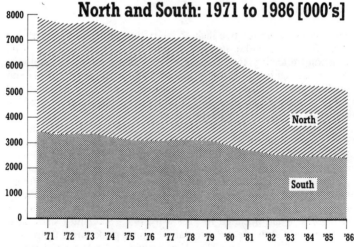

Source: Employment Gazette, Vol. 95 No. 2, Historical Supplement No. 1, February 1987.

drink and tobacco and pharmaceuticals. So, for example, the electronics industry in Scotland has since 1979 provided only one job for every fifty lost elsewhere in manufacturing; and in the period 1981 to 1984 *each* of nine manufacturing industries lost more jobs than the number gained in electronics.[14] Indeed, it is precisely because so few jobs have been created in the "high-tech" industries in Scotland compared with their contribution to output, that manufacturing productivity has risen so quickly over the last few years. Moreover, when jobs are created in these industries relatively few indirect jobs are created elsewhere in the Scottish economy. Employment multipliers estimated from the 1979 Scottish Input-Output Tables show that for every one job created in computers, instrument engineering and aerospace, only 0.33, 0.22 and 0.13 jobs, respectively, are created via linkages to other Scottish firms. In contrast, a traditional Scottish industry such as whisky generates two other jobs for every one direct job created in the industry.

Figure 4 shows that the service sector, in sharp contrast to manufacturing, has experienced a sustained expansion of employment. This rapid growth in service employment is, however, seen in figure 6 to be gradually concentrating in the south, with the north's share declining from 45.9% in 1977 to 44.1% in 1986. In Scotland, for example, service sector

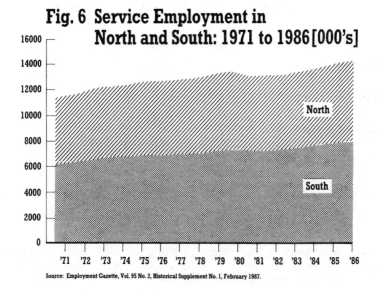

Fig. 6 Service Employment in North and South: 1971 to 1986 [000's]

Source: Employment Gazette, Vol. 95 No. 2, Historical Supplement No. 1, February 1987.

employment increased by 1.1% between 1980 and 1986, whereas in the South East service jobs rose by 7.6%. Moreover, over the same period the jobs in this sector actually fell in two of the northern regions, the North West and Wales, by 2.6% and 3%, respectively. All southern regions, in contrast, posted an increase.

There are also clear differences in performance within the service sector. Table 2, breaks down employment change in services between 1971 and 1986 into six broad groupings. The three fastest growing sectors in Great Britain all grew more quickly in the south. In Scotland two of the three fastest growing sectors also grew appreciably slower than the northern average, although this may in part be due to both Banking, Insurance and Finance, and Wholesale distribution, Hotels and Catering, being disproportionately represented in Scotland at the beginning of the period. At the other extreme, Transport and Communciations, which actually lost jobs during the period, contracted significantly more rapidly in the north than the south. Retail distribution, which experienced low positive growth in Britain as a whole, also contracted in the north while experiencing a positive rate of growth in the south over twice as fast as the national average. Only Public administration and Defence grew more quickly in the north than the south and this must in part reflect the limited dispersal of civil servants to northern regions in the 1970s and particularly the early 1980s.

Table 2: Employment Change in Service Sector Industries, June 1971 to June 1986 (Percentages)

	GB	South	North	Scotland
Banking, Insurance & Finance	65.5	67.4	62.2	52.9
Education, Health &Other	37.5	40.3	34.5	39.5
Wholesale distribution Hotels & Catering	35.3	36.9	33.5	25.9
Public administration & Defence	11.2	9.8	13.1	18.4
Retail distribution	5.3	11.7	−1.5	−2.6
Transport & Communications	−13.7	−5.4	−23.7	−23.6

Notes: the "south" is East Anglia, South East, South West and East Midlands; the "north" is Scotland, North, North West, Yorks & Humber, Wales and West Midlands.

Source: Employment Gazette, Historical Supplement No. 1, Vol. 95 No.2, Department of Employment, February 1987.

There is some suggestion here that tradeable services which generate high value added and offer highly skilled employment may be tending to be concentrated in the south. Examples include the intermediate producer services, such as finance, legal, insurance, professional, technical, distribution and maintenance activities, and the intermediate consumer services, such as the production of television programmes, computer software, and cable communications. "Low-level" services which directly serve local consumers and offer low skilled, often part-time, and usually female employment, may conversely be performing relatively better in the north. However, the disaggregated data necessary to evaluate this contention is limited. Nevertheless, recent data for Scotland does appear to point in this direction. Between 1981 and 1984, the Scottish share of GB employment *increased* in Personal Services by 1% point and in the Repair of Consumer Goods by 1.1% points, while Scotland's share of employment in Banking and Finance, Posts and Telecommunications, and Insurance *fell* by 1.4%, 0.9% and 0.2% points, respectively. But, Scotland's share of Business Services increased very slightly by 0.1% points, which is contrary to the suggested trend.

The relatively poorer performance of manufacturing and service employment in the north may partly be explained by the concentration of declining traditional activities in northern locations. However, this cannot account for the unequal spatial incidence of the location of new jobs both at the aggregate level in manufacturing and services and in particular sub-sectors. Although industries depending on local demand which tend largely to be in the service sector will have performed less well in the north as the traditional economic base contracted. That apart, other explanations are required to account for the relative imbalance in job opportunities.

One possibility is the failure of regional wages to adjust to geographical shifts in the demand for labour. On this view it is the downward wage rigidity in northern labour markets that is mainly responsible for the relative lack of job creation in areas of high unemployment.[15] Indeed the present government's policies towards the labour market are based on this belief, as can be seen by this pronouncement from the Trade and Industry Secretary in 1983:

.... real wages that are incompatible with the demand for labour create unemployment both regionally and nationally ..... wage flexibility could and should be increased.[16]

There is clearly some substance in the view that wages have failed to respond to variations in the regional demand for labour. Firms with plants in several regions tend to pay similar rates for the same occupations irrespective of the location. Wage rates are usually set at the national rather than the regional level through the collective bargaining process. And research into regional wage inflation suggests that earnings growth spreads from regions such as the South East, where the demand for labour is relatively high, to occupations and industries in regions where labour demand is relatively low.

The significance of downward wage rigidity to the comparative lack of job opportunities in northern labour markets has been overstated. In theory, firms will take on more workers if the value of production obtained from the extra employment is at least as great as the wages paid. However, if the value of the extra production that can be sold falls in proportion to the wage cut because workers reduce their expenditures on local goods and services then there will be litle effect on employment. In technical terms the *real* wages paid by firms remain unchanged even though *nominal* wages have been reduced.[17] Moreover, even if real wages were reduced in northern regions there is no guarantee in the short run that firms either will be able to sell more goods to warrant the extra employment, or that they would seize the opportunity to hire more labour at the lower wage cost.

First, the insensitivity of the demand for goods and services to changes in price could mean that wage cuts would have to be draconian before there was much impact on employment and this would have obvious consequences for industrial relations and the morale and living standards of workers. Secondly, and perhaps more importantly, it is unlikely that any feasible wage cuts would be sufficient to overcome firms' perceptions of the advantages of a location in the south. There is a wealth of academic evidence to suggest that businessmen and other individuals give a disproportionate weight to those areas with which they are familiar.[18] The level of knowledge about other areas diminishes rapidly as distance increases, resulting in what can only be described as regional myopia. UK firms have traditionally exhibited a metropolitan and southern bias in the location of their headquarters and production facilities. Evidence on the effects of regional policy in the 1960s and 1970s suggests that regional financial incentives had little impact in inducing firms to move out of the south. However, once firms had to consider a re-location because of shortages of space, skilled labour, or the refusal of an Industrial Development Certificate, then the incentives did play a role in diverting firms to the assisted areas.[19] In essence, regional myopia or metropolitan bias led many firms in the south to discount the regional incentives and much the same outcome can be expected if real wages were lower in the north. Furthermore, changes in the structure and organisation of firms' production would appear to have increased the potential for a concentration of key economic activities in the south.

The growth in the size of companies, often operating on a world scale, and technical developments in both communications and production processes, have raised the potential for functional specialisation within companies. This specialisation has in turn led to spatial divisions in the location of functions. At its simplest this means that key managerial control

– or headquarters – functions, such as investment planning, and key operating functions, such as marketing and R & D, can be located in one location, while firms' production facilities may, if necessary, be located elsewhere. In consequence, different types of employment can be offered: more highly skilled labour being required to satisfy the needs of the key control and operating functions, while less qualified labour is needed at the point of production.

It can be argued that spatial specialisation by function has been occurring, that it intensified in the 1970s and early 1980s, largely through a process of acquisitions and rationalisations, and perhaps inevitably this process has worked to the advantage of the south.[20] Headquarters and key operating functions are increasingly to be found in the south, while the quality of labour available in the north has probably suffered, following the outmigration of workers as the demand for key skills diminished.[21] This process has also been overlaid on a pattern of sectoral specialisation which, as noted above, has been changing, again to the probable long-run disadvantage of the north.

In sum, this argument contends that the trends discussed above appear to have led to a concentration of the more modern, technologically-advanced, high value added, and research-oriented sectors in the south. Specialisation within sectors and companies has also favoured the south through the location and re-location of key control and operating functions. Moreover, when the north and particularly Scotland has attracted modern growth industries such as electronics, it has largely been through the siting of production facilities without the key control and operating functions which are so necessary to regional development. The attraction of new "high- tech" industries to the regions therefore appears to provide little guarantee of a narrowing of the division. However, data on the geographical incidence and effects of industrial restructuring in Britain, is limited. It seems unlikely that the strong centripetal forces favouring southern locations will rigidly benefit the South East, East Anglia and the South West to the exclusion of all other regions. It can also be disputed whether any imbalance that exists between north and south is a long-run phenomenon. The decline in manufacturing industry which historically concentrated in the north will be of diminishing importance as its relative size contracts. All regions might be expected to benefit from increased growth in the service sector. But, the position of London and therefore the South East as the key UK financial and commercial centre suggests that financial and business services, the fastest growing parts of the service sector, are more likely to be concentrated there.

The present government in its public pronouncements has shown little recognition of the social, political and economic consequences if the suggested polarising tendencies of industrial restructuring produce their expected effect. Indeed it can be argued that the government's increased reliance on market forces compared with its predecessors has probably served to widen regional disparities in the UK to the detriment of the north.

One example usually cited is the progressive decline in regional policy expenditures and the relaxation of Industrial Development Certificate control since the late 1970s, followed by the radical cutback in planned outlays since 1984.[22] The run-down since the mid-70s of New Town and overspill policies and the growth of inner-city and urban initiatives may also have diminished the relative attractiveness of northern locations. Furthermore, the existing and planned concentration of major infrastructure investments in London and the south east: London's third airport at Stansted; the construction of the M25 and future completion of the M11 motorways; the regeneration of London's dockland; and the construction of the Channel Tunnel, all serve to increase the relative attractiveness of the south east of England to new jobs in manufacturing and service industry. One recent study has forecast that by 1995 these developments will result in almost half the projected net gain of 0.9 million UK jobs being concentrated in the south east of England.[23]

Competition policy and the corporate tax environment has under the present government moved in favour of takeovers and mergers. In 1983 the government overruled the findings of the Monopolies and Mergers Commission which had found against the takeover of Anderson Strathclyde by Charter Consolidated partly because of the anticipated detrimental effect to the Scottish economy. This was subsequently followed by a statement from the then Industry Minister, Norman Tebbit, that future takeover bids would only be referred to the Commission on competitive grounds. In addition, following the phased abolition in 1984 of investment allowances, investment in plant and machinery effectively became more expensive. This biased the choice faced by some companies against investment in new plant and machinery in favour of the takeover of firms' existing assets. For these and other reasons, takeovers have increased dramatically in the last few years, with the proportion of UK merger expenditure accounted for by the acquisition of Scottish companies rising from 2.4% in 1984, to 14.4% in 1985 and 26.1% in the first three quarters of 1986. The acquisition of only three companies: Bells, Distillers and Coats Paton obviously contributed significantly to this increase, nevertheless it is clear that the level of external takeover of Scottish owned companies has risen appreciably in the last few years.

The available evidence on the effects of the external takeover of Scottish companies suggests that the companies themselves tend on balance to benefit in terms of improved sales performance and growth. On average employment is little affected. However, external takeovers are a cause for concern because the associated loss of key control functions and the loss of operating functions such as R & D and marketing, coupled with the general transfer of business away from local suppliers, particularly professional services, will almost certainly be to the detriment of the wider Scottish economy.[24] The unrestricted growth of external takeovers, with no prior government evaluation of the potential internal company benefits against the likely cost to the wider regional economy, could well have contributed to a worsening of regional disparities in the UK and hence the so-called north-south divide.

Government policy in favour of the develoment of small firms has expanded in recent years, yet recent research suggests that this too may be worsening regional differentials.[25] Prosperous regions in the south with high levels of potential entrepreneurship were found to benefit most in terms of the take-up of the Business Expansion, Enterprise Allowance and Loan Guarantee schemes. The policy therefore appears to be reinforcing existing regional differences in entrepreneurship.

Finally, it should be remembered that the government's initial adoption of what is usually described as a "monetarist" macro-economic policy stance and its refusal to use discretionary fiscal policy to smooth the path of the business cycle, led to a contraction of output in 1979 to 1981 that was much more pronounced than would otherwise have occurred. The combination of a tight monetary policy, rising oil prices and the increased significance of North Sea oil precipitated a significant increase in the exchange rate which seriously affected the competitiveness of manufacturing industry. The resulting contraction of manufacturing output and employment served to widen regional disparities in the UK.

It cannot, however, be guaranteed that the current economic upturn will simply reverse the effects of the 1979 to 1981 recession. The scale of the recession in those years was so severe that many manufacturers were forced to review all aspects of their activities. With regional policy contracting, many firms took advantage of the recession to make a desired locational adjustment to the pattern of their production in favour of locations at or near their headquarters in the south. Moreover, many parts of manufacturing industry closed during the recession never to reopen again. Changes in the pattern of comparative advantage between Britain and the rest of the world meant that industries such as coal, shipbuilding, steel, textiles, and mechanical engineering, would never again attain the position they had in the economy even in 1979. And, as the earlier discussion suggested, the north is attracting a smaller share of the jobs being created in the fast growing service industries. The north has of course had some success in attracting the "new" manufacturing industries with, for example, almost £2 billion of inward investment being attracted to Scotland alone since the early 1980s. But it is clear that these industries will never be able to provide jobs on the scale of traditional industry, nor will this new industry favour northern locations as its predecessors did in the past.

4. Conclusions

The evidence presented in this chapter suggests that on the conventional indicator of economic well being, GDP per head, there is no simple division between north and south. Over the ten years from 1975, Scotland retained its position as the region with the third highest level of GDP per head. Nevertheless, changes in that indicator since 1975 have clearly been most favourable in the three most southerly regions: East Anglia, the South West and the South East. A consideration of employment performance does suggest, however, that a clear distinction can be made between the job opportunities available in regions above and below a line drawn from the Humber to the Severn. Variations in economic performance do occur within regions but recent research suggests that once extremes are excluded the range of variation hardly overlaps in the five northern regions and the three regions of the extreme south. The range of variation in the Midland regions tends to straddle this divide, although the average employment performance of the West Midlands and the East Midlands is more closely related to regions further north in the former and to regions further south in the latter.

Of the polarising forces likely to have contributed to the division, the effects of industrial restructuring aided by a more permissive policy environment appear to be of most significance. The failure of wages in northern labour markets to adjust to geographical shifts in demand may have played a contributory role but it appears unlikely that increased flexibility in regional wages would have much impact on the problem.

Can the government play a positive role in restricting the tendency to economic polarisation between the north and south of Britain while preserving an environment favourable to national economic growth?

The prescriptions on offer from the present government and the opposition political parties leave much to be desired. A somewhat, crude characterisation of their positions sees the government pursuing a policy of increasing reliance on market forces. State intervention, in the form of an improvement in the presentation and delivery of existing policies and the removal of bureaucratic constraints, is to be used to encourage initiative and enterprise. For the opposition, increased state intervention would channel greater financial resources through new and existing political structures in an attempt to stimulate development generally in the north and in the inner cities in the south. Both positions appear to betray a lack of understanding of the processes generating the division in employment opportunities between north and south.

The central thesis of this chapter is that the processes of industrial restructuring during the last decade have shifted the locus of control over economic activity in the UK even more in favour of the south. As the operation of the market gradually shifts control to the south, so managerial and professional staff are drawn away from the north and the prospects for the stimulation of enterprise in those regions diminishes. Increasing concentration in the south in turn provides increased market opportunities which sustains the development process in a potentially cumulative spiral. Polarisation between north and south increases as a result.

It is of course possible to argue that the process of concentration will only go so far, that problems of congestion, increasing rents and rising property prices will reverse the process, resulting in growth spreading back to the north. But even if this does occur the costs of the adjustment to both national and regional economies will be high. Costs which might be avoided if the government would add a determination to encourage the decentralisation of economic control to its commitment to stimulate local enterprise.

Nor does the solution to the lack of employment opportunities in the north depend solely on expanding the resources available to deal with the problem, although increased resources would almost certainly help. Greater resources channelled through Urban Development Corporations, Local Authorities, and regional agencies such as the SDA, in partnership with private developers, can do much to remove the dereliction and improve the infrastructure of the inner cities and other urban areas. The fabric of many British cities, both in the south and particularly the north, has deteriorated markedly during the last few years owing to the significant number of factory closures. Improved infrastructure in the urban areas would appear to be a necessary condition for economic development and much needed, if temporary, local jobs would be created in the process of urban renewal. In addition, increased regional policy incentives would, given the academic evidence on the effects of the policy, increase the flow of mobile jobs to northern locations and stimulate indigenous employment.

However, it is unlikely that the increased expenditures, both public and private, would do much to reverse the increasing centralisation of company headquarters functions in the south. Valuable jobs would be created but they would be largely confined to the semi-skilled, the unskilled, and often part-time female employees. If the northern regions are to increase their economic independence then large numbers of jobs must be created in the managerial and professional categories. And if this is to be achieved policy must address the question of how best to effect the decentralisation of economic control. Political and administrative devolution could help, but that in itself will not be a complete answer to the problem. What is required is nothing less than a radical change in attitudes by key decision makers in government and industry who currently perceive that economic, political and cultural activity can only be satisfactorily conducted in the south. Until that time the so-called north-south divide will remain on the political agenda.

Brian Ashcroft, Fraser of Allander Institute and Department of Economics, University of Strathclyde.

I am grateful to Iain Jenkins for his comments on an earlier draft of this chapter. Errors and omissions remain my own.

References

1. See for example: Christopher Huhne "Census shows south's grip on jobs", *The Guardian*, January 8, 1987; Hazel Duffy "Jobs divide brought sharply into focus", *Financial Times*, January 8, 1987.

2. See for example, Fraser of Allander Institute, *Quarterly Economic Commentary*, Vol.12, No.3, February 1987.

3. See Scottish Office Press Release, 26 February 1987.

4. Fraser of Allander Institute, *Quarterly Economic Commentary*, Vol.13, No.1, August 1987.

5. Regional Studies Association (1983) "Report of an Inquiry into Britain's Regional Problems", Geo Books, Norwich.

6. See Scottish Office Press Release, 26 February 1987.

7. The employment data presented in the chapter are based primarily on counts of National Insurance cards up to 1971. After 1971 employment data were based on Census of Employment estimates. To preserve consistency, pre 1971 data have been adjusted using the ratio of the estimates produced by the two series for 1971, the only year in which the two overlap. It should be noted that after 1970, improved information on the location of employees in the distributive trades became available. Post 1970 data are therefore not strictly comparable with data for the earlier period.

8. The period 1966 to 1970 should be treated as an exception to the general pattern since regional policy was very active in this period. The differential is therefore narrower than in later periods of more rapid national employment growth.

9. For a discussion of changes in the regional unemployment differential in Britain since 1965 see H Armstrong and J Taylor *Regional Policy: The Way Forward*, Employment Institute, 1987.

10. See for example S Fothergill & G Gudgin *Unequal Growth: Urban and Regional Employment Change in the UK*, Heinemann, 1982.

11. J B Goddard & M G Coombes *The North-South Divide: Local Perspectives*, Centre for Urban and Regional Development Studies, University of Newcastle upon Tyne, 1987.

12. The index for each area was constructed from five variables: population change, 1971-81; employment change, 1971-78; employment change, 1978-81; unemployment rate, May 1985; households with 2 cars, 1981. The unemployment rate was given double weight.

13. J B Goddard & M G Coombes *op cit*, pp.8 and 20.

14. See the article by S Boyle & I Jenkins in *Quarterly Economic Commentary*, Fraser of Allander Institute, Vol.12, No.3, February, 1987.

15. See for example, S Brittan "The fool's paradise on jobs", *Financial Times*, December 4, 1986.

16. Cited in R L Martin "In what sense a 'jobs boom'. Employment recovery, government policy and the regions". *Regional Studies*, Vol.20, No.5, 1986.

17. In principle, the negative effect on the demand for local goods and services following wage cuts could be offset by increased government expenditures in the region to maintain the level of demand.

18. See for example J R Gold *An introduction to Behavioural Geography*, Oxford: Oxford University Press, 1980.

19. B Ashcroft & J Taylor "The movement of manufacturing industry and the effect of regional policy", *Oxford Economic Papers*, Vol.29, 1977, pp 84-101; and B Ashcroft & K Ingham, "The comparative impact of UK regional policy on foreign and indigenous firm movement", *Applied Economics*, Vol.14, No.1, 1982, pp 81-100.

20. For an assessment of the effects of external takeovers on acquired Scottish companies and the wider economy see B Ashcroft, J H Love & J Scouller *The Economic Effects of the Inward Acquisition of Scottish Manufacturing Companies, 1965 to 1980*, Industry Department for Scotland, ESU Research Paper No.11, 1987.

21. By 1985, 22.6% of those employed in the South-East were in the managerial and professional category, compared with 11.4% in the North.

22. For a discussion of recent changes in British regional policy and the

likely effects see H Armstrong and J Taylor *op cit*.

23. J Rhodes and P Tyler *South East Employment and Housing Study*, Department of Land Economy, University of Cambridge, 1987.

24. See the discussion and evidence in B Ashcroft, J H Love & J Scouller, *op cit*.

25. D J Storey & S Johnson "Regional variations in entrepreneurship in the UK" *Scottish Journal of Political Economy*, Vol.34, No.2, 1987, pp 161-173.

THE SCOTTISH ECONOMY DECLINE AND RESPONSE

Peter Smith

Malcolm Burns

1 TRENDS IN THE SCOTTISH ECONOMY

RECENT TRENDS

"1986 was a difficult year for the Scottish economy".[1]

That is the official view, expressed in the *Scottish Economic Bulletin* in June 1987. Growth of 3.1% in Gross Domestic Product in 1985 was followed by little growth if any in 1986 with possibly some resumption in 1987. Excluding oil and gas, output in Scottish production and construction industries for 1986 was 2.9% down on 1985, with a further fall of 3.1% in the first quarter of 1987. The UK figures show an increase of 1.8% between 1985 and 1986, and 1% growth in the first quarter of 1987. The April 1987 New Earnings Survey suggests that average male earnings in Scotland had fallen back in 1986 to 97.0% of British levels from 98.6% in 1985.[2]

The Fraser of Allander Institute *Quarterly Economic Commentary* seems to concur with the official view:

"...the short-term outlook for the Scottish economy continues to be favourable. Output growth was expected to be greater in 1987 than in 1986 but will fall short of that achieved throughout the UK. Continued improvement in 1988 would largely depend on developments in the world economy and on the extent to which the UK economy avoids overheating and an accelerating rate of inflation."[3]

Nevertheless, while the Institute notes that "prospects for employment were encouraging"[4], unemployment remains stubbornly high. Seasonally adjusted unemployment (which excludes school leavers) has fallen from 14.1% in January 1987 to 13.2% in August. The fall of about 23,000 from January's peak is dwarfed by the 326,000 who remain unemployed.[5] Changes in statistical methods have helped reduce the totals. The Restart scheme and availability for work tests played a part in attenuating the rise in the figures in late 1986 and accentuating the fall in early 1987. Real unemployment remains massive and intractable.

It is thus extremely disappointing that what growth there has been in the UK economy should make so little difference to unemployment in Scotland. The South East of England shed 15% of its jobless in the year to August 1987. Scotland's proportionately greater problem was only reduced by 5%. The rate of decline of Scottish unemployment in the first half of 1987 was only about two-thirds that of the UK as a whole.[6] The *Quarterly Economic Commentary* notes that:

"The extent to which the Scottish economy can lag behind developments elsewhere in the UK is clearly seen in recent data from the construction industry on housing starts which were nearly 17% down on the corresponding quarter in 1986 whereas in the UK they were 20% higher overall."[7]

Thus although Scottish GDP is expected to grow a little in 1987 and manufacturing output has recovered its 1979 level (still well below its 1975 peak), there seems little prospect of a return to anything like full employment in the Scottish economy.

LONGER TERM CHANGES

The Scottish economy has generally speaking never enjoyed the same success as most other areas of the UK in the post-war period. Up until 1960, even as the economy experienced mild 'boom' conditions, with the heavy industrial sector experiencing "relative buoyancy of orders, profitability and employment"[8], the unemployment rate was usually twice the national average. Scotland's contribution to the National Income actually fell from 8.9% in 1948 to 8.7% in 1960.

The marked regional disparities of the thirties began to re-emerge in Scotland and elsewhere, as traditional heavy industries entered their period of almost terminal decline. These problems gave rise after 1960 to an extremely active and relatively well-funded regional policy. This may simply have been a recognition that centralised Keynesian demand management could not of itself maintain the full employment and low regional disparities of the late 40s and 50s. In theory the surplus labour in the disadvantaged regions was to be linked to foreign multinational companies looking for production sites. One advantage was that unemployment blackspots could be mopped up while the general level of unemployment was allowed to rise. The change to an active regional policy in 1960 could therefore be seen, perhaps cynically, as an attempt to maintain the Tory vote in the regions.[9]

Whatever the reasons, Scotland entered a period of sustained economic growth which narrowed the difference between Scotland and the rest of the country. However it can be seen from Table 1 that the margins of growth in Scotland's favour virtually disappeared after 1973. The troubled

Table 1: Gross Domestic Product: Growth of Aggregate Output and Output by Sector in Scotland 1963-1984
(constant prices %pa)

| Period | Growth of Aggregate Output[1] | | Growth of Sector in Scotland | | | | |
	Scotland	UK	Agriculture Forestry & Fishing	Production & Construction	Distribution Hotels & Catering & Repairs	Transport & Communications	Other Services
1963-73	3.5	3.0	3.2	4.0	3.1	3.7	2.9
1973-84	0.6	0.5	1.4	−1.3	1.2	1.3	2.5
1973-79	0.8	0.7	−1.4	−1.0	1.5	1.8	2.8
1979-81	−1.8	−2.7	6.5	−5.5	−3.3	−1.2	2.2
1981-84	1.8	2.3	4.0	0.9	3.5	1.8	2.0

Source: Scottish Office, Scottish Economic Bulletin (quoted in N. Buxton, op.cit.)

[1] By far the greater part of the GDP of the Oil and Gas Industry is attributed to the Continental Shelf Region. In order, therefore to obtain valid comparisons between Scotland and the UK, class 13 of the 1980 Standard Industrial Classification has been omitted from the above estimates. This class includes mainland as well as Continental Shelf Region activity in the extraction of mineral oil and natural gas.

rise of the oil and gas sector did little to alleviate this. A diminution in the breadth of the 'active' component in regional policy, the beginnings of the international recession related to the oil price hike, and the multinationals' responses are at the root of the slowdown.

A comparison between the two periods, before and after the mid-seventies, shows the positive success of the 'active' period in sustaining economic growth. However, the concentration on large lumps of investment – like car and aluminium plants – may be seen as an inherent weakness, as many of these investments failed in the late 70s and early 80s. Regional policy has not been sufficiently supportive of its major projects.

The 'active' period also accentuated a change already under way in both the ownership and structure of Scottish industry, especially in manufacturing. Of all US companies established in the UK after 1945, one third were sited in Scotland. Between 1958 and 1968 overseas companies accounted for 30% of all new employment in new enterprises in Scotland. By 1975, only 41% of manufacturing employment in Scotland was controlled from within the country.[10]

In terms of structure the trend was for non-Scottish companies to move into the minerals, textiles, light engineering and electronics sectors. These changes continued into the 70s and early 80s and were accompanied by a slow decline in total manufacturing employment and a strong rise in service sector employment. The decline in manufacturing was accelerated into a collapse by the domestic depression in the UK after 1979. The rise in service sector employment was almost completely halted.

A long term trend towards service sector employment cannot be denied. But the question arises whether a service sector dominant in terms of output and employment can maintain full employment income, or whether it needs a major manufacturing sector to underpin it in terms of tradeable output.

The employment figures since 1979 tell a rather sorry story. Between 1979 and 1986 Scottish manufacturing lost nearly 190,000 jobs – nearly 30%. Agriculture, forestry and fishing lost 17,000, energy and water lost 21,000, and construction lost 15,000. Against losses of almost quarter of a million jobs, the service sector gained only 30,000.

Over the same period, 'employers and self-employed' rose by 45,000 while the total of 'employees in employment' fell by 210,000 to 1,892,000. Males in employment fell by 173,000 to 1,032,000. There are no figures for part-time males. Females in full-time employment fell by 36,000 to 861,000 while part-time women workers increased by 29,000 to 361,000. This has taken place during what the Government assures us is a period of necessary 'shake-out' and subsequent strong growth in the UK economy. There is no clear evidence that enough growth will take place to create jobs for more than a modest proportion of those already 'shaken out' of work.

What then are the problems in Scotland? Two stand out above all others. Firstly, the trend to centralisation in the British economy, coupled to increased overseas control of Scottish industry and the lack of a comprehensive regional policy which would counteract the centripetal pull of the South East of England and the North of continental Europe. Secondly, and closely related, is the de-industrialisation of Scotland.

2 SCOTTISH RESPONSES

THE STANDING COMMISSION

One Scottish response to the changes of the last two years has been the establishment of an independent Standing Commission on the Scottish Economy. The Commission was launched on 18 November 1986. The decision to establish it had been taken at the Scottish Economic Summit convened jointly by Strathclyde Regional Council and the STUC on 1 July. Public support came from Summit participants ranging from churches to businessmen, local authorities to trade unions. Running on the lines of a parliamentary select committee, it was to present a case after taking evidence from a variety of organisations, institutions, indidivuals and experts. In the words of Sir Kenneth Alexander, previously chairman of the HIDB, principal of Stirling University and presently Chancellor of Aberdeen University, the Commission he was to chair would be "hungry for ideas, suggestions, information and research in any area relevant to its work."[11]

What kind of initiative is this? And what solutions can it offer to the problems which are recognised by its very existence?

Some answers to these questions may be developed by looking at how and why the Standing Commission was set up, considering some of the historical and economic background, identifying the major participants and the interests which they represent, and tracing these strands through the main events of the past two years.

Press reaction to the July Summit had been largely favourable. A *Scotsman* editorial the next day proclaimed a:

"DEMONSTRATION OF SCOTTISH WILL

It worked....That such a consensus could be constructed by a conference representing much of Scottish life was a substantial achievement which cannot be disregarded. In itself it defines, despite Government protestations to the contrary, the existence of a debilitating malaise as

Table 2: Changes in employment by industry: Scotland, 1979-1986

	1979	1980	1981	Sept 1981	1982	1983	1984	Sept 1984	1985	1986	thousands[1] % change 1979-86
Employers and self-employed	160	154	149	–	164	179	185	–	200	205	+28
Employees in employment[2]											
Total	2,102	2,082	2,002	1,985	1,950	1,899	1,901	1,904	1,906	1,892	–10
Males	1,205	1,186	1,128	1,113	1,090	1,060	1,043	1,053	1,043	1,032	–14
Females	897	896	874	872	860	839	858	851	862	861	–4
Part-time females	332	335	336	338	337	337	347	346	361	361	+9
Analysis by sector (1980 SIC)											
0 Agriculture, forestry, fishing[3]	48	45	45	39	39	37	35	37	34	31	–35
1 Energy & water supply	72	74	73	73	72	68	65	65	59	51	–29
2-4 Manufacturing industries	604	564	510	502	477	444	434	434	433	416	–31
5 Construction	155	155	141	138	135	134	136	139	139	140	–10
6-9 Service Industries	1,224	1,244	1,233	1,234	1,228	1,216	1,231	1,229	1,241	1,254	+2
Analysis by industry classes (1980 SIC)											
01-03 Agriculture, forestry, fishing[3]	48	45	45	39.1	39	37	35	36.7	34	31	–35
11-14 Fuel extraction, processing				44.2				39.5			
15-17 Other energy and water	72	74	73	28.9	72	68	65	25.7	59	51	–29
21-24 Metal manufacturing, ore other mineral extraction	82	77	67	42.7	63	55	53	32.2	53	52	–37
25-26 Chemicals, man-made fibres				24.1				20.1			
32 Mechanical engineering				77.1				69.2			
33-34, 37 Office machinery, electrical engineering, electrical machinery, electrical engineering, instruments				62.5				62.4			

SIC	Industry											Change
35	Motor vehicles and parts	258	239	215	11.2	204	195	6.8	189	187	181	−30
36	Other transport equipment				41.7			34.1				
31	Metal goods nes	265	248	229	18.7	209	194	15.1	192	193	184	−31
41-42	Food, drink & tobacco				87.1			73.1				
43-45	Textiles, leather, clothing	155	155	141	68.3	135	134	58.1	136	139	140	−10
46,48,49	Timber, rubber, plastics etc				30.0			28.0				
47	Paper, printing, publishing	197	201	193	38.9	200	188	34.3	193	193	194	−2
50	Construction				137.8			138.9				
61-63,67	Wholesale distrib., repairs	194	194	191	85.5	184	183	89.6	186	182	178	−8
66	Hotels and catering				107.1			103.7				
64-65	Retail distribution	135	134	129	190.2	124	119	186.3	115	117	114	−16
71-77	Transport				92.0			85.6				
79	Post, telecommunications	123	126	129	35.9	135	140	29.5	141	146	153	+24
81-85	Banking, finance, insurance				131.0			146.2				
91-92	Public administrat., defence[4]	170	171	167	167.6	168	171	169.7	170	171	176	+4
93	Education				144.4			133.4				
95	Health, veterinary services	403	419	422	145.2	417	416	143.5	425	433	438	+9
94,96-98					134.0			142.1				

1. Changes rounded to nearest whole number.
2. At June except for September 1981 and 1984 Census of Employment figures. 1985 and 1986 are provisional figure.
3. From September 1981 excludes non-principal tenant farmers who are now counted as self-employed.
4. Excludes members of H.M. Forces.
5. Domestic servants are excluded. Locally engaged staff working in diplomatic and other overseas organisations are included.

Source: Scottish Office, *Scottish Economic Bulletin*

well as the belief that the means of affecting a cure are available."[12]

However, a practical problem might arise if the Scottish Office withheld support. The Commission "could exist without the blessing of the Secretary of State but it could not survive the disdain of his senior officials."[12] But Malcolm Rifkind in a press statement said that the Summit "appears to have struck a positive and constructive vein" and he would listen to "sensible and realistic proposals to tackle our economic problems."

Encouraged by the unanimity which they had discovered, a steering committee made up of Strathclyde Region, the STUC and the Scottish Council (Development & Industry) pressed ahead with putting the Standing Commission together. A number of well-known, influential people from a variety of backgrounds agreed to join.

Press response to the November launch of the Standing Commission was slightly more equivocal. The *Glasgow Herald* argued that the Commission might serve as a useful forum for ideas "if it succeeds in getting its act together and avoiding the political pitfalls" and concluded that "the result may or may not be a consensus in favour of policies to reverse the decline but the effort seems worth making."[13] Hardly a ringing endorsement. To the practical and political pitfalls, a cautionary historical dimension was added. Alf Young, writing in the *Herald*, found

"ALEXANDER FACING A CREDIBILITY OBSTACLE

....even the combination of Alexander, the practical economist, with formidable talents and time on his hands, the great and the good gathered around him, an annual budget of £50,000, and a collective determination to define our economic future, is no guarantee that the Standing Commission on the Scottish Economy will succeed where so many before it have failed."[14]

This was a reference in particular to the Toothill Commission of twenty-five years earlier, which had the indulgence of an expansionist Tory government, directing car and aluminium plants into Scotland, "turning its back on traditional heavy industry". But the Toothill prescription failed, it is generally agreed. The proof of that is unemployment "at levels which Toothill could only have conceived of in some apocalyptic nightmare".[15]

The politics are different now, too. The only party ever to have gained more than half the votes in a General Election in Scotland was the Conservative Party, in 1955. But shortly after that it became apparent, most of all in regions like Scotland, that full employment was not going to remain an achievable objective. Ravenscraig and regional policy were ways in which the Conservatives hoped to hold Scotland. Today, the Tories are not fighting to win British elections in Scotland, and the economic orthodoxy belongs to Margaret Thatcher, not Harold Macmillan. One of her first targets was British Steel, the loss-making nationalised giant, to be made profitable not by investment, but by rationalisation. Ravenscraig was under threat.

GARTCOSH AND THE STANDING COMMITTEE ON STEEL

The steel industry campaign was unique. A conference in Motherwell in June 1985, specifically to campaign for investment in Ravenscraig was attended by over 200, representing virtually every organisation in public life in Scotland. There was unanimous consensus that a £90m investment should be made in the coke ovens. It is interesting that such a specific act (investment in a particular part of a steelworks) should have been so important to such a wide and representative constituency.

A recall conference in August 1985 in response to the Gartcosh closure announcement signalled the campaign to save the steel mill, an integral component of the Ravenscraig complex. Strathclyde Region were heavily involved in the unofficial Standing Committee which had been set up. Rallies, marches, demonstrations and lobbies were organised. At the lobby of Parliament in November 1985 Michael Forsyth, now a Scottish Office minister, was the only wholehearted dissenter in a group of Scottish Tories who met the delegation. Hector Munro and Anna McCurley provided sterling support for the Gartcosh case.

In January 1986, during the Commons debate on closure, the (Conservative) chairman of the Select Committee on Trade and Industry made a significant intervention, asking the government to look again at the case. McCurley and Munro both voted against the government.

Malcolm Rifkind, on the other hand, abruptly elevated to Scottish Secretary after the Westland affair had airlifted George Younger to the relative safety of the Defence Ministry, refused to intervene in what he described as a commercial decision by British Steel.

Against a depressing background of falling oil prices and spiralling unemployment, Gartcosh was a bitter defeat. But as popular opposition to closure grew with each conference, demonstration and lobby, the broad representative consensus was more and more remarkable. Perhaps only the UCS work-in mobilised greater support in recent times. The Government's stock had never been lower. At the Regional elections held in May 1986, the Conservatives were hammered. By contrast, Labour improved on their already impressive gains in the District poll two years earlier. With half the population of Scotland, many of the most pressing economic and social problems, and with what appeared to be an overwhelming mandate, Strathclyde Labour politicians felt frustration at the poor response from government to a series of specific crises in the Scottish economy.

Gartcosh was one. But from early 1986 there was no shortage of contenders for closure headlines: British Rail Engineering at Springburn; the shipbuilding industry – especially Ailsa at Troon and Govan Shipbuilders; the clothing and textiles industries due to a lack of Government support on an equal scale with European competitors; coal and oil-related industries as a result of the collapse in the price of oil.

THE STUC SETS AN AGENDA

At the STUC Congress in April 1986, a discussion document, *Scotland – A Strategy for the Future* was presented. The new General Secretary, Campbell Christie, indicated its origins in his speech:

"This document arises as a direct result of the Gartcosh closure. Despite the great concern in Scotland, despite the massive unity in favour of retention of the Gartcosh works, the Government has refused to listen".[16]

The document was "not a solution, but an agenda" for discussion with "those who know how our economy can be set right". Responses would be sought from affiliated unions and Trades Councils, but also crucially, from local authorities and other bodies representing Scottish opinion.

"What we will have to do is establish the consensus we had over Gartcosh in looking forward, in pressing forward, in creating the jobs we need here in Scotland. That is why I am pleased to welcome here the local authority representatives from the Regional Councils, from the District Councils, from the Scottish Council (Development & Industry), and from the churches in order to forge that way ahead."[17]

Shortly after the May elections, Strathclyde Region called on Malcolm Rifkind to convene a conference on the Scottish economy. He refused. The Labour administration in Strathclyde was prepared to break with traditional conceptions of the role of a local authority. It was quickly decided, picking up from the Gartcosh campaign and good press reaction, to go ahead and convene a Summit in association with the STUC.

Both organisations had decided that the crisis was older and deeper than the single issues of particular closures, and required broader, more positive action.

3 THE ECONOMIC SUMMIT – THE WAY FORWARD?

DE-INDUSTRIALISATION

The Way Forward, the paper which was presented to the Summit in July 1986, detailed the immediate crisis in the Scottish economy, and the longer term problems.

"After almost a decade of closures, contraction and mounting unemployment, a growing body of Scottish opinion appears to share the view that a fresh approach is needed to solve Scotland's deep-seated economic and industrial problems."[18]

Some of the main themes of *Scotland – A Strategy for the Future* were picked up. The decline in manufacturing was taken as the main indicator of catastrophe. It was noted that service sector employment had risen, and in fact the total of employees in employment was up slightly (in 1985 from a low in 1983 – see Table 1) – but that this was due to an increase in part-time, low-paid jobs and made no impact on the still-growing unemployment problem. The Government has argued that its critics are obsessed with manufacturing employment, that the service sector is healthy and growing and that service jobs are every bit as good as manufacturing jobs. *The Way Forward* faced up to this head on.

"...it is important to note that there are serious problems in relying on the service sector to fill the gap left by the collapse of manufacturing."

It was pointed out that there is a strong inter-relationship between the manufacturing and the service sectors. A big manufacturing closure affects suppliers and local services. Secondly, and quite crucially:

"...only a small proportion of services are 'tradeable', i.e. bring income into Scotland, rather than just recycling income within communities in Scotland."

Further, much service employment is in the public sector, where spending restrictions, pressure on pay, deregulation, and privatisation threaten jobs and curb growth in hard-hit areas. For all these reasons:

"...it is important to be clear that economic recovery in Scotland will to a large extent depend on a healthy manufacturing sector, even if manufacturing employment may not itself grow substantially."

But in economic reality Britain was suffering de-industrialisation. This was defined (quoting Cambridge economist Ajit Singh) as the absence of an "efficient" manufacturing sector, which:

"...currently as well as potentially not only satisfies the demands of consumers at home, but is also able to sell enough of its products to pay for the nation's import requirements...at socially acceptable levels of output, employment and the exchange rate."

In short, North Sea oil has bailed out the UK balance of payments but these revenues are no longer growing and will shortly begin to decline. "Invisible" traded services like tourism and banking can make only a limited contribution. If the relative decline of manufacturing continues this contribution will not be enough and a permanent trade deficit will result. In regional terms, a similar argument applies.

"For a healthy regional economy, attention needs to be given to strengthening the 'basic' or 'tradeable' sector to generate income, and in Scottish context this means manufacturing must not be neglected."

THE SUMMIT CONSENSUS

The Summit achieved broad agreement around the need for immediate action on the crisis industries, and also on some basic principles:

"1. The economic and industrial situation in Scotland cannot be allowed to deteriorate any further.

"2. Recovery cannot be relied on to come about unassisted, and the task of reconstruction must begin as of now.

"3. Striking an appropriate balance in public policy between reliance on oil, services, the new high technology industries, and a modernised and re-invigorated manufacturing industry is important.

"4. Fresh policies are required to help bridge the growing gap between those in work and those out of work."[19]

A Standing Commission comprising "a small number of people chosen for their familiarity with and experience of some of the areas of enquiry" would generate proposals on rebuilding the Scottish economy and stimulate constructive debate about the way forward. A variety of issues should be included in the Standing Commission's rolling programme of work: investment; research and development; skills and training; exports; energy; and policies to redistribute benefits of re-industrialisation and thus tackle low pay and unemployment. The Commission should make an interim report back to a reconvened Summit.

The Summit discussions were frank and fascinating, with participants drawing lessons from the past and agreeing on many fundamental points.[20]

Hamish Morrison of the Scottish Council (Development & Industry) felt that "Scotland's full potential as an industrial economy has been inhibited...centralisation has been acting against Scotland's industrial vitality for half a century".[21]

One reason for the success of the Summit was the weight which representatives of private enterprise put behind the initiative. The "total lack of a coherent industrial policy" should be addressed by the Standing Commission, thought Ewan Marwick of the Association of Scottish Chambers of Commerce. John Davidson of the CBI said he "shared without reservation the concerns expressed in the document". He also referred to *Oceanspan*. This was a 1970 Scottish Council plan to make central Scotland, facing out to North America over the Atlantic, an "export oriented conversion economy...a new industrial doorway to Europe".[22] In June 1986 the CBI was proposing "Eurowestport" in Scotland linked to the forthcoming Channel Tunnel – an essentially similar idea. The Toothill report and the *West Central Scotland Plan* of 1974 were also spoken of.

The references to Toothill, *Oceanspan*, and "coherent industrial policy", the implicit corporatism which they represent, underline the crucial political differences between the Scottish business sector and Conservative politicians in the Scottish Office and in London. Ian Grieve of Babcock Power stated that management and workers had to make a joint effort. He suggested that perhaps we should "call ourselves Scotland PLC and work together". At that time Babcock was investing heavily in new plant in Renfrew. However, they also faced a severe shortage of orders – in large part precisely because the government operates no "coherent industrial policy". It is clear why such businessmen should favour planning for the regeneration of locally-owned industry within a corporative state framework. "Stop-go" in the late 50s caused problems to regional businesses; how much more so, now that we seem to have swapped it for permanent stop.

Yet it would be wrong to claim too much for the consensus. Babcock, for example, is not a Scottish company, despite its long association with Renfrew. It was recently taken over by a much smaller English concern – just one of the spate of mergers and takeovers mentioned earlier which have affected Scotland. The largest of these were Coats Patons/Vantona Viyella and the Guinness takeover of Distillers. In the eighteen months to January 1987, Inbucon the management consultants found that total capital employed by Scottish industrial and manufacturing companies had fallen by more than half, from £4¾ bn to £2¼ bn.[22] Of course, Distillers had been headquartered in London for years. The very process of centralisation which the Summit identified as being so important, has over a long time substantially undermined the regional basis of the consensus.

The political base of the Conservative party in Scotland has suffered as a function of the reduced status of Scottish-owned industry and the mounting regional economic problem. While all political parties claim to represent the Scottish interest, it has become progressively less clear to their instinctive supporters in the professions, management and small business that the Conservatives can do that. It was not just Tory MPs who voted against their own government on Gartcosh – there were significant defections from the ranks of local councillors and activists. But the leaders of the Scottish Conservative party could not offer, as they did in 1969, a party commission report in favour of an elected Assembly, albeit with only consultative powers. Malcolm Rifkind was once in favour of devolution but can now only defuse the demands of business for regional policies. It was to this end that the invitation to the Scottish Office to be represented at the Summit was declined.

The other elements in the national consensus were all in place at the Summit. Rev. Kenyon Wright, secretary of the Scottish Council of Churches felt that the Summit was a symptom of something broader, an opportunity to produce a "total view of Scotland as a nation in the world – economic, political, moral." All the political parties and many academic institutions were represented. The local authority representatives drew attention to their record in economic development. They were not all municipal socialists. The Tory councillor for Troon, where the Ailsa shipyard was under threat, was obviously concerned with the shipbuilding industry, but had a wider view too. New investment had to be attracted he stated, but "the multinationals come and go – it is important for the SDA to attract the right kind of investment". He hoped that individuals in his party would participate in the Standing Commission and that his party would support it.

4 THE CRISIS DEEPENS

GUINNESS, CATERPILLAR AND THE SCOTTISH 'VOICE'

At the annual International Forum organised by the Scottish Council (Development & Industry) in November 1986, an important position paper was presented: *Performance and Problems of Scotland's Industrial Economy*. A personal view by Neil Buxton at that time depute director of Glasgow College of Technology, it was also an authoritative and rigorous academic assessment of the Scottish economy which largely echoed the themes addressed at the Summit. Buxton's main conclusions were that the Scottish economy suffers from de-industrialisation and from the growth of centralised decision making. He felt that the problems he had identified could usefully be taken up by the Standing Commission, which represented "a powerful alliance of Scottish opinion".[24]

A few days later, the Standing Commission was launched. It was the end of 1986, with Scottish unemployment at 370,000. Just when it looked as though things couldn't get worse, a series of hammer blows hit the Scottish economy. The year which had begun with the loss of Gartcosh and continued with the closure of BREL and Ailsa ended with a welter of redundancy announcements. Guinness were rationalising whisky production and the Black and White plant at Stepps was to go. Babcocks could no longer keep men on in the absence of orders. Scott Lithgow, along with most of the shipbuilding industry, faced the New Year with an empty order book and large redundancies. At Britoil's Glasgow headquarters the low oil price had worked its way back from the North Sea and staff were paid off. Burroughs announced the closure of their Cumbernauld electronics plant.

All sections of Scottish industry were in trouble. In January 1987, two interesting developments took place. The Department of Trade and Industry launched an investigation into the Guinness/Distillers merger and Scots businessman Sir Norman MacFarlane became chairman – but the fear was whether Guinness would keep Ernest Saunders' promise to set up the corporate headquarters in Edinburgh? And Caterpillar announced that they were closing their Uddingston factory just weeks after a major investment programme had been trumpeted by the beleaguered Secretary of State Malcolm Rifkind – to which the workers immediately responded by occupying the factory. These events confirmed fears which had been expressed at the Summit by all participants.

At a conference convened by Edinburgh District Council in January 1987, a wide representation of Scottish life came together to look at the lessons to be learned from the Guinness affair. Would Guinness keep its promise? What should be done to try to control mergers so that the Scottish economy did not suffer?

Professor Jack Shaw, executive director of Scottish Financial Enterprise, outlined a vision of a service based future where Scots could "export their personal skills technologically". But he agreed with the general analysis of the problem: "Scottish based businesses are an endangered species". And he called for a "crusade" to achieve the new Scotland.

"We have our own Scottish Office and our own Scottish Development Agency, and in Scotland as this Conference demonstrates, we do at least speak to each other to identify solutions to problems."[25]

While the STUC and Edinburgh District Council favoured pressure on Guinness to keep its promise, Professor Shaw thought it would be counter-productive to appear strident. Economic journalist Alf Young, another contributor to the conference, reflected this dissonance.

"There is no such thing as a Scottish voice. The Scottish lobby just doesn't exist. It is simply a chimera, and doesn't operate as a reality or an entity. Scotland didn't express any great concern at Distillers' inability to manage their whisky operations; nor that their old headquarters were in London; nor that most of the board were London based. There was no united voice during either the Bells or Distillers takeover battles. Also, the Scottish financial community's perspective has always been international and does not gel neatly with the Scottish political community's commitment to the Scottish economy. Thus the perspectives of the Scottish 'lobby' are themselves divergent. It has never been a united forum speaking on Scotland's behalf. So it is going to be hard to build up a unified Scottish voice – on this occasion stimulated by Guinness' failure to meet Scottish aspirations – without first of all appearing to be threateningly vocal and then learning lessons for future action. It is heartening to see such a representative group as this Conference. The only comparison is the Scottish Council's Annual Forum."[26]

Much of this may be soberingly realistic. Certainly there was no united voice during the takeover battles. And to say that the interest of the Scottish financial community "does not gel neatly" with that of the Scottish economy at once politely understates the distinction between financial and industrial capital; and gives some understanding of the political problem in Scotland. But apart from those who have faith in the Scottish Office,there are many Scottish voices all saying essentially the same things. This was clearer during the Caterpillar occupation.

Caterpillar illustrates the weakness of the increasing Scottish dependence on overseas-owned manufacturing plants. Much of what is true about Caterpillar is also true of newer inward investments. In the face of Japanese competition the American giant was having to cut capacity. But it was *easier* to pull out of Uddingston than its other European plants because there were no strings attached to the British investment. And since there were no higher corporate functions whatsoever at the factory, there were no deep roots in Scotland.

The Scottish reaction was unequivocal. Even Malcolm Rifkind praised the occupation as a "spirited and determined" effort to preserve employment which has "won wide support." His criticism of Caterpillar was partly due to personal embarrassment, but also to shrewd political calculation. With the Scottish Tories at an all-time low in the polls and an election looming, it could have been suicidal not to line up with public outrage. Certainly the business community, particularly the supplier companies, wanted Government intervention. Again, lobbies of Parliament took place, and Conservative politicians lined up on the platforms to support the Caterpillar workers. But the Government did nothing, despite a range of options and the protestation of virtually the whole Scottish community.

SCOTLAND – A LAND FIT FOR PEOPLE

In this tense political atmosphere the STUC published, in April 1987,

Scotland – A Land Fit for People, the outcome of the consultation begun the previous year. This document was forward-looking and positive. The main proposal was a radical new policy framework for the future of Scotland's economy. But many elements of the strategy, it claimed, could be implemented without a change of Government.

The success of regional policy since the early sixties had been the large number of jobs created over a long period. The failure has been the progressive weakening of Scotland's industrial base. The original role of the Scottish Development Agency – stimulation of the indigenous manufacturing sector with public assistance and accountability – had to be restored:

> "The SDA's direct investment budget needs to be greatly augmented. Its investment guidelines must be rewritten enabling it in sectors where growth is likely to provide: publicly accountable assistance and direction; loans or equity to companies which cannot get them from the private financial sector because of its narrow and short-sighted obsession with quick returns; and a vital link between the realities of competitive commercial life and the more abstract world of the planners."[27]

Recognising that inward investment is necessary but aware of the historic problems created, a new approach to multinationals was suggested. Multinationals have been welcomed on their own terms as providers of jobs. But Scotland (with access to UK and European markets, specific labour skills, a pleasant environment) has something to bargain with. In order to gain long term benefits from at least a proportion of inward investments, there should be:

> "a flexible approach to negotiations on such questions as the location of R&D facilities and other higher corporate functions, and the development of technology transfer agreements".

A Scottish takeovers watchdog was proposed, and a campaign to sell Scotland as a location for company headquarters. One of the areas which combines high tech manufacturing with valuable tradeable services is offshore technology. This expertise needs new markets abroad if it is to survive the decline of North Sea reserves. For this and many other sectors where small but good Scottish companies compete, a Scottish International Trading Agency was proposed, with offices in potential customer states, which could provide marketing on a commission basis.

At a local level, English experience with Enterprise Boards should be applied in Scotland. Despite the existence of the SDA, and because of its changing role, exemplified by increasing concentration on property marketing, there is much which can be done by councils to help local enterprises meet demand for goods and services.

This adds up to an executive planning function for a Scottish Assembly. Without such powers, nothing can challenge the freedom of the markets to further damage the Scottish economy.

THE 1987 ELECTION AND THE SUMMER OF DISCONTENT

The Tories in Scotland fought a low key, defensive election, a damage limitation exercise. They ended with only 10 MPs to Labour's 50. Since the election, the unemployment figures have fallen back, but not as greatly as the UK fall, and the production industries' output has finally regained its 1979 level, all on the back of the consumer boom. However, the balance of trade, both Scottish and British, is worsening. More redundancies in traditional industries are offsetting the few new inward investments. Guinness has finally reneged on its promise of corporate headquarters, and Caterpillar has gone.

The traumatic experience of the Scottish economy over the past few years has not diverted the Government. During the summer, a radical right-wing programme has been pressed ahead. Along with policies on schools, housing, poll tax, local authorities, trade unions, all of which were decisively rejected by the Scottish electorate, comes yet another review of regional policy. The effect of the last review in 1984 is only just taking its toll. Then, many areas were removed from development status, regional development grants were cut from 22% to 15% of capital costs, and a limit of £10,000 per job created was applied. Regional policy expenditure has been cut back severely. The most likely effect of the review will be further restrictions designed ostensibly to target resources more efficiently, but in reality to cut total expenditure even further.

Potentially the most important single arm of regional policy, the Scottish Development Agency has spent a progressively more insignificant proportion of its budget on industrial investment in recent years due to rewriting of its investment guidelines after the 1979 election. The SDA has never been allowed to fulfill the main role it was conceived for in 1975. It has certainly been used as a means to channel public money into private companies, but the resources and political will have never been applied to make it a tool which could direct the economic development of the country.

The fact that it is needed at all is an indictment of the Scottish financial sector.

"Charlotte Square in Edinburgh is the fifth largest financial centre in Europe, but its links with indigenous industry are perhaps not always strong as they might be, and a large proportion of funds placed with it are invested overseas."[28]

As Scottish manufacturing is increasingly owned and controlled by multinationals so the multinationals increasingly reap the remaining benefits of Scottish regional policy. Scottish industrialists are not likely to benefit from the review of regional policy.

Finally, the sudden realization by world stock markets that the USA has been running colossal budget and balance of payments deficits looks likely to cause at least a slowdown in the growth of world trade. Britain and more so Scotland, as open economies, could suffer more than most. Despite some recent inward investment announcements, the Scottish economy has taken further knocks with large redundancies at Babcock and Scott Lithgow.

5. THE STANDING COMMISSION

STRUCTURE AND SECRETARIAT

The structure of the Standing Commission has been evolved to fit the demands and constraints of the resources available. It was originally to have a dual purpose. Firstly, in the short term to do some lobbying on specific urgent issues. In the end this has not happened – due to teething troubles the hastily constructed special delegation really had no forum within which to develop. However, through a variety of traumatic events, the consensus has developed, perhaps hardened, and the longer term objective looks as though it can be achieved.

The Fraser of Allander Institute has taken on the role of secretariat. As reputable independent economic analysts their involvement adds to the already impressive academic credentials of the Commission. The setting up of working groups has given the Standing Commission a structure. When the Summit is reconvened with winter, these groups will make reports and recommendations. Specific events are being organised, like the recent oil-related industries conference, where participants included Shell UK and former Energy Minister Alick Buchanan-Smith.

INTERIM REPORT

While it is impossible to predict what the interim reports of the working groups will contain in detail, much of what will concern them has been discussed here.

The employment and manpower group is pulling together useful work which is being done in academic institutions on the labour market using 'job gap' calculations. This is being related to practical work which has been done by various agencies, for example, Strathclyde Region's *Jobs Plan*[29]. The case for further administrative devolution of the MSC will be considered in the light of STUC and Scottish Council proposals for greater Scottish and local control over training.[30]

The trade issues group may also pick up similar STUC and Scottish Council proposals for some form of Scottish export body.[31] Work done by the Scottish Council[32] suggests that Scotland has a relatively narrow export base, depending heavily on just two goods – computers and whisky. The thought is that the successful Locate in Scotland bureau may be replicated in reverse, in order to develop markets for a broader range of Scottish products.

The investment issues group will obviously concentrate on regional policy and the SDA, both of which are subject to Government review. The Standing Commission's proposals will be important inputs to these reviews.

SCOTTISH PROSPECT – WHAT CAN THE STANDING COMMISSION ACHIEVE?

What has already been achieved is a most remarkable degree of consensus about the nature of Scotland's economic problems, and a surprising willingness of the nation's experts – the Commissioners themselves, the extensive team of academic assessors, the working group participants and contributors – to get their hands dirty in trying to thrash out realistic ways forward.

The consensus implies that all concerned are in this together, that there are at least *some* mutually agreeable courses of action which can be taken. It follows, of course, that if there are solutions available, but they have not yet been adequately argued for and tried, there has been a failure on the part of the representatives of sections of society. It is precisely this failure that the Standing Commission seeks to redress by building a consensus.

One institution that has failed to address the economy is the Government itself. The Government is also refusing to become part of the consensus which the Standing Commission hopes to develop. This displays two problems: one for the Government and one for the Standing Commission. The Commission problem is twofold: first that official expertise and assistance would greatly help the project; and secondly, and much more important, that official approval has to be won before any of its schemes ever leave the drawing board.

That approval is unlikely to be forthcoming. The official case against will probably be that the Standing Commission is not representative. The CBI, represented at the Summit in July 1986, is not involved in the Standing Commission. The Scottish Office, which controls the Industry Department for Scotland, has refused to assist. The SDA is unable to appoint an assessor. Pressure has been put on Government departments and business people not to participate.

The problem for the Government is easy to state: it has no mandate in Scotland. Right across the political spectrum in the country, up to (and including many members of) the Conservative Party there is broad opposition to the Government's handling of the economy. As John Davidson of the Scottish CBI put it colloquially, "things is no right".[33]

The question of how this will be resolved has a complicated and by no means clear political answer.

By what criteria can the success of the Standing Commission be judged? For a start, there is the very fact that work has been done, that the Summit is reconvening. If the Standing Commission's success is to be defined in terms of changes in Government policy, then it is likely to have been a failure, at least for the present. If however, success is seen more realistically, as the provision of a genuine and authoritative Scottish voice on the economy, the Standing Commission looks set fair to achieve it.

The reconvened Summit will consider what are, of necessity, preliminary reports. Its recommendations are likely to be less important than the directions which are identified for future work. The long term prospects for the Standing Commission are good. The prospects for the Scottish economy look distinctly less promising.

Peter Smith, Head of Trade Union Research Unit, Scotland
Malcolm Burns, Research Assistant, Trade Union Research Unit, Scotland.

The Unit is based in Glasgow College og Technology.

References

1.   *Scottish Economic Bulletin*, HMSO, Edinburgh, June 1987.

2.   Quoted in *Scottish Economic Bulletin*.

3.   *Quarterly Economic Commentary*, Fraser of Allander Institute, Glasgow, August 1987.

4.   *Ibid*

5.   *Unemployment in Scotland 1987*, Alistair Smith, unpublished STUC paper. Official figures from *Employment Gazette*, HMSO, London, monthly.

6.   *Quarterly Economic Commentary*, August 1987.

7.   *Ibid.*

8.   P Smith and J Brown, 'Economic crisis, foreign capital and working class response' in T Dickson (ed.) *Scottish Capitalism*, Lawrence & Wishart, London, 1980, p292.

9.   See J Foster and C Woolfson, *The Politics of the UCS Work-in*, Lawrence & Wishart, London, 1986, esp. chapters 1 and 2.

10.   Smith and Brown, *op.cit.* See also N Buxton, *Scotland in a rapidly changing world: Performance and problems of Scotland's Industrial Economy*, a position paper for the Scottish Council Development and Industry's International Forum at Gleneagles in 1986.

11.   *Scotsman*, 17 November 1986.

12.   *ibid.* 2 July 1986.

13.   *Glasgow Herald*, 18 November 1986.

14.   *ibid*, 19 November 1986.

15.   *ibid.*

16.   *89th Annual Report, Aberdeen 1986*, STUC, Glasgow, 1986.

17.   *ibid.*

18.   *The Way Forward*, a paper presented to Scottish Economic Summit, 1 July 1986, Strathclyde Regional Council and STUC. Following quotes from same source unless otherwise noted.

19.   Summit communique to press, 1 July 1986.

20.   This and following quotes are contributions to Summit discussion, 1 July 1986, unless otherwise noted.

21.   This picks up a Scottish Council theme from the sixties. See *Centralisation of industrial control: the twentieth century nine of diamonds – the curse of Scotland*. Scottish Council Development and Industry paper, Glasgow, 1969.

22.   *Oceanspan: a maritime-based development strategy for a European Scotland 1970-2000*, Scottish Council Development and Industry, Edinburgh, 1970. See also *Inquiry into the Scottish Economy 1960-61*,

usually called the *Toothill Report*, Scottish Council Development and Industry, Paisley, 1961, and *West Central Scotland Plan*, WCSP, Glasgow 1974.

23.   Quoted in *Financial Times*, 7 January 1987.

24.   N Buxton, *op.cit*.

25.   *Guinness plc and the Scottish economy: broadening the debate*, conference report, Edinburgh District Council, January 1987.

26.   *ibid*.

27.   *Scotland – A Land Fit for People*, STUC, Glasgow, 1987. Following quotes from same source unless otherwise noted.

28.   *The Way Forward, op.cit*.

29.   *The Region's Economy – The Regional Council's Platform for Growth*, Strathclyde Regional Council, Glasgow, 1987.

30.   *Scotland – A Land Fit for People, op.cit*. and *Industrial Development Incentives*, consultative paper on reform of regional policy, Scottish Council Development and Industry, Edinburgh, 1987.

31.   *ibid*.

32.   Mark Cox, 'Scotland's export performance – a closer look' in *Quarterly Economic Commentary*, May 1986.

33.   Quoted in *Scottish Business Insider*, May 1987.

LOCAL AUTHORITY RESPONSES TO ECONOMIC UNCERTAINTY IN SCOTLAND

M G Lloyd and J Rowan-Robinson

Introduction

In England and Wales a substantial number of local authorities have responded positively to the localised effects of economic recession, industrial collapse and rising unemployment by devising and implementing their own economic development initiatives. This present interest by local authorities stands in direct contrast to their more traditionally passive role with respect to economic policy. A survey carried out over the period 1982-1984 by the Association of District Councils found, for example, that, of the responding authorities, only a comparatively small proportion (11%) of district councils had no involvement with local economic development policies.[1] The survey also revealed that economic development activity was increasing as local authorities in England and Wales responded to the localised effects of deteriorating economic conditions. Until recently there has been little comparable evidence rgarding the economic development activities of Scottish local authorities. In 1980, the Convention of Scottish Local Authorities (COSLA) carried out a survey of local authority assistance to industry. The results of the COSLA survey, which were never published, confirmed that Scottish local authorities were beginning to encourage industrial development and indigenous economic aactivity.[2] In 1986 a more comprehensive survey was carried out by the authors to determine the nature and extent of local authority economic development activity in Scotland.[3] This article sets out the context within which local authority economic development activity in Scotland takes place, describes the nature of the economic initiatives and reports on the findings of the 1986 survey.

The Changing Context of Local Authority Economic Intervention

Traditionally central government has assumed the main responsibility for domestic and international economic policy making and implementation. This is particularly the case with respect to controlling inflation, managing unemployment and industrial development, and influencing the balance of trade. As a consequence local authorities have tended to assume a relatively passive role with respect to economic policy. This is illustrated by the institutional arrangements for regional development. Whilst central government provides the regional policy framework which is concerned with the geographical distribution of industrial development and employment creation, local authorities have fulfilled an important supporting role in facilitating the regional policies. Thus, in the areas designated by central government as eligible for regional assistance, local authorities provided the supporting housing and education services and ensured an adequate land supply for the industrial, residential and commercial development that formed part of the regional development strategy. There have, however, been exceptions to this traditional distribution of functions. For example, during the inter-war period some local authorities initiated public works programmes and provided land and buildings for local industry in an attempt to offset the considerable difficulties associated with severe localised unemployment.[4]

In the 1970's however, the traditional pattern began to change. Local authorities started to address the localised problems of economic decline and unemployment with which they were confronted. The most important factor contributing to the increased involvement by local authorities in the formulation of local economic policy was the prevailing national economic recession. Two further, and not entirely unrelated, factors may also be identified as having had a significant influence on local authority involvement in this area. First of all, there was the process of 'co-option' by central government which involved local authorities in facilitating its economic development policies. Secondly, and running counter to co-option, there was a process of 'alienation', local authorities found they were becoming more isolated from central government's economic policy and were increasingly exposed to the localised effects of economic restructuring in Britain. These two, apparently contradictory, processes deserve closer examination.

First of all, the 'co-option' of local authorities into the economic development arena was essentially a response by central government to the rapidly deteriorating economic circumstances in the later 1970's. There was an effective 'rethinking' of economic and industrial policy and, as a consequence, local authorities were encouraged to contribute to the national industrial strategy by formulating local policies to promote economic development.[5] Concern was expressed in particular about the geographical distribution of unemployment and economic opportunities throughout Britain. This led to a recognition of what is commonly referred to as the inner city crisis, as distinct from the more conventional regional development problem. Local authorities in the older, larger conurbations were being forced to address the concentrated problems of unemployment and industrial decline effectively within a policy vacuum. Furthermore, the localised economic difficulties in the inner cities were compounded by an outworn physical property base and infrastructure fabric together with a deteriorating fiscal position on the part of the local authorities.[6]

The Labour government's response was the Inner Urban Areas Act 1978 which "marked the introduction of the most ambitious and comprehensive attack on inner city problems. It embodied the reformist-structuralist view that policy be directed towards economic development while the agents of change were to be partnerships between central government, local authorities and private enterprise. The underlying premise of the policy was that inner city economies had inherent structural weaknesses which market forces alone could not overcome. The programme offered various forms of financial aid for land acquisition, provision of amenities, rent and interest relief and so forth. In addition, the programme was intended to 'bend' other development programmes in order to favour the inner cities".[7] The inner city legislation proved to be a considerable stimulus to local authorities and as a consequence there was an increase in local authority involvement in economic development activity. Local authorities in the designated inner cities were now given resources so as to provide some assistance to local industry, establish co-operatives, undertake land development and designate industrial area improvement initiatives.[8] At the same time, the nature of the local economic initiatives changed. Local authorities recognised the futility of conventional policy measures that attempted to attract available mobile investment to their respective areas. The national economic recession meant that the supply of such investment was rapidly diminishing and as a consequence local authorities developed policies targetted at indigenous economic activity. Local authorities set out to protect existing industry, to provide premises and other facilities for established firms to enable them to expand in situ, and to provide financial aid to encourage the establishment of small firms.[9]

Although the co-option of local authorities commenced with a Labour government, the process continued with the subsequent Conservative administration. The nature of the co-option process has changed, however, and now reflects the prevailing 'supply side' philosophy of the present government. Since 1980, for example, central government has issued advice to local authorities cautioning them against placing restrictive obstacles in the way of economic growth and the development of private enterprise. Thus in Circular 22/80, the Department of the Environment stated that the development control process "must avoid placing unjustified obstacles in the way of any development especially if it is for industry, commerce, housing or any other purpose relevant to the economic regeneration of the country". Similarly Circular 14/85, which is concerned with development and employment, emphasises that "new development contributes to economic activity and to the provision of jobs. It is in the national interest to promote and encourage it. The planning system must respond positively and promptly to proposals for development". The process of co-option has therefore encouraged local authorities to become more involved in local economic development activity.

The second factor which influenced local authority involvement in economic development activity was the process of 'alienation'. This stemmed directly from the present government's economic philosophy and industrial strategy. It was a consequence in part of the rejection of the conventional Keynesian policy framework which had dominated post-war economic policy making. Economic policy has effectively been redrawn along stricter financial, commercial and market lines, criteria described as a reaction "against the cost and dubious justifiability of various state expenditures".[10] As a consequence, government intervention and public sector expenditure has been subject to monetary targets and public expenditure restraint.[11] The main elements of the government's economic strategy are financial stringency, monetary controls and targets, privatisation and the de-regulation of economic activity. As a consequence many local authorities in the early 1980's became increasingly isolated from the 'safety net' of economic policy measures as the government attempted to reduce the extent of intervention in order to permit the market greater influence in economic development. Regional policy illustrates this trend. The map of assisted areas was redrawn and rationalised in line with the government's philosophy and a number of areas in Scotland lost designation for regional assistance. The level of financial support and the nature of the regional development incentives available in the areas remaining eligible for assistance were reduced and stringent cost/job criteria were introduced.[12] Many local authorities were thus radically and adversely affected by the implementation of the new market based philosophy and were effectively left to tackle the problems of local economic decline in the absence of central government support. As a result of the effective policy vacuum, many local authorities felt they had little choice but to undertake a more active interest in local economic development activity.

Local authorities have been further 'alienated' from central government economic policy as a result of a marked shift towards centralisation in public policy making. This has involved "imposing specific duties on local authorities, curtailing administrative discretion by imposing detailed statutory procedures on local decision making and by centralising discretionary decision making by vesting broad powers of intervention in the Secretary of State".[13] In Scotland, the attempts by the Scottish Office to curb spending by local authorities has led to a deterioration in their relationship which is expected to worsen with proposals for the privatisation of local services.[14] A number of specific economic measures introduced by the present government have also served to alienate local authorities by effectively reducing their ability to devise and implement local economic strategies. Such measures include the designation of enterprise zones, the setting up of urban development corporations, and to a lesser extent, the proposals for 'simplified planning zones'. Each of these measures are effectively imposed on the local authorities involved, and each designation results in a diminution of local control, as the local authorities are called upon to fulfill an important supporting role in the initiative. Thus, for example, the London Docklands Development Corporation has involved a high level of public sector infrastructure investment in order to support private sector financial investments but there has also been a concomitant corruption of local control and public benefit.[15] In similar fashion, the government's proposals to introduce simplified planning zones reflect its view that planning controls inhibit private economic activity. The intention is that simplified planning zones should be designated for a wide range of new development, including areas for housing, industrial and commercial purposes. Within the designated zones conditions and limitations over development and other activities will be kept to a minimum, and a zone designation may be initiated by a private developer.[16]

These measures have all served to alienate local authorities from mainstream economic and planning policy making and have encouraged them to intervene in an attempt to offset the localised difficulties associated with economic restructuring and uncertainty. Their ability to do so, however, has been considerably hampered by legal and financial constraints.

Legal and Financial Constraints on Local Authority Economic Development Activity.

Local authorities are not vested with a general economic function, their traditional responsibilities being primarily concerned with the protection of the community and the provision of personal services, such as education and housing.[17] The provisional findings of a survey of local authorities in England and Wales suggests, however, that there has been a substantial extension in the past twenty years in the statutory provisions available to local authorities for economic purposes and in the flexibility with which they have been interpreted.[18] It is important to recognise however that this conclusion refers to the indirect powers available to local authorities. Local authorities do not themselves have an explicit power to undertake economic policy but they do have certain indirect economic powers and are able to use other general powers for economic purposes, such as those relating to town and country planning.[19]

Thus, although the power for local authorities to engage in local economic development activity is ambiguous, local authorities have long been involved in facilitating economic development through the land allocation process in their statutory develoment plans. Furthermore, local authorities can provide an important supporting role for economic development through the provision of infrastructure and the construction of buildings and other works. Section 78 of the Local Government (Scotland) Act 1973, for example, enables local authorities to construct, alter or improve buildings or execute works on land owned or leased by them for the purpose of any of their functions or for the benefit or improvement of their area. The Local Government (Development and Finance) (Scotland) Act 1964, as amended, empowers local authorities to carry out, or to support the carrying out by others, of building restoration and other works on land for the benefit and improvement of their areas. And Part VI of the Town and Country Planning (Scotland) Act 1972 permits local authorities to acquire and develop land for planning purposes.

Despite the range of indirect powers, the evidence suggests that in the early 1980's the ambiguity and uncertainty regarding what was permitted under the legislation acted as a major constraint on local authority involvement in economic affairs. The COSLA survey carried out in 1980, for example, noted that local authorities were uncertain as to what they could achieve under the wide but indistinct range of powers and instruments available to them. What appears to have happened since then has been a growing awareness on the part of local authorities of the potential of the indirect powers available to them. It remains the case, however, that the indirect powers do not readily lend themselves to stimulating local economic development and this has inhibited the activity of many local authorities. The severity of the localised economic problems would seem to be one of the principal factors which has encouraged some authorities to adopt what might be termed a 'creative' approach to their powers.[20] Nonetheless, despite a willingness to exercise these powers, they remain a less than perfect means of pursuing a sustained programme of local economic development activity. Thus, for example, whilst land use planning powers may form the basis upon which to construct a local industrial strategy, the strategy is limited by the fact that the "main powers of the planners are permissive and reactive rather than interventionist and directive".[21]

In the absence of a clearly distinguished power to undertake local economic development initiatives, local authorities wishing to implement direct measures to alleviate local economic problems have had to have recourse to the general power in s.83 of the Local Government (Scotland) Act 1973. This enables local authorities "to incur expenditure which in their opinion is in the interests of their area or any part of it or all or some of its inhabitants". Section 83, it should be noted, may not be used for purposes for which an alternative power already exists. Research shows that there has been a substantial increase in recent years in the number of authorities using this power and in the occasions upon which it is used.[22] There are, however, two main drawbacks to the use of s. 83 for local economic development activity. First of all, the expenditure is subject to a financial ceiling. The Abolition of Domestic Rates Etc (Scotland) Act 1987 will peg this ceiling hereafter to the product of a 2p. rate for the financial year 1988-1989. The real value of this product will clearly fall over time and this will influence the level of economic development activity as some Scottish local authorities are already close to their s.83 limit and others are likely to become so over the next year or so. Without a change in the 2p. limit or in the legislation, it has been suggested that more staff time will have to be devoted to distinguishing between expenditure which must be classified under s.83 and expenditure which may be classified under other legislative provisions.[23] Secondly, there remains considerable uncertainty about the scope of s.83. The COSLA survey showed this to be a matter of considerable concern amongst Scottish local authorities, and it has been suggested that the use of s.83 has been constrained by legal opinion in Scotland and by its interpretation by local authority solicitors. For example, the action of guaranteeing a small factory development was apparently considered to be ultra vires on the grounds that the main benefit accrued to the developer and not to the area or its inhabitants.[24]

Notwithstanding these constraints, recent years have seen increasing involvement by local authorities in Scotland in local economic development activity and it is now appropriate to examine the nature of this activity.

The Nature of Local Authority Economic Initiatives

Most of the discussion relating to the nature, extent and trends in local authority involvement with local economic development activity draws on survey evidence and case study material carried out in England and Wales. Until recently, there was little comparable evidence for Scotland although there was perhaps enough to draw some very general inferences. Reference has already been made to the survey of local authority assistance to industry carried out by COSLA in 1980-1981. This survey set out to establish, first of all, the scope of involvement by local authorities in Scotland in providing such assistance, and, secondly, the main constraints on that involvement and the ways in which available powers might be amended or supplemented. The COSLA survey confirmed the general position in England and Wales of increasing involvement by local authorities in local economic intervention. Significantly the COSLA survey suggested that local authorities in Scotland now perceived the active encouragement of local industrial development to be one of their main responsibilities. Clearly there was a greater awareness of the relationship of the local authority to its local economy than had existed some five or ten years earlier. The COSLA survey also revealed that Scottish local authorities were primarily interested in developing the small firm sector and concluded that "almost all the initiatives taken by local authorities, and many of the additional powers they would like to have, are aimed not at the attraction of mobile industry but at the encouragement and creation of local industry". The survey, therefore, had a very practical purpose but it was confined to one specific area of local authority involvement in their local economies.

The authors carried out a more comprehensive questionnaire survey of Scottish local authorities in 1986. The full findings of that survey are presented elsewhere.[25] In this article, we pick out some of the main findings and consider them in the light of evidence derived from other sources.

First of all, our survey confirms that there is a continuing and increasing interest by local authorities in Scotland in economic development initiatives noted by COSLA. The way in which this manifests itself is discussed below.

Secondly, it is clear that the main characteristic of the policy initiatives being adopted by the majority of local authorities in England and Wales is that they are 'property led'. The focus is on the provision of sites and premises for local industrial development by the private sector.[26] This strategy is supported by a number of associated measures such as the building and letting of factory units, the carrying out of environmental improvements, the reclamation of derelict land and the designation of industrial improvement areas. This approach would seem to follow from the traditional concern of local authorities with the use and development of land in their areas. It is interesting to note, however, that local authority interest in property as an economic policy instrument is no longer confined to industrial development alone. Research shows that local authorities are now "usually willing to provide on an equal basis for warehouse and service activity and to supply sites to speculative industrial developers as well as industrialists having premises built for their own use".[27]

The response to our questionnaire shows a similar interest in such conventional land and property based economic development initiatives amongst Scottish local authorities. There is a clear preference for the traditional provision and improvement of sites and buildings for the private sector. This approach, however, is sufficiently flexible to permit targeting of indigenous industry as well as facilitating the expansion needs of firms choosing to relocate. The extent of the involvement by Scottish local authorities in this traditional area of activity is given in Table 1.

The Table also shows the extent to which Scottish local authorities undertake property led development initiatives in conjunction with the private sector and other public sector agencies, notably the Scottish Development Agency whose particular concern has been with the reclamation of land and environmental improvements. It would seem that the relationship between local authorities and the private sector has been limited. A number of regions and district councils have formalised their activity in this field to the extent of developing a property strategy as part of their overall economic development policies. Strathclyde Regional Council, for example, prepared an industrial property strategy in 1983.

Recent research in England and Wales shows the development of a more sophisticated property led strategy on the part of local authorities through the provision of financial support and incentives to the private

TABLE 1

Provision of and Improvement of Sites and Buildings

Activity	%of respondents					
	Authority		Authority with Private Sector		Authority with Private Agency	
	R	D	R	D	R	D
Provision of serviced sites	80	58	0	12	30	38
Site assembly	30	62	0	12	0	31
Reclamation of derelict land	50	23	0	8	70	54
Environmental improvement	70	50	20	19	80	31
Conversion for commercial/ industrial units	60	46	30	12	10	15
Provision of new buildings	90	70	0	19	10	23

sector. There has been "considerable innovation in the organisation and financing of industrial development".[28] Local authorities now provide financial support to firms, through direct or indirect subsidies, which are often for the specific purposes of land acquisition. The Scottish survey confirms that local authorities similarly provide financial assistance, mainly in the form of grants and loans but also, in some instances through guarantees and the acquisition of shares in local businesses. The evidence suggests that regional authorities provide grants and loans for private firms largely for the purposes of purchasing plant and machinery, the conversion and improvement of land and buildings and for market research and business consultancy advice. Financial assistance from district councils, tends to be limited to the more traditional forms of support, for example, the provision of grants and loans mainly for the conversion of land and buildings, the construction and purchase of premises and for rent and rate relief.

Thirdly, it is a characteristic of local authority economic development activity that the initiatives are primarily 'market and business related' – being geared for the most part to attract and stimulate the private sector.[29] In this sense such activity is entirely compatible with central government's emphasis on the private sector as the dominant force in economic development and regeneration. The evidence shows that Scottish local authorities undertake a considerable amount of business development activity. Regions and district councils provide business information services and advice to the private sector, particularly on the price and availability of sites and premises. Significantly, however, there is increasing interest by all authorities in the opportunities for economic development offered by enterprise trusts, community businesses, and, in the remoter local authorities, worker co-operatives. Resource restrictions on local authorities may explain their interest in the encouragement and development of such 'arms length' organisational arrangements.[30] Agencies such as the enterprise trust concept are also popular among local authorities in England and Wales because, it is suggested they are free of the procedural constraints that make local authority decision making cumbersome and unpredictable.[31] Furthermore, the concept has received tacit encouragement from central government and is politically attractive because it involves the private sector.

Fourthly, it appears that in England and Wales local authority interest in economic development activity has tended to concentrate on the encouragement of indigenous small firm economic activity.[32] The Scottish survey confirms this interest, with an emphasis on firms employing less than 50 employees. Indeed, one criticism that has been levelled at the general thrust of local authority development initiatives is that employment considerations have become a secondary consideration for many local authorities[33], the emphasis being on the development and expansion of the local business sector. It is also argued that by concentrating on small firms local authorities are effectively increasing the competition between authorities for the available small firms wishing to expand or possibly relocate.[34] This argument is familiar and recalls the earlier conventional approach of local authorities to economic development through the promotion of their areas so as effectively to bid for and attract inward investment. However, a different view is that local authorities have redirected their policies to concentrate on the encouragement and stimulation of indigenous economic activity.[35]

Finally, there are a limited number of local authorities in England and Wales that have developed more radical or interventionist local economic initiatives. These local economic development initiatives have emerged for the most part in areas of severe social and economic deprivation and have been described as "unorthodox" in approach.[36] The authorities are Labour controlled and they have chosen to confront the policies of central government and provide an alternative local economic strategy in order to address localised problems of unemployment and industrial collapse. This interventionist approach rejects the conventional attitude of local authorities which is, as we have seen, very largely property led and replaces it with "a pro-active approach to their role in the local economy which utilises a wide range of assistance targeted at specific locations, client groups within the labour market, and particular types of firm".[37] The measures associated with this approach include the setting up of local enterprise boards, co-operatives and community businesses, training initiatives, explicit support for equal opportunities, low pay and welfare rights lobbies and attempts to implement contract compliance as a means of promoting local economic growth. The distinctive characteristics of this alternative approach to local economic development are "a clear policy framework; (the authorities) chose to expand their activity rapidly and committed substantial resources and staff in comparison with the majority of local authorities; they developed a range of new initiatives; and they introduced an explicit political dimension in their work".[38] Keating and Boyle argue that there is little evidence of such an "ideological dimension" in Scotland[39], and the survey findings confirm this observation. The reason for this, it has been suggested, is the 'crowding out' effect of the activities of the Scottish Development Agency which has assumed the central responsibility for economic development work in Scotland.[40]

Economic Development Statements and Policies

It has been argued that "the most sophisticated level of (economic development) activity involves the decision to produce an economic development plan within the corporate policy framework of the authority".[41] One of the most interesting findings of our survey is that local authorities in Scotland are increasingly institutionalising that activity as a part of their general responsibilities and operations. Of the authorities responding to our questionnaire, all of the regional councils and more than 60% of the district councils stated that they have prepared or are in the process of preparing economic development statements. This finding may be contrasted with the conclusion of a study of economic development activity on Clydeside.[42] This suggests that "adopting a rational planning approach to economic policy is a largely undeveloped strategy. Only one authority actually produced a statement, although other authorities have moved towards strategic programme documents for key elements of their activities".

We found that several of the responding local authorities had prepared separate policy statements. An example of such a statement is the Economic Development Plan prepared by the Economic Development and Employment Committee of Glasgow District Council. This sets out the aims of the District Council with respect to economic development as follows:

(i)   to promote the city as a place to invest;

(ii) to support industries already in the city and particularly those under threat of rundown or closure;

(iii) to support small businesses through the provision of advice, information, training and financial help where appropriate;

(iv) to provide more specific support to community businesses, offices, retailing and tourism in order to give special help relevant to their distinctive character and potential development;

(v) to improve the infrastructure for business development by encouraging energy efficiency, a better physical environment, and an adequate supply of premises and land;

(vi) to develop co-ordinated approaches to business development in areas of the city identified as having development potential or where remedial action is required to solve particular problems of disadvantage;

(vii) to seek to improve the situation of those at a disadvantage in the city's workforce by encouraging training, support for the unemployed, and measures to improve pay and conditions and combat discrimination.

In general, however, most economic development policies are contained in the appropriate structure and local plans. The function of a structure plan is to set out policies and proposals to resolve or ameliorate the major land use problems that are identified by the authority as being strategic issues. It is acknowledged that these strategic issues are likely to include the scale and location of industry and employment.[43] The use of structure and local plans as the primary means of setting out economic development policies emphasises the adoption by Scottish local authorities of conventional means and instruments. Thus local economic development activity in Scotland is primarily land use based, and land use will remain the main lever by which local authorities attempt to stimulate economic activity. The nature of the economic development policies in the structure plans, however, vary widely. The Western Isles Structure Plan (1986), for example, argues that "the promotion of economic development will assume greater importance than the need to resolve competing land use issues or to restrict or control change in some other way". The Grampian Region (Part) Structure Plan: Rural Area (1985) also adopts an unusual approach to local economic development. The structure plan sets out to promote economic development in the rural area and to consolidate existing services, facilities and investment. These objectives are necessary in order to maintain the economic and social well being of the rural communities in the landward areas of the region and also to manage the resources and environment.[44] The plan establishes a dispersal strategy for investment and sets out "to counteract the tendency for the remoter parts of the Region to decline relative to the more prosperous areas, while still accommodating growth wherever it can be reasonably accepted". It also sets out a policy of positive discrimination for the rural area, as illustrated in its economic development strategy. This sets out "to discriminate positively in favour with regard to public sector promotion and development, and secondly, to concentrate particularly on indigenous industry and community based solutions to employment problems". The policy of positive discrimination is translated into practical terms by the 60/40 distribution of public sector resources to rural Grampian. The commitment to foster the growth and development of indigenous industry is supported by a policy of restraint of the major settlements, so as to facilitate integrated development throughout the rural area, together with the protection of prime quality agricultural land and protection of the environment so as to encourage tourism.

Recent years have seen the preparation of non-statutory economic development policy instruments by a number of authorities. These policy statements tend to focus specifically on economic development issues and represent an alternative, but not mutually exclusive, approach to economic development policy making. The non-statutory documents permit a more corporate or comprehensive approach to economic development than is possible in the relatively narrowly defined land use based structure and local plans. A good example of this approach is the Economic Review prepared by East Lothian District Council (1984-1985). This summarises the major events and trends that took place in the district during 1984, rehearses the District Council's economic development strategy and sets out a detailed development programme for the forthcoming financial year. The Economic Review does not confine itself to matters of industrial development but broadens its analysis, policies and programme to all aspects of economic development and employment. Another example is the report made by the Director of Economic Development and Estates to the Policy and Resources Committee of Edinburgh District Council in intervening in the local industrial base of the city over a four year period and makes recommendations for an expansion and refinement of that strategy including the development of area-specific initiatives.

Our survey also enables us to say something about the subject matter of the land use planning policies adopted for economic development purposes. The findings are presented in Table 2. The evidence shows that for both regional and district councils there was a clear emphasis on the 'priority for allocating and safeguarding land for industry' in the structure plans and local plans. There is some divergence between the regional and district authorities regarding the other policies – a divergence that reflects their different statutory responsibilities and powers. Thus, the regional authorities place considerable emphasis on 'fostering schools/industry links', in their capacity as education authorities. The district authorities, on the other hand, place a relatively high priority on the 'provision of housing for key workers', an approach that reflects their statutory responsibility as housing authority. There are two other important points suggested by the survey evidence. First of all, both regional and district councils recognise the importance of the local plans in facilitating economic development activity. Both levels of authority place emphasis on the 'provision in local plans for small business development'. Although it is the district councils that have the responsibility for the preparation of the local plans, the regional authorities clearly recognise the importance of maintaining a continuity of strategy from the structure plan down to the detailed implementation of proposals in the local plans. Secondly, it is interesting to note that there is relatively little priority afforded the 'relaxing of development control policies in certain areas'. This is effectively in opposition to central government advice contained, for example, in SDD Circular 17/1985 "Development Control – Priorities and Procedures" and represents a vote of confidence by the authorities in the planning system. The overwhelming view of the authorities was, perhaps not surprisingly, that the development control process did not operate to inhibit private economic activity.

TABLE 2

Planning Policies for Economic Development

Policy	% of respondents	
	Regions & Islands	Districts
Priority in allocating/safeguarding land for industry in structure and local plans.	90	85
Provision in local plans for small business development	60	75
Relaxing development control policies in certain areas	40	15
Priority to industrial/commercial planning applications	40	55
Provision of housing for key workers	10	75
Fostering schools/industry links	80	–

The survey also shows that local authorities in Scotland are giving serious attention to the internal institutional arrangements for implementing local economic development policies. In contrast, a study of the Clydeside region found that none of the authorities in the study area had adjusted their organisational arrangements to accommodate economic development activity.[45] The Scottish wide survey shows that, with one exception, all the regional councils have established a special department or unit within an existing department so as to co-ordinate their economic development activity. There is a tendency for such arrangements to be associated with the physical planning departments. A relatively smaller proportion of district councils have carried out such changes, but the main emphasis at the district council level is with the establishment of special committees or sub-committees. In 1986, for example, the sub-committee on Employment in Glasgow District Council was upgraded to the full Economic Development and Employment Committee.

Conclusions

This article has examined the context within which local authorities in Scotland have increasingly devised and implemented local economic development initiatives. Such activity mirrors that which has taken place in England and Wales. In common with the majority of local authorities in England and Wales, Scottish authorities have tended to rely on conventional policy instruments to attain local economic development. These are drawn largely from land and property measures which reflect in part, the authorities' statutory responsibilities for land use planning controls and the preparation of development plans.

Notwithstanding the increase in local authority activity it is important to recognise the limitations to such initiatives. It was suggested that local authorities were initially co-opted by central government so as to provide additional support in tackling such localised problems as are concentrated in the inner cities. Later, local authorities were increasingly alienated by central government in the economic sphere, and much of the increased local authority involvement is an attempt to compensate for the increasing centralisation and selectivity in central government's economic policy. This relationship between the two tiers of government is a critical one. Notwithstanding considerable ingenuity on the part of local authorities in the interpretation of their powers and in the devising of economic development initiatives, there is no doubt that the final arbiter over the extent of local authority involvement in this area is central government. Our survey shows that financial constraints have very considerably curtailed the scope of local authority activity in recent years and we referred earlier to the difficulties arising from reliance upon the general power in s.83 of the Local Government (Scotland) Act 1973. The Local Government Bill presently before Parliament will further curtail the activities of local authorities by promoting the privatisation of certain services, by limiting obligations imposed by local authorities in contracts for the supply of goods and services and for the carrying out of works to purely commercial matters and by further defining the scope of the power to engage in publicity. It seems likely that the impact of legal and financial constraints in this area will become more pronounced in the future.

Nonetheless, local authority involvement in this sphere of activity may be seen to some extent as implementing the government's supply side philosophy. This is particularly the case with the supply of land and buildings to the private sector. We think that local authorities will, therefore, continue to have a role to play in economic development but that its focus will be narrower and they will effectively be restricted to providing goods and services to the business community.

M G Lloyd, Department of Land Economy, University of Aberdeen.

J Rowan-Robinson, Department of Land Economy, University of Aberdeen.

References

1. Association of District Councils, *Economic Development Initiatives and Innovations*. Association of District Councils, London, 1985.

2. Convention of Scottish Local Authorities, *Review of Local Authority Assistance to Industry*. COSLA, Edinburgh, 1980.

3. J Rowan-Robinson and M G Lloyd, *Local Authority Economic Development Activity in Scotland*. Planning Exchange, Glasgow, Occasional Paper 32, 1987.

4. S V Ward, 'Inter War Britain: A Study of Government Spending, Planning and Uneven Economic Development', *Built Environment*, 7 (2), 1983, pp.96-108.

5. M Loughlin, *Local Government in the Modern State*. Sweet and Maxwell, London, 1986.

6. M Boddy and S Barratt, *Local Government and the Industrial Development Process*. School for Advanced Urban Studies, Bristol, Working Paper No.6, 1979.

7. C Hasluck, *Urban Unemployment: Local Labour Markets and Employment Initiatives*. Longman, London, 1987.

8. L Mills and K Young, 'Local Authorities and Economic Development: A Preliminary Analysis', in V A Hausner (ed) *Critical Issues in Urban Economic Development, Volume 1*. Clarendon Press, Oxford, 1986, pp.89- 144.

9. M Boddy and S Barratt, *op.cit.*.

10. J Tomlinson, *Monetarism: Is there an alternative*. Basil Blackwell, Oxford, 1986.

11. M Bleaney, *The Rise and Fall of Keynesian Economics – An Investigation of its Contribution to Capitalist Development*. Macmillan, London, 1985, pp.141.

12. R Martin, 'Monetarism masquerading as regional policy? The government's new system of regional aid'. *Regional Studies*, 19(4), 1985, pp.379-388.

13. M Loughlin, *op.cit.*, pp.14.

14. D Scott, 'Local v. Central Government: the spending conflict', in D McCrone (ed) *The Scottish Government Yearbook 1986*. Unit for the Study of Government in Scotland, Edinburgh, 1986, pp.36-48.

15. D Klausner, 'Infrastructure Investment and Political Ends: The Case of London's Docklands', *Local Economy*, 1(4), 1987, pp.47-59.

16. J Rowan-Robinson and M G Lloyd, 'Lifting the Burden of Planning: A Means or an End?, *Local Government Studies*, 12(3), 1986, pp.51-64.

17. T Byrne, *Local Government in Britain*. Penguin, Harmondsworth, 1981.

18. L Mills and K Young, *op.cit.*

19. M Loughlin, *op.cit.*

20. P B Rogers and C R Smith, 'The Local Authority's Role in Economic Development: The Tyne and Wear Act 1976', *Regional Studies*, 11, pp.153- 163.

21. N Johnson and A Cochrane, *Economic Policy Making by Local Authorities in Britain and Western Germany*, Allen and Unwin, London, 1981.

22. C Crawford and V Moore, *The Free Two Pence*, CIPFA, London, 1983.

23. D Johnstone, *Discretionary Powers for Economic Development*, Planning Exchange, Glasgow, Occasional Paper 31, 1987.

24. D Johnstone, *ibid*.

25. J Rowan-Robinson and M G Lloyd, 1987, *op.cit.*

26. M Boddy, 'Local Economic and Employment Strategies', in M Boddy and C Fudge (eds) *Local Socialism? Labour Councils and the New Left Alternatives*. Macmillan, London, 1984, pp.160-191.

27. M Boddy, 'Changing Public – Private Sector Relationships in the Industrial Development Process', in K Young and C Mason (eds) *Urban Economic Development*. Macmillan, London, 1983, pp.34-52.

28. L Mills and K Young, *op.cit.*, pp.95.

29. M Boddy, 1984, *op.cit.*

30. M G Lloyd and J Rowan-Robinson, 'Local Authority Economic Development Activity in Scotland: Further Evidence', *Local Economy*, 2(1), 1987, pp.49-84.

31. L Mills and K Young, *op.cit.*

32. M Boddy and S Barratt, *op.cit.*

33. M Boddy, 1984, *op.cit.*

34. M Boddy, 1984, *ibid.*

35. J Bennington, 'Local Economic Initiatives', *Local Government Studies*, 11(5), 1985.

36. S Cameron, 'Economic Development: The Changing Public – Private Sector Relationship', *Planning Outlook*, 26(2), 1983, pp.75-79.

37. J Mawson and D Miller, 'Interventionist Approaches in Local Employment and Economic Development: The Experience of Labour Local Authorities', in V A Hausner (ed) *Critical Issues in Urban Economic Development: Volume 1*. Clarendon Press, Oxford, 1986, pp.145-199.

38. J Mawson and D Miller, *ibid.*

39. M Keating and R Boyle, *Remaking Urban Scotland*. Edinburgh University Press, Edinburgh, 1986.

40. C Moore and S Booth, 'The Scottish Development Agency: Market Consensus, Public Planning and Local Enterprise', *Local Economy*, 1(3), 1986, pp.7-19.

41. C Moore and S Booth, 'Urban Policy Contradictions: the market versus redistributive approaches', *Policy and Politics*, 14(3), 1986, pp.361- 387.

42. C Moore and S Booth, *ibid.*

43. Scottish Development Department, *Structure Planning*. Scottish Development Department, Edinburgh, Planning Advice Note 27, 1981.

44. A Stark, 'The Grampian Rural Area Structure Plan', in D Johnstone

(ed) *Rural Economic Development Policies and Initiatives*. Planning Exchange, Glasgow, 1985, pp.18-26.

45. C Moore and S Booth, 'The Pragmatic Approach: Local Political Models of Regeneration', in W Lever and C Moore (eds) *The City in Transition: Policies and Agencies for the Economic Regeneration of Clydeside*. Clarendon Press, Oxford, 1986, pp.92-106.

SCOTTISH LEGISLATION 1986

Hamish McN Henderson

Nearly 70 Public General Acts were passed in 1986. Four of these were consolidation Acts of which three are of interest to Scotland. These are the *Insolvency Act (c.45)*, which brings together recent legislation, especially from the *Companies Act 1985 (c.6)* and *Insolvency Act 1985 (c.65)*, relating to corporate insolvency throughout Great Britain and to individual insolvency in England and Wales, the *Company Directors Disqualification Act (c.46)* and the *Parliamentary Constituencies Act (c.56)*. The *Building Societies Act (c.53)* applies throughout the United Kingdom and introduces the first major reforms of the law relating to these institutions for over a century. Despite its length, much detail is still left to be completed by Statutory Instruments.

Although there were only four "Scotland only" Acts in 1986, two others are included in this article: the *Marriage (Prohibited Degrees of Relationship) Act*, because it amends the *Marriage (Scotland) Act 1977* in important details, and the *Salmon Act*, because some of its provisions applying to England and Wales are essentially designed to complement the Scottish provisions as to the licensing of salmon dealers, and to secure more effective law enforcement.

Altogether three of the Acts will be seen to continue the progressive reform of Scottish family law that has been piloted by the Scottish Law Commission throughout the past decade.

Chapter Number

9 *Law Reform (Parent and Child) (Scotland) Act*. This short Act implements the report of the Scottish Law Commission on *Illegitimacy* (Scot Law Com No 82) published in January 1984.

Perhaps the most important provision is the effective abolition of the concept of illegitimacy for most purposes, except in relation to the transmission of hereditary titles, coats of arms and other hereditary honours or dignities.

Otherwise, the fact that a person's parents are not, or have not been, married to each other is to be ignored in establishing the legal relationship between that person and any other person. Future documents are to be interpreted according to this rule, unless they manifest a contrary intention. The provisions are not retrospective, so that existing documents are not affected. Several statutes passed before the commencement of this Act are however amended.

While a mother has full parental rights automatically (unless they are modified by an order of the court), a child's father has them only if he is married to the child's mother, or was married to her at the time of the child's conception, or subsequently. Parental rights means rights of tutory, curatory, custody or access, and any right or authority relating to the welfare or upbringing of a child conferred on a parent by any rule of law.

These rights may be modified by a court, and may be given to any person claiming interest. Such a person may be a grandparent, a foster parent, or anyone who has been in fact looking after a child. The statutory right to claim custody given to relatives, step and foster parents by the *Children Act 1975 (c.72)* is replaced by these more general provisions.

The presumption that a man is the father of a child if he was married to its mother at any time from its conception to its birth continues, even if the marriage is later held to be void or voidable. Otherwise, if both a man and the child's mother have acknowledged that he is the father and he has been so registered in any register of births kept in any part of the United Kingdom, the presumption applies.

Consent to the taking of blood samples to determine parentage may be given on behalf of a pupil child (that is, a boy under the age of 14 years and a girl under the age of 12 years) by the child's tutor, or by anyone having custody or care and control of the child. Where a person is incapable of giving consent, the court may do so if no-one else is entitled to do so, or if it is not reasonably practicable to obtain consent from the person entitled, or if that person refuses to accept responsibility for giving or withholding consent. The Court does not appear to have power to overrule a positive refusal of consent.

Lawyers will have to get used to an extended meaning of the word "parentage" and its opposite, "non-parentage". "Parentage" means that a person is or was the parent, or is or was the child, of another person. But in an age when American visitors come back to the old country to meet with their ancestors, this is not surprising.

Actions for declarator of parentage, non-parentage, legitimacy, legitimation or illegitimacy (formerly bastardy), are competent in both the Court of Session and the sheriff court. These actions may be necessary because of the express words of future deeds such as wills, excluding "illegitimate" issue from bequests, or in questions of succession to titles of honour. It is just conceivable that, because of the circumstances in a special case, a grant of a title of honour might expressly permit devolution of the title to an individual born outwith marriage.

16 *Marriage (Prohibited Degrees of Relationship) Act.* This Act contains provisions for England and Wales on the one hand and for Scotland on the other, in tandem, so as to amend the *Marriage (Scotland) Act 1977 (c.15).*

It amends the rules relating to the prohibition of marriage between persons related by affinity.

Marriage between an individual and his or her step-child, step-grandchild, step-parent or step-grandparent is prohibited unless both parties are over 21 and unless the younger party has never before the age of 18 lived in the same household as the older party and never been treated by him or her as a child of his or her family. It is not clear whether or not holiday visits to a step-grandparent constitutes living in that person's household, nor precisely how one distinguishes between treating a step-grandchild as a child of one's family as opposed to treating him or her as a grandchild.

There are now no restrictions on marriage between grandparents-in-law and grandchildren-in-law (e.g., a man of 70 may marry the grandmother of his former teenage wife or the teenage ex-wife of his grandson). But a parent-in-law may marry a son or daughter-in-law only if both parties are over 21 and if the former spouses of both are dead.

The Act should work reasonably satisfactorily in most cases, but it is not impossible to envisage some bizarre situations, both within and without the law.

36 *Incest and Related Offences (Scotland) Act.* In Scotland the law of incest has for over four centuries been governed by the Incest Act 1567 (c.15), which incorporated the eighteenth chapter of the Book of Leviticus as the law of the land. In modern times charges of incest have been restricted to cases falling within the terms of that Act, because of uncertainty as to the scope of the relevant common law.

However, the extensive prohibitions of intercourse based on affinity, which endured after death or divorce, were limited where legislation permitted the marriage of persons so related, on the principle that if persons were free to marry intercourse between them could not be incestuous, expressed in the *Criminal Procedure (Scotland) Act* 1938 (c.48) s.13, now repealed. But the law of incest generally ignored illegitimate relationships, and those arising from adoption.

The Scottish Law Commission in 1981 produced a *Report on the Law of Incest in Scotland (Cmnd 8422)* and a draft Bill was appended to the Report.

The *Incest and Related Offences (Scotland) Act 1986* gives effect to the proposals in the Report and the draft Bill, by textual amendment of the *Sexual Offences (Scotland) Act 1976 (c.67)*. Incest is now restricted to normal hetero-sexual intercourse between persons who are related by consanguinity in a degree listed in the Act, whether of the full or the half blood, or by adoption; or between an adoptive or a former adoptive parent and child. So such intercourse between persons related by affinity no longer constitutes incest. No account is taken of the fact that the relationship is traced through, or to, any person whose parents are not or have not been married to one another. In other words, the natural genetic relationship is regarded in establishing the consanguinity.

Intercourse between step-parents and step-children, and between step-grandparents and step-grandchildren, no longer constitutes incest. But a step-parent or former step-parent who has sexual intercourse with a step-child or former step-child will be guilty of an offence if the step-child is under 21 or has, before the age of 18, lived in the same household and been treated as a child of the step-parent's family. Anomalously intercourse between step-grandparents and step-grandchildren is not a criminal offence in similar circumstances, yet these individuals may fall within the prohibited degrees of marriage set out in the *Marriage (Prohibited Degrees of Relationship) Act 1986 (c.16)*. Thus these provisions are somewhat imperfect mirror images of the rules relating to the prohibition of marriage between persons related by affinity, contained in the *Marriage (Scotland) Act 1977 (c.15)* as amended by the *Marriage (Prohibited Degrees of Relationship) Act 1986 (c.16)*.

The Act creates a new offence, where a person of or over the age of 16 years has intercourse with a child under the age of 16, if he or she is a member of the same household as the child and stands in a position of trust in relation to that child.

There are certain defences to charges of contravention of this Act, based mainly on ignorance of the relevant facts or lack of consent on the part of an accused person. The Act may be criticised because it tends to shift the burden of proof on to the accused to prove his ignorance and therefore his innocence. In the *English Sexual Offences Act 1956 (c.69)* the onus is on the prosecution to prove the accused's knowledge of the relationship

The sheriff court is given jurisdiction to try alleged offences under this Act. Formerly the High Court had exclusive jurisdiction. Although the sheriff may sentence a person convicted of an offence under this Act to up to 2 years imprisonment on conviction on indictment, or only three months on summary conviction, he may, if he considers his powers to be inadequate, remit the convicted person to the High Court, which may impose a sentence of life imprisonment.

47 *Legal Aid (Scotland) Act.* Since 1949 the administration of legal aid in Scotland has been the responsibility of the Law Society of Scotland. The Royal Commission on Legal Services in Scotland, in its report published in May 1980 (Cmnd. 7846), recommended that the Law Society should cease to have this responsibility. Most members of the Commission favoured an independent authority. In March 1985 the Scottish Home and Health Department, having considered the Commission's Report, issued a consultation paper with proposals for changes in the administration of legal aid. The *Legal Aid (Scotland) Act 1986* gives effect to these proposals, and repeals the *Legal Aid (Scotland) Act 1967 (c.43)* in its entirety, and the *Legal Advice and Assistance Act 1972 (c.11)* so far as Scotland is concerned. However, any schemes, regulations, orders or rules of court made under these Acts remain in force until replaced.

The Act transfers responsibility for the provision of legal aid to the newly established Scottish Legal Aid Board. The Board has between 11 and 15 members, appointed by the Secretary of State who also appoints one of them as chairman. Members must include at least two members of the Faculty of Advocates, at least two members of the Law Society of Scotland, appointed after consultation with these two professional bodies, and at least one person with experience of the procedure and practice of the courts.

Much of the existing legislation on legal aid is re-enacted, with appropriate modifications. Virtually all details of the scheme will be covered by regulations made by the Secretary of State, as in the past. He does not appear to be required to enter into consultations with the legal professions before making regulations, but it is understood that these take place. Many regulations require to be laid before each House of Parliament and to be approved by a resolution of each House. Although this procedure does not permit amendments to be made, it ensures that the regulations will be subjected to more than the usual rather limited scrutiny in Parliament, and to consequent publicity.

Rules of Court, regulating procedure in relation to legal aid, are made by way of Acts of Adjournal by the High Court of Justiciary and Acts of Sederunt by the Court of Session.

All the provisions of the Act had come into force by 1st April 1987, except those relating to legal aid in contempt proceedings and Part V. This Part authorises the employment of solicitors by the Board to give advice and assistance, to act for persons receiving legal aid, generally to give advice to local organisations such as Citizens' Advice Bureaux, to promote contact between these organisations and local solicitors, and to give advice orally in cases where that should suffice. In matters of professional conduct, the same rules apply to solicitors employed by the Board as would apply if the Board were a firm of solicitors. However, they may act separately for different individuals who may have conflicting interests. Similar provisions in the 1972 Act have never been operated, and the Lord Advocate indicated, at the Second Reading in the House of Lords on 20 February 1986, that this Part is unlikely to come into force in the foreseeable future.

62 *Salmon Act*. In form this is a "GB" Act, but the greater part of it applies to Scotland only. The Government's Bill was preceded by the Second Report on Scottish Salmon and Trout Fisheries (by a committee chaired by Lord Hunter) in 1965 (Cmnd. 2691), and the District Salmon Fishery Boards (Scotland) Bill, introduced in the House of Lords by Lord Thurso in February 1985. The Act makes fresh provision for the administration of salmon fisheries in Scotland, and for the licensing and regulation of salmon dealing throughout Great Britain. Seven entire Acts, from 1696 to 1882, are repealed, but in order to understand the new Act it is still necessary to have access to some of the older legislation.

Salmon angling contributes many millions of pounds to the economy of remoter rural areas, but there appears to be some uncertainty as to how many. The Parliamentary Under-Secretary of State, moving the Second Reading of the Bill, is reported in Hansard as giving the figure as being between £22 million and £140 million per annum. Clearly, the industry provides a significant amount of employment in these areas, but the anglers will continue to come only so long as they find a reasonable chance of catching fish. This Act aims to secure the improvement of salmon fisheries throughout Great Britain, and protect them more effectively from criminal activities.

For the most part, this Act does not apply to the River Tweed, where fisheries are administered by a Council on behalf of the Tweed Commissioners, under the *Tweed Fisheries Act 1969 (c.xxiv)*. There are also special provisions relating to the River Esk (Dumfriesshire).

The new legislation is designed to bring all rivers flowing directly or indirectly into the sea within a salmon fishery district, based on the districts established under older legislation, and extending seaward for three miles from mean low water springs. Existing legislation affecting any particular district is reapplied to the new district for that area. The Secretary of State may make a designation order following an application to him by a district salmon fishery board, or, in the absence of a board, by two proprietors in the area affected by the proposed order, or by a combination of any of these. The order may abolish districts and create new ones, including amalgamations. It will designate the annual close time and the periods within that time when fishing for salmon by rod and line is permitted, with different provisions for different parts of a district, if desired.

The Secretary of State has extensive powers to make regulations after consultation concerning the due observance of the weekly close time, construction of dams, meshes, materials and dimensions of nets, etc. (The weekly close time is from 12 noon on Saturday to 6 a.m. on Monday. During this time no fishing at all is permitted, except by rod and line on Saturday and Monday).

The exercise of other powers depends on the initiative of a district salmon fishery board, or, where there is no board, of two proprietors. These relate to the making of orders prescribing the precise dates of the annual close time, which must be not less than 168 days, and the fixing and variation of estuary limits. Boards may also apply to him for the making of regulations specifying baits and lures.

Proprietors continue to be classified as "upper proprietors" and "lower proprietors", above and below a dividing line fixed by the Secretary of State or under earlier legislation, or taken as the normal tide limit. This is to identify the angling and the netting proprietors. Any individual proprietor may of course on occasion come within both categories.

The former district salmon fishery boards continue as "transitional district boards", and will be phased out over three years and replaced by new boards, holding office for three years.

These new boards are in fact the committees of associations of the proprietors of salmon fishery districts. Upper and lower proprietors have separate representation, with not more than three from each category, plus a chairman. Each proprietor may have up to four votes depending on the valuation of the fishery as entered in the valuation role.

Where there are joint proprietors or several persons with fishery rights, they must choose one of their number to be the proprietor for the purposes of this Act, e.g. voting. There are special provisions for the rare occasion where there is only one proprietor in a district.

The boards are required, if practical, to co-opt up to three representatives of salmon anglers and also three of the tenant netsmen in the district. The number must be the same for each category.

The Act sets out in detail the financial and other powers and duties of district salmon boards, which may be established even for a district with no salmon in its waters, because steps may be taken to clean up and restock a river. Boards are financed by way of a "fishery assessment" at a rate based on the valuation of individual fisheries as entered on the valuation roll. The general powers and duties of boards are essentially to protect and improve fisheries within their district and increase the stock of salmon. They include the power to appoint water bailiffs.

One important power given to boards is to authorise expenditure for the purchase of heritable property out of money accruing from the fishery assessment, or borrowed, or from elsewhere. Boards have already bought the netting rights of lower proprietors, in order to abandon them for the benefit of salmon anglers.

The permitted methods of fishing for salmon in the sea are by rod and line, net and coble or bag net, fly net or other stake net. The *Salmon and Freshwater Fisheries (Protection) (Scotland) Act 1951* restricts salmon fishing in inland waters to rod and line or net and coble.

A system for licensing dealers in salmon (which includes sea trout) will be brought in by order of the Secretary of State within the licensing machinery of the *Civic Government (Scotland) Act 1982 (c.45)*. Similar provisions, appropriately adapted, apply to England and Wales.

While the common law may be adequate to deal with the theft or reset of farmed salmon, since wild salmon are the property of no-one legislation must create specific offences. The Act creates the new offence of being in possession of salmon, believing that it has been taken unlawfully anywhere in Great Britain, or possessing it in circumstances where it would be reasonable for the accused to suspect that it had been so taken. For reasons of urgency, a constable may search any premises other than a dwellinghouse without warrant if he has reasonable grounds for suspecting that this offence has been committed.

The gathering of evidence is further facilitated by extending the list of offences for which powers of search may be granted to a water bailiff, constable or person appointed by the Secretary of State. The power of a water bailiff to search vehicles on private land near to water without warrant is extended to cover stationary vehicles parked on roads near water or private land.

Corroboration is not required in order to secure a conviction. The need for it is also no longer required in relation to those offences under the *Salmon Fisheries (Scotland) Act 1868 (c.123)* where private prosecution was previously permitted. Now these prosecutions will be brought only by the procurator-fiscal.

It is an offence to introduce salmon or salmon eggs into inland waters without the written consent of the district salmon fishery board (if there is one for the district), or if the waters form part of a fish farm.

Exemption from certain offences may be made by the Secretary of State if every affected proprietor and the relevant district salmon fishery board (if there is one) agree, e.g. to allow salmon ranching or other developments in salmon fishing.

Acts or omissions done for scientific purposes or for the protection or improvement of salmon stocks are exempted, if written permission has been given by the relevant district salmon fishery board or the Secretary of State, as appropriate.

The Secretary of State and the Minister of Agriculture, Fisheries and Food, are required by early November 1989 to prepare a report for Parliament reviewing the nature and extent of fishing in the areas of the Yorkshire and Northumbrian water authorities, and the salmon fishery districts from the River Tweed to the River Ugie. This will involve monitoring the migration of salmon from the salmon net fisheries off the north east coast of England and the east coast of Scotland towards Scottish rivers. The purpose is to ensure that, in these areas and districts, sufficient salmon return to spawn in rivers, and that fishing for salmon by nets there is properly managed.

65 *Housing (Scotland) Act.* This Act consists of a series of textual amendments to earlier legislation, mainly the *Tenants' Rights, Etc. (Scotland) Act 1980 (c.52)*. To this extent, it parallels provisions for England and Wales in the *Housing and Planning Act 1986 (c.63)*.

Secure tenure and the right to buy are extended to the tenants of regional councils, police authorities and fire authorities, subject to safeguards for "operational" houses belonging to these authorities.

The minimum discounts on flats are increased to 44% after two years up to a maximum of 70% after thirty years, because these have been selling more slowly than other types of houses. The *Housing and Planning Act 1986* contains complementary provisions, enabling the Secretary of State (by order, subject to Parliamentary approval of the draft order) to increase these, and the percentage increase for each complete year after the first two.

These increases are not retrospective to affect negotiations already in train, but a tenant could withdraw his application to buy, submit a new one, and risk the valuation's having increased in the mean time.

Restrictions on the discount on the sale of recently built houses are relaxed, being moved forward from houses first let after 15 May 1975 to those first let after 31 December 1978, and affect houses let before that date but improved after it. A later date may be substituted by an order of the Secretary of State, with Treasury consent, and modifications made in relation to different areas, cases or classes of case.

The period within which the discount is recoverable by the landlord authority on re-sale by the former tenant is reduced from five years to three years, the amounts due in the second and third years being altered to 66% and 33% respectively. Disposals by the executor of a deceased owner, or by an owner by way of gift to a member of his family who has already lived with him for a year are exempt.

The principle behind the reduction in the time is that the previous rules about repayment were an unnecessary barrier to mobility. An additional aid to mobility will be the power given to the Secretary of State to contribute by way of grants or claims towards the cost of schemes to make it easier for tenants to move to a house in the area of a different authority by way of transfer or exchange of houses.

In order to avoid the need for intending purchasers to complain to the Lands Tribunal for Scotland against what may be considered to be unreasonable conditions to a sale imposed by landlord authorities, the Secretary of State may issue a direction requiring them not to include these conditions. If they are included, they will have no effect as regards the offer to sell. There are further minor provisions associated with the continuing game of leap-frog between recalcitrant authorities and the Secretary of State in his efforts to counter devices adopted by those authorities who attempt to put difficulties in the way of intending purchasers.

While a local authority may be able to afford to fight a case in the Lands Tribunal and appeal to the Court of Session, the tenant of modest means is unlikely to be able to do so. Accordingly the Secretary of State is given discretion to give financial or other assistance to a tenant or purchaser in relation to any proceedings, prospective or actual, under Part I of the 1980 Act (the right to purchase). The case must normally raise a question of principle and the giving of assistance must be in the public interest.

A number of machinery provisions amending the *Housing Associations Act 1985 (c.69)* deal with the administration of these associations. Certain controls under the *Building (Scotland) Act 1959 (c.24)* are relaxed by way of amendments arising from a Statement of Intent by the Secretary of State placed in the Library of the House of Commons on November 29, 1984, following consideration of the responses to a consultative paper issued in October 1983. Small additions to buildings such as porches and car-ports may be excluded by regulations from the full requirement of the Building Standards Regulations; class warrants may be issued to the effect that particular designs conform to particular provisions of the Building Standards Regulations; in certain cases under what is known as "self-certification of design", an applicant will be able to certify that the design of a building complies with these Regulations. Arrangements for remission of fees are made more flexible. The intention is to grant exemptions from fees where work is carried out entirely for the benefit of disabled people.

To sum up. This might have been more aptly entitled the *Housing (Miscellaneous Provisions) (Scotland) Act*.

Hamish McN Henderson, Department of Scots Law, University of Edinburgh.

SUMMARY OF OPINION POLLS 1986/87

Allan Macartney

Following the established pattern of this Appendix, the invaluable monthly series of polls on voting intention carried out by System Three (Scotland), and commissioned by the *Glasgow Herald*, is reproduced in graphic form for the year June 1986/June 1987. However, given that June 1987 was the month of the General Election, the six-monthly trend between the 1983 and 1987 election is also reproduced, courtesy of System Three. For comparison the MORI polls carried out for *The Scotsman* are reproduced in bar chart form. All these figures should be self-explanatory.

One of the most interesting aspects of polling in 1987 concerned their effect (if any) on voting behaviour. Attention was focussed on opinion polls in three marginal seats, carried out by System Three on behalf of Scottish Television and the *Herald*.

Table 1 below gives the figures for the three constituencies, with the preceding and ensuing General Election results for comparison.

TABLE 1

Constituency Polls %

a) Edinburgh South

	General Election 1983	27 May 1987	General Election 1987	Change 1983-87 Local	National
Con	37	27	34	−3	−4
Lab	29	38	38	+9	+7
Lib/SDP	29	24	23	−6	−6
SNP	5	10	5	0	+2
Green/Ecol	1	1	1	0	0

b) Stirling

	General Election 1983	31 May 1987	General Election 1987		
Con	40	29	38	−2	−4
Lab	28	39	37	+9	+7
Lib/SDP	24	18	15	−6	−6
SNP	8	13	11	+3	+2

c)Strathkelvin & Bearsden

	General Election 1983	5 June 1987	General Election 1987		
Con	37	31	33	−4	−4
Lab	26	37	38	+12	+7
Lib/SDP	29	24	21	−8	−6
SNP	9	9	7	−2	+2

One of the talking points of the Election campaign concerned the "Doomsday Scenario", i.e. what happens if Scotland were to return a substantial majority of non-Conservative (particularly Labour) MPs while the position in England, and therefore the UK as a whole, was reversed. (This outcome was of course correctly anticipated by those suggesting the Doomsday Scenario.) Two opinion polls carried out by System Three (one for *Radical Scotland*, one for STV/Channel 4) produced virtually identical results: only one Scot in three was prepared to accept that the Tories in such a situation had a mandate to govern Scotland. Both polls indicated, through different wording, substantial support (a majority of those expressing a view) for the attempt to have a Scottish Assembly set up.

On the preferred constitutional options for Scotland, the poll carried out for Scottish Television/Channel 4 found 26% in favour of "a completely independent Scotland", 54% for a devolved Assembly "with substantial powers" and 19% for the status quo. In the past, against similar expressions of preference had usually to be offset the low saliency of the issue of constitutional change. In 1987 however the importance attached to this issue increased. In the poll just cited those who saw the issue as important outnumbered those who saw it as unimportant by 5:2 (and, into the bargain, those prepared to pay higher taxes to a Scottish Assembly outnumbered the contrary view by 55:45). A further survey by System Three for BBC Scotland found that the setting up of a Scottish Assembly came sixth out of 14 issues in terms of importance; and – perhaps unsurprisingly – 56% thought the Scottish National Party the best party to support in order to achieve an Assembly (although in the Election the SNP received only 14% of the total vote).

Technical note

As usual, percentages have been rounded; "don't knows", "won't votes" and refusals have been ignored: and where dates are given they refer to the completion of fieldwork rather than publication.

Achnowledgements

Grateful thanks are due to all the opinion polling and mass media organisations mentioned above for their cooperation and permission to quote and republish data. Without such help the production of this Appendix would be impossible. Finally, our thanks are due to the Audio-Visual Services Department of Edinburgh University for the production of Figures 1-3.

Allan Macartney is Staff Tutor in Politics, The Open University in Scotland, and Hon. Fellow in Politics, University of Edinburgh.

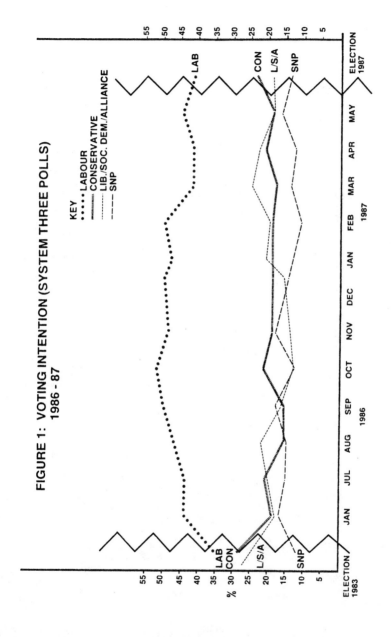

FIGURE 1: VOTING INTENTION (SYSTEM THREE POLLS) 1986 - 87

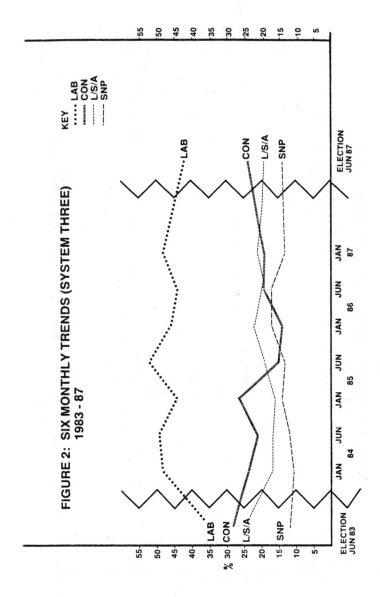

FIGURE 2: SIX MONTHLY TRENDS (SYSTEM THREE) 1983 - 87

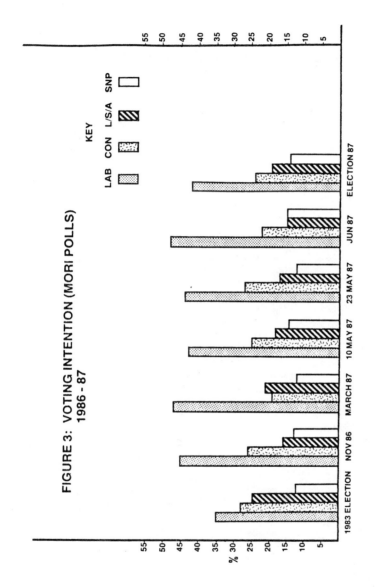

FIGURE 3: VOTING INTENTION (MORI POLLS)
1986 - 87

SECTION 1

SCOTTISH OFFICE MINISTERS

Private Secretary*

Secretary of State   Rt Hon Malcolm Rifkind MP   D J Crawley Ext 4011
Assistants:
   A Rinning DH Ext 6738‡
   C Weatherston Ext 4021

Minister of State   Lord Sanderson (Lords)   A C MacLaren Ext 4023
(Agriculture, Fisheries,
Forestry, Highlands and
Islands and Tourism)

Minister of State   Ian Lang MP (Commons)   I W Jardine Ext 4015
(Minister for Industry
and Local Government
Finance)

Parliamentary   Lord James Douglas-Hamilton MP I J C Howie Ext 4012
Under-Secretaries (Minister for Home Affairs
of State   and the Environment)

   Michael Forsyth MP   D B Binnie Ext 4107**
(Minister for Education
and Health)

* at New St Andrew's House, Edinburgh EH1 3SX
(031-244text) except
** at St Andrew's House, Edinburgh EH1 3DE
‡ Dover House, London (01-270 3000)

SECTION 2

REGIONAL COUNCILS

Names and Addresses of Convenors and Chief Officers

	Convener/ Population	Chief Executive	Director of Administration	Director of Finance	Director of Education	Director of Social Work	Director of Planning	Director of Roads
BORDERS Newton St Boswells TD60SA 083523301	Tom Hunter (Ind) 102,000	K J Clark		P Jeary	J McLean	D A Macdonald	D P Douglas	R I Hill
CENTRAL Viewforth Stirling FK82ET 07863111	Charles Sneddon (Lab) 272,000	J Broadfoot	P W Buchanan		I Collie	J A Ross	F Bracewell	G I McCrindle
DUMFRIES & GALLOWAY Council Offices Dumfries DG12DD 038753141	John Jameson (Ind) 147,000	M W D McIntosh	G M Sinclair	J C Stewart 038769191	J K Purves 30 Edinburgh Rd Dumfries 038763822	T McMenaway 8 Gordon St Dumfries 038763022	A H Dobbie	H D B Murray
FIFE Fife House North Street Glenrothes KY75LT 0592754411	Robert Gough (Lab) 344,000	J A Markland	W Breslin	D T Mitchell	M More	M A Gillespie	W Taylor	J T Rowson (Engineering) 0592754411

	Convener/ Population	Chief Executive	Director of Administration	Director of Finance	Director of Education	Director of Social Work	Director of Planning	Director of Roads
GRAMPIAN Woodhill House Ashgrove Rd West Aberdeen AB9 2LU 0224 682222	Geoffrey Hadley (Ind) 503,000	J D Macnaughton	A Campbell	T E Carter	J A D Michie	Miss M Hartnoll	T F Sprott	G Kirkbride
HIGHLAND Regional Buildings Glenurquhart Road Inverness IV3 5NX 0463 234121	Alexander Russell (Ind) 201,000	R H Stevenson	H Farquhar	J W Bremner	C E Stewart		R Cameron	G K M Macfarlane
LOTHIAN George IV Bridge Edinburgh EH1 1UQ 031-229 9292	James Cook (Lab) 742,000	G Bowie		D B Chynoweth	W D C Semple 40 Torphichen St Edinburgh EH3 8JJ	R W Kent Shrubhill House Edinburgh EH7 4DP 031-554 4301	D M Jamie 1 Parliament Sq Edinburgh EH1 1TU	P J Mason 19 Market St Edinburgh EH1 1BL
STRATHCLYDE Strathclyde House 20 India Street Glasgow G2 4PF 041-204 2900	James Jennings (Lab) 2,345,000	R Calderwood		A Gillespie	E Miller	F E Edwards	R G Maund	W S McAlonan
TAYSIDE Tayside House 26-28 Crichton St Dundee DD1 3RA 0382 23281	Ron Tosh (Lab) 392,000	J A Wallace		I B McIver	D G Robertson	S J Moxley	H Ramsay	J F White

	Convener/ Population	Chief Executive	Director of Administration	Director of Finance	Director of Education	Director of Social Work	Director of Planning	Director of Roads
ISLANDS COUNCILS								
ORKNEY County Offices Kirkwall KW15 1NY 0856 3535	Edwin Eunson (Ind) 19,000	R H Gilbert	R McCallum	R H Gilbert	A Bain	H MacGillivray	T W Eggeling	
SHETLAND Town Hall Lerwick Z%l61 0HB 0595 3535	Edward Thomason (Ind) 24,000	M Gerrard	P B Regan 31 Commercial St Lerwick	M Green 4 Market St Lerwick	R A B Barnes Brentham Ho Harbour St Lerwick	P Malcolmson 64 St Olaf St Lerwick	G L Mann Victoria Bldgs Esplanade Lerwick	
WESTERN ISLES Council Office South Beach Stornoway PA87 2BW 0851 3773	Sandy Matheson (Ind) 32,000	G Macleod	R Barnett	D G Macleod	N R Galbraith 0851 3992	Mrs N E Macleod 0851 3664	J R Haworth	

SECTION 3

DISTRICT COUNCILS

Names and Addresses of Conveners and Chief Executives

	Convener/Provost/ Chairman	Chief Executive (unless stated)
BORDERS		
Berwickshire	J Evans	R Christie District Offices, Duns TD11 3DU (03618 2600)
Ettrick & Lauderdale	A L Tulley	C Anderson, PO Box 4 Council Chambers, Paton St., Galashiels TD1 3AS (0896 4751)
Roxburgh	J R Irvine	K W Cramond District Office, High St. Hawick TD9 9EF (04507 5991)
Tweeddale	J Campbell	G H T Garvie District Offices, Peebles EH45 8GH (0721 20153)
CENTRAL		
Clackmannan	J Millar	I F Smith The Whins, Alloa FK10 3SA (0259 722160)
Falkirk	J Docherty	J P H Paton Municipal Buildings, Falkirk FK1 5RS (0324 24911)
Stirling	J Wyles	R Black Municipal Buildings, Corn Exchange Road, Stirling FK8 2HU (0786 79000)
DUMFRIES & GALLOWAY		
Annandale & Eskdale	R G Greenhow	J A Whitecross High Street, Annan DG12 6AQ (04612 3311)

Nithdale	K Cameron	W W Japp Municipal Chambers, Dumfries DG1 2AD (0387 3166)
Stewartry	J Nelson	W L Dick-Smith Council Offices, Kircudbright DG6 4PJ (0557 30291)
Wigtown	D R Robinson	A Geddes Sun Street, Stranraer DG9 3JJ (0776 2151)

FIFE

Dunfermline	R Mill	G Brown City Chambers, Dunfermline KY12 7ND (03837 22711)
Kirkcaldy	R King	J M Smith (Director of Administration) Town House, Kirkcaldy KY1 1XW (05922 61144)
North-East Fife	D Barrie	R Brotherton County Buildings, Cupar KY15 4TA (03345 3722)

GRAMPIAN

City of Aberdeen	H E Rae	J M Wilson Town House, Aberdeen AB9 1AQ (0224 642121)
Banff & Buchan	N Cowie	R W Jackson (Director of Administration and Legal Services) St Leonards, Sandyhill Rd., Banff AB4 1BH (026 12 2521)
Gordon	J B Presly	M C Barron Gordon House Blackhall Rd., Inverurie AB5 9WA (0467 20981)
Kincardine & Deeside	D J MacKenzie	T Hyder Arduthie Rd, Stonehaven AB3 2DQ (056 92 62001)

Moray	E Aldridge	J P C Bell High Street, Elgin IV30 1BX (0343 3451)

HIGHLAND

Badenoch & Strathspey	J A McCook	H G McCulloch Council Offices, Ruthven Road Kingussie, Inverness PH21 1EJ (054 02 555)
Caithness	J M Young	A Beattie Council Offices, Wick KW1 4AB (0955 3761)
Inverness	A G Sellar	B Wilson Town House, Inverness IV1 1JJ (0463 239111)
Lochaber	C Neilson	D A B Blair Lochaber House, Fort William PH33 6EL (0397 3881)
Nairn	H McLean	A M Kerr (Director of Law and Administration) The Courthouse, High Street, Nairn IV12 4AU (0667 52056)
Ross & Cromarty	G D Finlayson	Douglas Sinclair Council Offices, Dingwall IV15 9QN (0349 63381)
Skye & Lochalsh	J F Munro	D H Noble Park Road, Portree IV51 9EP (0478 2341)
Sutherland	Mrs L Mackenzie	D W Martin District Office, Golspie KW10 6RB (040 833192)

LOTHIAN

City of Edinburgh	J H Mackay	A Hepburn City Chambers, High St., Edinburgh EH1 1YJ (031 225 2424)

East Lothian	T Wilson	Malcolm Duncan Council Buildings, Haddington EH41 3HA (062 082 4161)
Midlothian	D Lennie	D W Duguid 1 Eskdaill Court, Dalkeith EH22 1DJ (031 663 2881)
West Lothian	D McCauley	W N Fordyce South Bridge St., Bathgate EH48 1TS (Bathgate 53631)

STRATHCLYDE

Argyll & Bute	D C Currie	M A J Gossip Kilmory, Lochgilphead PA31 8RT (0546 2127)
Bearsden & Milngavie	R W Robinson	A U Laurie Boclair, Bearsden G61 2TQ (041 942 2262)
City of Glasgow	R Gray	S Hamilton City Chambers, Glasgow G2 1DU (041 221 9600)
Clydebank	D S Grainger	J T McNally District Council Offices Clydebank G81 1TG (041 941 1331)
Clydesdale	Miss M T Hodgson	P W Daniels District Offices, Lanark ML11 7JT (0555 61511)
Cumbernauld & Kilsyth	J Pollock	J Hutton Bron Way, Cumbernauld G67 1DZ (02367 22131)
Cumnock & Doon Valley	D Shankland	D T Hemmings Lugar, Cumnock KA18 3JQ (0290 22111)
Cunninghame	Mrs T Beattie	B Devine Cunninghame House, Irvine KA12 8EE (0294 74166)

Dumbarton	R McNamara	L MacKinnon Crosslet House, Dumbarton G82 3NS (0389 65100)
East Kilbride	G McKillop	W G McNay Civic Centre, East Kilbride G74 1AB (035 52 28777)
Eastwood	Mrs J M Edmondson	M D Henry Eastwood Park, Rouken Glen Road, Glasgow G46 6UG (041 638 6511)
Hamilton	S. Casserly	Alister Baird 102 Cadzow Street, Hamilton ML3 6HH (0698 282323)
Inverclyde	Sir Simpson Stevenson	I C Wilson Municipal Buidings, Greenock PA15 1LY (0475 24400)
Kilmarnock & Loudon	T Ferguson	R W Jenner Civic Centre, Kilmarnock KA1 1BY (0563 21140)
Kyle & Carrick	G MacDonald	I R D Smillie Burns House, Ayr KA7 1UT (0292 81511)
Monklands	E Cairns	J S Ness Dunbeth Road, Coatbridge ML5 3LF (0263 24941)
Motherwell	J McGhee	J Bonomy P.O. Box 14, Motherwell ML1 1TW (0698 66166)
Renfrew	W McCready	Miss M C Thomson (District Administrator) Cotton Street, Paisley PA1 1BU (041 889 5400)
Strathkelvin	R M Coyle	C Mallon P.O. Box 4, Kirkintilloch G66 4TJ (041 776 7171)

TAYSIDE

Angus BMC Milne

Patrick B Regan
County Buildings, Forfar
DD8 3LG (0307 65101)

City of Dundee T Mitchell

J F Hoey
City Chambers Dundee
DD1 3BY (0382 23141)

Perth & Kinross J M Mathieson

J E D Cormie
1-3 High Street, Perth
PH1 5JU (0738 21161)

Source: Scottish Development Department

SECTION 4

GENERAL ELECTION RESULTS
11 JUNE 1987

ABERDEEN NORTH 63,229   **(Turnout 70.0%)**

				%
*	R Hughes	Lab	24,145	54.7
	R Smith	SDP	7,867	17.8
	Ms G E C Scanlan	Con	6,330	14.3
	P B Greenhorn	SNP	5,827	13.2
	Majority		16,278	

ABERDEEN SOUTH 62,956   **(Turnout 67.2%)**

				%
	F Doran	Lab	15,917	37.7
*	P G Malone	Con	14,719	34.8
	I G Philip	SDP	8,844	20.9
	M F Weir	SNP	2,776	6.6
	Majority		1,198	

ANGUS EAST 61,069   **(Turnout 75.5%)**

				%
	A Welsh	SNP	19,536	42.4
*	P.L. Fraser	Con	17,992	39.0
	R A Mennie	Lab	4,971	10.8
	I N Mortimer	SDP	3,592	7.8
	Majority		1,544	

ARGYLL & BUTE 48,846   **(Turnout 75.4%)**

				%
	Ms J R Michie	Lib	13,726	37.3
*	J J MacKay	Con	12,332	33.5
	R R Shaw	SNP	6,297	17.1
	D Tierney	Lab	4,437	12.1
	Majority		1,394	

AYR   66,498   **(turnout 80.0%)**

				%
*	G Younger	Con	20,942	39.4
	K Macdonald	Lab	20,760	39.1
	K W Moody	Lib	7,859	14.8
	C T Weir	SNP	3,548	6.7
	Majority		182	

BANFF & BUCHAN 62,165   **(Turnout 70.8%)**

				%
	A E A Salmond	SNP	19,462	44.2
*	A McQuarrie	Con	17,021	38.7
	G M Burness	SDP	4,211	9.6
	J M Livie	Lab	3,281	7.5
		Majority	2,441	

CAITHNESS & SUTHERLAND 31,315   **(Turnout 73.6%)**

				%
*	R A R Maclennan	SDP	12,338	53.6
	R L Hamilton	Con	3,844	16.7
	A Byron	Lab	3,347	14.9
	A W K MacGregor	SNP	2,371	10.3
	W A Mowat	IndLib	686	3.0
	B R Planterose	Green	333	1.5
		Majority	8,494	

CARRICK,CUMNOCK & DOON VALLEY 56,373   **(Turnout 75.8%)**

				%
*	G Foukes	Lab/Co-op	25,669	60.1
	S Stevenson	Con	8,867	20.7
	Ms M Ali	SDP	4,106	9.6
	C D Calman	SNP	4,094	9.6
		Majority	16,802	

CLACKMANNAN 49,332   **(Turnout 76.7%)**

				%
*	M J O'Neill	Lab	20,317	53.7
	A Macartney	SNP	7,916	20.9
	J Parker	Con	5,620	14.9
	Ms A M Watters	SDP	3,961	10.5
		Majority	12,401	

CLYDEBANK & MILGAVIE 50,219   **(Turnout 78.9%)**

				%
	A Worthington	Lab	22,528	56.9
	K Hirstwood	Con	6,224	15.7
	R Ackland	SDP	5,891	14.9
	S F Fisher	SNP	4,935	12.5
		Majority	16,304	

CLYDESDALE   61,691   (Turnout 78.1%)

			%
J Hood	Lab	21,826	45.3
R S Robertson	Con	11,324	23.5
J Boyle	SDP	7,909	16.4
M W Russell	SNP	7,125	14.8
	Majority	10,502	

CUMBERNAULD & KILSYTH   45,451   (Turnout 78.5%)

			%
* N Hogg	Lab	21,385	60.0
T R Johnston	SNP	6,982	19.6
C S Deans	SDP	4,059	11.4
Ms A E Thomson	Con	3,227	9.0
	Majority	14,403	

CUNNINGHAME NORTH 54,876   (Turnout 78.2%)

			%
B D H Wilson	Lab	19,016	44.4
* J A Corrie	Con	14,594	34.0
D J Herbison	SDP	5,185	12.1
M Brown	SNP	4,076	9.5
	Majority	4,422	

CUNNINGHAME SOUTH 49,917   (Turnout 74.9%)

			%
* D Lambie	Lab	22,728	60.8
E R Gibson	Con	6,095	16.3
J A Boss	Lib	4,426	11.9
Ms K Ullrich	SNP	4,115	11.0
	Majority	16,633	

DUMBARTON   58,810   (Turnout 78.2%)

			%
J McFall	Lab/Co-op	19,778	43.0
R F Graham	Con	14,556	31.7
R A Mowbray	SDP	6,060	13.2
Ms J Herriot	SNP	5,564	12.1
	Majority	5,222	

DUMFRIES 59,392   (Turnout 75.6%)

			%
* Sir H S P Monro	Con	18,785	41.8
Ms C W Phillips	Lab	11,292	25.2
J R McCall	SDP	8,064	18.0
T McAlpine	SNP	6,391	14.2
P M Thomas	Green	349	0.8
	Majority	7,493	

DUNDEE EAST   60,830   (Turnout 75.9%)

				%
	J McAllion	Lab	19,539	42.3
*	G Wilson	SNP	18,524	40.2
	P.S. Cook	Con	5,938	12.9
	Ms M K von Romberg	Lib	2,143	4.6
		Majority	1,015	

DUNDEE WEST   61,944   (Turnout 75.5%)

				%
*	E Ross	Lab	24,916	53.3
	J A Donnelly	Con	8,390	18.0
	A N Morgan	SNP	7,164	15.3
	Ms R Lonie	SDP	5,922	12.7
	S R Mathewson	Comm	308	0.7
		Majority	16,526	

DUNFERMLINE EAST   51,285   (Turnout 76.5%)

				%
*	J G Brown	Lab	25,381	64.7
	C Shenton	Con	5,792	14.8
	Ms E B A Harris	Lib	4,122	10.5
	Ms A McGarry	SNP	3,901	10.0
		Majority	19,589	

DUNFERMLINE WEST 51,115   (Turnout 76.9%)

				%
*	R G Douglas	Lab	18,493	47.1
	P Gallie	Con	9,091	23.1
	F Moyes	SDP	8,288	21.1
	G Hughes	SNP	3,435	8.7
		Majority	9,402	

EAST KILBRIDE   63,144   (Turnout 79.2%)

			%
A P Ingram	Lab	24,491	49.0
D R E Sullivan	SDP	11,867	23.7
P M Walker	Con	7,344	14.7
J H Taggart	SNP	6,275	12.6
	Majority	12,624	

EAST LOTHIAN   65,059   (Turnout 78.7%)

				%
*	J D Home Robertson	Lab	24,583	48.0
	S M Langdon	Con	14,478	28.3
	A W Robinson	Lib	7,929	15.5
	A Burgon-Lyon	SNP	3,727	7.3
	A E Marland	Green	451	0.9
		Majority	10,105	

EASTWOOD   61,691   (Turnout 79.3%)

				%
*	J A Stewart	Con	19,388	39.5
	R M Leishman	SDP	13,374	27.2
	P A Grant-Hutchison	Lab	12,305	25.1
	J A M Findlay	SNP	4,033	8.2
		Majority	6,014	

EDINBURGH CENTRAL   59,672   (Turnout 68.9%)

				%
	A Darling	Lab	16,502	40.2
*	Sir A M Fletcher	Con	14,240	34.7
	A B Myles	Lib	7,333	17.9
	B Shaw	SNP	2,559	6.2
	Ms L M Hendry	Green	430	1.0
		Majority	2,262	

EDINBURGH EAST 48,952   (Turnout 74.1%)

				%
*	G S Strang	Lab	18,257	50.4
	J F Renz	Con	8,962	24.7
	Ms J C Aitken	Lib	5,592	15.4
	M Bovey	SNP	3,434	9.5
		Majority	9,295	

EDINBURGH LEITH 60,425   (Turnout 70.8%)

				%
*	R D M Brown	Lab	21,104	49.3
	D A Y Menzies	Con	9,777	22.9
	Ms S R Wells	SDP	7,843	18.3
	W S Morrison	SNP	4,045	9.5
		Majority	11,327	

EDINBURGH PENTLANDS   58,200   (Turnout 77.6%

				%
*	M L Rifkind	Con	17,278	38.3
	M J Lazarowicz	Lab	13,533	30.0
	K A Smith	SDP	11,072	24.5
	D N MacCormick	SNP	3,264	7.2
		Majority	3,745	

EDINBURGH SOUTH   63,953   (Turnout 75.7%)

				%
	N Griffiths	Lab	18,211	37.7
*	M A Ancram	Con	16,352	33.8
	D A Graham	SDP	10.900	22.5
	Ms C M Moore	SNP	2,455	5.1
	Ms R V Clark	Green	440	0.9
		Majority	1,859	

EDINBURGH WEST   62,293   (Turnout 79.3%)

				%
*	J A Douglas-Hamilton	Con	18,450	37.3
	D G King	Lib	17,216	34.9
	M C B McGregor	Lab	10,957	22.2
	N Irons	SNP	2,774	5.6
		Majority	1,234	

FALKIRK EAST   52,781   (Turnout 74.8%)

				%
*	H Ewing	Lab	21,379	54.2
	K H Brookes	Con	7,356	18.7
	R N F Halliday	SNP	6,056	15.4
	Ms E G Dick	SDP	4,624	11.7
		Majority	14,023	

FALKIRK WEST   50,442   (Turnout 75.6%)

				%
*	D A Canavan	Lab	20,256	53.2
	D R B Thomas	Con	6,704	17.6
	I R Goldie	SNP	6,296	16.5
	M J Harris	Lib	4,841	12.7
		Majority	13,552	

FIFE CENTRAL 56,120   (Turnout 76.2%)

				%
	H B McLeish	Lab	22,827	53.4
	R E Aird	Con	7,118	16.7
	T M Little	Lib	6,487	15.2
	D Hood	SNP	6,296	14.7
		Majority	15,709	

NORTH EAST FIFE   52,303   (Turnout 76.2%)

			%
W M Campbell	Lib	17,868	44.8
* J S B Henderson	Con	16,421	41.2
A M E Gannon	Lab	2,947	7.4
F D Roche	SNP	2,616	6.6
	Majority	1,447	

GALLOWAY & UPPER NITHSDALE   53,466   (Turnout 76.8%)

			%
* I B Lang	Con	16,592	40.4
S F Norris	SNP	12,919	31.5
J E McKerchar	Lib	6,001	14.6
J W Gray	Lab	5,298	12.9
D Kenny	Ind	230	0.6
	Majority	3,673	

GLASGOW CATHCART   49,362   (Turnout 76.3%)

			%
* J A Maxton	Lab	19,623	52.1
W A Harvey	Con	8,420	22.4
Ms M Craig	SDP	5,722	15.2
W A Steven	SNP	3,883	10.3
	Majority	11,203	

GLASGOW CENTRAL   51,195   (Turnout 65.6%)

			%
* R McTaggart	Lab	21,619	64.5
B C Jenkins	Con	4,366	13.0
J S Bryden	Lib	3,528	10.5
A B Wilson	SNP	3,339	9.9
A Brooks	Green	290	0.9
J P McGoldrick	Comm	265	0.8
D Owen	RF	126	0.4
	Majority	17,253	

GLASGOW GARSCADDEN   47,997   (Turnout 71.4%)

			%
* D C Dewar	Lab	23,178	67.7
A Brophy	SNP	4,201	12.2
T Begg	Con	3,660	10.7
J S Callison	SDP	3,211	9.4
	Majority	18,977	

GLASGOW GOVAN 50,634   (Turnout 73.4%)

				%
*	B Millan	Lab	24,071	64.8
	A Ferguson	SDP	4,562	12.3
	Ms J R Girsman	Con	4,411	11.9
	F McCabe	SNP	3,851	10.4
	D Chalmers	Comm	237	0.6
		Majority	19,509	

GLASGOW HILLHEAD   57,932   (Turnout 72.3%)

				%
	G Galloway	Lab	17,958	42.9
*	R H Jenkins	SDP	14,707	35.1
	B D Cooklin	Con	6,048	14.4
	B Kidd	SNP	2,713	6.5
	A Whitelaw	Green	443	1.1
		Majority	3,251	

GLASGOW MARYHILL 52,443   (Turnout 67.5%)

			%
Ms M Fyfe	Lab	23,482	66.4
Ms E M Attwooll	Lib	4,118	11.7
G Roberts	SNP	3.895	11.0
S R R Kirk	Con	3,307	9.4
D L Spaven	Green	539	1.5
	Majority	19,364	

GLASGOW POLLOCK 62,293   (Turnout 79.3%)

			%
J F Dunnachie	Lab	23,239	63.1
Ms G R French	Con	5,256	14.3
J C Shearer	Lib	4,445	12.0
A Doig	SNP	3,528	9.6
D Fogg	Green	362	1.0
	Majority	17,983	

GLASGOW PROVAN   43,775   (Turnout 69.1%)

			%
J Wray	Lab	22,032	72.9
W Ramsay	SNP	3,660	12.1
Ms A Strutt	Con	2,336	7.7
J Morrison	SDP	2,189	7.3
	Majority	18,372	

GLASGOW RUTHERGLEN   57,370   (Turnout 77.2%)

			%
T McAvoy	Lab/Co-op	24,790	56.0
R E Brown	Lib	10,795	24.4
G M Hamilton	Con	5,088	11.5
J Higgins	SNP	3,584	8.1
	Majority	13,995	

GLASGOW SHETTLESTON 53,650   (Turnout 70.4%)

				%
*	D Marshall	Lab	23,991	63.6
	M Fisher	Con	5,010	13.3
	J A MacVicar	SNP	4,807	12.7
	Ms P A M Clarke	Lib	3,942	10.4
		Majority	18,981	

GLASGOW SPRINGBURN   51,590   (Turnout 67.5%)

				%
*	M J Martin	Lab	25,617	73.6
	B O'Hara	SNP	3,554	10.2
	M Call	Con	2,870	8.3
	D Rennie	Lib	2,746	7.9
		Majority	22,063	

GORDON   73,520   (Turnout 73.7%)

				%
*	M G Bruce	Lib	26,770	49.4
	P R Leckie	Con	17,251	31.9
	Ms M C Morrell	Lab	6,228	11.5
	G E Wright	SNP	3,876	7.2
		Majority	9,519	

GREENOCK & PORT GLASGOW   57,811   (Turnout 75.4%)

				%
*	N A Godman	Lab	27,848	63.9
	J H Moody	Lib	7,793	17.9
	T J D Pearson	Con	4,199	9.6
	T Lenehan	SNP	3,721	8.6
		Majority	20,055	

HAMILTON   62,288   (Turnout 76.9%)

				%
*	G I M Robertson	Lab	28,563	59.7
	G S Mond	Con	6,901	14.4
	T McKay	Lib	6,302	13.2
	C Crossley	SNP	6,093	12.7
		Majority	21,662	

INVERNESS,NAIRN & LOCHABER 66,817   (Turnout 70.9%)

				%
*	Sir R Johnston	Lib	17,422	36.8
	D Stewart	Lab	11,991	25.4
	Ms A T Keswick	Con	10,901	23.0
	N P. Johnson	SNP	7,001	14.8
		Majority	5,431	

KILMARNOCK & LOUDOUN 62,725   (Turnout 78.0%)

				%
*	W McKelvey	Lab	23,713	48.5
	Ms A K Bates	Con	9,586	19.6
	G Leslie	SNP	8,881	18.2
	P E Kerr	SDP	6,698	13.7
		Majority	14,127	

KINCARDINE & DEESIDE 63,598   (Turnout 75.3%)

				%
*	A L Buchanan-Smith	Con	19,438	40.6
	N R Stephen	Lib	17,375	36.3
	J K A Thomaneck	Lab	7,624	16.0
	Ms F E Duncan	SNP	3,082	6.5
	Ms L M Perica	Green	229	0.6
		Majority	2,063	

KIRKCALDY 53,473   (Turnout 76.5%)

				%
	L G Moonie	Lab	20,281	49.6
	I G Mitchell	Con	8,711	21.3
	D Stewart	SDP	7,118	17.4
	W A R Mullin	SNP	4,794	11.7
		Majority	11,570	

LINLITHGOW 59,656   (Turnout 77.5%)

				%
*	T Dalyell	Lab	21,869	47.4
	J Sillars	SNP	11,496	24.9
	T R Armstrong Wilson	Con	6,828	14.8
	Ms H A McDade	SDP	5,840	12.6
	J Glassford	Comm	154	0.3
		Majority	10,373	

LIVINGSTON 56,659   (Turnout 74.1%)

				%
*	R F Cook	Lab	19,110	45.6
	R A McCreadie	Lib	8,005	19.1
	M N A Mayall	Con	7,860	18.7

LIVINGSTON   56,659   (Turnout 74.1%)

				%
*	R F Cook	Lab	19,110	45.6
	R A McCreadie	Lib	8,005	19.1
	M N A Mayall	Con	7,860	18.7
	K W MacAskill	SNP	6,969	16.6
		Majority	11,105	

MIDLOTHIAN   60,588   (Turnout 77.2%)

				%
*	A Eadie	Lab	22,553	48.3
	A R Dewar	SDP	10,300	22.0
	F G Riddell	Con	8,527	18.2
	I M Chisholm	SNP	4,947	10.6
	I Smith	Green	412	0.9
		Majority	12,253	

MONKLANDS EAST 49,672   (Turnout 74.8%)

				%
*	J Smith	Lab	22,649	61.0
	J Love	Con	6,260	16.8
	K J Gibson	SNP	4,790	12.9
	Ms S M Grieve	SDP	3,442	9.3
		Majority	16,389	

MONKLANDS WEST   50,938   (Turnout 77.2%)

				%
*	T Clarke	Lab	24,499	62.3
	G Lind	Con	6,166	15.7
	Ms A McQueen	SDP	4,408	11.2
	K Bovey	SNP	4,260	10.8
		Majority	18,333	

MORAY   62,210   (Turnout 72.7%)

				%
	Ms M A Ewing	SNP	19,510	43.2
*	A Pollock	Con	15,825	35.0
	C R C Smith	Lab	5,118	11.3
	D G M Skene	Lib	4,724	10.5
		Majority	3,685	

MOTHERWELL NORTH   57,657   (Turnout 77.3%)

				%
	J Reid	Lab	29,825	66.9
	A Currie	SNP	6,230	14.0
	R Hargrave	Con	4,939	11.1
	G Swift	Lib	3,558	8.0
		Majority	23,595	

MOTHERWELL SOUTH   52,164   (Turnout 75.5%)

				%
*	J W Bray	Lab	22,957	58.3
	J Wright	SNP	6,027	15.3
	J S Bercow	Con	5,704	14.5
	R MacGregor	SDP	4,463	11.3
	R Somerville	Comm	223	0.6
		Majority	16,930	

ORKNEY & SHETLAND 31,093   (Turnout 68.7%)

				%
*	J R Wallace	Lib	8,881	41.7
	R W A Jenkins	Con	4,959	23.3
	J H Aberdein	Lab	3,995	18.7
	J Goodlad	OSM	3,095	14.5
	G K Collister	Green	389	1.8
		Majority	3,922	

PAISLEY NORTH 49,518   (Turnout 73.5%)

				%
*	A S Adams	Lab	20,193	55.5
	Ms E P McCartin	SDP	5,751	15.8
	Ms E F P Laing	Con	5,741	15.8
	I Taylor	SNP	4,696	12.9
		Majority	14,442	

PAISLEY SOUTH   51,152   (Turnout 75.3%

				%
*	N F Buchan	Lab	21,611	56.2
	A M Carmichael	Lib	5,826	15.1
	Ms D A Williamson	Con	5,644	14.7
	J R Mitchell	SNP	5,398	14.0
		Majority	15,785	

PERTH & KINROSS   63,484   (Turnout 74.4%)

				%
*	N H Fairbairn	Con	18,716	39.6
	J M Fairlie	SNP	13,040	27.6
	S Donaldson	Lib	7,969	16.9
	J W McConnell	Lab	7,490	15.9
		Majority	5,676	

RENFREW WEST & INVERCLYDE 56,233   (Turnout 80.5%)

				%
	T Graham	Lab	17,525	38.7
*	Ms A A McCurley	Con	13,462	29.8
	J D Mabon	SDP	9,669	21.4
	C M Campbell	SNP	4,578	10.1
		Majority	4,063	

ROSS, CROMARTY & SKYE 52,816   (Turnout 72.2%)

				%
*	C P Kennedy	SDP	18,809	49.4
	C F Spencer Nairn	Con	7,490	19.7
	M M MacMillan	Lab	7,287	19.1
	R M Gibson	SNP	4,492	11.8
		Majority	11,319	

ROXBURGH & BERWICKSHIRE 43,350   (Turnout 76.8%)

				%
*	A J Kirkwood	Lib	16,388	49.2
	L Fox	Con	12,380	37.2
	T C H Luckhurst	Lab	2,944	8.8
	M N Douglas	SNP	1,586	4.6
		Majority	4,008	

STIRLING 58,350   (Turnout 78.1%)

				%
*	M B Forsyth	Con	17,191	37.8
	M Connarty	Lab	16,643	36.5
	I B McFarlane	Lib	6,804	14.9
	I M Lawson	SNP	4,897	10.8
		Majority	548	

STRATHKELVIN & BEARSDEN 62,743   (Turnout 82.1%)

				%
	S L Galbraith	Lab	19,639	38.1
*	M W Hirst	Con	17,187	33.4
	J Bannerman	Lib	11,034	21.4
	G Paterson	SNP	3,654	7.1
		Majority	2,452	

TAYSIDE NORTH 54,024   (Turnout 74.7%)

				%
*	W C Walker	Con	18,307	45.4
	K J N Guild	SNP	13,291	32.9
	P F Regent	Lib	5,201	12.9
	J Whytock	Lab	3,550	8.8
		Majority	5,016	

TWEEDDALE, ETTRICK & LAUDERDALE 38,235   (Turnout 76.5%)

				%
*	D M S Steele	Lib	14,599	49.9
	Ms C S Finlay-Maxwell	Con	8,657	29.6
	N Glen	Lab	3,320	11.4
	A Lumsden	SNP	2,660	9.1
		Majority	5,942	

WESTERN ISLES   23,535   **(Turnout 70.1%)**

			%
C A MacDonald	Lab	7,041	42.7
I Smith	SNP	4,701	28.5
K A McIver	SDP	3,419	20.7
M Morrison	Con	1,336	8.1
	Majority	2,340	

An Asterisk denotes a member of the previous Parliament.
Source: Election Studies, University of Dundee.

SECTION 5

MAJOR POLITICAL AND SOCIAL ORGANISATIONS IN SCOTLAND

1. **Political Parties**
    Communist Party, 44 Carlton Place, Glasgow G5 9TW
    (041-429 2558)

    Scottish Conservative Party, 3 Chester Street, Edinburgh EH3 7RN
    (031-226 4426)

    The Labour Party (Scottish Council), Keir Hardie House,
    1 Lynedoch Place, Glasgow G3 6AB (041-332 8946)

    Scottish Liberal Party, 4 Clifton Terrace, Edinburgh EH12 5DR
    (031-337 2314)

    Scottish National Party, 6 North Charlotte Street,
    Edinburgh EH2 4JH (031-226 3661)

    Social Democratic Party, 5 Royal Exchange Square, Glagow
    G1 3AH (041-221 8871)

2. **Government Agencies**
    Crofters Commission, 4-6 Castle Wynd, Inverness IV2 3EQ
    (0463 23731)

    Highlands and Islands Development Board, 27 Bank Street,
    Inverness IV1 1QR (0463 234171)

    The Housing Corporation, Scottish Head Office, Rosebery House,
    9 Haymarket Terrace, Edinburgh EH3 7AF (031-226 3153)

    Manpower Services Commission for Scotland, 4 Jeffrey Street,
    Edinburgh EH1 1UU (031-556 0233)

    Scottish Development Agency, 120 Bothwell Street, Glasgow G2 JP
    (041-248 2700)

    Scottish Special Housing Association, 37-41 Manor Place,
    Edinburgh EH3 7EE (031-226 4401)

3. **Industrial and Social Organisations**
    Church of Scotland, 121 George Street, Edinburgh EH2 4YN
    (031-225 5722)

    Confederation of British Industry (Scottish Office), 5 Claremont
    Terrace, Glasgow G3 (041-332 8661)

Scottish Consumer Council, 314 St Vincent Street, Glasgow G3 8XW (041-226 5261)

Scottish Council (Development and Industry), 1 Castle Street, Edinburgh EH2 3AJ (031-225 7911)

Scottish Council for Community and Voluntary Organisations, 18/19 Claremont Crescent, Edinburgh EH7 4QD (031-556 3882)

Scottish Trades Union Congress, 16 Woodlands Terrace, Glasgow G3 6DF (041-332 4946)

RECENT PUBLICATIONS IN SCOTTISH GOVERNMENT AND POLITICS

C H Allen

The list below covers material omitted from previous listing, and material published since the last list in the period 1.6.86 to 31.5.87. Where a publisher is not specified, the publisher and author are the same. I would be grateful to be told of any errors or omissions.

To make it easier to obtain theses on inter-library loan, I have included where possible the British Library (Lending Division) or University Microfilm numbers; these should be quoted when applying for a loan copy.

As there now exists a current index to the *Scotsman* (contact Ted Lloyd-Gwilt, Scotsman Index Project, 21 Buccleuch Place, Edinburgh) I no longer cite newspaper feature articles in the index. I also do not list reports of investigations by the local Government Ombudsman.

1. ABERDEEN BEYOND 2000, *Aberdeen beyond 2000*. Aberdeen, 1987, 44pp
2. ABRAMS, B A *Scottish nationalism and the British response: a critical analysis of the devolution debate*. Ph.D. thesis, Brandeis University, 1986, 260pp
3. ADAMS, D "A new driving force in the economy", *Scottish Economic Development Review* 2 (1985) 4-7 (service sector)
4. ADLER, M, PETCH, A & TWEEDIE, J, "The Parents' Charter in Scotland", *Scottish Government Yearbook* 1987, 289-331
5. ADLER, M & RAAB, G, *Survival of the fittest? The impact of parental choice on admission to primary and secondary schools in Dundee*. Edinburgh: Edinburgh University Dept. of Social Policy, 1986
6. AGE CONCERN *Housing facts and figures*. Edinburgh, 2nd edition, 1985, 32pp
7. AGNEW, J A "Place and political behaviour: the geography of Scottish nationalism", *Political Geography Quarterly*, 3,3 (1984) 191-206
8. AITKEN, J J "Community councils: the first decade", *Scottish Planning Law and Practice* 19 (1986), 69
9. ALEXANDER, A *Local governmment in Britain since reorganisation*. London: Allen & Unwin, 1982, 191pp; see chapter 6
10. ALLEN, C H "Recent publications in Scottish government and

politics", *Scottish Government Yearbook* 1987, 378-403

11. ALLEN, F R *New Towns, old habits: freedom of information in New Town Development Corporations.* Glasgow: SCC, 1986, 21pp
12. ALLISON, M *et al, Unemployed workers' centres in Strathclyde.* Paisley: Paisley College of Technology, 1986
13. AL-QUADDO, H M A, *An analysis of organisational change: a study of the SSHA.* Ph.D. thesis, CNAA (Robert Gordon's Institute) 1986, 498pp (British Library No. D68257/86)
14. AMSEL, A *et al, Housing cooperatives in Scotland.* London: Cooperative Union Ltd/TPAS, 1983, 27pp
15. ANGUS DISTRICT COUNCIL, *Housing plans and programmes 1986/7 to 1990-91.* Forfar, 1986, 109pp
16. ANON "Anderston Quay", *Radical Scotland* 31 (1986) 14-15
17. ANON "Gearing up for another ten years", *Planning*, 17.4.87, 10-11
18. ANON "Review of the oil related industry in Highland Region", *Highland Economic Review* 7 (1986)
19. ARMSTRONG, H & TAYLOR, J "Regional policy", *Developments in economics*, ed. G B J Atkinson (Causeway Press, 1985)
20. ARMSTRONG, H & TAYLOR, J "Regional policy: dead or alive?", *Economic Review*, 4,2 (1986) 2-7
21. ASHCROFT, B K, LOVE, J H, & SCOULLER, J, *The economic effects of the inward acquisition of Scottish manufacturing companies 1965-80.* Edinburgh: I.D.S. (ESU Research paper 11), 1987, 148pp
22. BAGGOTT, M "Scotland's Silicon Glen", *Scottish Economic Development Review* 3 (1985) 16-19
23. BAILEY, S J *Assessing need to spend for Scottish local authorities.* Glasgow: Glasgow College of Technology, Policy Analysis Research Unit Discussion paper 12, 1984, 18pp
24. BALDERRAMA, R J *The North Sea oil activities in the context of Scottish development.* M.Sc. dissertatioin, Manchester University, 1983
25. BARLOW, J "The housing crisis and its local dimensions", *Housing Studies*, 2, 1 (1987) 28-41
26. BEESLEY, M E & HAMILTON, R T "Births and deaths of manufacturing firms in the Scottish regions", *Regional Studies*, 20, 4 (1986) 281- 88
27. BEGG, H M *Regional policy under review.* Dundee: Duncan of Jordanstone College, Dept. of Town and Regional Planning Occasional paper 17, 1984
28. BEGG, H M & POLLOCK, S H A "The future of development plans in Scotland", *Scottish Planning Law and Practice* 21 (1987) 40-41
29. BEGG, H M & WILSON, I B (Eds) *Planning in Tayside: past, present and future.* Dundee: Duncan of Jordanstone College of Art, Dept. of Town and Regional Planning, Occasional paper 18, 1985,

67pp

30. BELL, D N F *Regional econometric modelling with special reference to Scotland*. Ph.D. thesis, Strathclyde, 1983, 351pp (British Library No. D68570/86)

31. BENLEY, C "Industrial survey: Kilmarnock and Loudon", *Business Scotland*, Oct. 1986, 31-38

32. BIRTWHISTLE, A & HARVEY, A J, "Output-based estimates of GDP for Scotland 1963-84", *Scottish Economic Bulletin* 33 (1986)

33. BLACK, J "We did it our way", *Roof*, 11, 4 (1986) (Pilton)

34. BOCHEL, J & DENVER, D "Labour predominance reasserted: the Regional elections of 1986", *Scottish Government Yearbook* 1987, 23- 31

35. BOCHEL, J & DENVER, D *Scottish regional election 1986: result and statistics*. Dundee: Dundee University Dept. of Politics, 1986, 54pp

36. BONNEY, N *Social and economic change in Aberdeen 1971-81*. ESRC Report GOO/23/2090, 1987(?)

37. BORDERS REGIONAL COUNCIL/SDA *Pilot rural development areas study*. Newtown St Boswells, 1986

38. BOUNDARY COMMISSION FOR SCOTLAND *Report on interim review of parliamentary constituencies*. London: House of Commons Paper HC 141, 1987, 7pp

39. BOYLE, R "Urban initiative in Scotland", *Planner*, June 1987, 27-30

40. BOYLE, S & JENKINS, I "Census of employment 1984: an assessment", *Quarterly Economic Commentary*, 12, 3 (1987) 70-76

41. BRAND, J "Political parties and the referendum on national sovereignty: the 1979 Scottish referendum on devolution", *Canadian Review of Studies in Nationalism*, 13, 1 (1986) 31-43

42. BROWN, A & FAIRLEY, J "A Scottish labour market board?", *Scottish Government Yearbook* 1987, 219-38

43. BROWN, C *The social history of religion in modern Scotland*. London: Methuen, 1987; see pp 209-48

44. BROWN, R "Special survey: Strathclyde", *Scottish Business Insider*, 3, 8 (1986) 28-33

45. BRYANT, I, BURNHILL, P & RAFFE, D *Report on the 1984 pilot of the Scottish young people's survey*. Edinburgh: Edinburgh University Centre for Educational Sociology, 1984

46. BURNS, M "Housing in Scotland", *Scottish Trade Union Review* 31 (1986) 21

47. BUXTON, N *Performance and problems of Scotland's industrial economy*. Scottish Council (Development and Industry) International Forum, 1986

48. CAIRNS, J A, HARRIS, A H & WILLIAMS, H C *Barrier to entry in the North Sea offshore oil industry*. Aberdeen: Aberdeen University Dept. of Political Economy Occasional paper 24, 1987

49. CARTER, C J *The Scottish New Towns: their contribution to post-*

war growth and urban development in central Scotland. Dundee: Duncan of Jordanstone College, Dept. of Town and Regional Planning Occasional paper 19, 1985

50. CARTER, J J & KEATING, M *The designation of Cumbernauld New Town. A study of central-local government relationships in Scotland during the 1950s.* Milton Keynes: Open University Faculty of Social Sciences Working paper 2, 1986

51. CARTY, T "Land reform for Scotland", *Radical Scotland* 22 (1986) 10-11

52. CENTRAL REGIONAL COUNCIL *Transport policy and programme 6B: 1985-86.* Stirling, 1985, 52pp

53. CENTRAL REGIONAL COUNCIL *Transport policy and programme 6C: 1985-86.* Stirling, 1986, 56pp

54. CENTRAL REGIONAL COUNCIL *Transport policy and programme 1987-88.* Stirling, 1986, 110pp

55. CENTRE FOR HOUSING RESEARCH *Area management and community planning.* Glasgow: Glasgow University CHR (Centre for Urban and Regional Research discussion paper 23), 1985, 53pp

56. CHALMERS, M (ed) *New communities: did they get it right?.* Edinburgh: Royal Town Planning Institute Scottish Branch, Women and Planning Committee, 1986, 41pp

57. CHAPMAN, J "Scottish society: the prospects for girls", *Yearbook '85* (Modern Studies Association), 69-75

58. CLARK, C "Community responses on unemployment", *Scottish Government Yearbook* 1987, 174-202

59. COLE, J "Scotland's alienation", *Listener*, 5.6.86, 6

60. COLLEGE OF ESTATE MANAGEMENT *The contractor's principle of valuation for rating: a comparison study of rateable value and rates paid on properties in Scotland and England.* Reading, 1986, 68pp

61. COLWELL, R "Urban regeneration", *Scottish Economic Development Review* 1 (1985) 4-5, 10-11

62. COMMISSIONER FOR LOCAL ADMINISTRATION IN SCOTLAND *Report...for the year ended 31.3.1987.* Edinburgh, 1987, 28pp

63. COMMISSIONER FOR LOCAL AUTHORITY ACCOUNTS IN SCOTLAND *Annual report 1985.* Edinburgh, 1986, 48pp

64. COMMITTEE ON PUBLIC ACCOUNTS *Review of the SSHA: minutes of evidence.* London: House of Commons paper HC 349-i, 1987

65. COMMITTEE ON SCOTTISH AFFAIRS *Hospital provision: minutes of evidence.* London: House of Commons paper HC 331-I&II, 1987, 41pp, 298pp

66. COMMITTEE ON SCOTTISH AFFAIRS *Public expenditure to 1989/90: commentary on the Scottish programme.* London: House of Commons paper HC 305, 1987

67. COMMITTEE ON SCOTTISH AFFAIRS *The Committee's work*

Dec. 1983 to May 1987. London: House of Commons paper HC 385, 1987

68. COMMUNIST PARTY (SCOTTISH COMMITTEE) *Scotland's future.* Glasgow, 1987

69. COMMUNITY DEVELOPMENT HOUSING GROUP *But will it fly, Mr Wright? Tenant participation in practice.* Glasgow: TPAS, 1986, 28pp

70. COON, A C (ed) *Keeping local plans up to date.* Glasgow: Glasgow School of Art Dept. of Planning, Occasional paper 9, 1986, 35pp

71. COOPER, J "Japanese investment in Scotland", *Scottish Trade Union Review* 32 (1986) 19-21

72. C.O.S.L.A. *Paying for local government: the Convention's response.* Edinburgh, 1987, 21pp

73. C.O.S.L.A. *The need for investment in Scottish council housing.* Edinburgh, 1986, 12pp

74. COUNTRYSIDE COMMISSION FOR SCOTLAND *Forestry in Scotland: a policy paper.* Perth, 1986, 42pp

75. COWAN, M M "Development of owner-occupied housing in Strathclyde Region 1975-85: the greenfield-brownfield debate", *Scottish Planning Law and Practice* 17 (1986) 5-6

76. COX, M "Scotland's export performance: a closer look", *Quarterly Economic Commentary*, 12, 4 (1987) 63-66

77. CRANMER, F *Select committees: the Scottish dimension.* London: the author, 1987, 15pp

78. CROFTERS COMMISSION *Annual report 1986.* Edinburgh: HMSO, 1987, 39pp

79. CROSSROADS YOUTH AND COMMUNITY ASSOCIATION *The 492 story: a tenant's horror story.* Glasgow: SFHA, 1986, 28pp

80. CUMBERNAULD & KILSYTH DISTRICT COUNCIL *Statistical trends 1984- 85.* Cumbernauld, 1986, 57pp

81. CUMBERNAULD & KILSYTH DISTRICT COUNCIL *Statistical trends 1985- 86.* Cumbernauld, 1987, 57pp

82. CUMBERNAULD & KILSYTH DISTRICT COUNCIL *Housing plan 6: 1983/84- 1987/88.* Cumbernauld, 1982, 46pp

83. DARTINGTON AMENITY TRUST *Countryside around towns in Scotland: a review of change 1976-85.* Perth: Countryside Commission for Scotland, 1987, 79pp

84. DANSON, M & LLOYD, G *Changing local economies: response and initiatives in Tayside and Grampian.* Glasgow: Planning Exchange, 1987, 71pp

85. DENVER, D "Scotland", *Electoral change in Western democracies – patterns and sources of electoral volatility*, ed. I Crewe and D Denver (London: Croom Helm, 1985)

86. DEWHURST, J H C, LYTHE, C M & PETERSON, J C *An analysis of trends in output and employment in the service sector in Scotland.* Edinburgh: I.D.S. (ESU Research paper 10), 1986, 82pp

87. DIDIER-HACHE, J "The politics of island transport", *Scottish*

Government Yearbook 1987, 124-42

88. DORAN, F et al *North Sea oil: issues for the Labour Party*. Dundee, 1986
89. DOW, S C "The capital account and regional balance of payments problem", *Urban Studies*, 23, 3 (1986) 173-84
90. DOWLE, M "The year at Westminster", *Scottish Government Yearbook* 1987, 12-22
91. DUNION, K "The philosopher's stone", *Radical Scotland* 21 (1986) 31-32
92. DYER, M C & JORDAN, A G *Who votes in Aberdeen: marked electoral registers as a data source.* Glasgow: Strathclyde University Department of Politics (Strathclyde Papers in Government and Politics 42) 1986
93. EAGLES, M "The neglected regional dimension in Scottish ethnic nationalism", *Canadian Review of Studies in Nationalism*, 12, 1 (1985) 81-98
94. EAST LOTHIAN DISTRICT COUNCIL *East Lothian economic development review 1985-86*. Haddington, 1986, 28pp
95. EDGAR, B & MACNAUGHT, M "Policies for palaces: a radical view of housing in Scotland", *Radical Scotland* 21 (1986) 11-13
96. EDINBURGH DISTRICT COUNCIL *Economic and employment review*, No.1. Edinburgh, 1986-
97. EDINBURGH DISTRICT COUNCIL *Edinburgh District Planning report 1986. Background paper 1: population*. Edinburgh, 1987, 27pp
98. EDINBURGH DISTRICT COUNCIL *Financial report and abstract of accounts 1985-86*. Edinburgh, 1986
99. EDINBURGH DISTRICT COUNCIL *Guinness and the Scottish economy: broadening the debate*. Edinburgh, 1987
100. EDINBURGH DISTRICT COUNCIL *Poverty in Edinburgh*. Edinburgh, 1987, 44pp
101. EDINBURGH DISTRICT COUNCIL *Unemployment in Edinburgh: ward data: Oct. 1985*. Edinburgh, 1986, 32pp
102. EDINBURGH DISTRICT COUNCIL *Unemployment in Edinburgh: ward data: Jan. 1986*. Edinburgh, 1986, 39pp
103. EDWARDES, M *Back from the brink*. London: Collins, 1983, 301pp (see pp 75-77, 159-61)
104. EDWARDS, R *No say? No way! A review of Tenants Participatory Advisory Service 1980-86*. Edinburgh: SCVO, 1986, 48pp
105. EDWARDS, R "The enquiry is a farce", *New Statesman*, 16.5.86, 12-13
106. ENGLISH, B "The RSG settlement for Scotland", *Public Finance and Accountancy*, 9.1.87, 8-9
107. ENGLISH, J "Housing", *Yearbook '85* (Modern Studies Association), 64-68
108. ERMISH, S & MACLENNAN, D "Housing policies, markets and urban economic change", *Critical issues in urban economic*

development Vol.2, ed. V Hausner (Oxford: OUP, 1987), 160-200

109. FAIRLEY, M "Action for jobs?", *Radical Scotland* 21 (1986) 10-12

110. FARRINGTON, J H & MCKENZIE, R P "Bus deregulation in Scotland: a preliminary review", *Scottish Geographical Magazine*, 103, 1 (1987) 50- 53

111. FIFE REGIONAL COUNCIL *Strategic projections 5*. Glenrothes, 1986, 31pp

112. FIRN, J R "Industry", *Strategic planning in action*, ed R Smith & U Wannop, 100-138

113. FIRN, CRICHTON, ROBERTS *et al Employment opportunities for Wester Hailes: final report*. Edinburgh. 1986, 93pp

114. FORBES, S & PADDISON, R (eds) *Area management and community planning*. Glasgow: Glasgow University Centre for Urban and Regional Research, Discussion paper 23, 1985, 58pp

115. FOSTER, H "Dumbarton District", *Business Scotland*, March 1987, 13-18

116. FOSTER, J & WOOLFSON, C *The politics of the UCS work-in*. London: Lawrence & Wishart, 1986, 446pp

117. FRASER, N & SINFIELD, A "The Scottish labour force in recession", *Scottish Government Yearbook* 1987, 143-73

118. FRY, M *Patronage and principle: a political history of modern Scotland*. Aberdeen: Aberdeen University Press, 1987, 299pp

119. GATHERER, W A "Education and poverty", *Scottish Education Review*, 18, 1 (1986) 5-14

120. GATHERER, W A & WALLACE, B (eds) *Educating for tomorrow: a Lothian perspective*. Edinburgh: Holmes Macdougall, 1984

121. GEAR APPRAISAL GROUP *GEAR: a job half done*. Glasgow, 1986(?), 16pp

122. GETZ, D "Tourism and population change: longterm impacts of tourism in the Badenoch and Strathspey District", *Scottish Geographical Magazine*, 102, 3 (1986) 113-26

123. GLASGOW DISTRICT COUNCIL *Annual housing review 1985*. Glasgow, 1986. 208pp

124. GLASGOW DISTRICT COUNCIL *Annual housing review 1986*. Glasgow, 1987, 179pp

125. GLASGOW DISTRICT COUNCIL *Homesteading and rehabilitation for sale in Glasgow*. Glasgow, 1987

126. GLASGOW DISTRICT COUNCIL *Glasgow house condition survey 1985. Vol. 1: the condition of Glasgow's homes*. Glasgow, 1987, 82pp

127. GLASGOW DISTRICT COUNCIL *People and households in Glasgow, current estimates and expected changes 1985-82*. Glasgow, 1986, 22pp

128. GLASGOW DISTRICT COUNCIL *Report of the proceedings of the community councils convention ... 1982*. Glasgow, 1982, 16pp

129. GLASGOW DISTRICT COUNCIL *The Glasgow database project;*

the second report on the incidence and effects of housing rehabilitation spending in the City of Glasgow 1974-84. Glasgow, 1986

130. GLASGOW DISTRICT COUNCIL Unemployment in Glasgow by local area. Research memorandum, April 1986. Glasgow, 1986, 49pp
131. GLASGOW DISTRICT COUNCIL Unemployment in Glasgow by local area, July 1986. Glasgow, 1986, 54pp
132. GLASGOW DISTRICT COUNCIL Unemployment in Glasgow by local area, October 1986. Glasgow, 1987, 55pp
133. GOLDSMITH, M "Managing the periphery in a period of fiscal stress", New research in central-local relations, M Goldsmith (Aldershot: Gower, 1986), 152-72
134. GOODLAD, J "The SIC and the future of Shetland", New Shetlander, 159 (1987) 9-11
135. GRAHAM, L Shetlander crofters: a hundred years of island crofting. Lerwick: Scottish Crofters Union (Shetland Branch), 1987
136. GRAMPIAN REGIONAL COUNCIL Annual report and accounts 1985/6. Aberdeen, 1986
137. GRAMPIAN REGIONAL COUNCIL Grampian Region (Part) structure plan: Aberdeen area review 1986. Aberdeen, 1986, 3 vols
138. GRAMPIAN REGIONAL COUNCIL Strategic forecasts: employment, population, housing – 1986 update. Aberdeen, 1986, 42pp
139. GRAMPIAN REGIONAL COUNCIL "The Grampian employment survey 1986". Grampian Quarterly Economic Review, Spring 1987, 1-13
140. GRANT, R A history of recent deprivation initiatives. Edinburgh: SDD, 1986, 51pp
141. GRIEVE, R et al Inquiry into housing in Glasgow. Glasgow: Glasgow District Council, 1986, 67pp
142. GUNN, L "Lanarkshire", Business Scotland. Nov.1986, 40- 42
143. HADDON, A The conditions of Glasgow's housing; homesteading and rehabilitation for sale – report of two surveys. Glasgow: Glasgow District Council, 1987, 32pp
144. HAMILTON, R T "The influence of unemployment on the level and rate of company formation in Scotland 1950-85", Environment and Planning A, 18, 10 (1986) 1401-1404
145. HARRIS, A H "The future of the Aberdeen economy and the need for new policy directions", Changing local economies ed. Danson & Lloyd, 43-55
146. HARRIS, A H, LLOYD, M G et al "Incoming industry and structural change: oil and the Aberdeen economy", Scottish Journal of Political Economy, 34, 1 (1987) 69-90
147. HARVEY, J Bridging the gap. Edinburgh: St Andrews Press, 1987
148. HARVIE, C "Legalism, myth and national identity in Scotland in the imperial epoch", Cencrastus 26 (1987) 35-41
149. HARVIE, C "Time now for a new politics for Scotland", Radical

Scotland 26 (1987) 6-7

150. HAUSNER, V A (ed) *Urban economic change: five city studies*. Oxford: OUP, 1987, 256pp

151. HAWORTH, N "Making tracks: Caterpillar's crawl from Scotland", *Quarterly Economic Commentary*, 12, 4 (1987) 67-71

152. HEATWISE *Bernard Street: a case study on the estate rate heating addition*. Glasgow, 1986, 11pp

153. HOGWOOD, B W *Recent developments in British regional policy*. Glasgow: Strathclyde University Dept of Politics Papers in Government and Politics 51, 1987, 51pp

154. HOLDEN, D R, NAIRN, A G M & SWALES, K *Shift-share: seconds out, round two*. Glasgow: Glasgow University Centre for Urban and Regional Research, Discussion paper 25, 1986, 38pp

155. HOLLINGSWORTH, J "Population", *Yearbook '85* (Modern Studies Association) 442-47

156. HOOD, N, HAUG, P & YOUNG, S, *R & D intensity in the affiliates of US-owned electronics companies manufacturing in Scotland*. Glasgow: Strathclyde University, Strathclyde Business School Working paper 8207, 1982

157. HOOD, N, STEWART, D & YOUNG, S *Monitoring multinationals in Scotland: some preliminary evidence in appraising corporate behaviour*. Glasgow: Strathclyde University, Strathclyde Business School Working paper 8107, 1981

158. HOOD, N & YOUNG, S *Local small business development schemes in Scotland*. Glasgow: SDA, 2 vols, 1981

159. HOOD, N & YOUNG, S *The engineering industry in Scotland: comparisons with other small European economies*. Glasgow: SDA, 1985

160. HOOD, N & YOUNG, S, *US electronics industry in Scotland: a contextual assessment*. Glasgow: SDA, 1978

161. HOOD, N, YOUNG, S & MILNER, M *Growth and development in small successful manufacturing firms in Scotland*. Edinburgh: SEPD, 1982

162. HOOD, N, YOUNG, S & REEVES, A *European manufacturing investment in Scotland*. Glasgow: SDA, 1980

163. HOUSE OF COMMONS LIBRARY *Abolition of domestic rates etc (Scotland) Bill*. London: House of Commons Library (Reference Sheet 86/16) 1986, 20pp

164. HOUSE OF COMMONS LIBRARY *Regional policy and the North-South divide*. London: House of Commons Library (Reference Sheet 198), 1987, 25pp

165. HOUSING CORPORATION (SCOTLAND) *Race and housing*. Edinburgh: Housing Corporation (Scottish guidance note 22/86), 1986

166. HOUSING CORPORATION (SCOTLAND) *Report 1986/6. Scottish statistical supplement*. Edinburgh, 1986

167. HOUSTON, L & SELMAN, P *Environmental surveys by local*

authorities in Scotland. Glasgow: Planning Exchange (Occasional paper 29), 1986

168. HUGHES, G A *Community charge ... at what cost?* Glasgow: Scottish Local Government Information Unit, 1987

169. HUGHES, G A *The abolition of domestic rates and the distribution of income in Scotland.* Edinburgh: Edinburgh University Department of Economics Discussion paper, 1986

170. HUGHES, J "Some dimensions of regional inequality", *Poverty* 61 (1985) 32-38

171. HULBERT, J (ed). *Land ownership and use.* Longforgan by Dundee: Andrew Fletcher Society, 1986, 64pp

172. HUNTER, J "Crofting's comeback", *Radical Scotland* 26 (1987) 26-27

173. HUNTER, J & MACLEAN, C *Skye: the island.* Edinburgh: Mainstream, 1986, 224pp

174. HUTCHISON, D "Political writing in the Scottish press", *Scottish Government Yearbook* 1987, 239-56

175. HUTTON, N *Lay participation in a public local enquiry.* Aldershot: Gower, 1986, 203pp (Mossmoran)

176. INDUSTRY DEPARTMENT FOR SCOTLAND *1986 review of the SDA: final report.* Edinburgh, 1987, 138pp

177. INDUSTRY DEPARTMENT FOR SCOTLAND *1986 review of the SDA: summary report.* Edinburgh, 1986, 19pp

178. INSTITUTE OF HOUSING, SCOTTISH TRAINING UNIT *Going local in Scotland.* Edinburgh, 1986, 54pp

179. INSTITUTE OF HOUSING, SCOTTISH TRAINING UNIT *House sales: the management implications.* Edinburgh, 1986

180. INTERNATIONAL NEW TOWNS ASSOCIATION *New partnerships in urban development.* The Hague, 1986, 120pp

181. JACOBS, M "Local economic development by community business", *Local Economy* 2 (1986) 17-34

182. JOHNSON, J "Public management of the private sector", *Architects Journal*, 20.8.86, 66-72 & 27.8.76, 74-75

183. JOHNSTONE, D *Discretionary powers for economic development in Scotland.* Glasgow: Planning Exchange (Occasional paper 31), 1987

184. JONES, C & MACLENNAN, D "The impact of North Sea oil on the Aberdeen housing market", *Land Development Studies* 3 (1986) 113-26

185. JONES, P "Scotland's urban fringe", *Planner*, 72, 8 (1986) 12-14

186. KAY, B "A sense of identity: a conversation", *Radical Scotland* 25 (1987) 33-35

187. KEATING, M "Devolution and the parliamentary state", *The politics of legislative reform*, ed. D Judge (London: Heinemann, 1983)

188. KEATING, M "Scottish politics", *Yearbook '85 (Modern Studies Association)*, 83-85

189. KEATING, M *Territorial management and the British state: the case of Scotland and Wales*. Conference paper, Midwest Political Science Convention, Chicago, 1986

190. KEATING, M *Territorial management and regionalism nationalism – Britain, France, Italy and Spain*. Conference paper, Conference on Minority Nationalisms in the 1980s, Gregynog, 1986

191. KEATING, M "The political debate on the housing crisis", *Municipal Journal*, 3.4.87, 633-34

192. KEATING, M & BOYLE, R *Remaking urban Scotland*. Edinburgh: Edinburgh University Press, 1987, 175pp

193. KEATING, M & MITCHELL, J *Easterhouse: an urban crisis*. Glasgow: Strathclyde University Department of Politics (Strathclyde Papers in Government and Politics 47) 1986, 36pp

194. KEATING, M & MITCHELL, J "Glasgow's neglected periphery: the Easterhouse and Drumchapel initiatives", *Scottish Government Yearbook* 1987, 203-18

195. KEATING, M & MITCHELL, J "Inner city decay: Glasgow sees need to look beyond the fringe", *Municipal Journal*, 1.8.86, 1312-1313

196. KEATING, M & MITCHELL, J "Scottish politics", *Yearbook '86* (Modern Studies Association), 16-23

197. KEEBLE, D & KEELY, T, "New firms and high-technology industry in the UK: the case of computer electronics", *New firms and regional development in Europe*, ed. D Keeble & E Wever (London: Croom Helm, 1986), 75-104

198. KELLAS, J D *Scotland: political aspects of ethnicity*. Conference paper, IPSA Round Table in Politics and Ethnicity, Glasgow, 1984

199. KELLAS, J D "The politics of constitution making: the experience of the UK", *The politics of constitutional change in industrial nations*, ed. K G Banting & R Simeon (London: Macmillan, 1985), 146- 59

200. KELLAS, J D *The Scottish and Welsh Offices as territorial managers*. Conference paper, ECPR Joint Sessions, Amsterdam, 1987, 12pp

201. KELLAS, J D & BRAND, J *Politics and ethnicity and nationalism in Western Europe*. Conference paper, IPSA Research Committee on Politics and Ethnicity, Paris, 1985

202. KELLAS, J D & ELDER, J M *The legal, administrative and financial impact in Scotland (outside Orkney and Shetland) of North Sea oil develoments*. Glasgow, paper for SSRC North Sea Oil Panel, 1980

203. KENDRICK, S, BECHHOFER, F, & MCCRONE, D "Is Scotland different? Industrial and occupational change in Scotland and Britain", *Restructuring capital*, ed. H Newby, J Bujra *et al* (London: Macmillan, 1985), 63-102

204. LAMB, B "Inquiries put paid to tablets of stone image", *Planning*, 17.4.87, 8-9

205. LAMONT, D, MACLENNAN, D & MUNRO, M, *New private housing in the East End of Glasgow*. Glasgow: Glasgow University Centre for Housing Research, 1985

206. LAWRIE, G "Political education in Scottish schools", *Scottish Government Yearbook* 1987, 331-46

207. LEWIS, J & FOORD, J, "New Towns and gender relationships in old industrial regions: women's employment in Peterlee and East Kilbride", *Built Environment*, 10, 1 (1984) 42-52

208. LLOYD, M G "Enterprize zones: emerging evidence and criticisms", *Quarterly Economic Commentary*, 12,2 (1986) 70-74

209. LLOYD, M G "The enterprize zone experiment in Scotland", *Scottish Planning Law and Practice* 18 (1986) 43-45

210. LLOYD, M G & ROWAN ROBINSON, J "Local authority economic development activity in Scotland: further evidence", *Local Economy*, 2, 1 (1987) 49-54

211. LLOYD, M G & SHUCKSMITH, D "Economic development and land policies in the Highlands and Islands of Scotland", *Land Use Policy* 2 (1985) 114-25

212. LOCAL ENTERPRISE ADVISORY UNIT *Community business in Scotland directory 1986*. Paisley : Paisley College Local Enterprise Advisory Programme, 1986, 64pp

213. LOCKERBIE, C "Scottish radio", *Scottish Government Yearbook* 1987, 270-82

214. LOTHIAN REGIONAL COUNCIL *Annual report and accounts 1985/86*. Edinburgh, 1986

215. LOTHIAN REGIONAL COUNCIL *Structure plan 1985: policy abstract*. Edinburgh, 1986, 55pp

216. LOTHIAN REGIONAL COUNCIL *Transport policies and programme 8A: 1986-91*. Edinburgh, 1986, 44pp

217. LOTHIAN WOMENS SUPPORT GROUP, *Women during the strike*. Dalkeith, 1987, 63pp

218. LOVE, J "Fraser of Allender file", *Scottish Business Insider*, 3, 8 (1986) 25

219. LOVE, J "Scottish economy", *Yearbook '85 (Modern Studies Association)*, 86-91

220. LOVE, J *The whiskey industry in the Scottish economy*. Glasgow: Fraser of Allender Institute Working Paper 41, 1986, 33pp

221. LUTZ, J M "Community context in the spread of voter support for the SNP", *Western Political Quarterly*, 39, 3 (1986) 455-63

222. McARTHUR, A A "An unconventional approach to economic development: the role of community business", *Town Planning Review*, 57,1 (1986) 87-100

223. MACARTNEY, W J A "Summary of opinion polls 1985/86", *Scottish Government Yearbook* A 1987, 360-64

224. MACBETH, A, STRACHAN, D, & MACAULAY, C *Parental choice of school in Scotland*. Glasgow: Glasgow University Dept. of Education, 1986

225. McCALLUM, N *Report of the committee of inquiry into structure, organisation and constitution of the SNP*. Edinburgh, SNP, 1984

226. McCALMAN, J "What's wrong with Scottish firms? Local sourcing in electronics". *Quarterly Economic Commentary*, 12,3 (1987) 62-69

227. McCLUSKEY, S "Shroud for the Scottish landscape", *Landscape Design*, Dec. 1986, 48-51

228. McCONNELL, J "Labour's assembly commitment", *Radical Scotland* 25 (1987) 7-8

229. McCRONE, D "A commentary", *Scottish Government Yearbook* 1987, 7-11

230. McCULLOCH, N A *The structure of the Scottish electronics industry*. BSc. dissertation, Edinburgh University Dept. of Electrical Engineering, 1985

231. MACDONALD, R "Report from the STUC women's conference", *Scottish Trade Union Review* 33 (1987) 20-21

232. MACEWAN, M *Racial harassment, council housing and the law*. Edinburgh: Edinburgh College of Art, Scottish Ethnic Minorities Research Unit paper 1, 1986, 62pp

233. MACEWAN, M, HASHMI, H & WORTHINGTON, T "Race relations", *Yearbook '85* (Modern Studies Association), 76-82

234. MACGAHEY, M "Interview", *Scottish Trade Union Review* 34 (1987) 4-8

235. McGIVERN, S "Kyle and Carrick District", *Business Scotland*, March 1987, 39-46

236. McGIVERN, S "Livingston", *Business Scotland*, April 1987, 31- 32

237. MACGREGOR, B D "Land development and employment creation on landed estates in the Northern Highlands", *Planning Outlook*, 28,2 (1985), 98-104

238. MACGREGOR, J "The people's gathering", *Radical Scotland* 26 (1987) 34-35 (Interview)

239. McINNES, J "What's wrong with services?", *Scottish Trade Union Review* 33 (1987) 25-26

240. McINNES, J & SPROULL, A "Electronics employment in Scotland", *Quarterly Economic Commentary*, 12, 3 (1987) 77-82

241. McINNES, J & SPROULL, A *Union recognition in the electronics industry in Scotland*, Glasgow: Glasgow University CRIDP Research Report 4, 1986

242. McINTOSH, S "The Kingdom Strikes back", *Scottish Business Insider*, 4, 4 (1987) 26-28 (Fife)

243. MACKENZIE, W J "Peripheries and nation-building: the case of Scotland", *Mobilisation: centre-periphery structures and nationbuilding* ec. P Torsvik (Bergen: Bergen Universitetvorlaget, 1981), 153-80

244. MACLENNAN, D *The demand for housing: economic perspectives and planning practices*. Edinburgh: SDD, 1986, 33

245. MACLENNAN, D & MUNRO, M "Evaluating the new approach to home improvement", *Housing Review*, 35, 5 (1986) 153-55

246. MACLENNAN, D & MUNRO, M "Intra-urban changes in housing prices: Glasgow 1972-83", *Housing Studies*, April 1987, 65-81

247. McNICOLL, I H "Input-output planning in Shetland", *Planner*, June 1986, 39-42

248. MACPHERSON, E "The Scottish police complaints procedure", *Scottish Government Yearbook* 1987, 99-123

249. MANN, L "In the front line at a forgotten inquiry", *Town and Country Planning*, 55, 12 (1986) 348-49

250. MANN, S "Smiling better", *Building Support*, 5.9.86, 4- 11

251. MANSON, B *The institutional basis of rural development: a comparative study of Lozere in South-Central France and Grampian in NE Scotland.* Langholm: Arkleton Trust, 1986, 110pp

252. MASTERSON, M *Community councils after seven years.* Dundee: Dundee University Dept of Political Science, 1984, 25pp

253. MARTLEW, C *Democracy, policy and implementation: decentralisation in Strathclyde Regional Council.* Glasgow: Planning Exchange (Occasional paper 23), 1986, 41pp

254. MARTLEW, C & BAILEY, S *Local taxation and accountability: an assessment of the 1986 Green Paper 'Paying for local government' and its effects on Scotland.* London: Public Finance Foundation, 1986, 39pp

255. MARTLEY, C & BUCHANAN, G *Councillors in Scotland: a research report on their work and background.* Glasgow: Planning Exchange (Research Report 28), 1986, 77pp

256. MASSIE, A "Scottish Labour begs for scraps", *Spectator*, 17.1.87, 14-15

257. MAXWELL, S *Facing the facts: Scotland and the social security reviews.* Edinburgh: SCVO, 1985, 5 parts

258. MAXWELL, S "The politics of poverty in Scotland", *Scottish Government Yearbook* 1987, 81-98

259. MEECH, P "Television in Scotland", *Scottish Government Yearbook* 1987, 257-69

260. MIDWINTER, A "Disastrous effect on the island communities", *Local Government Chronicle*, 8.5.87, 16 (of a national business rate)

261. MIDWINTER, A "Local government", *Yearbook '86* (Modern Studies Association), 24-26

262. MIDWINTER, A "The need for consensus campaigning", *Local Government Chronicle*, 27.3.87, 28 (COSLA)

263. MIDWINTER, A *The Scottish local government system: structure, management and finance.* Birmingham: Birmingham University Institute of Local Government Studies, Future of Local Government Project, Study paper 11, 1986

264. MIDWINTER, A, MAIR, C & FORD, C "Rating revaluation revisited", *Scottish Government Yearbook* 1987, 32-56

265. MIDWINTER, A, MAIR, C & FORD, C "Regression analysis and the assessment of local expenditure need: a reconsideration", *Local Government Studies*, 13, 1 (1987) 35-51

266. MILLS, L & YOUNG, K "Local authorities and economic development: a preliminary analysis", *Critical issues in urban economic development* ed. V Hausner (Oxford: OUP, 1986), 89-144
267. MITCHELL, A *Is Pliatzky alive and well?* Conference paper, Political Science Association conference, 1987, 14pp
268. MOIR, J *The impact of oil-related development on Aberdeen in the 1970s.* Dundee: Duncan of Jordanstone College of Art Dept of Town and Regional Planning, Occasional paper 14, 1983, 58pp
269. MONKLANDS DISTRICT COUNCIL *Urban programme: progress report 1.* Coatbridge, 1985, 41pp
270. MOORE, C & BOOTH, S "Accountability and regional control: options for reform", *Quarterly Economic Commentary*, 12, 4 (1987) 75-79
271. MOORE, C & BOOTH, S "The SDA: market consensus, public planning and local enterprise", *Local Economy*, 1, 3 (1986) 7-19
272. MOORE, C & BOOTH, S "Urban policy contradictions: the market versus redistributive approaches", *Policy & Politics*, 14, 3 (1986) 361-88
273. MORENO, L F *Decentralisation in Britain and Spain: the case of Scotland and Catalonia.* PhD. thesis, Edinburgh University, 1986, 547 pp (British Library No. D71331/87)
274. M.O.R.I. *Public opinion in Glasgow.* London, 1985, 137pp app
275. MORISON, H *The regeneration of local economies.* Oxford: OUP, 1987, 216pp
276. MORTON, J "Scottish housing merger?", *Local Government News*, Oct. 1986, 10-11
277. MUNRO, M *Testing for segmentation in the Glasgow private housing market.* Glasgsow: Glasgow University Centre for Housing Research, Discussion paper 8, 1986
278. NAIRN, A G M *GEAR and New Town policy: conflict or complement?* Glasgow: Strathclyde University Dept. of Urban and Regional Planning, Papers in planing 10, 1987, 26pp
279. NAIRN, A G M & SWALES, J K "Area policy impacts: a multiplier analysis of GEAR", *Urban Studies*, 24, 1 (1987) 31-45
280. NATIONAL AUDIT OFFICE, *SDD's review of the SSHA.* London: House of Commons paper 102, 1986, 23pp
281. NITHSDALE DISTRICT COUNCIL *Annual report and financial statement.* Dumfries, 1986
282. ORKNEY MOVEMENT *Policy paper 1986.* Kirkwall, 1986
283. PACIONE, M "Inner-city regeneration: perspectives on GEAR", *Planning Outlook*, 28, 2 (1985) 65-69
284. PACIONE, M "Quality of life in Glasgow: an applied geographic analysis", *Environment & Planning* A, 18 (1986) 1499-1520
285. PACIONE, M "The changing pattern of deprivation in Glasgow", *Scottish Geographical Magazine*, 102, 2 (1986) 97-109
286. PARRY, R "The centralisation of the Scottish Office", *Ministers and ministries* ed. R Rose (Oxford: OUP, 1987), 97-141

287. PAYNE, G *Employment and opportunity*. London: Macmillan, 1987, 215pp

288. PERCY, M "Dream and realities", *Listener*, 3.4.86, 8-10, 17

289. PIEDA *Industry's early reaction to the new regional development grant*. Edinburgh, 1986

290. PIEDA *Land supply and house prices in Scotland*. Edinburgh, 1986, 49pp

291. PILKINGTON, M "Industrial survey: Fife", *Business Scotland*. Oct. 1986, 16-30

292. PLANNING EXCHANGE *Prospects for private finance for housing associations: report of a seminar*. Glasgow: Planning Exchange (Occasional paper 30), 1986, 26pp

293. PORTWOOD, D "Local authorities' unemployment strategies", *Social Policy and Administration*, 20, 3 (1986) 217-24

294. RAAB, C "The 'leadership' class dismissed: Humes' critique of Scottish education", *Scottish Government Yearbook* 1987, 283-88

295. RAAB, G & ADLER, M *Exploding some myths about the uniqueness of Edinburgh: the impact of parental choice on admission to primary and secondary schools in Edinburgh*. Edinburgh: Edinburgh University Dept. of Social Policy, 1986

296. RADICAL SCOTLAND "Hoping for the best ... preparing for the worst", *Radical Scotland* 25 (1987) 9-11

297. RADICAL SCOTLAND "Hung Parliament, PR and the Scottish Assembly", *Radical Scotland* 21 (1986) 8-10

298. RADICAL SCOTLAND "Preparing for the Assembly", *Radical Scotland* 22 (1986) 8-9

299. RADICAL SCOTLAND "Tactical voting: turning off the Tories", *Radical Scotland* 26 (1987) 8-9

300. RAFFE, D "Unemployment among 16 and 17 year old school leavers in Scotland", *Employment Gazette*, 94,6 (1986) 274-80.

301. RAGIN, C C "The impact of Celtic nationalism on class politics in Scotland and Wales", *Competitive ethnic relations*, ed. S Olzak & J Nagel (New York: Academic Press, 1986)

302. RANDALL, J "Scotland", *Regional problems, problem regions and public policy in the United Kingdom*, ed. P Damesick & P Wood (Oxford: OUP, 1987)

303. REGISTRAR GENERAL (SCOTLAND) *Population estimates Scotland 1986*. London: HMSO, 1987, 16pp

304. RENFREW DISTRICT COUNCIL *Annual report and financial statement 1985-86*. Paisley, 1986, 108pp

305. RENFREW DISTRICT COUNCIL *Renfrew District's community development strategy*. Paisley, 1986, 23pp

306. RENWANTZ, M E *From crofters to Shetlanders: the social history of a Shetland Islands community's self-image 1872-1978*. PhD. thesis, Stanford University, 1981, 362pp (University Microfilms order no. 8108983)

307. ROBERTSON, D S *The Glasgow database project: the second*

report on the incidence and effects of housing rehabilitation spending on the City of Glasgow 1974-84. Glasgow: Glasgow University Centre for Housing Research, 1986, 344pp

308. ROBERTSON, D S & CUNNINGHAM, C "Merging in the background", *Housing*, June 1987, 12-13

309. ROBERTSON, J G *The Western Isles Integrated Development Programme: further lessons in human ecology.* Portree: Habitat Scotland, 1986, 63pp

310. ROSENGARD, A *The development of community-based housing in Glasgow: an experiment in the social control of housing.* PhD. thesis, Strathclyde University, 1981, 957pp (BLLD order no. D 68467/86)

311. ROSS, D *An unlikely anger: Scottish teachers in action.* Edinburgh: Mainstream, 1986

312. RUSSELL, J & SHANKS, P "The Edinburgh Western Relief road: by-pass of planing proceedures?" *Scottish Planning Law & Practice*, 19 (1986) 73-74

313. RUTHERFORD, A *et al Community councils in Scotland: a review after five years.* Glasgow: Community Councils Resources Centre, 1984, 26pp

314. RYDER, A "Dounreay Inquiry: jumble sale funding v. 50 staff", *Town and Country Planning*, 56, 1 (1987) 20-21

315. RYDER, A "The Dounreay Inquiry: public participation in practice", *Scottish Geographical Magazine*, 103, 1 (1987), 54-57

316. RYDER, A "The Dounreay public inquiry", *Planner*, Jan.1987, 24-26

317. SADLER, D "Works closure at British Steel and the nature of the state", *Political Geography Quarterly*, 3,4 (1984) 297-311 (esp. 304-306)

318. SALMOND, A & WALKER, J "The oil price collapse : some effects on the Scottish economy", *Quarterly Economic Commentary*, 12, 2 (1986) 63-69

319. SCOTBIC *Scottish Business in the Community: a year of development. Chairman's statement 1985/86.* Edinburgh, 1986, 10pp

320. SCOTT, D "Changes are unwelcome and unacceptable", *Local Government Chronicle*, 5.9.86, 1001

321. SCOTTISH ANTIRACIST MOVEMENT "Which side are you on?" *Scottish Trade Union Review* 34 (1987) 32

322. SCOTTISH BUSINESS INSIDER "Scotland's top 100 companies", *Scottish Business Insider*, 4, 1 (1987) 2-44 passim

323. SCOTTISH COMMISSION FOR RACIAL EQUALITY *Annual report 1985/6.* Glasgow, 1986

324. SCOTTISH CONSERVATIVE PARTY *Leading Scotland.* Edinburgh, 1986, 24pp

325. SCOTTISH CONSUMER COUNCIL *The community charge.* Glasgow, 1986, 75pp

326. SCOTTISH COUNCIL FOR THE SINGLE HOMELESS *Annual*

report 1985/6. Edinburgh, 1986

327. SCOTTISH DEVELOPMENT AGENCY *Accounts 1985-86.* London: House of Commons paper 598, 1986, 24pp

328. SCOTTISH DEVELOPMENT AGENCY *Agency of opportunity. SDA annual report 1986.* Glasgow, 1986

329. SCOTTISH DEVELOPMENT AGENCY *North American companies manufacturing in Scotland.* Glasgow, 1987, 58pp

330. SCOTTISH DEVELOPMENT AGENCY *Scottish local enterprise trusts.* Edinburgh: Scotbic, 1986

331. SCOTTISH DEVELOPMENT AGENCY *The potential of Glasgow city centre.* Glasgow, 1986, 56pp

332. SCOTTISH DEVELOPMENT DEPARTMENT *Annual estimates of households.* Edinburgh: SDD (Statistical Bulletin HSIU 26), 1987

333. SCOTTISH DEVELOPMENT DEPARTMENT *Changes to local plan proceedure in Scotland.* Edinburgh, 1986

334. SCOTTISH DEVELOPMENT DEPARTMENT *Government's response to Rural Forum's June 1985 policy statement on Scotland's rural housing.* Edinburgh: SIO, 1986, 11pp

335. SCOTTISH DEVELOPMENT DEPARTMENT *Grants to the private sector for the improvement of dwellings 1976-85.* Edinburgh: SDD (Statistical Bulletin HSIU 25), 1986, 12pp

336. SCOTTISH DEVELOPMENT DEPARTMENT *House condition survey of private sector interwar stock in the four Scottish cities.* Edinburgh, 1985, 40pp + appendices

337. SCOTTISH DEVELOPMENT DEPARTMENT *Policy review of the SSHA 1985-86.* Edinburgh, 1986, 50pp

338. SCOTTISH DEVELOPMENT DEPARTMENT *Public sector rents in Scotland 1986-87.* Edinburgh: SDD (Statistical Bulletin HSIU 29), 1987, 12pp

339. SCOTTISH DEVELOPMENT DEPARTMENT *Scottish Homes, a new agency for housing in Scotland.* Edinburgh, 1987, 23pp

340. SCOTTISH DEVELOPMENT DEPARTMENT *Scottish household projections, 1983 based.* Edinburgh: SDD (Statistical Bulletin HSIU 23), 1986, 8 pp

341. SCOTTISH DEVELOPMENT DEPARTMENT *The Urban Programme in Scotland. Annual report 1986.* Edinburgh, 1986, 22pp

342. SCOTTISH HEALTH SERVICE PLANNING COUNCIL *Report for 1985.* Edinburgh: HMSO, 1986, 24pp

343. SCOTTISH HOME AND HEALTH DEPARTMENT *Health in Scotland 1985.* Edinburgh, 1986, 103pp

344. SCOTTISH INFORMATION OFFICE *Ethnic minorities in Scotland.* Edinburgh: SIO (Factsheet 30) 1987, 7pp

345. SCOTTISH INFORMATION OFFICE *Local government in Scotland.* Edinburgh: SIO (Factsheet 28; revised edition) 1986, 40pp

346. SCOTTISH LOCAL FINANCE GROUP *The role of the Accounts Commission.* Glasgow: Glasgow University Centre for Urban and Regional Research Discussion paper 27, 1986, 58pp

5Scottish Government Yearbook 1988

347. SCOTTISH LOCAL GOVERNMENT INFORMATION UNIT
Local authorities as employers: seminar report. Glasgow, 1987, 16pp
348. SCOTTISH LOCAL GOVERNMENT INFORMATION UNIT
Rates reform and the poll tax, a guide to the issues. Glasgow, 1987, 13pp
349. SCOTTISH LOCAL GOVERENMENT INFORMATION UNIT
Scottish homes and jobs: conference report. Glasgow, 1987, 56pp
350. SCOTTISH NATIONAL PARTY *Play the Scottish card.* Edinburgh, 1987, 27pp
351. SCOTTISH OFFICE *Bus deregulation in Scotland: survey results.* Edinburgh: SIO, 1987, 5pp
352. SCOTTISH OFFICE *Paying for local government: the community charge – operational issues.* Edinburgh, 1986, 13pp
353. SCOTTISH OFFICE *Public expenditure to 1989/90: a commentary on the Scotland programme.* Edinburgh, 1987, 155pp
354. SCOTTISH OFFICE *Scottish local government financial statistics 1982-83.* Edinburgh, 1986, 27pp
355. SCOTTISH OFFICE (CENTRAL RESEARCH UNIT) *Bus deregulation: an interim report.* Edinburgh, 1987
356. SCOTTISH OFFICE (CENTRAL RESEARCH UNIT) *Low cost home ownership initiatives in Scotland.* Edinburgh, 1986, 91pp
357. SCOTTISH SOCIETY OF DIRECTORS OF PLANNING *Annual General Meeting and conference.* Glasgow, 1986, 61pp
358. SCOTTISH SOCIETY OF DIRECTORS OF PLANNING *Consultation by government on: changes to local plan proceedures in Scotland; the future of development plans (England and Wales): observations of SSDP.* Glasgow, 1987
359. SCOTTISH SPECIAL HOUSING ASSOCIATION *Annual report for the year ended 31.3.86.* Edinburgh, 1986, 20 16pp
360. SCOTTISH TERTIARY EDUCATION ADVISORY COUNCIL *Future strategy for higher education in Scotland.* Edinburgh: HMSO, 1985
361. SCOTTISH TRADES UNION CONGRESS *89th annual report.* Glasgow 1987
362. SCOTTISH TRADES UNION CONGRESS *Scotland: a strategy for the future.* Glasgow 1986
363. SECRETARY OF STATE FOR SCOTLAND *The Rates Support Grant (Scotland) Order 1986. Report.* London: House of Commons paper 542, 1986, 13pp
364. SECRETARY OF STATE FOR SCOTLAND *The Rates Support Grant (Scotland) Order 1987. Report.* London: House of Commons paper 174, 1987, 28pp
365. SEWEL, J, TWINE, F & WILLIAMS, N "Council house allocation and tenant incomes", *Area*, 18, 2 (1986) 131-40
366. SHAPIRO, D "Explaining peripheral change" *Localities, class and gender*, ed. Lancaster Regionalism Group (London: Pion, 1985), 77-95

362

367. SHAPIRO, D "Policy, planning and peripheral developments", *Ibid*, 96-120

368. SHELTER *Council housing waiting lists survey*. Edinburgh, 1986, 5pp

369. SHELTER *Scots children's health at serious risk from damp housing*. Edinburgh, 1986, 7pp

370. SHETLAND MOVEMENT *Are you interested in Shetland's future? Summary of policy discussions*. Lerwick, 1985

371. SHUCKSMITH, M, ROBERTSON, D & MACGREGOR, B (eds) *Rural housing: rural research and policy issues*. Aberdeen: Aberdeen University Press, 1987

372. SMAIL, R *Breadline Scotland: low pay and inequality north of the border*. London: Low Pay Unit/Glasgow: STUC (Low Pay pamphlet 43), 1986, 32pp

373. SMITH, C "Attitudes to the NHS", *Scottish Trade Union Review* 32 (1986) 24-25

374. SMITH, P *Young people's attitudes to YTS*. Edinburgh: Edinburgh University Centre for Educational Sociology, 1986

375. SMITH, R "The setting up of the Clyde Valley Regional planning Team and agencies for implementation", *Strategic planning in action*, ed. R Smith & U Wannop (Aldershot: Gower, 1985) 17-40

376. SMITH, R & FARMER, E "Housing, population and decentralisation", *Strategic planning in action*, ed. R Smith & U Wannop (Aldershot: Gower, 1985)

377. SPAVEN, F D N "The geographer and the HIDB", *Geography, planning and policy-making*, ed. P T Kivell (Norwich: Geo Books, 1986), 271-7

378. SPAVEN, F D N "The work of the HIDB 1965-78", *A contemporary account* (Inverness: HIDB, 1979)

379. STEAD, J *Women and the miners' strike 1984-85*. London: Womens Press, 1987, 177, passim

380. STEEL, D "Towards a Scottish Assembly?" *Radical Scotland* 21 (1986) 6-7

381. STOVALL, J G *The Scottish press and nationalism: a content analysis of newspaper attention to nationalism 1966-76*. PhD. thesis, University of Tennessee, 1978

382. STRATHCLYDE COMMUNITY BUSINESS *SBC annual report 1985/86*. Glasgow, 1986, 23pp

383. STRATHCLYDE FEDERATION OF UNEMPLOYED WORKERS CENTRES *Report on Glasgow unemployed workers centres*. Glasgow, 1985

384. STRATHCLYDE REGIONAL COUNCIL *Clothing and textiles in Strathclyde and the Multi-fibre Agreement*. Glasgow, 1985, 31pp

385. STRATHCLYDE REGIONAL COUNCIL *Strathclyde-built in the 1990s*. Glasgow: Shipbuilding Working Group, 1987, 27pp

386. STRATHCLYDE REGIONAL COUNCIL "Strathclyde's divisional community development committees", *Strathclyde Digest*

62 (1986)
387. STRATHCLYDE REGIONAL COUNCIL *Strathclyde structure plan handbook*. Glasgow, 1986, 125pp
388. STRATHCLYDE REGIONAL COUNCIL *Strathclyde structure plan: monitoring report (1986)*. Glasgow, 1986, 155pp
389. STRATHCLYDE REGIONAL COUNCIL *Strathclyde structure plan: second written review and alteration – the decision letter*. Glasgow, 1986, 16pp
390. STRATHCLYDE REGIONAL COUNCIL *Strathclyde structure plan update (1986): consultation report*. Glasgow, 1986, 62pp
391. STRATHCLYDE REGIONAL COUNCIL *Strathclyde structure plan update (1986): written statement*. Glasgow, 1986, 50pp
392. STRATHCLYDE REGIONAL COUNCIL *Transport policies and programmes 7, 1987-92*. Glasgow, 1987, 200pp
393. STRATHCLYDE REGIONAL COUNCIL/SCOTTISH TRADES UNION CONGRESS *The summit: the way forward*. Glasgow, 1986, 19pp
394. STRATHKELVIN DISTRICT COUNCIL *Changing for the better: Strathkelvin housing plan 1987-92*. Kirkintilloch, 1986
395. SUTHERLAND, I "Left high and dry", *New Society*, 11.7.86, 7-8
396. TAYLOR, A C C *Overseas owned firms in Scottish manufacturing industry – an overview*. Edinburgh: Industry Department for Scotland (Statistical Bulletin A3.1), 1986, 10pp
397. TAYLOR, A C C "Overseas ownership in Scottish manufacturing industry 1950-85", *Scottish Economic Bulletin* 33 (1986)
398. TAYSIDE REGIONAL COUNCIL *Transport policies and programme 1986-91*. Dundee, 1986, 55pp
399. TAYSIDE REGIONAL COUNCIL *Transport policies and programme 1986-91: second supplement*. Dundee, 1986, 57pp
400. THOMAS, D E "Socialism and nationalism for our times", *Radical Scotland* 22 (1986) 24-26
401. THOMPSON, J *et al* "Abolition of the Scottish domestic rates bill", *Rating and Valuation*, Jan.1987, 7-15, 20
402. TOMPKINS, S C *The theft of the hills: afforestation in Scotland*. London: Ramblers Association, 1986, 32pp
403. ULAS, M *Trends in education, class and mobility: the experience of Scottish males 1925-70*. MPhil. dissertation, CNAA (Plymouth Polytechnic), 1986
404. VOLANS, K (ed) *The future of agriculture in the hills and uplands*. Edinburgh: Edinburgh University Dept. of Agricultural Resources, 1986, 87pp
405. VOORHEES, D J *The Shetland Islands: social change and psychiatric symptoms*. PhD. thesis, California School of Professional Psychology (Berkeley), 1985, 180pp (University Microfilms no. A8512620)
406. WALKER, C A & MCCLEERY, A "Economic and social change in the Highlands and Islands", *Scottish Economic Bulletin* 35 (1987) 8-

20

407. WALKER, J *International trade and the Scottish economy: a 'pattern' model of the published data on Scottish trade 1968-79*. PhD. thesis, Strathclyde University, 1985, 551pp (BLLD No. D69613/86)

408. WALKER, J "Storm clouds on Scots economic horizon", *Scottish Business Insider*, 3,8 (1986) 12-13

409. WALKER J "The Scottish 'electronics' industry", *Scottish Government Yearbook* 1987, 57-80

410. WALLACE, J "The S.I.C. and local development", *New Shetlander* 156 (1986) 27-29

411. WALLER, R *The almanac of British politics*. London: Croom Helm, 1987, 640pp (constituency data)

412. WANNOP, U "Strategic and development planing: Scottish implications of English innovations", *Scottish Planning Law and Practice* 20 (1987) 8-9

413. WANNOP, U & SMITH, R "Robustness in regional planning: an evaluation of the Clyde Valey Regional Plan", *Strategic planning in action*, ed. R Smith & U Wannop (Aldershot: Gower 1985), 210-40

414. WATT, G "Racism and education in Scotland", *Radical Scotland* 21 (1986) 20-21

415. WEST, R "The Scottish Klondike", *Spectator*, 16.8.86, 13-14

416. WESTER HAILES EMPLOYMENT INITIATIVE *Information Pack*, Edinburgh, 1986

417. WHITTON, D "The 'famous five' head towards maturity with youthful vigour", *Scottish Business Insider*, 4, 2 (1987) 28-30

418. WHYTE, R *Aspects of the employment structure in the electronics industry in Scotland in 1985*. Edinburgh: Industry Department for Scotland (Statistical Bulletin C3.1), 1987, 15pp

419. WHYTE, R *Employment in the Scottish electronics industry 1978-85*. Edinburgh: Industry Department for Scotland (Statistical Bulletin C2.1), 1986, 13pp

420. WHYTE, R "The Scottish textile and clothing industry", *Scottish Economic Bulletin* 34 (1986) 12-18

421. WYLLIE, D *The impact of a new extractive resource on a declined industrial region: Scotland and North Sea oil*. PhD. thesis, University of Connecticut, 1978

422. YOUNG, E & ROWAN ROBINSON, J "Planning control in Scotland", *Planning control: philosophy, prospects and practice*, ed. M L Harrison & R Mordey (London: Croom Helm, 1987)

423. YOUNG, J "*The Advisory Council on Education in Scotland 1920-61*. PhD. thesis, Edinburgh University, 1986, 462pp (BLLD no. D69740/86)

424. YOUNG, N "Read all about it", *Scottish Economic Development Review* 8 (1986) 13-14, 17

425. YOUNG, R "Social strategy in Strathclyde: where now?" *Local Government Studies*, 13, 3 (1987) 1-19

426. YOUNG, S *Scottish multinationals and the Scottish economy*.

Glasgow, Conference on 'Scotland and the multinationals'. 1986

INDEX TO BIBLIOGRAPHY

Glasgow: 285
Wester Hailes: 113
Urban renewal (see also GEAR): 39, 55, 61, 108, 140, 150, 180, 188, 192-
95, 250, 269, 271, 272, 278, 282, 341
Voting: see Elections
Women: 16, 56, 57, 207, 217, 231, 379
Y.T.S.: 374

THE SCOTTISH GOVERNMENT YEARBOOK 1976-7
Ed. by M.G. Clarke and H.M. Drucker
CONTENTS

THE SCOTTISH GOVERNMENT YEARBOOK 1978
Ed. by H.M. Drucker and M.G. Clarke
CONTENTS

THE SCOTTISH GOVERNMENT YEARBOOK 1979
Ed. by N. Drucker and H.M. Drucker
CONTENTS

THE SCOTTISH GOVERNMENT YEARBOOK 1980
Ed. by H.M. Drucker and N. Drucker
CONTENTS

Colin Wiseman
10. More and Less Coercive Ways of Settling Debts – Mike Adler and Edward Wozniak
11. The Scottish Fishing Industry: Technical Opportunities and Political Constraints – John Godfrey and Norman Godman
12. Energy Demand and Energy Policy in Scotland – G.A. Mackay

THE SCOTTISH GOVERNMENT YEARBOOK 1981
Ed. by H.M. Drucker and N. Drucker
CONTENTS

1. The Political Physiognomy of Jekyll and Hyde – The Editors
2. The Select Committee on Scottish Affairs – Donald Dewar
3. The Year at Westminster – James Naughtie
4. The Social Structure of Modern Scotland – David McCrone
5. Scotland's Public Expenditure 'Needs' – David Heald
6. The Rise and Fall of Civil Service Dispersion to Scotland – Richard Parry
7. COSLA: A Silent Voice for Local Government? – Carol Craig
8. Subverting Housing Plans: Some Institutional Realities – Paul Crompton
9. Policy-making in Area Health Boards: The Role of the Board Member – David Hunter
10. Children's Panels: A Strathclyde Member's View – Alf Young
11. The Birth and Development of the Shetland Movement 197780 – Martin Dowle
12. Scotland in Europe – Ian Dalziel
13. Parties' Progress: The District Council Elections of May 1980 – John Bochel and David Denver
14. Scottish Legislation in the Seventies – H. McN. Henderson

THE SCOTTISH GOVERNMENT YEARBOOK 1982
Ed. by H.M. Drucker and N. Drucker
CONTENTS

1. Valedictory – The Editors
2. The Year at Westminster – James Naughtie
3. Braking Mr Younger's Runaway Train: The Conflict Between the Scottish Office and Local Authorities over Local Government Expenditure – D.A. Heald, C.A. Jones and D.W. Lamont
4. Reflections of a Scottish Office Minister – Malcolm Rifkind

SCOTTISH GOVERNMENT YEARBOOK 1983
Ed. David McCrone
CONTENTS

SCOTTISH GOVERNMENT YEARBOOK 1984
Ed. David McCrone
CONTENTS

SCOTTISH GOVERNMENT YEARBOOK 1985
Ed. David McCrone
CONTENTS

SCOTTISH GOVERNMENT YEARBOOK 1986
Ed. by David McCrone
CONTENTS

SCOTTISH GOVERNMENT YEARBOOK 1987
Ed. David McCrone
CONTENTS

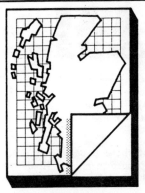
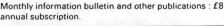